MONSARRAT AT SEA

NICHOLAS MONSARRAT

Monsarrat at Sea

WILLIAM MORROW and COMPANY, Inc.
NEW YORK   1976

Contents

The Longest Love,
The Longest Hate

IT STARTED WITH PADDLING, IN THE SMALL YEARS OF 1912, when I was two, and so beautiful (according to a fond or myopic mother) that I would never reach maturity. Paddling was then, in common with almost everything else, a formal occasion; I had to be specially dressed for it, like a princeling at a coronation, in a romper suit, sun-bonnet, vest, underpants, and a thing called a 'binder'—a miniature version of the cholera belt which guarded the middle section of every white man in India or Africa.

The sea air, we were told, was notably treacherous: and this was said to be as true in Anglesey, where we paddled during certain set weeks of August, as in the freezing Arctic, the hot and humid Ivory Coast, or the sinister sea-board of Java and Sumatra.

This was my first touch of salt water, which proved to be cold, and intrusive to the toes, and then fascinating. There was so much going on. Tiny crabs, not Britain, ruled these waves, and then pale see-through shrimps, and then the shoals of little fish, changing course miraculously at the slightest alarm, which I later identified as embryo mackerel.

But above the tide-mark, under the sun, everything seemed to be dying, or dead, or decayed. Here the little crabs, which could nip and run, were spread-eagled in forlorn defeat. Mounds of baby shrimps lay careened on their sides, wriggling no more. Even the fronded seaweed had taken on the musty smell of death.

Under a blue sunbonnet, a small brain like a spongy walnut had sucked in its newest lesson: the abundant life and huge mortality of the sea.

But soon we were ready to take our own toll of this mortality. We began with shrimps which, caught, boiled, and eaten within the hour, were a prime dividend for children permanently ravenous. There was a small technical snag here, in that I was unable to extract the shrimps, when caught, from the net; they squirmed, they were cold and slimy, they might even bite. But my elder sister, brave as a lion, had no such qualms; without undue family taunting—just simple references to cowardice and the feebleness of boys—she was always ready to lift out what I caught.

Then we were given a rowing boat, our dearest possession for many years. It was 'safe' because it was virtually oblong: eight feet long by four feet wide—the nearest approximation to the wicker coracle of 2,000 BC which my father could have obtained without recourse to the National Maritime Museum. It was not 'safe' because it had a leak in the stem. Sometimes we had to bail for our lives. Thus I embarked upon the sea, and landed on islands at least fifty yards away, and caught uneatable spiny bass, and the grown-up mackerel which swarmed into the bay in September and contributed the best breakfast in the world.

But first I had to learn to swim. There was a war on, that old remorseless war, and 'You can't join the Navy if you can't swim' was the family catch-phrase. Already it was established that any British boy worth his salt would make a bee-line for the Senior Service as soon as he was tall enough to trigger a torpedo. But swimming, even with the 'water wings' which were then the trendy maritime wear, never appealed. It took me nearly naked into much deeper water: there must be great shoals of fish searching and hungry beneath me: perhaps not actual sharks, but certainly dogfish, and possibly a lobster with claws like iron snatch-blocks, scouting the surface.

One was vulnerable all over. A confirmed water-funk already, I disposed of this test of manhood as quickly as I could; and then the rowing boat—'The Tub'—became a 14-foot sailing dinghy, and racing engrossed us for three days a week, and the long love affair really began.

The sea was in our blood, I was constantly assured even by so realistic a man as my father, who was a busy Liverpool surgeon and dealt quite coolly in real blood and the real tissue that went with it. I believed it then, and believe it now: an island race does breed like this; the British, when in doubt, either of duty or of pleasure, swarm to the sea. It was as true for me as for any gallant admiral, any jolly jack tar, or any Blackpool tripper.

When the summer holidays were over, and I could not sail on it, I walked towards it; down to the salty dirty old Mersey River, and the 'pier head' where the giant Cunard and White Star liners, with the famous names like *Mauretania* and *Olympic*, docked and stored and embarked their new passengers and sailed away again—away from our own Liver birds to a fabled Statue of Liberty which any Liverpool boy knew was 3,080 nautical miles west-south-west.

The world turned: the sun moved north again: always blessed July and August and September came round, and the boats grew bigger. The 'racing season' at Trearddur Bay in Anglesey was still a sacrosanct summer date; but now I went cruising and crewing with richer young men in *real* yachts, up to Stornaway, down to Portree in the Isle of Skye, out of the Hamble River and Burnham-on-Crouch and Lymington and even Bordeaux.

Once I crewed in the Mersey Race, which started in the Menai Straits, took us across to Dublin, and then back to Holyhead. We lost our way—it was enough to say that I was still 'learning navigation'— and fetched up, miles and even days astern of the fleet, on an unknown coast which just had to be somewhere in Ireland.

I rowed ashore in the pram dinghy, and asked the first policeman where I was. 'Balbriggan' was the answer; I could only identify it from the A.A. handbook which was luckily part of my equipment. We were 25 miles off course. Perhaps the sea wasn't in my blood after all.

That was August 1939; the last year of innocence and love. After that, hatred and fear took over. For the world turned again, mortally, and now it was another war—this time mine and my brother's instead of my father's—and the Navy claimed me at last, after a long wait, and 'the sea in their blood' proved exactly true.

I have written enough about the war at sea; 200 words can now take the place of 200,000. It was just *there*, thirty years ago, like a disgusting cockroach in an innocent bowl of soup. I spent it on the Atlantic convoy run, then the Gibraltar, then the east coast of England, then the Atlantic again. To begin with, I dealt mostly with survivors, because my father was a surgeon, and his loving and expert care must (the Captain thought) have rubbed off on me. How often I wished my sister had been there as well, to take these bedraggled gasping fish out of their net.

But though appalling and hateful, it was all so *natural*. Our wardroom consisted, apart from a superb professional in the captain, of one Australian motor-car salesman, one gas-company cashier, one barrister, and me. 'Me' was a holiday sailor, a freelance writing hack with his shirt-tails hanging out of his trousers; but when my private world turned again, and I grew up like everyone else, I was a First Lieutenant, and then a corvette Captain, and then a frigate Captain, and my landfalls were not the little rocks of Trearddur Bay, but Newfoundland or the Clyde or Gibraltar, or a spot in mid-Atlantic which had to be, not 25 miles wrong, nor ten miles wrong, but right.

The sea was in our blood, and our blood was in the sea, and that's enough about those five martial years, which made a man out of me and a corpse of my brother.

Post-war, a minor diplomatic job took me out to South Africa. We

sailed down Channel, and across the Bay of Biscay, and out into the
loathed Atlantic again, and ever southward towards Cape Town. The
sun shone, and dreary rationing was over, and I wasn't the captain, with
all the worries.

But I could never forget that we were sailing, peacefully at last, over
ground literally strewn with dead sailors, blown up, burned to death,
shredded by the sea, sucked down, *drowned*—the most awful word in a
sailor's word-book. 'Full fathom five thy father lies'—the fathers and
sons were all there, just under our keel. The sea now seemed poisoned
for ever, and I never touched the stuff for another seven years.

It came all right again, like a ferocious quarrel between lovers who,
surviving bitter years, unforgivable insults, find that for good or ill they
cannot endure a life apart. I began to live on islands: first a private
one—my very own—in the middle of the broad St Lawrence Seaway:
two miles from Canada, three from America.

Here I took up ship-watching once more and logged the ensigns of 29
different nations, from Taiwan to Liberia, South Africa to Iceland, and
learned for the first time that there was a Swiss merchant marine, and
that a ship could be registered 'Zürich' and still float instead of being
embalmed in landlocked ice.

The Swiss? Zürich? God bless my soul! Liverpool for ever!

I also returned to sailing again: racing in Dragons, which proved
superb machines for this purpose, though their helmsmen grew
quarrelsome as the Olympics approached, and dirty tactics became the
fashion and the need, and protests flew round the club like bats at
sunset. Sadly, it turned out that sail-people can be like horse-
people—contemptuous, arrogant, and crook. But so can the sea itself.

After that it was Guernsey, where even a car left out at night might
wake up encrusted with briny spray, and finally Malta: set in a tideless
ocean which is a salt sea none the less. A side-trip to Japan, to witness the
launching and maiden voyage of the *Globtik Tokyo*, a half-million-ton
tanker and the biggest in the world, proved at least one thing: that one
can grow a little too old for sea-going—too old, at least, to walk a
quarter of a mile from the bridge to the pointed end, passing on the way
a swimming-pool about five times as long as that first adored 'Tub'
rowing boat.

It all started with paddling, and seems likely to end like that. I still
don't like swimming, and now it's gentle wading for me. Though I shall
love the sea for ever, like every second man to be met on the streets and
lanes of Britain, my love, in terms of intimate contact, is confined to the
first six inches of it.

Three Corvettes

This collection of three short books—all originally published during the war—covers time spent afloat from 1940 to 1943. It is not a complete picture (nor anything like it) of the whole of the Battle of the Atlantic during that period; it is an account of one man's naval service during three critical years of the battle, when I had the luck to be serving in small ships in this crucial theatre of war.

All these books started as 'notes'—notes for a future war novel. That was why I started keeping a diary, early in 1940; that, and for the pleasure and relief of writing, in the middle of bloody war, when I was a watch-keeping officer in a corvette on Atlantic escort, and the whole world seemed composed exclusively of violence, fatigue, and worry.

The notes—though I didn't know this at the time— were intended to be the basis of *The Cruel Sea*. But *The Cruel Sea* turned out to be quite a different book, and a long way ahead in any case—ten years, in fact, though again I didn't know it at the time. Finally, I had the notes published as a series of smaller books, for a reason that impels many men to write and to publish—I thought I was going to be killed.

Basically, it's an arrogant idea—that you have something to say, and must say it while you can. But the Battle of the Atlantic was like that—death and fear at sea, and then, in harbour, the wish to tell people about it before you went out on convoy again. (It was a battle we had to win, if we were to exist at all—and that was something we *did* know at the time.) In addition, we *all* thought we were going to be killed: the war book that would shake the world seemed a very long time ahead: perhaps too long for one's current chances of survival. Meanwhile, here was a story.

Here is the story now—incomplete, disjointed, but first-hand. The three books are progressive, because by 1943 we had stopped losing the Battle of the Atlantic, and had started, very slowly and painfully, to win.

If you detect too much pride in this progression, or too much pleasure at having survived three years of watch-keeping at sea, or too much astonishment at attaining command, you may put it down to relief.

1945   N. M.

H.M. Corvette

1 COMMISSIONING

OUR DRAFT-CHIT HAD BEEN ENDORSED, MAGNIFICENTLY, 'Report on arrival to Admiral Superintending Contract-built Ships', which conjured up a picture of a penetrating eye and an acre of gold lace on either arm; but after a tour of a small shipyard which, noise for size, must have rated one of the highest in the business, we could not escape the conviction that our No. 1 suits (of warranted superfine pilot cloth), our gloves, our correctly slung respirators, our factory-fresh turn-out, was a dangerous waste of elegance. For the place was undeniably dirty, full of such hazards as girders, coils of rusty wire, cranes taking swings at the passers-by, red-hot rivets describing arcs through the air overhead, and bunches of men aiming baulks of oily wood, like battering-rams. Now and then there would be a dull splash as a ship was launched—or so it seemed. To preserve that elegance of ours we had continually to draw ourselves aside, like old ladies scandalized in Piccadilly; and, unlike old ladies, often wonderfully immune in the most dubious of situations, sooner or later we were going to be soiled by contact with our surroundings.

'There'll be no admirals in this joint,' said M. to me. 'It's expecting too much altogether.'

There seemed to be almost everything else: above all, there was a stupefying row going on the whole time, with everyone contributing according to his means: most of it was riveting, but even small boys with nothing else to do would be idly hammering on sheets of iron as they talked. (I dare say they were training for the more responsible jobs: I swear they deserved them.) To make ourselves heard at all we had to shout; and it is foolish (and unhelpful) to shout, 'What a horrible noise!' so we mostly kept silent and looked for our quarry.

There was, as we had suspected, no admiral, but instead a helpful works-foreman who directed us to a hut labelled, dauntingly, 'NAVAL OFFICERS KEEP OUT'; and installed there we found an R.N.V.R. officer, with a red face and a square chin, dressed in a working suit which made us look and feel like the First and Second Dudes in a tastelessly lavish production. He had two stripes to our one, and was in fact the First Lieutenant. After we had announced ourselves he looked us over carefully, from a good many angles: it was difficult to tell which, if any, he liked. (We were both ex-amateur yachtsmen granted commissions by an Admiralty Selection Board very likely persuaded to a sense of crucial emergency by Dunkirk.) After a bit the First Lieutenant said: 'What can you do?' and after we had told him he said: 'Well, well.' He was an Australian, accustomed to herds of dumb animals.

M. and I toured the ship together, as green as grass. Neither of us had seen a corvette before, though there were certainly enough of them about: indeed, it seemed as if, up and down the Clyde, anyone who had ever handled a hammer had set a pole up in his back garden and started building a corvette. Ours was afloat, almost finished, and jammed with workmen: the chief noise was supplied by some last-minute riveting going on on the after gun-platform, but there were several minor performers of note among the welders, caulkers, joiners, carpenters, and plain crash-and-bangers employed on board. We were an hour on our tour, mostly climbing over obstacles and avoiding paintwork, but examining every discoverable corner and going over the ground from bridge to magazine and forepeak to tiller-flat: we liked the look of her, though she was as yet more like an unfinished factory than a ship. Here and there ratings were at work—the advance guard of the crew drafted from barracks, mostly leading-hands testing out their departments: in the W/T cabinet the Leading Telegraphist, caught in a maze of different-coloured wires, was having a cup of tea. M. said: 'Getting it all shipshape?' and the Leading Tel. answered: 'No, sir.'

Aft, the Torpedoman was arguing over the depth-charge rails with a welder, a Clydeside dockyard-matey with an accent like a roll of drums. This was my department, and I listened, while M., who was taking over Gunnery Officer, went forward to look at his gun and presently came back nursing a bleeding hand. It seemed he had closed the breech in a new and wrong way.

When we returned to the hut the First Lieutenant said: 'Well, what do you think of corvettes?' I said I liked them: M., a reserved character, said it had all been very interesting. The First Lieutenant said: 'I've been in trawlers up to this,' and added: 'Now you can get busy correcting King's Regulations and Admiralty Instructions, Part One.' The corrections lay in a neat pile of printed booklets, not more than five inches high. Alongside was a pen and two bottles of ink.

Odd sight: Stoker Petty Officer making a sort of doormat-bootscraper out of metal beer-bottle tops nailed upside down on a board. He claimed it his own idea, and no hardship to provide for.

We came to know K.R. and A.I., and those interminable corrections, and we came to know that hut, our headquarters for ten days. Until we were formally in commission it was the hub of everything: of checking stores, of ammunitioning, of conferences with dockyard officials, of the formidable amount of paper-work—signals, correspondence, watch-and quarter-bills, chart folios—in which we were all soon involved. The crew arrived in driblets, more guns arrived by crane and alighted on their mountings like settling sea-gulls: the Chief Engine-Room Artificer arrived and was immediately involved in a technical blizzard over the suction-and-outlet system. The Captain arrived—no, he had been there all the time.

On the ship, progress could be measured by the decreasing amount of noise aboard; soon we were able to enjoy as much as half an hour of tranquillity at a time. Carpets appeared in our cabins, the wardroom lost its carpenter's-shop look and became habitable: a man went round on a float painting in our pendant numbers, a key-board with not less than sixty bunches of keys made its appearance and was, inevitably, put in my charge. The coxswain, a West-countryman of broad accent, broader beam, and humour broadest of all, emerged as a character, a directive force of outstanding value in handling the crew. (I liked some of his expressions. 'He wears a green coat sir,' he once said of a rating very lively in the mess-decks and very slow at tackling a job of work; and again, less elegantly, of one of the duller seamen: 'He's wood from the —— up,' and yet again: 'He's very seldom up top'—signifying 'He's bald.') Bit by bit, the ship's heart moved across from the hut and started beating in the ship itself.

Said the Captain, staring out of the window across the dock, to the First Lieutenant:

'Put the ship in commission at midday today.'

It was only a matter of saluting while the spotless ensign was hoisted, sending a signalman to the mast-head with the commissioning pendant, and mounting an armed sentry on the jetty alongside; but what a difference it seemed to make, that transfer from floating shell to one of His Majesty's ships of war in commission. We walked differently when we were aboard, we sat in the wardroom with a sense of formal proprietorship; we even came to resent the dock-workers crowding the decks and strolling about without care or caution. That was no way to treat the ship. . . . She was ours now: anyone else was there on sufferance, and no one else mattered.

When I signed the first wine-chit of the commission—'Two Plymouth gins'—I felt as if I were founding a dynasty. As time went by, this turned out to be true.

We broke more new ground that same day and night, initiating ourselves and the ship into the Navy's apt ceremonial. There was Colours at sunset—hoisting our own Preparative for the benefit of the two other corvettes in the dock-basin, saluting as the bosun's pipe shrilled, dividing the summer evening air, and the ensign came slowly down—all of it was new, and all moving for a score of reasons. And I made the ship's first Rounds the same night, tailing a small procession of the quartermaster, leading hand of the watch, and duty Petty Officer: through the mess-decks (crowded, silent, attentive), up on the fo'c'sle-head to look at the shore-wires, aft to the galley where some sort of tea-party was in progress (though not after I had left). All that, again, was new, and something one could enjoy for unanalysable reasons, somehow bound up with the compelling phrase 'in a seaman-like manner': to write in the Night Rounds book: '21.00, Rounds Correct', and initial the entry was to stand warranty for an orderly and disciplined tribute to tradition.

'06.15, Call Officer-of-the-Day.
06.30, Hands fall in: Wash down.'
This was the sting in the tail of the First Lieutenant's night orders; it stung me, and after a late session in the wardroom to celebrate commissioning, I could have done without it. But duty (and a certain remembered glitter in the First Lieutenant's eye) got me turned out, hurriedly dressed, with such compromises as sea-boots for ordinary shoes and a scarf instead of a collar and tie, and put me on a cold, windswept upper deck as the fall-in was piped, to stare at a muster of nineteen seamen who stared reproachfully back. Then the duty leading-hand reported the watches correct, the sweepers were told off and hoses rigged, and presently those rather bleak early morning noises, of bristles and squeegees and the gurgle of water in the scuppers and freeing-ports, made themselves heard.

The rating in charge of the hose brought to his job an energy and a scrupulous zeal not always appreciated by the upper-deck sweepers,

whose sea-boots now and then took the full force of the attack and who
were inclined to hurry the job and get below to the comparative holiday
known as 'squaring off mess-decks and flats'. I dodged the main stream
and went aft to the galley, where the Leading Cook was heating up a
good quart of dripping-fat in a saucepan and the wardroom steward
making a brew of tea, from which I claimed a hand-out. The Stoker
Petty Officer of the morning watch came up the ladder, took six puffs at
a cigarette, crushed it out against the depth-charge rails, and went below
again, followed by the black cat which had already attached itself to the
ship, with the obvious promise of more to come. Ashore, a trickle of
workers was coming through the dock-gates, some of them making for
our gangway where the sentry, counting aloud, was practising his own
stylized version of 'Present Arms'. The cold haze which had overhung
the dock-basin when I first came up was already beginning to disappear.

I waved to the Sub. on the neighbouring corvette, and he answered
with a semaphore message of which I could only read the first
word—'what'. I repeated it back, and there, in frustrated confusion, the
matter rested. . . . When, from forrard, I heard 'Cooks to the galley'
being piped, I went below to shave and finish dressing, and make
myself fit to see Colours hoisted at eight.

A second gigantic assortment of charts was delivered shortly before
we sailed. At the top of the box was the 'Arctic Pilot', and underneath a
chart of the navigable parts of the Danube. Said the Leading Signalman,
looking over my shoulder as I unpacked the consignment:

'Seems like we're going to get some variety, sir. I could just do with a
slice of Old Vienna.'

'Pipe "Stations for leaving harbour" in five minutes,' said the First
Lieutenant to the quartermaster; and to me he added: 'You take the
after-part, and if you get a wire round the screw, God help you.'

My foreboding that only with God's help would I avoid turning the
screw into something like one of those old-fashioned frame-aerials was
not borne out, probably because the leading-hand of the after-party was
a leading-seaman of extreme competence, clearly accustomed to the
code of whistle-blasts and mystical signs which came in a steady flow
from the bridge. It was he who translated into action the first technical
obscurity, 'Single up to the breast and spring!'—i.e. let go all ropes
except a single breast-rope and a single rope running from aft to a shore-
bollard about amidships: without him I might have plunged about for
hours and still guessed wrong. (Hitherto, in my experience, one had
simply said 'About time to cast off', and suited the action to the word,

fending off the jetty with one's leg.) Judging from the uproar forrard, M. was having trouble with the windlass, which gave me time to reel some of the spare wire out of the way, before the next manœuvre.

We needed a tug at each end to get us out of the dock-basin and into the stream, and it took us some time to hook on to ours, the heaving-line being brand-new and the seaman in charge of it a painstaking worker who was not going to be flurried by a mistake or two. The deep silence from the bridge which attended our efforts made an effective commentary. . . . But presently the tow was secure, and we were out in the narrow tributary stream which ran into the Clyde—a stream lined with dockyard workers from our own and other yards, who had left their jobs to give us a cheer and a wave as we passed. It was their last moment, and our first: I wished I could go up on the bridge to get the full savour of it, but my job was aft, in case we had for any reason to cast off the tow. So down-stream we went, slowly and evenly, not yet in our own element or under our own power, but setting out on our journey none the less: a Clyde-built ship leaving the Clyde, with her builders watching her and wishing her God-speed.

I had time to watch my after-party at work, and to like the way they got down to it. About half the crew were Active Service—i.e. regulars, and the rest were 'Hostilities Only' ratings, or as the coxswain called them, with more humour than truth, 'Hostile Ordinary Seamen'. But whatever their background—and the H.O.s ranged from van-boy to statistical accountant—they buckled to their new job with admirable keenness. I think that all of us, officers and men alike, felt the same about the ship: that she was something between a brand-new toy and a—well, almost a sacred charge, a unit whose reputation had to be made and whose laurels won. We had to work, from now on, to get going, to tune up, to perfect the fighting instrument that had been given us: she was a good ship, a grand ship—corvettes *are* attractive and workmanlike— but we had to deserve her, and that meant hard work. The Clyde had done its famous best for us: from now on the charge was ours.

There is a process known as 'signing for the ship'. It is one of the higher mysteries, conducted behind drawn curtains, but roughly speaking it happens after full-power trials, the working of the windlass, and the firing of every gun and depth-charge thrower carried, and is a contest between the contractors, who say everything is marvellous, and the Captain, who has a list a mile long of defects and shortcomings he wants put right before he will finally take the ship over. As can be imagined, it may be a very tense occasion indeed.

But when it is concluded, as sometime it must be, all is love again, and double gins. And soon after, the first sailing-orders arrive; they are endorsed 'SECRET', and begin: 'Being in all respects ready for sea, H.M.S. *Flower* will proceed . . .'

2 WORKING-UP

I shared the morning watch (4 to 8) with the First Lieutenant on the passage to our base, after keeping the first watch (8 to midnight) as well. In these early days, we worked watch-and-watch about, until the two children (M. and I) could be trusted with weapons of war; later, of course, we were in three watches, of which I kept the Middle (midnight to 4 a.m.) for seventeen months. To be perfectly frank, this was not the hardship it may sound: in fact I preferred this arrangement, for the main reason that I was left alone unless (or until) all hell broke loose, and could run the watch as I liked, without interference and in peace: the Captain was turned in, in his sea-cabin, the First Lieutenant did not relieve me till four, and I was free of the odd assortment of visitors who were inclined to crowd the bridge at other times. (I *hate* being watched or supervised, when I am doing my best and making no mistakes.) But all those personal problems and arrangements, of course, were still to come, on that first night at sea.

The log-entries when we took over at four o'clock read:

'WIND: Direction 270, Force 2–3.
WEATHER AND VISIBILITY: bc 7.
SEA AND SWELL: 21.
CORRECTED BAROMETRIC PRESSURE IN MILLIBARS: 1002.'

all of which is the dull sea-language for a lovely night. We had passed an inward-bound convoy in the first watch, before the moon got up, being challenged out of complete blackness by a very wide-awake destroyer; but now it was clearer, with a smudge of land just visible, and the ship progressed steadily, finding her easy speed, having nothing to deal with as regards weather, but behaving admirably under helm and promising a ready and able performance in the future. From the wing of the bridge I could distinguish the hard outline of the fo'c'sle-head, the sky cut by the mast and forestay, the line of foam at the bow: beyond was a brilliant spread of moonlit water, silver on black, and beyond that the ring of darkness, retreating before us, closing in astern. The 'group-flashing' light we had picked up half an hour earlier was just coming abeam, and fine on the bow a cluster of lights low in the water marked a line of fishing-boats working the inshore tide. I reckoned we could just about pass them without altering course, though I didn't suppose I should have any say in the matter.

From the other wing of the bridge came the First Lieutenant's voice: 'I'm going inside to log that light and have a smoke. Sing out if you see anything.'

He disappeared inside the compass-house, and I had the ship and the watch to myself.

I moved across to the centre of the bridge, stirred to an odd exhilaration. Behind me a faint—a very faint—glow from the screened binnacle showed the face of the Asdic rating, intent and serious: at my side the signalman of the watch was fiddling with his Aldis-lamp, and out on the bridge-sponsons the two look-outs stared ahead, the pointed capes of their duffle-coats in sharp outline against the sky. Centred thus, with fifty-odd men sleeping between decks, with the whole ship entrusted to me as a kind of intricate going concern, I felt tremendously responsible, and tremendously alert too. She was all mine: from this nerve-centre on the bridge—myself—could go out a pulse that would be felt from end to end of the ship: she would respond to it, and she would do what I told her, she would move at my word. Magic moment of authority! Quite possessed by the idea, prompted to pure foolishness by this novelty of power, I bent to the voice-pipe.

'Port ten.'

From below came the quartermaster's answering voice: 'Port ten, sir.' And then: 'Ten of port wheel on, sir.'

'Midships.'

'Midships. . . . Wheel's amidships, sir.'

'Steady.'

'Steady. . . . Course South, eighty West, sir.'

'Very good.' I waited perhaps twenty seconds. 'Starboard ten. Steer North, eighty-five West.'

'Steer North, eighty-five West, sir.'

The First Lieutenant made himself heard from behind the chart-table screen: 'What's going on out there?'

'We passed a floating log,' I called back, feeling slightly silly. 'It looked too big to hit.'

A vague grumble indicated that the explanation passed muster. Only the starboard look-out, peering over the dodger at virgin sea, seemed to betray an injured incredulity. No logs, big or small, had got past *him*.

Up another voice-pipe came the Captain's voice.'Fore-bridge!'

'Bridge, sir.'

'Who's that?'

'Monsarrat, sir.'

'Where's the First Lieutenant?'

'Just looking at the chart, sir.'

'M'm . . . How far have we got?'

I gave the last light abeam, and the time.

'M'm . . . See anything?'

'The next light just looming, sir: the bearing's all right. Ship to port, going our way. Fishing-boats inshore.'

'Quite a party.' And then, surprisingly: 'Feel all right up there?'

'Yes, sir.'

'Very good. Tell the Bosun's Mate to call me at a quarter to eight.'

'Aye, aye, sir.' Below, the voice-pipe cover clicked shut, cutting me off. Of such small exchanges, lit with sudden humanity, is homage born.

It grew lighter. The best thing about the morning watch, this, the thing one looked forward to from four o'clock onwards, the thing I was to miss greatly in the middle watch later on: dawn coming up, ships in station, and all secure. . . . There is, at sea, a certain swift change from moonlight to dawnlight that is very easily recognizable; at one moment, it seems, the water is silvery, glowing, with each breaking wave throwing off a small wash of phosphorescence, and then when next you look it has taken on a livid hue, a cold, dull grey which is the day's first signal. The ship's outlines fill in suddenly, and all the bridge-personnel becomes figures and faces instead of shadows—grey, tired faces, mostly, but welcome for their return to normality. Then up comes the sun, to complete the colour-process and dry off the damp shoulders of your duffle-coat; and up comes tea, with the steward foraging for the cups and plates of the night's picnic; and lastly up comes your relief, which is best of all.

You've earned your breakfast, and it's those lovely soused herrings again.

We arrived at our destination.

'What a grand place,' said M. to me as soon as we were moored. 'It's a pity we've got to work.'

Work we did. Daily we exercised everything, with a wild sense of crisis. We abandoned ship, we repelled boarders, we got out the kedge-anchor (an intolerable operation, this): we closed up action-stations against the stop-watch, we fought fires, we prepared to tow, we put an armed landing-party ashore amid a hurricane of cheers. There was even a suggestion, happily suppressed, that we should exercise the Confidential Books, throwing them overboard to see if they sank, in accordance with the regulations. . . . We fired guns, and signalled, and took soundings; we demolished the target at gun-practice, but on the other hand we made a supreme hash of our first depth-charge drill, due to a fault in the electric buzzer-system. ('Really, sir, you don't know whether to laugh or cry,' murmured the coxswain to me, as we surveyed one thrower-crew awaiting the order to fire, and another arguing the toss as to whether two rings meant 'Fire' or 'Fall out'.) But we learnt quickly during those weeks: almost before we knew it had happened, we emerged as a ship's company instead of a crowd of individuals, we took shape as a disciplined force with a routine, practised and practised again, for any and every eventuality. It was hard work, and we wasted no time, but we could see the results from day to day, and they were encouraging in every particular.

Our first defaulter.
'Halt! Left turn! Off caps! Ordinary Seaman Jones, sir: one, was absent over leave two and a half hours, two, did return on board drunk, three, did create vandalism in the mess-decks.'
'What—er—vandalism was this, coxswain?'
'Broke up a mess-stool, sir, and tried to light the stove with it.'
'What have you got to say, Jones?'
'Had a few drinks, sir.'
'Is that all?'
'Yes, sir.'
'Serious offences, all these. And you made a nuisance of yourself, too, keeping a lot of people awake. First Lieutenant's report.'
'First Lieutenant's report. On caps! Right turn! Quick march!'
'Spoilt our record, coxswain.'
'Got to sometime, sir. Human nature.'

Sunday morning brought us Divisions on the fo'c'sle, the only space large enough to accommodate the whole ship's company; and a very smart turn-out it was, too, the two ranks facing in-board, the wind stirring the seamen's collars and ruffling our hair as we stood bareheaded for prayers. And afterwards came the Captain's Rounds, a most thorough progress through every part of the ship, which looked (on that occasion) like a millionaire's yacht—a millionaire with an inquisitive eye and a passion for spit-and-polish.

Later in the morning I attended 'Up Spirits', though the sight of the
rum going down, tot by tot, was tantalizing to a degree. And then 'Pipe
down' was sounded, and a true Sunday calm fell on the ship: we lay to
our moorings in shelter and warm sun, and revelled in our hard-won
peace.

Alas, to have one's afternoon nap interrupted by the ominous words:
'Leading Seaman Black, sir, reports the loss of a salt-fish, and wishes to
state a complaint.'
This is going to be a long one.

We went out on exercises with a submarine, but all that, save for one
innocent oddment, must be shrouded in mystery. The oddment is this.
To help an inexperienced ship, and to avoid waste of time, the
submarine at first sometimes tows what are called 'buffs'—mark-buoys
at the end of a warp—when it is submerged; and it must be related that
during my first Asdic attack the machinery failed, and I looked up (after
a lengthy and profitless sweep all round the horizon) to see the buffs
coming in at high speed and delivering a smashing attack on our
starboard quarter. Said the Captain, as we scraped clear with a thin
ripple to spare: 'I don't think you've quite got the idea. This practice is
for our benefit, not the submarine's. They're meant to be strictly neutral
down there.'

When we dropped a test depth-charge the explosion killed half a
dozen guillemots which must have been diving nearby. The dead birds
lay breast downwards on the water, with bowed heads and flat,
outstretched wings: they seemed to be praying, or making an
exaggerated satirical obeisance.

By way of a change, I swapped horses and had a day out in the
submarine before we left.
All of it was interesting, and unexpected too. I thought I would be
conscious of being under water, and possibly nervous—indeed, at the
very beginning I had been mortally afraid of turning claustrophobic,
and possibly disgracing myself; but at no time was it possible to realize
that we *were* submerged. The occasional noise of the hunting corvettes,
sounding oddly like goods trains, passing overhead, was the only
indication that we were under water: otherwise (save for the cramped
space) it was no different from being, say, in the forrard mess-deck of a
corvette. And it was all amazingly quiet: there was no vibration and no

engine noise, and orders were given almost in a whisper, instead of the wind-quelling shout we had to use on our own bridge. It had been rough on top before we dived, but down here there was a deep peace; nothing threatened, no one stirred save the two men at the hydroplane controls, their eyes on the depth-gauges, their hands fingering the wheel-spokes like harp-players reading an intricate score.

The minute wardroom, with everything neatly slipped into place, was no more than a passage-way from one end of the boat to the other; and the cramped space made for a recognizable comradeship between officers and men, of special value when one man's mistake might mean disaster for all of them. But one could not help being struck by the adroitness and the marked competence of everyone aboard: when the klaxon sounded for diving-stations nothing much seemed to happen, and yet, when one looked round the control-room, every lever and wheel and knob had been closed up by a crew which slipped into place like pieces of the same machinery.

Only when the order 'Periscope depth!' was given, preparatory to surfacing, was a slight sense of crisis to be observed: it was conceivable that a blunder might be made and one or other of the hunting craft would be in the way: one could feel a certain tenseness in each person—the Officer-of-the-Watch staring at his gauges, the crew with their hands ready on the Kingston-valve levers, the Captain (a young lieutenant) gripping the periscope training gear. Then the periscope broke the surface, and the Captain, suddenly relaxing, gave an order over his shoulder and climbed up to the conning-tower; and presently, touched by a breath of fresh air, I looked up, and there above us was a square of blue sky.

It is, perhaps, worth remarking that, with my eyes on the future, I noted that the view of the surrounding surface craft through the periscope was distressingly sharp and clear.

It was the energetic habit of the Senior Officer of the base to put out in a fast motor-launch directly after lunch, and, choosing his victim, approach at speed on the blind side of the ship, in the hope of catching the Officer-of-the-Day off his guard or the Captain literally napping. As he was almost a professional Angry Man, it is good to be able to relate that, thanks to luck and a series of reliable quartermasters, we were never caught out.

Our 'passing-out' day at the end of our working-up period also went off without mishap, though there was one moment, when the order 'Pressure on the fire-hoses!' produced a trickle that would not have quelled a daisy, when the situation looked dynamic. But it passed: we were officially congratulated on the day's performance; and the same evening a bunch of reports, on the ship and on each officer, made their appearance. They were rather like school-reports, and induced the same expectant nervousness.

The Captain came off best: then the First Lieutenant: then M.: then me. Some sort of coincidence, no doubt.

Off again, nearer the war and our job; at anchor, awaiting sailing orders.

On a nearby shoal, with her mast and one funnel showing above water, there lay a sunk destroyer full of dead Frenchmen. Her story had been one of the brief horrors of the war: an explosion aboard had been followed by a fire, and the ship gradually became one vast incandescent torch. Now she lay there, a rusty, weed-washed charnel-house, marked by a green wreck-buoy; and many times later, as we came up the river at dusk and drew nearer that green, winking eye, I would project my mind below the surface of the water, and try to picture the horror's details, and what it was our anchor saw as it shattered the still water and plunged below. Indeed, I could not help this imagining, which always persisted long after we had swung and settled to our anchor: the mast proclaimed an ugly angle in the near-darkness, the green eye accused me—'You are alive,' it said: 'we are dead, very dead—charred, swollen, abandoned—and there are scores of us within a few hundred feet of you.' It was the other side of the medal, frightful in its detail, final in its implication. It was not the R.N.V.R.: it was our introduction to war.

I came aboard by the last liberty-boat after a spell ashore, and went down to the wardroom, where M. was correcting charts.

'Our orders have come,' he said. 'We're off tomorrow morning.'

'What are we getting?' I asked. 'Iceland? Alexandria? Or some nice soft job, defending a pier in North Wales?'

'None of those. Convoy escort, North Atlantic.'

'Oh . . .' I picked up the wine chit-book. 'What are all these double gins?'

He smiled. 'Convoy escort, North Atlantic. And winter coming on.'

3 WORKING

A corvette would roll on wet grass.

Our measure of rough weather is domestic, but reliable. Moderate sea, the lavatory-seat falls down when it is tipped up; rough sea, the radio-set tumbles off its bracket in the wardroom.

Some trips are good, some not. There was one, in calm weather, with an easy-going Gibraltar convoy, that was a picnic, the kind of jaunt which costs a guinea a day, with fancy-dress thrown in, in peace-time; there was another, that took us far North and West, which was a long nightmare. For when, seven days out, we turned round to go home, an easterly gale set in: we went five hundred miles in the teeth of it before it moderated—five hundred miles, and six days, of screaming wind and massed, tumbling water, of sleet and snow-storms, of a sort of frozen malice in the weather which refused us all progress. Nothing could keep it out: helmets, mittens, duffle-coats, sea-boot stockings—all were like so much tissue paper. 'Cold?' said the signalman, as he pulled his hand away from the morse-lamp and left a patch of skin on the handle: 'Cold? I reckon this would freeze the ears off a brass monkey.'

There are cumulative miseries to be endured during a really wet night on the bridge: icy water finds its way everywhere—neck, wrists, trouser-legs, boots: one stands out there like a sodden automaton, ducking behind the rail as every other wave sends spray flying over the compass-house, and then standing up to face, with eyes that feel raw and salt-caked and streaming, the wind and the rain and the treachery of the sea. Of course, heavy weather need not always make life so miserable: if corvettes are in no hurry, and can afford to ease down and lie-to with their bows just off the wind, they do very well—as far as that's concerned, they are prime sea-boats; but if they have to proceed with any determination, they put their nose smack into it every time. Twice we have had windows smashed up on the bridge by seas which curled up and broke right on top of them: surprise-packets we could have done without. We're not complaining: just remarking on the facts. . . .

Cheerful dialogue on being called for the middle watch, rough weather:

'Is it raining?'

'No, sir—just washing over.'

Midnight means taking it all on again: mounting the ladder with an effort, watching for the square of sky (sometimes scarcely perceptible) which will tell you what the visibility is going to be like; listening to see if it is still blowing as hard as when you were last on watch. It usually is.

Apart from the noise it produces, rolling has a maddening rhythm that is one of the minor tortures of rough weather. It never stops or misses a beat, it cannot be escaped anywhere. If you go through a doorway, it hits you hard: if you sit down, you fall over; you get hurt, knocked about continuously, and it makes for extreme and childish anger. When you drink, the liquid rises towards you and slops over: at meals, the food spills off your plate, the cutlery will not stay in place. Things roll about, and bang, and slide away crazily: and then come back and *hurt* you again. The wind doesn't howl, it *screams* at you, and tears at your clothes, and throws you against things and drives your breath down your throat again. And off watch, below, there is no peace: only noise, furniture adrift, clothes and boots sculling about on the deck, a wet and dirty chaos. Even one's cabin can be a vicious cage, full of sly tricks and booby-traps: not a refuge at all, rather a more subtle danger-spot, catching you relaxed and unawares and too dead-tired to guard your balance. Sometimes, at the worst height of a gale, you may be hove-to in this sort of fury for days on end, and all the time you can't forget that you are no nearer shelter than you were twenty-four hours before: you are gaining nothing, simply holding your own: the normal rigours of the trip are still piled up, mountains high, in front of you.

A most unholy chaos can be caused on the upper deck when, in bad weather, things get adrift and are not immediately secured. We once had some heavy oil drums which broke away aft, and were washing about with a tremendous noise, dragging all sorts of odd-ments—planks, fenders, heaving-lines—in their train: to get them under control again we had almost to stalk them, dodging out of the way as they crashed to leeward, gradually getting more and more ropes secured and finally smothering them. And another time, a rough, pitch-dark night, one of the boats which was swung out rolled itself right under water, smashing the griping-spar and jumping its releasing gear at one end: it hung down by the after falls, its bows in the water at one moment and then lifting and crashing against the ship's side as we rolled. It looked, and sounded, nasty.

'Have a crack at securing that,' said the Captain, after watching it for a couple of minutes. 'But don't kill yourself. If it's no good, cut it adrift.'

The right order. . . . . It took an hour, and the six toughest hands of the watch, but we got it inboard in the end, not much the worse for wear, and securely lashed in its chocks. I think I almost enjoyed that struggle, floundering about on the boat-deck with the seas washing over, leaning outboard at the end of a life-line to try and get the falls hooked on again. It was nearer the sea-going of the past, less official, less organized, less war-like.

Discussion on the bridge, at the height of a gale, of how we came to be drafted to corvettes.
Captain: 'I was told it would be like luxury motoring.'
Self: 'I was told I was damned lucky to get one.'
Voice of Asdic rating: 'I was detailed off, sir.'

When the ship crosses the storm-centre, there comes a sudden lull, and then the wind starts to blow from the opposite direction, setting up a baffling sea. It seems to come at you from all angles, rather like the meeting of the tides in Pentland Firth at the top of Scotland: shapeless humps of water are thrown together crazily, and when the wave-tops break they are caught and blown back like a horse's mane, or a crest of white hair suddenly whipped up.

Running with a heavy following sea at night has its own hard-won loveliness. The long streaks of foam are lit eerily by the moonlight: the enormous pile-up of water which collects, hissing and roaring, under the bow, seems suddenly to explode into a broad phosphorescent smother which in a moment is left behind. Looking aft, one sees the stern cant up before a black wall of water: the water overtakes, slides underneath and past, and breaks at the bow, its attack spent. The ship yaws, the compass swings: from below comes the quartermaster's muttered curse as he braces his feet and hauls the wheel over to meet the next ponderous weight of sea.

Simile-spinning in the middle watch.
Northern lights—like giant streamers stirred by a sky-wide fan: like an amateur-operatic rendering of Don Giovanni's purgatory: like the fake flames of a pale electric fire. . . .

'Bosun's Mate!'
'Bosun's Mate, sir.'
'Get me a cup of tea and the note-book in my top drawer.

It is pleasant to notice the first patch of drying deck after a storm. It spreads. It means peace. But it covers, between decks, a chaos which until then there has been no chance to set to rights. In the mess-decks, water is everywhere: there are benches broken, things washing about on the deck, off-watch stokers trying to sleep and cursing the sweepers at work cleaning up. The wardroom is like an abandoned battle-field: armchairs have slipped their moorings and crashed the whole length of it, packed bookcases have burst open, and in the pantry all the steward's cunning has not prevented a formidable expense of crockery.

There's a respite now, anyway: hot meals again instead of tea and corned-beef sandwiches; sleep without being tipped out of your bunk, a whole watch without once getting wet. The upper-deck petty officer gets to work squaring up, the seaman-gunner of the watch cleans the Lewis and Hotchkiss guns, the leading signalman checks over his rockets and flares, the torpedoman greases the depth-charge releasing gear, examines all the primers, tests the electric circuits. Work comes as a relief, after the discomfort and the cramping inactivity of the past few days.

In the calm darkness, there sounds the beat of an unseen bird's wings, flailing the water as it evades the ship. We seem to be moving through a bath of phosphorescence; our bow-wave can be seen, streaming away into the darkness on either side, and ships in company, even half a mile away, have a luminous line from stem to stern along their water-line.

When you are in convoy, station-keeping at night becomes an endurance test, a matter of staring without respite, concentrating on a little blurred image far ahead or abeam which may be the right ship—or a smudge on one's binoculars. If, in poor visibility, a zigzag is ordered, it has to be worked out on time instead of on distance, and becomes a sort of qualified guess-work: you run the outward course for so many minutes, until the convoy is right out of sight, and then you turn and run back till you meet them again; the whole manœuvre is a recurrent act of faith.

There is tremendous difficulty, sometimes, in hanging on for hours to a ship which seems to fade devilishly to nothing if you relax for a moment; but the difficulty gradually lessens and is at last forgotten, if you are lucky, in the joys of the morning watch, with the light coming up and showing the convoy still there, still in formation, still ploughing on, and one day nearer delivery. And there is a certain satisfaction, too, in rounding up stragglers, shepherding them, grading your signals between 'Can you squeeze a few more revs?' and a forthright 'Keep better station in future.'

But on the whole the compensations of watch-keeping at night are few, and tremendously realized: the comfort of a small, wavering stern-light, of a big ship easily seen and recognized: of a duffle coat: of a cup of near-solid cocoa half-way through the watch. They are the things you count on and cling to, the things that seem to be on your side against the enemy. You grow, almost, to love them.

A ship may be so blurred by darkness and rain that its outline, even close to, is no more than a dubious smudge in the gloom; and that is what you have to hold on to for four long hours, under orders to remain at an exact bearing and distance from it. And all that time the weather can best be summed up in the coxswain's phrase: 'Dark, sir? You couldn't see a new sixpence on a sweep's ——.'

There is something completely satisfying in the attention, the loving care even, that one can give to a watch, especially at night: keeping an all-round, all-time look-out, keeping mathematical station and a fast, wide-angle zigzag, doing your very best for four hours and handing over the watch as if it were a neat and shipshape package.

Sometimes, even when there is nothing doing, the Captain comes up in the middle watch; saying nothing at first, noticing everything, and then perhaps settling down to talk, with relays of tea at intervals to sweeten the session. (Some watches, indeed, are so boring that a cup of tea is an event, a banging door a relief from flat monotony.) The coxswain also is an occasional visitor, usually introducing himself with a bar of chocolate or some home-made titbit from the Petty Officers' mess; perhaps to season his advice, discreetly and often very indirectly tendered.

In default of visitors or emergencies, one talks to the duty signalman—a different one every night. The talk ranges widely, most of it concerned with the future, some of it (as is natural at 3 a.m.) highly pessimistic. I remember one such discussion, of what it would be like after the war, where we would live and what job we would go for. The signalman favoured a country pub, with just enough custom to keep things going. . . . But the talk had, as usual, a nostalgic air about it—it was dependent on so many things, so many chances of fortune, so many hazards: it might even stand or fall by something that was going to happen in the next five minutes. . . . Even to use the phrase 'after the war' took for granted the twin unmentionable doubts, of victory and of personal survival.

Strain and tiredness at sea induce a sort of hypnosis: you seem to be moving in a bad dream, pursued not by terrors but by an intolerable routine. You come off watch at midnight, soaked, twitching, your eyes raw with the wind and with staring at shadows; you brew a cup of tea in the wardroom pantry and strip off the top layer of sodden clothes; you do, say, an hour's intricate ciphering, and thereafter snatch a few hours' sleep between wet blankets, with the inflated life-belt in your ribs reminding you all the time that things happen quickly; and then, every night for seventeen nights on end, you're woken up at ten to four by the bosun's mate, and you stare at the deck-head and think: My God, I *can't* go up there again in the dark and filthy rain, and stand another four hours of it. But you can, of course: it becomes automatic in the end. And besides, there are people watching you.

But when you are working in three watches, and have eight hours off at a time, there is luxury in coming off watch: the luxury of relaxing, smoking, putting on bedroom slippers, turning on the electric heater and feeling your face thawing and losing its stiffness; all with no sense of hurry. It can be comforting below: one *can* forget all the menaces outside. So far I have been lucky in having had only one acute attack of nerves—lying down, strained, alert, unable to sleep, just waiting for it: waiting for those shouts, that rush of water, that iron clang. . . . But that was in the middle of a rough party, when another escort-vessel had been sunk, and I don't imagine I was alone. I hope not, anyway.

There is a steady deterioration of food during a trip: we have five days or so of comparative comfort, and then beans set in, and corned beef, and tinned sausages, and biscuits ominously labelled with the name of a firm which, in peace-time, was famous among dog-lovers the world over.

'Steward, is this bread fresh?'
'No, sir—reconstructed.'

Satisfaction, after a ten days' outward battle, of once more giving helm-orders with 'East' in them.

As with convoys, so with watches: they can be specially good as well as specially bad. The first landfall of the return journey makes one of the best—it is comforting to meet the friendship of coast-lights again, to be (as they say) under the Fighter Umbrella, to be on the map and an ascertainable spot on it too, instead of staring eternally at stars and the last ship of the wing column and anonymous unidentifiable water. Besides, the watch goes quickly: there are lights to be picked up and checked, bearings to be taken, little sums in Four-Points and Running Fixes to be added up: possibly the convoy alters its formation, and there is some chivvying to be done: one is at work as a sailor instead of as a pair of bored eyes. Above all, it means that there will not be many more watches; another day of it, thirty-six hours perhaps, and one will be tied up to something solid and enjoying sleep without a miserly limit to it.

Near land, the porpoises and the sea-gulls play round the ship, giving us the first welcome. The sea-gulls have a trick of skimming round the bows close to the water, ready to plane upwards if there is a second player coming the other way. Human beings need four sets of traffic lights, and slavish obedience thereto, to do this in safety.

Now and then there comes a quiet sunny afternoon watch, with the Captain and all other officers turned in below, with nothing for me to do but take one Meridian Altitude sight and see that the quartermaster keeps his course, with the signalman washing out an ensign in a bucket of suds. And sometimes it is a prelude to a whole row of luxuries within a few hours: tying up to the oiler and ringing off engines: the silence and peace which descends on the ship when the mail comes over the side and is distributed: the first night in port, the first drink, first undressing, first sleep.

At our usual base there is one small dock, nicknamed 'The Garage', that has become Corvette Headquarters. At the end of a convoy it is crammed with ships; and this recurrent association, and the chance of exchanging visits, is remarkably pleasant, particularly at the end of a trip which may have been rough in one way or another. The various visiting captains usually forgather in the C.O.'s cabin: down in the wardroom some moderate junketing sets in; it is good to relax, and tell competitive lies about the one that got away.

Of course, this lotus-eating doesn't last for ever: the mail will have brought enough paper-work to last a dozen good men a fortnight. Reports, as long as your arm, are called for if a ship has as much as had a queer look from a porpoise; and internal peace in the dock is very likely shattered by a snooty blast from the Senior Officer about jetty-sentries, or about the Guard Corvette being responsible for cleaning up the very nasty rubbish-dump left by the preceding escort-group. But while quiet reigns, it is just what we want. We're possibly going out again in a matter of hours, anyway.

Snow in the navigation-lights going down river: driving past the bridge, glowing green or red for an instant and then disappearing.

More satisfying to the lover of nature than to the Navigating Officer.

Rounding up a big convoy and getting it into shape, particularly in bad weather, can be hard work, and doubly so if you are canteen-boat—i.e. the junior corvette, detailed for the odd jobs.

There has come to be, among merchant ships, a very high standard of convoy discipline, and the greater part of the 'forming up' can safely be left to them; but even so there are always plenty of oddments to attend to. You may be sent up and down the lines counting heads: you may be detailed to close one of the ships and give him last-minute instructions on the loud-hailer—and he is invariably a foreigner with neither English nor megaphone: you may be sent to chivvy an outlying straggler; and all the time you are getting a steady trickle of signals from the Senior Officer—'Tell the fourth tanker to fly his pendants'—'Find out where that little one is straying to'—'Has So-and-so dropped his pilot?'—'So-and-so reports steering defect: close and investigate.' Sometimes, from the upper deck of a bigger ship, you see a long line of khaki or Air Force blue, faces staring down, hands waving, and you know you've got something even more worth escorting than usual.

Incensed by some free-style manoeuvring on the part of his charges, the Commodore hoisted the signal for 'Manoeuvre badly executed': the hoist was repeated (no doubt with full hearts) by all the other ships in convoy, with the exception of half a dozen confirmed stragglers and wanderers in the rear, whose hoists were incorrect and signalled instead 'Manoeuvre well executed'. . . . I should like to think they did it on purpose.

The last sight of land impresses the mind as much as the first landfall of the homeward journey.

The convoy is now in shape, the escorts correctly stationed: each ship knows its proper position, its opposite number, the amount of room it has to play with; all we now have to do, every ship in company, is to stay in station, make no smoke, keep on going, turn the right corners, and make our number prettily on arrival. . . . We're on the job once more, and it's a job we know (and I suppose) like; and when one looks about and sees the faint line of land, our last contact with the normal world, slipping away on the quarter, and the convoy proceeding as an orderly unit on a journey wherein it must make its own tracks and meet such emergencies as come its way, one is aware of the moment as a memorable and significant one.

By now there is probably no ship in company that does not know of these emergencies at first hand, and will acquit itself in seamanlike fashion if any of them arise; but for good or ill we are on our way, for the *n*th time challenging the sea and the malice of the enemy: the convoy to make the journey against all hazards, and we to see that it does not fail for want of a show of teeth. When land fades astern the party is on once again, the ring is formed.

There is a certain comradely pleasure in meeting an aircraft on long-range reconnaissance. A wide-awake look-out picks it up, the signal-man of the watch challenges and is answered; and then it flies past, sometimes quite close, giving little dips of its wings and flirts of its tail; the pilot waves, and you wave back, and you think: 'My God, I wouldn't care to be so far out in an aeroplane,' and he is probably thinking: 'My God, I wouldn't care to be down there in that sea.' The sense of being on the job together is a very strong one. Some of them are well worth looking at, too, especially the Catalinas, extraordinarily graceful in flight, and the squared-off business like Whitleys.

Usually they are most energetic, going away into corners to look at suspicious waves and then scampering back to report. And, of course, as a means of keeping submarines out of harm's way below the surface they have, time and again, proved themselves invaluable.

Cross-talk:
Destroyer: 'Can't you keep up?'
Corvette: 'We have been investigating astern.'
Destroyer: 'Well done.'

A big convoy at sea, well closed up and keeping good station, has an immense air of purpose: seen as a whole, it is a fine and rewarding spectacle. Lines of ships—big ships, loaded deep: ships crammed with deck-cargo, ships with aeroplanes all over their upper-works, like peeled almonds stuck in a pudding; bluff, good-looking tankers (a modern tanker is probably the best-kept and best-looking ship of all)—they make up a whole fleet, an Armada which no onslaught of the enemy can scatter. Round them the corvettes and destroyers play, almost in droves: a ring hard to crack, harder still to pierce. One can only feel proud to be one of the company, to be trusted with a watch and a ship when there is so much at stake, and when such grim efficiency is the rule.

Some of the destroyers in company may have famous names, many of the corvettes a string of successes to their credit. Often we know some of the customers, too: there may be ships in the convoy that we have escorted half a dozen times before, old friends who have survived many a rough party and are still coming up for more. Sometimes they recognize us, and send individual greetings. We like that. But it is the convoy as a whole that takes the eye and the imagination. Making its steady and determined way, having limitless reserves of power and nerve to call on, it is, somehow, such a good thing to belong to.

Christmas at sea brings no holly, no turkey: only the snow is seasonable, only the lovely Christmas surprise may still make its appearance. 'I've sent a hand aft to read the Yule log,' said M. to me as I came up on the bridge at midnight, 'and I've been saving that joke since ten o'clock. A happy Christmas to you!'

In the morning, a festive signal from the Commodore: 'Happy Christmas. Keep well closed up.' In the afternoon, a long-range Santa Claus, showering seasonable gifts rather wide of the mark, with no one's name on them this time. In the evening, a rising sea which filled our stockings for us. Never mind: one day nearer home.

After checking depth-charges:
'Next time we drop one of these it may not kill a submarine—it may not even explode—but by God! we'll have its right number.'

One incredibly dreary slow convoy, which sometimes seemed to be no more than drifting in with the Gulf Stream, was redeemed and indeed glorified by the fact that the Commodore had had a difference of opinion with the leading ship of the nearest column, and the two of them spent their time enlivening the watch and each other by exchanging cracks, of which, 'Pay more attention to station-keeping,' and, 'Your signal is wrongly hoisted and meaningless,' were the least objectionable.

'What's the hoist?' I would ask the signalman, as an effervescent burst of bunting fluttered up, covering all halyards and overflowing to the triatic stay. 'Another alter-course?'

The signalman, examining a little-used part of the code-book, shook his head.

'No, sir—they're just chewing each other's ears off again. Something about "discharge of offensive waste matter".'

Satisfactory sight: two convoys, outward and inward bound, meeting within half a mile of each other, nearly half-way across the Atlantic. Naval navigation!

The first time we met an American escort-group at sea, and took over their convoy from them, was an occasion which should have been dramatic, and was of course nothing of the sort. There *was* a small exchange of international courtesies, including (from them): 'Hope the convoy itself will be American one of these days,' which we thought handsome of them, as well as accurately prophetic; but there the hands-across-the-sea stuff began and ended. (I'm not sure what I had been expecting: something heroic in the 'March of Time' style, possibly.) But it was good to see the Stars and Stripes again, for the first time in this war, and to know that a potent ally was, officially or not, ranged on our side at last. I had latterly been meeting a certain number of Americans ashore, mostly ferry-pilots resting between transatlantic trips delivering bombers—men, outspokenly partisan, who had certainly known their own mind and translated it into action: doubly welcome were their sea-going counterparts, blessed by authority and free to wear their uniforms.

Ordeal for an officer-of-the-watch: corvettes and destroyers (of unequal speed, turning-circle, and general manœuvrability) hurrying to a rendezvous in line abreast: set speed, zigzag an exact number of degrees every few minutes, and damn your eyes (with the widest publicity) if you get out of station.

In any case the rendezvous is very likely an impossible one: 300 miles at 15 knots in half a gale, on the offchance of finding twenty ships that have been hove-to for three days in a position depending on a week-old estimate: with visibility less than two miles, and about six hours of daylight to play with. No wonder the senior officers of escort-groups are men of half-humorous despair.

For a convoy to heave-to in bad weather, especially if it has to turn to face a following gale, endless care is needed, and a good slice of luck as well. There may be sixty ships or more, close together and with unequal and sometimes very large turning-circles, swinging round 180 degrees into the wind, and many of them may have been yawing wildly for the past hour. Getting round is a slow operation—for the smaller ships dangerously so; and when it is accomplished there is usually a good deal of trimming up to be done before the convoy is in shape again.

In the night they separate for safety's sake, perhaps clinging to one consort, one pin-point stern-light in a howling wilderness, shouldering the waves, shaking themselves free of water when they ship a heavy one, their screws turning just enough to keep steerage-way. On watch in a corvette, it is a matter of patience and a damned good look-out; for there is usually some smart Alec who decides that he's had enough of it, and squares away before the gale and comes roaring down-wind at fourteen knots, leaving it to the other bloke to get out of the way.

When daylight comes, if the weather has moderated, we look hopefully round, sight one ship and then a couple more, dash backwards and forwards persuading them to form up; and then, with, say, six tankers and a couple of merchant packets in company, comes the job of guessing the night's drift, roughing out some sort of D.R. position and laying a course for the next rendezvous or landfall. If you sight other ships on the way, you coax them into the party; sometimes it is a case of two corvettes, each with a miniature convoy in tow, trying to attract custom by bluffing about the sights they haven't taken or by specious promises of joining the main body in two hours at the outside. . . . And, of course, you pray all the time for improving weather and a sight of the sun, which will put an end to guess-work and prevent the whole issue running ashore at either Namsos or Ostend.

Terrific calculations take place as soon as we make our first landfall, calculations as intricate and as dependent on fortune as any Delphic prophecy.

The stake is a high one—the saving of a tide. If the main diverted portion causes no delay when it breaks off: if the convoy can increase speed by at least half a knot: if we are not landed with the X, Y, or Z portions, bound for different ports: if we can find the Outer Buoy quickly and part company there instead of escorting all the way home (usually the canteen-boat's job): if we can then break the port speed-limit without attracting the attention of an examination vessel: if there is no fog in the approaches: if we can get up river in an hour and a quarter and oil in two and a half—then we'll just get through the dock-gates with ten minutes to spare and gain a whole night ashore.

Signal from air-escort over convoy:
'Fancy escorting a bloody Irishman.'

Destroyers sometimes lose the convoy. Then, having been unseen for three days, they dash up when the convoy is just going up river and start signalling all round the horizon. In the end, you come to think that they have been there the whole time without any unaccountable gaps.

Perhaps they even deceive themselves.

Once, when we were nearing home, we had a signal that mines had been laid in the approach-channel, and that ships were to anchor until the fairway was clear. Escort vessels congregated while sweeping was going on, seemingly impatient, but when the port was declared open there was no sort of competition to be first down the line. A great deal of cumbersome manœuvring took place, and such signals as 'Please pass ahead of me'—'I am not oiling now—go ahead'—'My speed reduced to three knots—will go up last' passed to and fro like smooth drawing-room courtesies. . . . Finally a large, baleful destroyer signalled to the junior corvette: 'Proceed up river forthwith,' and the rest of us fell gracefully into line. Dinner with the Borgias was served.

There is satisfaction in delivering a big convoy: a long line of laden ships that have been in company for thousands of miles, now moving slowly up river at the end of their journey, is one of the finest sights that the war can offer. No wonder one watches them with pride and a certain proprietary pleasure as well; they have been a responsibility for many days and nights, and now the responsibility is discharged. Even if there are gaps they are not big ones; they have been closed and forgotten in the routine triumph of the majority.

That's why we like our job, I suppose: it shows results. We are proud of those results and of a lot of other things besides. And why not? We *are* proud of our ship, of the way she can take it and the tough answers she can hand out in return: we think she's a good outfit to belong to. We are proud of our crack guns'-crews, and of our immensely resourceful signalmen. (I myself am proud of my depth-charge section: the last time it was in action it tossed the things overboard like chicken-feed and, in rough weather, broke its own *harbour* record for firing and reloading.)

We are proud of the scores of convoys we have escorted; proud of being a good ship's company. We have to be: the job calls for nothing less. We have seamen aboard who can meet any emergency and deal with it; and the Captain is the best seaman of all. We are proud of that, too.

We like reading about ourselves in the newspapers: we enjoy what one might call their highly coloured understatements. We are the smallest ships that operate regularly in the North Atlantic in winter: we have to keep going in appalling weather, weather that must really be seen to be believed. After a long and rough trip, when everything in the mess-decks—bedding, lockers, spare gear—has been wet through for days, and cooking anything but tea has been out of the question, we may have to oil, store, and go out again all in a matter of hours. We may be closed up at action-stations for days on end: certainly we are often never out of our clothes for a fortnight or more at a stretch.

Why not be proud? Destroyers are all right, of course; but corvettes are the tough babies, and we're in corvettes.

For a variety of reasons the job is very much easier in summer: the weather is kind, the sun a blessing, the nights short and (up North) barely dark. With only three hours or so to develop their attack, submarines can by day be kept below the surface by our aircraft and made unable to catch the convoy up in the short time when surface progress is feasible for them. But against this, longer daylight gives the bombers far more chance: sometimes darkness is only the short respite between two attacks.

It is a harsh fate (or a harsh Admiral) which sends corvettes, not equipped with refrigerators or more than a limited supply of fresh meat and vegetables, on the south-bound run in summer—fifteen days or more of blinding heat, solaced by tinned beans and beautiful corned beef. Coming on top of Arctic weather all winter, it did seem that they were doing their worst for us. And how quickly summer was over: two Gibraltar runs and a boiler-clean, and we were back to the merry North Atlantic, and a particularly murderous party in vile weather to kick off with.

4 INTERLUDES

Going down to Gibraltar, in midsummer.

The sea became calmer than ever, the sky a deeper blue, the sun a hot caress; the barometer scaled unbelievable heights, and stayed there. Daily the sextant-angle at the meridian showed a more tropical figure.

We passed whales and basking sharks, and once a turtle, paddling manfully westward. M. swore to having seen flying-fish in his watch: a warm breeze, imaginatively spiced with oranges, blew from the southeast, and odd rigs were seen about the ship—bare legs, singlets, sandals, shameful tattooings. . . . Even the fact that, after ten days at sea, meals now consisted (in tropical heat) of tinned sausages and beans and smoking hot potatoes in their jackets, and that there was no limejuice or fruit of any kind, could not spoil the attraction of that southward journey.

It was the genuine summer begun at last, the relief and compensation we had all been waiting for throughout months of winter hardship; no wonder there were sing-songs and the drone of a mouth-organ in the dog-watches, no wonder there were naked stokers laid out like half-cooked bullocks on the after-deck, no wonder that, in the canvas bath rigged in the port waist, a noisy road-house gaiety was soon under way. This was what we had all been earning ever since the black onset of last October.

And what a landfall was granted us to finish up with—Spain on the port hand and Africa on the starboard: Cape Trafalgar and Cape Spartel, with a glow in the sky ahead marking the lit waterfront of Tangier. My watch ended with Tangier abeam, but I stayed on while it grew lighter, and Tarifa came into view and an extraordinary smell of burnt grass came out of Africa, and dawn broke and the Rock showed at last, and the failing lighthouse off Europa Point winked twice and then gave in to the sun.

The harbour was full of heavy stuff; the Rock, close to, was as impressive as I had expected, and always suggesting more than it revealed—stones that were something else, scrub that surely hid weapons, sunlight over all: a bristling fortress decked out as scenery. Gibraltar becomes a sort of Boom Town at night, the narrow streets crammed with Forces in white or khaki shorts. Standing, as I did, at a balcony window with a tallish glass of Tio Pepe sherry, one looks down on Main Street chockful of people, a parading stream eddying out at the corners and overflowing into shops and bars. The latter, luring customers with music and chorus-singing, do a roaring trade; and in the oddly-named shops everyone buys silk stockings and cosmetics and perfumes of considerable fame and rarity and suspicious abundance.

Travel, for the lazy or romantic, is by gharry, a species of crazy open four-wheel cab, very light and springy, which dash about like operatic chariots. There is (or was) no black-out: women are rare, and wary.

On our first night ashore we attended rather a good party given by some Merchant Navy survivors who seemed to think they owed us a drink or two. We met them in the Grand, all togged up in Gibraltar suits and rainbow shirts, and we had an uproarious polyglot session, with Swedes, Dutch, Belgians, and Danes bobbing up continuously to drink our healths and (presumably) return formal thanks to us. But we felt we needed none of that: theirs had been the ordeal and theirs the brave endurance.

Thoughts after a shopping expedition.

One cannot help being conscious of a certain futility in convoying, sometimes at great risk and loss of life, shiploads of goods to Gibraltar in order to buy them in the shops there and bring them back by corvette. Rough trips apart, I think this was one of the reasons why we came to dislike what some of us called 'The Gibraltar Packet' and others 'The Silk-Stocking Run'.

One of the best things about our stay at Gibraltar was wearing tropical kit—white shirt and shorts, white stockings and shoes, and white cap-cover: an extraordinarily cool rig which made one feel fresh and clean immediately one put it on. Forgotten were duffle-coats, sea-boot stockings, thick oiled-wool sweaters: this, at last, was the luxury life we had been born to. . . . We used to work in the morning, not very hard—since our mails had not caught us up there was hardly any official business: 'Pipe down' would be sounded after lunch, 'Liberty-men to clean' at four, and after that there was nothing to do but enjoy ourselves.

Usually we would bathe at Rosia Bay, swimming out into the Mediterranean as if it were once more an *haute monde* playground; and then, in the cool of the evening, we would walk down into the town, and there shop lazily, and sip sherry at the Embassy Bar or the Bristol, and dine *à l'espagnol* off onion soup and rice-with-trimmings and smooth Algerian wine: the kind of dinner that goes on and on. . . . It was out-of-the-war, of course, and almost traitorously escapist: too much of it would have made us feel guilty and destroyed its savour; but as a severely-rationed interlude we felt that we could take all that came our way.

We were lucky not to come in for a bloody job which fell to another corvette—taking another ship's dead to sea and burying them.

What with the hot weather and the fact that most of them had spent two days in an oil tank (where an explosion had blown them), the corpses were already nearly liquid; but they were yanked out. identified, sewn up in blankets and wheeled across to the corvette—oozy packets trundled by men with handkerchiefs tied over the nose and mouth. ... There they lay all night, leaking a vile and sickening fluid into the scuppers, sprayed at intervals, watched by a quartermaster (what a job for a young rating!), and on the following night they were buried; and for a week afterwards a stink hung about that ship that no effort or antidote could get rid of.

That must have been an odd burial: pitch darkness, the chaplain shining a torch on his prayer-book, the pipes shrilling as thirty-eight bodies went down the chute one by one, making their successive quick trails of phosphorescence. But if the opportunity offered on another occasion, I should still be willing to take the description at second-hand.

We were in collision, in thick fog, with a Portuguese trawler on one of our homeward trips; very little was damaged besides the port boat and a section of bow-plating, but while it lasted the encounter was impressive.

Fog tests the judgment very highly indeed, particularly in convoy, where the way in which a nearby ship can fade away as if washed over with dirty chalk, makes station-keeping half guess-work and half a sort of direction-finding by ear. All the senses are alert. You stand on the bridge, sniffing cold, vaporous air, listening to and trying to tabulate the various fog-horns, staring at the blank wall ahead. With the engines at 'Slow' and the oily sea making no noise against the bows, the silence is extraordinary. Deceptive also: fog blankets the sound in some directions, magnifies it in others. The look-out or the signalman will sing out 'Whistle on the starboard beam!' when you have just classified the sound as coming from dead astern, if not slightly to port. ... Either may be right: it's not a question of good hearing or even of practice; it is luck. The signalman may have heard the sound directly, you may have heard it reflected off a layer or a bank of colder air. You cannot know for certain: all that *is* certain is that you must make up your mind, and then act—decisively, unhesitatingly—one way or another.

But in this case confusions of sound did not enter into it: the trawler, lit but silent, came to us at right angles on the port bow. If she had not hit us she would have hit one of the ships in convoy. We sighted her lights about a minute before the collision; she was moving far too fast, and there came the instant realization (*felt* rather than calculated) that we could not miss each other. Having given all possible orders ('One short blast'—'Hard a-starboard'—'Full astern'—'Sound mess-deck alarm bell'—'Close watertight doors') we could only stand on the bridge and wait for it. There was a sound of air going into life-jackets at high pressure. . . . The lights, suddenly very near and menacing, seemed to throw themselves at us; there was one startled shout from the bridge of the trawler and then the crash.

Not a sharp crash but a long-drawn-out grinding. Due to our quick turn to starboard we had closed on a converging course, our port bow to his starboard one, instead of a right-angle cut which might well have sunk one or other of us. The two ships closed, surging against each other, parted momentarily, and then closed again: expensive smashing noises came from up forrard, and below me the port boat, splintered and stove-in, was forced over its griping spar and fell inboard. We could see the trawler clearly now, in the few moments before she sheered off: a big, heavily-built ship with high spoon bows and one man on the bridge staring up at us as if roughly awakened from a deep dream. Perhaps such was the case. Then we drifted apart and the trawler faded out once more till only her lights could be seen.

Sent below by the Captain to see what the damage was, I forced my way through a throng of half-asleep and rather reproachful ratings, and went into the messdecks. It was odd, and disconcerting, to see light through the bow-plating, but the main damage seemed to be well above the water-line, the forepeak being still quite dry and in fact remaining so for the rest of the trip. (Rough weather, of course, would have made it quite a different matter, but we were lucky in that respect.) I attended to one casualty, a surprised steward who had been thrown out of his cot and had cracked a rib, and then went up to the bridge to report.

Up on the bridge also was a leading stoker, a reputed linguist, who had been summoned to address the trawler through the loud-hailer. The exchange was a short one, and inconclusive at that. He called out: 'Barco! Habla Inglese?' and the answer came back: 'Portuguese ship! You damn' fool!' And that was really all. She claimed no damage, we were fit to proceed, and there was a convoy to attend to; so after we had prised her name and number out of her (a long and disjointed business, sounding rather like a badly translated play) we rang 'Slow ahead' and got back on our course. It might have been very much worse, and thoughts of leave while the ship was under repair certainly sweetened the rest of the watch.

The upper-works of an odd ship showed themselves above the horizon.

'Close me!' signalled the senior corvette decisively. 'I'm going to investigate.'

We wound up to something near our maximum speed, we turned to starboard and laid a course for the stranger. Within a quarter of an hour it was revealed as not one ship but rather a lot; battleships, cruisers, a big ring of destroyers, escorting aircraft droning overhead. . . . After a surprised moment: 'Resume previous course', signalled the senior corvette: 'Formation is friendly.' As we turned to port again we signalled back: 'What price glory?'

We had an engine breakdown one morning, when we were by ourselves and on our way to a rendezvous. A knock developed, slight at first and then growing and growing till it seemed to fill the whole ship. Before long it was obvious that we would have to stop engines and investigate: never a popular necessity in the Western Approaches. . . . The repairs took us about six hours, and during all that time we lay motionless, our sea-boats swung out, the perfect target for air or underwater attack. We had, of course, wirelessed our position, but a feeling of tension filled the whole ship—it was a very clear day and one looked round the immense circle of wide, flat sea and thought: somewhere in that circle there may be, at this very moment, a submarine looking at us through its periscope and shaping up for an attack. Perhaps more than one submarine; perhaps a clutch of half a dozen. . . . Said M. to me, reflectively: 'In the old days there used to be an order, "Down funnel, up sail!" I wish we could give it now.'

I remember going down to the engine-room to see if I could hurry things up at all, finding a ring of engine-room ratings, stoker petty officers, and the Chief gathered round the offending crankshaft, and withdrawing again without saying anything. Anxiety was excusable, but it was obvious that they were doing their utmost without any chivvying from the bridge.

When we got going again you could almost hear the ship sigh with relief. A straight scrap we don't mind: we do mind being at the wrong end of a target-practice.

The next time it happened to us we were in company, which made things a lot easier, and we could also manage slow speed without tearing things to bits. But as we had the prospect of at least ten days at sea, and the damage might easily become worse, we made a signal to the senior corvette, telling her the tale and requesting permission to return to harbour for adjustments or repairs. The reply came back: 'Approved.

Do you require an escort?' to which we answered: 'Would prefer it if possible.'

From the other corvettes through whom the exchange had been passed came an instant twitter of signals, full of resource and inventiveness. 'Am prepared to escort *Flower* to base,' was the generous offer of one. 'My A/S gear unsatisfactory, suggest I return with *Flower*,' said a second, in whom eagerness had induced some rather muddled thinking. 'Would be glad of chance to refuel,' was a third optimistic suggestion which would not stand even superficial scrutiny. . . . But it was the Senior Officer himself who made the great sacrifice. 'Follow me,' he signalled: 'returning to harbour in company. What is your maximum safe speed?'

Coming alongside a French-manned oiler.

I went aft in pitch darkness, trying to think of the exact French equivalent of 'Take that forespring forrard and make it fast'.

After strife. We sailed into the inlet in the dusk of early evening, and into a different world. There was a little village opposite our anchorage, with an unromantic name; but what a village! There were lights in its streets, there were windows uncurtained—or curtained in friendly yellows and blues and reds such as we had not seen for months; there were buses with unscreened lamps and yellow bicycle lights, and a bonfire or two. Dusk here was not the beginning of total gloom or the onset of danger, but the signal for lighting the hearth and the way, for the comfortable exchanges of neighbour and neighbour.

From the bridge we stared at it in astonishment, for it was violently against the law and it invited the contemporary horrors; and then we realized. It was not a defiant village, it was the other half of the world, the world free from fear and preserving its sanity: it was Ireland, Ireland still evading the toils; it was peace. . . . And often during the evening we could come up from below to look at it, staring in contemplative wonder at this strangest of all sights—dear normality; and in some degree or other we all thought: 'Christ, this war! If only we lived across there. . . .' The international aspect was (to me) obscure; for here we were at anchor, one of His Majesty's ships of war in commission which had somehow escaped hateful reality and come upon a haven. Was it a licensed haven, or was it the blind eye? And how little it mattered! Dear village, dear cottages lighted and unafraid, dear unharmed corner of a scarcely remembered world.

In the morning the international aspect became (again, to me) even

more obscure; for we signalled to the Irish side and presently took off an
Irish pilot. He was small, diffident, and efficient; and when I inquired
how it was that Irish pilots were allowed to pilot British men-of-war, he
made the entirely reasonable comment: 'Now why should you be
sending up the river for a Six-Counties man when there's a good Irish
pilot waiting for you on the doorstep itself?'

The channel was, at times, extremely narrow. Said the Captain,
standing by my side, unexpectedly: 'You've only got to give "hard a-
starboard" and we could all be interned for the duration.'

Conversation-piece in Northern Ireland.
'Go ashore and get me a paper.'
'Any special one, sir?'
'Yes, get me the *Independent*.'
'The *Independent*, sir?'
'Yes, there's sure to be an *Independent*.'
There was.

Northern Ireland was another place where we slackened off, in a
rather special way. For some reason our stay there developed into a
faintly mad-house session, the effect of Ireland on a normally hard-
working and routine-ridden ship's company being to induce a sort of
fairy-like unreality; in fact, we all became Irish, and made the most of it.

Odd, unexplained people came aboard, and ate their lunches on the
upper deck; disreputable children wandered about at will, hazarding
their teeth on ship's biscuit. A feud developed with the corvette
alongside: the rival quartermasters faced each other across the
gangway, muttering threats and fingering their side-arms. It was
nothing for respectable petty officers, returning from liberty via the
other ship's fo'c'sle, to report to the Officer-of-the-Day in some such
formula as, 'Returning on board, sir, with fender and heaving-line.' We
went for a bicycle ride past the Eire customs (a signpost by the road-
side, deserted after office hours), and returned, laden with eggs, butter,
and strawberries, and impelled by Guinness to a breakneck speed.
Couponless, I was able to buy some silk stockings by initiating a whip-
round among the shop-girls, who each contributed one coupon and a
brilliant smile. The Captain, drinking in a pub on the dock-side, found
himself joined by his four officers one after the other. I counted them as
they arrived, and presently realized that there was no one left on board.
(It was attributed to lack of liaison, excused, and very shortly
forgotten.) And among many other manifestations of the Irish spirit,
there was a second case of creating vandalism in the mess-decks.

On our last night I went ashore with H., our recently joined junior officer, a jovial ex-barrister of spacious build. I recall two things about that night. The first was seeing a huge church, almost a cathedral, with a lighted porch beckoning us across the street. On an impulse I said: 'Let's light a candle to the holy saints above' (that was how one talked in Ireland), and we tiptoed in, silent, slightly awe-struck, chockful of milk stout and religious feeling. Inside the porch the first thing we saw was a blue notice, 'YOU MAY TELEPHONE FROM HERE', and the second a placard: 'TOWN HALL A.R.P. STATION. FEMALE DECONTAMINATION CASES, FIRST ON THE RIGHT.' The other thing I remember was asking at the hotel if drinks were procurable after hours, and being cheerily answered: 'Sure they are, sir—there's a Naval Base upstairs.' There was, too—almost a floating one.

A boiler-clean seems to render the ship, and the duty-officer, quite derelict.

With the boilers blown down, the whole ship is very cold: she is lit by unreliable shore-lighting which has a habit of packing up when you need it most; she has a general air of disuse not lessened by most of her innards being spread out over the engine-room casing. All officers except yourself are on leave. You sit and sit (and drink and drink) and nibble at the enormous amount of paper-work before you: other corvette officers in the same position come over to grouse in company, friendly destroyer-blokes come aboard to borrow stationery and stay to commiserate; it is like a Chekhov play pushed sideways into the dock. And when, as sometimes happens, repairs take a long time; when you miss your group, when weeks elapse and there is still no sign of going to sea; then a positive rotting-away atmosphere seems to set in. Friends come back from long and hard trips, and make pointed remarks about depot ships; someone chalks H.M.S. *Wallflower* in a prominent position opposite the gangway; you find yourself looking round the wardroom and thinking; we can't move now—imagine the break with tradition. . . . And soon, in any case, there will not be enough oil left to go and get some more.

There are shore-blokes who come aboard when you are trying to work and expect a mid-morning gin as an inalienable right. There are shore-blokes who, having got that gin, lean comfortably back and enlarge on the theme: 'I *wish* I could get to sea instead of being stuck ashore.' Some, wistful ones, really mean it; others patently do not. H. and I developed a rather amusing game with people we thought were shooting a line in this respect. We would let them run on, telling us the sad tale of their frustration, and we would then profess ourselves willing, *and able*, to get them sea-going jobs any time they wanted them. 'My uncle, the Admiral, can easily fix it for you,' H. would say, with a great air of patronage. 'What job would you like? Mine-sweeping at Sierra Leone?' There would be halfhearted agreement and a pinned-on smile, and then, rather late in the day, the bad news that the speaker, after all, had a tendency to catarrh which unfortunately precluded war-like activity. Otherwise, of course . . .

You get sick of them in the end; you cannot help contrasting natural wire-pullers who get themselves snug jobs with natural co-operators who take whatever job is given them and get on with it. To the gin you pour out for them is added a fairly stiff measure of contempt.

And there is the other kind: the inshore hero, who sits at the end of the bar. He has one of those tiddley little yachts which breeze up and down the river bullying merchant-men and sending us silly signals like, 'You have given the wrong recognition letters', or, 'You are approaching a prohibited anchorage', or, 'You have a fender hanging over the stern'. He gets command-money, hard-lying money, and a reputation for coolness and courage. He is invariably in great form in the bar, as brave as a lion: explaining what is wrong with our convoy-screening system, using two tumblers and an ash-tray and gestures of unflinching defiance.

Later on, when we had run through despair and dull resignation, we became much more light-hearted about paper-work; doing our best with it, certainly, but refusing to be worried by accumulations which we could not avoid. Back from a ripe convoy, you can't exactly give a broadside of enthusiasm to preparing a memorandum on the advantages experienced from using wrapped bread: particularly when you are fresh (hardly the right word) from ten days' hacking at ship's biscuit. . . . To delve at random into the 'Pending' file, to pick out some likely-looking morsel, blow the dust off, and deal concisely with it—surely that's the most the paymaster branch can expect.

There are 'strong' characters among the crew who wear you down by doing things they shouldn't and always having to be told about it. One day you forget to tell them, or you get tired and think: 'Oh, hell, it'll all be the same in a hundred years,' and there you are: a precedent is established, and they have won yet another round. There are others who make vaguely insubordinate remarks just within hearing: they are trying it on, and unless checked will make a habit of it and get out of control; but how can you check a man for saying, 'I wouldn't pick a Jerry out of the water, orders or no orders.' Surely it would be better to wait till the occasion arises, and then take the appropriate strong action....

Alternatively, how difficult it is to tick off a good bloke, well-behaved and efficient, who suddenly goes wrong—or who, perhaps from carelessness, develops some habit you do not like. For by his good behaviour he had, almost, earned a privileged position, or at least the right to a certain latitude; you respect each other, and there is an undercurrent of friendship: is it worth spoiling this for something basically unimportant, some petty toe-the-line regulation? In a way, you yourself should make some effort and sacrifice towards the smooth working of the ship; and this acceptance of individual foibles may be part of that effort.

One finds difficulty also in ticking off someone like a Chief Engine-Room Artificer, old enough to be your father and at least as individualist.

Numbered among the crew are unknown humorists whom you only learn about accidentally, when you happen to go forrard in the dog-watches: there you find an able-seaman, whom you had set down as slow and none too bright, giving a mouth-organ recital or an exhibition dance to his enthralled mess-mates, or a cross-talk act good enough for the music halls, if quite unsuitable thereto. To be rated as humorists also, in a different tradition, were the two superior ordinary seamen, recommended for commissions, who put in a brief, enchanted period in our lower deck. Of them it is related that, on first coming aboard, they strode into the stokers' mess-deck and asked cheerily: 'Are there any other Cambridge chaps here?' I have had no reliable account of the stokers' reaction.

They came to fit in better than that later on, though there was one whose habit it was, when on look-out duty, to report anything of interest with the words, 'I say, sir, rather suspicious object over there!' (His best effort was: 'I say, sir—water-spout!' It was a lighthouse.)

It is perhaps worth touching on the problem (not applicable in this case) of what to do with a really useless rating of this sort—i.e. a 'gent' who simply does not satisfy naval standards of seamanship. Sooner or later you have to send in a report on him—an honest report which decides his future sphere of usefulness. To keep him in the ship as an A.B. is to keep so much dead wood: the status of officer might just enable him to pull his weight. But is promotion to be on these lines? Should good manners and lack of a localized accent draw the attention and give a man such a pull? Surely it should be the best *sailors* who are advanced to commissions, rather than men of gentle birth, about whose naval future one is in despair.

In my capacity as Senior Medical Officer (acting, unpaid), I once had occasion to send a chit to Naval Sick Quarters, to accompany 'So-and-so, Stoker First Class, who is believed to be suffering from the complaint commonly known as crabs'. The answer came back in due course, signed by a Surgeon-Lieutenant, R.N.V.R.: 'I confirm your diagnosis, and add that your stoker is also suffering from the complaint commonly known as the Itch (scabies). For your future reference, crabs, by the way, are called "Pediculosis Pubis", or Little Pattering Feet on the Private Parts.'
I should like to meet that man.

Our former leading steward, when rebuked (which was often), had the habit of going into the pantry and saying in a loud, carrying voice to the assistant steward: 'Steward, you've *let me down*! I told you to get tea and now the officers are *waiting*!'

Lighting up the boiler, the young stoker explained the process for my benefit as he went along.
He turned a few knobs, seemingly at random, and then took up a sort of long-handled pair of tongs with a piece of cotton-waste at the end. This he dipped in a can of oil, and lit with a match: then he opened a small door under the boiler, and thrust it within. There was a subdued roar, and then a glow through half a dozen small windows. He turned two more knobs, and then began to watch, carefully, a pressure-gauge above his head.
He looked very young, to be allowed to play about with machinery like that.

Sunday morning: returning from short leave, driving into the port after a bad blitz.
Outside the town, a lovely sunny day; but ahead there were billows of black smoke, and soon the air was fouled by smuts, charred paper drifting on the wind,[1] an over-all reek of destruction. As we made our

[1] During the morning a rating brought aboard a half-burned page from a Statute Book which he had picked up seven miles outside the town.

way the air grew darker and darker, shutting out the sun, the sky, the corners ahead: each street we traversed, by a dozen diversions, bumping over hoses, scuttering through broken glass and ruined woodwork, passing groups of intent rescue-workers or silent onlookers, showed a more appalling destruction. Tall houses lay in the street, flames showed through empty windows and gaping rents, shops and buildings sprawled over the roadways. The night must have been a fearful one.

When progress became impossible before the smoky chaos at the top of the main street, I tapped the taxi-driver on the shoulder and called out: 'That'll do—I'll walk the rest.' By force of habit he gave the correct traffic-signal and drew into the kerb—directly underneath a blazing building whose roof had already crashed through three flights. . . . Across the street it was the same, and farther on the same, and all the way to the ship the same: what was not still burning lay in red-hot piles of brick and wood; what was not torn to pieces was blasted into a vile disorder. Even to the casual observer it was a frightful scene—the mounting furnaces, the thick, smoke-filled air, the huge spaces laid waste; to a man born in that town it was heart-breaking.

We waited on board that same evening as the hands crawled round the clock towards another night, another testing-time. another ordeal. Hoses were rigged, sand-buckets filled and placed, wires run out to the opposite side of the dock in case the tall building alongside should take fire: the duty-watch were given their instructions and warned to stand by: but all these precautions seemed to be offset, rendered foolish even, by the opposing facts—the ship lay in the heart of the docks, and within a hundred yards two uncontrollable fires raged, unsubdued from the previous night, pointing beacons across the whole night sky. The day died, the fires showed stronger; at midnight the expected sirens went again.

It wasn't one of the worst raids; but it sufficed, it passed muster. We had a number of incendiary bombs on the fo'c'sle and on the warehouses alongside: some near-misses which fell in the dock made a disconcerting whistling sound. But the barrage, which had obviously been added to, was one of the most formidable things I had ever listened to; and at intervals the night-fighter boys tried their hand, the bursts of machine-gun fire being applauded by the crew. Then dawn, and a respite, and hot whisky all round.

We went down river at dusk, and anchored at the entrance, and from there watched the last heavy raid on the port. Occasionally a turning aircraft roared overhead, shaping up for another run over the target; but all one's attention was for the noise and the amazing display ashore—star-shells, flares, tracer from ships, the pin-point flicker of the barrage, the crash of bombs, the glow of fire spreading. A fine spectacle, and a sickening one.

Said the young Newfoundland rating at my side, slowly: 'I didn't reckon for this sort of war. There's women and children there.'

To be north-bound again, on one of the last fair-weather days of the year, came as a relief after the dusty havoc of our spell ashore.

It was a lovely day, of bright and warming sunshine, and we had the morning to waste. So we loitered: doing turning-trials in a smother of wake, altering course to look at pieces of drift-wood: flying home-made kites for machine-gun practice, firing off all the guns at once at an imaginary aeroplane which was brought down in spectral flames; sinking a mine by rifle-fire, dropping an adroit test-depth-charge and collecting the harvest of fish.

Second winter: rough weather again; but now we know all about it, now we've learned the drill, the routine of personal caution.

Hang on to something always: give no chances, secure everything movable, including the arm-chairs in the wardroom, clear your desk and wedge your books in the bookcase. When you are eating, watch with constant care the food and drink, which at any moment will dart for your lap. When you turn in, have your back against the bulkhead and crook your knees so that your thighs lie athwartships: this may keep you in place. But above all, if you don't want to be hurt, hang on to something, even if you're only taking a couple of steps: even if you are leaning against the bridge-rails having five minutes' inoffensive think-of-home.

Second winter, second year in corvettes. Yes, it's all the same now: the job is standardized; survivors are even wounded in the same way, and all corpses are alike.

There *was* one change, however, and a marked one: it grew out of the sharpening crisis in our corner of the war, the quickening *tempo* of the Atlantic fight.

For things woke up, with the intensification of the 'Battle of the Atlantic' that began in the turn of 1940–1; things came to the boil, and every phase of convoy-escort acquired a sharper edge to it. More danger for convoys, harder work for us; and more ships were sunk, though it wasn't a one-way affair by a long chalk—we drew more blood in the process, as the records will one day show. But this intensification brought with it a curious change in our outlook: it was, briefly, that we came to dislike everything that made sea-going easy and pleasant. To get convoys through, we wanted cover, and cover meant, in the last analysis, dirty weather.

It was odd to look forward, on setting out, to the chance of a gale—anyone who really wants the North Atlantic to do its worst in winter should be qualifying for a lunatic asylum—but that was what it amounted to. Before, all the emphasis of convoy work had been on navigation and station-keeping, and we had cursed the dark, moonless nights, the rain and mist, the lumpy seas that multiplied our difficulties; now we hated the moon, and wanted only a black night and a bit of flying scud to draw the curtains round us. It made it infinitely harder to hang on to the convoy, it turned zigzagging into tip-and-run in the dark, but it was harder still for the submarines to trail us, and that weighed more than all the hardship and the intolerable strain that bad weather brings.

Oddest, and in a way saddest, of all, was the fact that we tended to develop the same feeling about going off watch: it used to be so welcome, that tired descent, but now it meant not much more than going below the water-line and entering a possible trap. And to feel this about leaving the wet bridge and putting off the burden was another nut-house qualification which would, in any other circumstances, have been conclusive. . . . But above all, it was sad: it meant that we were being cheated, daily and nightly, of our just reward and recompense.

I'm not sure that I can truthfully talk of 'we' where all this is concerned: the others may not have felt it so strongly, or, indeed, at all. Better, perhaps, to say that one watch-keeping officer in corvettes came to prefer the fresh air, and the fresher the better.

5 ACTIONS: SURVIVORS

When 'Anti-aircraft stations' was sounded I put my tin hat on, and climbed up through the dusk to the after gun-turret: under a clear, frosty sky the gun's-crew stood silent, watching, waiting, possibly nervous. I said something or other, and they laughed, and relaxed: five young men, steel-helmeted and closely wrapped against the cold, the white tops of their seaboot stockings standing out in the gloom: five young men listening for sound above the ordinary disregarded sound of the ship and the sea, staring at the stars across which the mast swung a slow arc. To be together, and to see the stocky gun-barrel cocked up at the sky like a jauntily raised thumb, was to be reassured. . . . And then, head on one side, I heard the sound we were waiting for: far away on the other wing of the convoy a single line of tracer fled upwards; and without an order being given the crew closed up round their gun, the safety-catch clicked, and the layer slapped the breech with his mittened hand and said: 'Come on, Rosie, win me a medal.'

The brilliant fireworks of a dusk air attack: the bomber flies very low above the columns, pursued and harried by cross-fire from machine-gun tracer, by the quick pom-pom flashes, by the burst of flame as the destroyers' bigger guns go into action. Sometimes you may see a line of tracer bullets describing a complete semicircle, like a glowing fan opening and shutting, as a plane flies low over a ship.

Satisfactory (in default of bringing it down) was the sight of the day-bomber flying round and round the convoy in gradually widening circles, kept at bay and finally defeated by the escort's long-range guns, each ship turning to bark at it, like a bad-tempered farm-dog, as the plane entered its sector.

A huge column of water is thrown up after a near-miss: it rises grey and white, edged with foam, higher than the ship and hiding it completely, so that for all we know it may have been hit. But when the turmoil subsides, there is the ship still ploughing on: and you look at it and think: 'I bet that brought 'em up on deck with their braces dangling. . . .'

Sometimes a single bomb falls, very wide of the mark, and that is all—the ugly incident is closed: it's odd to think that a bomber may have flown a thousand miles to drop that one bomb 10,000 feet through the clouds a mile and a half from the nearest ship, after which it turns round and heads for home again. . . . But that doesn't seem to alter the score, as far as Goebbels is concerned. I remember one occasion when, after a profitless and none too intrepid attack on the convoy by two Junkers 88s, no damage of any sort being done, we tuned in to Haw-Haw the same evening. 'This morning,' said that snarling voice, 'aircraft of our gallant Luftwaffe attacked an important convoy 500 miles south-west of the Scilly Isles. Two ships were sunk, one of 5,000 and the other 2,000 tons, both having their whole sides ripped off; and others were damaged. Query: is this Goebbels's own make-up, or is it based on the actual report of the aircraft concerned? If it's the aircraft, how mutually embarrassing it must be for their crews, all of whom know it to be a pack of lies. And if it's Goebbels, how foolish the airmen must feel, to be given false credit: and how mistrustful of their own propaganda.

But now and then it is *they* who have the luck. After a quiet and unscathed journey of some 2,300 miles and fifteen days, it is depressing to lose a ship on your own front door-step, to some bloody little aircraft returning from a raid with one spare bomb.

When, in convoy, the sun goes down and the order 'Darken ship!' is piped, one has a feeling that the dividing line is being crossed, from the comparative tranquillity of daylight to the hazard and the startling crudity of things that go bump in the night. It's a sort of private signal that the party is once more on, a moment which has come to mean a great deal on board, and it is attended with care—deadlights are dropped and screwed home, screens rigged at the mess-deck entrances, the shutters of the bridge and the wheel-house put in place and secured. Then the duty petty officer makes his rounds—meticulous rounds, the most important made either at sea or in harbour; and when he comes up to the bridge and reports the ship darkened, one thinks: well, the convoy may be for it—we may be for it ourselves—but at least we're giving no chances and leaving no ends hanging out.

Among the minor trials of the middle watch are the porpoises which, with relish and great agility, play submarines at night—i.e. come darting at the ship's side at right angles, and then pass underneath with a swirl of phosphorescence. You get used to these April Fool torpedoes after a bit, and almost feel like joining in the fun yourself, but the first few times you find yourself ducking. . . .

There develops, unavoidably, a certain tension aboard as we approach the U-boat danger zone: we know that at any moment, from now on, we may be involved in some action which will test nerve and skill to the utmost: the feeling affects the whole ship, and it is almost a relief when the first explosion is heard and the first flare goes up, and you think: 'Oh, well, this is it. . . .'

But the tension for us is really nothing compared with what it must be for ships in convoy, and the amount of self-discipline and nerve needed

to remain in station after another ship has been torpedoed. We at least
have the relief—and possibly the safety—of action: we can crack on a
few revs, fling ourselves about a bit, strike back formidably if the
opportunity arises; but they have to wallow along as if nothing had
happened—same course and station, same inadequate speed, same
helpless target.

Imagine being on the bridge of a tanker, loaded deep with benzine
that a spark might send sky-high, and seeing the ship alongside struck
by a torpedo, or another torpedo slipping past your stern, *and doing
nothing at all about it*. Imagine being a stoker, working half-naked
many feet below the water-line, hearing the crack of explosions,
knowing exactly what they mean, and staying down there on the
job—shovelling coal or turning wheels, concentrating, making no
mistakes, disregarding what you *know* may be only a few yards away
and pointing straight at you.

No amount of publicity, no colourful write-ups, no guff about 'the
little silver badge', above all no medals, can do honour to men like these.
Buy them a drink ashore, if you like; but don't attempt an *adequate*
recompense. You won't get in the target area.

Going aft to my depth-charges, when 'Action stations' is sounded, is
now a routine which somehow never loses its significance or fails in its
effect; and the start of the routine has itself become almost a ritual.

Time, possibly, one a.m. (Good old middle watch: it gets all the
knocks there are.)

'Captain, sir!'

'What is it?'

'Second ship, starboard wing column, torpedoed, sir. They're firing
star-shell the other side.'

'Very good. Sound off "Action-stations". I'll be up in a second.'

When I am relieved of the watch I make my way down the ladder and
across the boat-deck: below me in the waist there is a clumping of sea-
boots as the thrower-crews run aft to close up and clear away for action.
There's time to look round as I cross the deck in darkness, ducking
under the funnel-guy which I cannot see but which comes two steps
after the last boiler-room grating, and always the view—or lack of
it—is the same: black water, now seeming very much closer, the
silhouette of a nearby ship, the glow from a flare: perhaps, already, the
flickering lights low down on the water which mean lowered boats and
rafts. Then the coxswain passes me, on his way forrard to take over the
wheel; and I say (as always): 'A fine night, coxswain,' and he says: 'Let's

drop a few for luck this time, sir'—another ritual which marks the occasion as an authentic one.

Leaning against the rail by the ensign-staff, I can see below me the thrower-crews standing by waiting for their orders; farther aft there is a group of spare numbers—off-watch stokers and communications-ratings—ready to bear a hand in reloading. Farthest aft of all, I can just make out the Seaman-Torpedoman bending over his depth-charge rails: as soon as he sees me silhouetted above him he calls out: 'All ready, sir,' in a voice half formal, half eager. I happen to know that he very much likes dropping depth-charges. . . .

Probably there is a murmur of voices, some of them angrily blasphemous—we all realize what those lights on the water mean, from long practice we can translate them accurately into loss of life, disablement, mutilation. Standing ready in the darkness, we hope for luck, and action.

Strange people come to the surface when 'Action-stations' is sounded—stokers I had no idea were on board, rare faces that never otherwise see the light of day.

The first thing you notice when a ship has gone down is a hateful smell of oil on the water. (We grew to loathe that smell: as well as a ship sunk, it meant survivors drenched with fuel oil, coughing it up, poisoned by it.) But there is always an amazing amount of stuff left on the surface—crates, planks, baulks of wood, coal-dust, doors, rope-ends, odd bits of clothing—a restless smear of debris, looking like a wrecked jumble-sale, on which the searchlight plays. Here and there lights may be flickering: too often they are not the ship's boats you are hoping for, but empty rafts with automatic calcium-flares attached to them, burning uselessly, mute witnesses to disaster.

As soon as you come upon the scene you feel you must search it all thoroughly; you feel you must prowl round and miss nothing: you also *know* that you are not the only prowler, that even as you circle a raft or wait for a laden boat to come alongside, someone in the dark outer ring may be taking a sight of you, preparing as you loiter to run a fish and teach you the same lesson. Perhaps among the wreckage a white face or a raised arm appears: can you afford to wait, are they worth the risk of salvage, or will one more chance, one more effort of mercy, forfeit your ship? Already she is sufficiently in hazard: how much margin is there still left?

In semi-darkness, we passed a dead man floating upright, supported by his life-jacket. We shouted at him, but he stared back in silence. To cover up, a stoker called out: 'So you won't talk, eh?' and there was a tiny laugh, a whisper of mirth drowned in pity.

Uncannily, some high, jabbering voices came out of the darkness: the engine-room telegraph rang 'SLOW', and then 'STOP', and presently we saw ahead of us a bobbing black spot—one of the ship's boats we were looking for. We hailed it from the bridge, and were answered by a torrent of Chinese: I thought, 'God, this is going to be difficult . . .' The wailing of high voices continued, almost operatic in its pattern—a slice of *Aida*, cut thin and slipped into a 20-foot boat in mid-Atlantic; and then, breaking through them like a soloist with a will of his own, a strong Welsh voice sang out: 'Shut up, the whole damn' lot of you.'

The boat came alongside, a Welsh second officer at the helm: someone in it started flashing a torch carelessly, and was stopped by a crisp order through a megaphone from the bridge. We took off twenty-two Chinese firemen—'They must have sunk a laundry,' said H. to me as we counted them coming over the side—and then the boat, with revolver bullets through her planking and buoyancy tanks, was set adrift, though not before a certain number of rescuers' perquisites—oars, blocks, shackles, a spare water-breaker—had been prudently salvaged and borne aboard.

They had that round score of Chinese sleeping in the mess-decks for the rest of the trip. Said a signalman to me one morning, reflectively: 'It's funny to wake up, sir, and see all those new faces.'

Valuable time is taken up in lowering a boat and bringing it in again, but it is often the quickest way of picking up men in the water, who may be too exhausted to climb aboard and too slippery with oil to be pulled up. I was once in charge of a boat which was sent away on this job, one dark night when a fairly high sea was running; and I remember the extraordinary difficulty we had in getting inboard men who had been in the water for nearly four hours, who were almost paralysed with cold, and whose clothes (and in some cases their naked bodies) were so saturated with fuel-oil that it was like trying to land enormous greasy fish with one's bare hands. A short, steep swell, that seemed to lift us up and flick us about like a chip of wood, didn't make things any easier.

This particular lot were lucky in having life-jackets with lights attached to them: otherwise we would never have seen them from the bridge in the first place. (These lights—they are small naked bulbs clipped to the life-jacket and connected to a battery in the breast-pocket—have been the salvation of countless men, and the lack of them must have been the death of countless more: a man in the water at night is almost impossible to see, and his voice, even in still weather, is lost in engine and water noises.) I forget how many we collected—about thirteen, I think, including a man so badly injured that it seemed hardly worth while giving him the extra agony of being handled. . . . When we got alongside again we bundled them over the side, the boat surging with every wave so that sometimes they could step straight aboard and sometimes could not even reach the foot of the ladder: the slightly nightmare quality of the occasion was heightened by the pitch darkness, the injured man's groans, and the thunderous noise of the chain ladder against the ship's side.

Soon there remained only the bad casualty to be dealt with. 'Send a stretcher down for this one,' I called up to the ship, and when it was passed we strapped him in, handling him as gently as the tossing boat allowed: he seemed unconscious at the end. Then a sling was rigged, and they started to heave in. But as he swung in mid-air the boat rose to a huge wave and lurched against the ship's side—or where it would have been if the stretcher had not been in the way. I felt that blow in my own guts. The man screamed once, sharply: I called out to the bow-oar: 'Hold her off, for Christ's sake,' and to the men on the tackle: 'Heave away all you know—get him clear.' It was, of course, too late, and I was glad it was dark: I didn't want to catch anyone's eye just then.

But the moment could be wiped out in action.

'Coxswain!'

'Yes, sir?'

'How many hands up there?'

'Cleared lower deck, sir.'

'Very good. . . . Pass the falls.' And to the hands with me in the boat: 'Hook on!'

'Hook on, sir.'

'Haul taut singly! . . . Hoist away!'

That was that: the best we could do.

We once had a Negro survivor who would not strip, or let himself be warmed, or drink anything: all he wanted to do—all he *would* do—was to curl up in a ball with his head between his legs, and be left to himself. We covered him up with a blanket (which he immediately drew over his head) and let him lie. Said the coxswain, looking down at him: 'It's his religion, sir'—which for some reason seemed a completely fitting explanation.

Another Negro was brought aboard dead: he was well-formed, stark naked, and already stiffening as he was hauled over the side. I put my hand out to feel his heart: the skin I touched was cold, but very smooth and well-muscled. 'Waste of time, sir?' said the sick-berth attendant, giving his voice a slight note of question. 'Waste of time,' I repeated: 'cover him up, and let's get on with the others.'

The body, lashed to the rail, made a dark smudge in the port waist all night, stirring when the ship rolled; now and then a patter of spray touched the sewn-up blanket. The cook, leaving his galley to bring the wardroom breakfast forrard, eyed it, retraced his steps, and came forrard by the starboard alley-way. . . . At ten o'clock, to the survivors' captain, three lascar seamen, and a small muster of hands, I read the burial service; and then at a signal to the bridge the telegraph rang, the engines paused for a moment, and the neat weighted package went over the side.

Survivors in the mess-decks, filling every available space: asleep on the deck, on benches, against bulkheads: sitting at tables with their heads between their hands, talking, shivering, wolfing food, staring at nothing. Some of them half-naked, wrapped in blankets and makeshift shoes: some with pathetic little cardboard suit-cases, hugged close: puzzled black faces, pinched yellow ones, tired bleary white masks that still muster a grin. Men half-dead, men cocky as bedamned: men suffering from exposure, frost-bite, oil-fuel poisoning, cuts, gashes, broken limbs: men hanging to life by a wet thread. The bravest man I have yet met was a survivor, a Yorkshire seaman with a broken thigh and a fearful gash across his face. As I paused in strapping up his leg, wondering whether he could stand any more of it, he said: 'Go on—I've a bit saved up yet'; and when I was unskilfully stitching his wound: 'Now then, lad, none of your hem-stitching—I'm not as particular as all that.' I can't remember any men who were *not* brave and patient in suffering, but he holds the record, so far.

Going forrard to attend to casualties was sometimes like stepping into a nightmare; but it was lit here and there by glimpses of the sheer nobility of man, such as could only beget confidence and pride.

Survivors in the wardroom, eating us out of house and home: their bare feet on the carpet, their odd scraps of uniform, their wet life-jackets which they do not discard—all these are stock properties in our theatre of war. They have a habit of dozing off in awkward attitudes, but they look up, and smile, when one of us comes off watch and puts his head inside the room. Often they yarn to us about their previous escapes, or produce photographs of their homes and families and hand them round: once, rather sadly, a Belgian captain talked of Leopold, and what his surrender had meant to Belgian merchant seamen then at sea. It was this captain who made us a formal speech of thanks, selfconscious but manifestly sincere, on the last night of the trip, when we had drinks all round in the wardroom and they toasted their rescuers.

People seize on odd things when the order 'Abandon ship!' is given. One third officer had left behind his note-case, containing all his papers and four months' pay, but had pocketed a large shoe-horn, quite unconsciously.

When I am ashore, and hear (as I have done) one man telling another that he can get as much petrol as he wants, by licensing all four of his cars and only using one of them: when I see photographs of thousands of cars at a race-meeting for which a special fast train-service is run: when I read a letter to a newspaper complaining that the writer has had difficulty in obtaining extra petrol for the grouse-shooting season: when I hear of *any* instance of more than the bare essential minimum of petrol being used, this is what I think of.

A torpedoed tanker ablaze at sea, with all its accompanying horrors.

That's your extra ten gallons of petrol, sir and madam: that's last week's little wangle with the garage on the corner. You might remember what you're burning, now and then: its *real* basic coupon is a corpse-strewn Atlantic.

It cannot be denied that the loss of another corvette had its effect on our behaviour when next we ran into trouble: there was certainly a return of that reluctance to go below which I have mentioned before. Many of the crew slept on the upper deck or the gun-platform; some of the officers dossed down on the bridge, and even failed to complain when they were relieved late. We took home two of her survivors, signalmen, and bloody thoughtful they looked the whole time. In fact it was an odd, faintly unpleasant, and almost affecting reminder of their ordeal and our own hazard, to come upon them at night, as I did when I came off watch: usually they would both be standing outside the wheel-house, sleepless, strained, silent, and (I suppose) remembering. I once tried to talk to one of them on my way down, and found it impossible. Staring at the water, he was out of small-talk altogether.

Notes on a Naval survivor, Lieutenant R.

R. was in the wheel-house, with a sub-lieutenant who was drowned. He told me that his ship, turning under half-helm, was hit on the port side, level with the boiler-room: there was a big explosion, the ship gave a tremendous lurch to starboard, right on to her beam-ends, and broke in half; both ends then started to sink, bows and stern upwards. R. climbed up till he was standing on the engine-room telegraph and when he was already under water, succeeded in opening the wheel-house door which was by that time above his head. He held his breath and shot to the surface.

There was a lot of oil about, but not much wreckage: he found a cordite-case to hang on to, and a seaman with him got astride a mine-sweeping float. They were then picked up by us. Others saved included all the bridge personnel, a look-out who was in the A.A. bandstand, and another look-out in the crow's-nest, who waited until the mast touched the water and then swam out. A large number of the crew were in the port waist, just over the explosion, and must have been killed by it. Very few were below.

Note.—R., who had swallowed a lot of oil, came aboard suffering from what I thought was oil-fuel poisoning. He was walking about normally (though of course feeling a bit under the weather) for at least twelve hours, but when a doctor from a destroyer came aboard to take over my three worst casualties, R. complained that he was feeling ill and was put to bed. Though he got rid of most of the oil, he became worse: the doctor diagnosed a ruptured kidney or some internal hæmorrhage, and we proceeded home at full speed.

He was in my cabin, and I spent a good deal of time with him: he asked perpetually: 'How long before we get in? Can't we go any faster? How far is it now?' and it was clear that he was simply fading out in a way very distressing to watch. He was conscious when taken ashore, but died in hospital the same night.

When he had survived so much, and had been actually walking about after his rescue, it was sad to hear that he had died after all.

We cruised slowly round the raft, looking at it through our binoculars. It seemed lifeless, and completely derelict: a tattered piece of cloth stuck up on a pole—the first thing to catch the look-out's attention—was all that stirred in a picture utterly forlorn.

I counted, as best I could, the untidy jumble of forms that lay round the pole in the centre. 'Seven, I think, sir. None of them moving.'

'We'll go alongside.'

When the raft was hooked on I jumped down and began turning them over, though as soon as I had touched the first one's arm I knew that it was hopeless. We were too late by many days and nights. . . . But there was something in their attitudes, not of strain but of longed-for abandon, which seemed to say that these men had not, after a time, fought against death. That was the only thing on the credit side: that whatever tortures they had experienced, they had also experienced release, and been able to realize it.

Another time, unrelieved by any compensations. Half a gale blowing, the sea very rough, and a raft with three survivors clinging to it: we got a line across and took two of them off, and then the line snubbed and parted. Coming as close as we could, we threw another which fell right across the raft, but the man made no effort to secure it and it was swept into the sea again. 'What's the matter with him?' I asked: 'we can't do anything unless he wakes up and takes a hand himself.' 'He's awake, all right,' answered one of the rescued men, 'but he can't move. Broken arm and leg. He told us to go first. He's the mate.'

We tried to get alongside, but it wasn't possible in that sea: and swimming was out of the question, though there was no lack of volunteers. In the end we had to leave him. . . . As we drew away, he waved to us: not a summons, but a sort of half salute. Then he lay down again.

Ships don't always sink, no matter how big a fish they have stopped. We once brought home a torpedoed tanker with a hole like Elijah's cave in her side, into which the sea washed like surf into a bay. But she was well built, and her bulkheads held: they held, in fact, for four hundred miles at three knots. On such a journey as this, you learn what patience is, and nervousness too.

It is rumoured that German submarines keep one of their torpedo-tubes packed with assorted 'wreckage'—clothing, woodwork, etc.—and when attacked discharge this in the hope of foiling the pursuit. But unless they keep a Jew or a Pole there as well, ready for discharge at the same time, I reckon our sister corvette sank that submarine. The 'human remains', collected and brought home in their refrigerator, were pronounced authentic.

6 ONE TO THEM

Short Account of a Seven-Day Party.

First Day. A couple of long-range reconnaissance planes showed up about midday, but as usual they would not come within range: instead they flew round and round the convoy making sure of our course and speed, and left us about four—having no doubt prepared a reliable and detailed report, and having incidentally kept us at action-stations the whole afternoon. Some of the destroyers tried shots at them now and then, but it was hardly serious shooting. There was an alarm that night, probably a false one: I don't think the U-boats had picked us up previously, and it takes a little time to collect the pack after it has been put on the scent.

Second Day. Aircraft came over fairly early, high-level bombers: they kept us on our toes, but didn't get nearer than a near miss. Nor did we. There were also a couple of Focke-Wulfs playing round most of the day: a routine shadowing, well out of range, but damned annoying all the time. There are thought to be '4 or 5' U-boats in the vicinity. Weather rather too good to be pleasant.

Third Day. Bombed by two Junkers 88s (?—too high to be certain) in the morning: they got rather close to one errant straggler who, having resisted all previous pleading, then and there caught up and resumed his station. A U-boat attack developed at night, and some ships were sunk: we were closed up at action-stations from ten o'clock till six-thirty in the morning, counter-attacking one contact without visible result but managing to collect some survivors. Not known how many submarines were involved: must have been two at least, judging by the conflicting reports of torpedo-tracks sighted.

Fourth Day. Unable to relax after the eventful night, as aircraft came over again on reconnaissance; but the good weather was starting to break and by nightfall it was blowing quite hard—the middle watch was, in fact, the thickest and blackest we've ever had. Coming as it did just at the right time, we bore it with a certain fortitude; and when daylight came again without any incident developing, we congratulated ourselves on having shaken the submarines off. Sometimes it happens like that.

Fifth Day. Those congratulations were too soon. We heard aircraft overhead, above cloud-level, during the morning, and in the afternoon watch the weather cleared and they picked us up once more. One has a feeling of impotent rage against spotting aircraft which can with so little trouble put the submarines on the scent again. The convoy has fooled them, by good luck or bad weather, so that they're hunting far off the course and hourly getting farther; and then along comes a reconnaissance plane and brings them back again in half a day.

Nothing developed that night, but it was certain that they would be back before long.

Sixth Day. Bombing during the morning, shadowing most of the day; during the afternoon a couple of really grand destroyers joined the escort-group, settling down astern like Rolls-Royces ticking over. We had an idea that we would be needing them.

A quiet night, notwithstanding; one or two scares, but maybe we gave a few back.

Seventh Day. Routine shadowing most of the day, keeping us on the alert all the time; but the real climax came, as usual, at night.

It started fairly early, too: the first attack came at ten o'clock. We heard two explosions, and rockets went up: after carrying out the sweep ordered by the Senior Officer we saw lights on the water and altered course towards them.

Soon we came upon the usual muck drifting about—oil, dust, pieces of wood, corpses, clothing: then we heard voices shouting out of the darkness, and saw a cluster of men swimming: they were singing 'Roll out the barrel' in chorus. We laughed when we heard that, and a rating in the waist called out: 'Good lads! We're coming!' and the men in the water shouted back: 'Three cheers for the Navy!' I think most of us aft thought it should be 'Three cheers for the Merchant Navy'. We lowered a boat and collected all we could find: some of them, wounded and swimming in oil up to three hours, were already survivors from another ship, torpedoed four days before and rescued by the ship which had now itself gone down. One of them, clinging to a life-buoy, had been calling out: 'Hurry up! I can't hold on much longer,' as we approached, and then, over and over again in a gasping voice: 'Christ, I'm done! Christ,

I'm done!' When he saw us drawing away again, not knowing that we had lowered a boat, he started screaming: 'Don't go away! You bloody cowards, don't go away!'

We collected about thirty all told, picked up our boat again, and set a course for the convoy. I was working for nearly two hours in the mess-decks, attending to casualties (two internal, two badly gashed in the head, five minor cuts, and some needing treatment for shock): half-way through, H. came forward and gave me a glass of whisky, which I needed. At about two o'clock, when I was on the bridge again standing my watch, two more ships were hit: from one of them flames shot into the air, and soon she was ablaze from end to end. Once more we went through the evolutions ordered, and once more dropped back to see if we could help the rescue ships.

The burning oil on the water now covered about a square half-mile, an immense wall of flame topped by a huge smoke-pall drifting away to leeward, which lit the sea for miles around. We closed this, looking for survivors which the others might have missed. If you want to know what tension is, or wish to gauge a captain's responsibility at such a moment, try stopping engines when silhouetted against solid flame, with an unknown number of submarines prowling round. We could see other corvettes, intent on the same job as ourselves, crossing and recrossing, black against red and yellow, and we could not help thinking: 'That's the sort of target *we're* making. . . .' But we finished it at last, and quitted the effective back-cloth and started off again; and then ahead of us we saw another explosion and flames going up in the air, and then sudden darkness. Someone said, aptly but unnecessarily: 'That was a quick one,' and almost immediately we got a signal to say that it had been one of the escorts, torpedoed and sunk.

I can recall the sense of shock which that signal brought to the bridge. Of course other ships had been sunk, but this was an escort vessel, one of our group, manned by fellow-sailors doing the same job as us and supposedly strong enough to be immune. . . . The blended feeling of rage and depression lasted till dawn—dawn, when another ship, a straggler far away from any effective cover, was shelled by a U-boat and had to be abandoned.

This was the last casualty, and it rounded off, with originality, an eventful night and (as it turned out) an eventful seven days.

I think we were all a little mad by the time we got in. We'd been at action-stations for virtually a week on end, missing hours of sleep, eating on the bridge or the upper deck, standing-to in the cold and wet and darkness. We'd had the aircraft plaguing us continually and the U-boats hunting, striking, losing, hunting, and striking again: we'd watched ships—too many ships—go down, and heard of our friends being killed and seen men drowning and had to leave them to it: we'd grown sick of destruction, light-headed with tiredness and strain. And above all we'd felt ineffective; even though we knew that other escorts had struck back with notable effect there'd probably been nine submarines round us, and you can't do miracles—they had simply played hide-and-seek with the convoy, and a ripe game it was. . . . By the end, we'd had enough of it; though if it had gone on I suppose we would have done the same.

In fact, I *know* we would. That's the main thing about a convoy: it doesn't retreat, or re-form on a new line or execute a strategic withdrawal to previously prepared positions. It sails on: having no choice and, in the last analysis, wishing none.

7 ONE TO US

Unexpectedly, the U-boat surfaced about two miles ahead of us.

I don't know why she came up: perhaps we had kept her down too long, or she thought she'd try her luck at a shooting-match, or she may even not have heard us; but we didn't waste time with speculations just then. Our first shot fell short, our second was dead in line but over, and our third ploughed the water just where she had crash-dived again. We dropped a pattern of depth-charges for luck on her estimated diving-position and then began a proper sweep.

We picked her up almost immediately, and ran in again and dropped another pattern; this brought up some oil. Out on a wide turn and in again; once more the charges went over the side, and once more, after a pause, there came that series of splitting crashes from below which told us they had well and truly earned their keep. Another run, and another still; the afterpart was a scene of vast activity—firing, reloading, priming, setting: then the awaited signal from the bridge, and down went the charges and presently the surface of the sea jumped and boiled, and the torpedoman rubbed his hands and called out happily: 'Next for shaving!'

More oil, and big air bubbles: we had the measure of him now. . . . I spoke on the bridge voice-pipe to H., who said we were doing well and ordered another rather special pattern. 'I'm not sure I can manage that,' I told him: 'I'll have to give you the nearest size to it.' Momentarily the

Chief popped his head out of the engine-room companionway. 'Isn't he sunk yet, sir?' he asked. 'We're getting properly shaken up down here.' One more run, one more series of thunderous cracks—and then the sea, spouting and boiling, threw up what we were waiting for: oil in a spreading stain, bits of wreckage, woodwork, clothing, scraps of humanity. . . . Contact failed after that, and though we waited till dusk, nothing else worth collecting made its appearance. We had enough, in any case.

It was a dog's death, but how triumphant we felt—a triumph clinched, later that night, by a signal of congratulation from the Commander-in-Chief. And in the morning came another moment—perhaps the real moment—of the sweetness of success. We found the convoy, from which we had been detached nearly twenty-four hours before; and as soon as we were in sight the Senior Officer signalled: 'Well met and well done. Steam down the centre of the convoy: they want to give you a big hand.' And so it was. When we came level with the head of the convoy the Commodore hoisted 'Congratulations'. It was repeated by every ship, and as we steamed down the ranks each ship waved and cheered. It made up for much of the preceding winter. . . . The last ship of all, a puzzled Greek, still had his answering pendant at the dip[1] as we passed—'Bunting-tosser's asleep', said our own signalman, outraged by the occurrence; but we took the will for the deed. Even congratulations at the dip contributed to the sum total.

We'd worked a long time for that signal: steamed thousands of miles, been bored for days and weeks on end, spent scores of nights at the alert in wet and freezing darkness, sent and received thousands of signals. Over three hundred middle watches had gone to it, weeks of eye-strain, filthy weather in plenty, and God knows how many blasts from Senior Officer, from Captain (D), from Flag Officer-in-Charge, from the heart of Whitehall. . . . Only one more submarine, when it came to notching the stick; but it settled a longer score than that, for us.

Another corvette in the same group had some U-boat prisoners aboard, whom she used to exercise every day on the upper deck. H. and I examined them one morning through our binoculars as we passed close by. They looked a scruffy lot, and most of them did not move about at all but stood in the waist, staring out at the convoy which was an exceptionally large one. Many of them, we could see, were frowning.

[1] Signifying 'Signal-flags seen but not yet understood.'

'Surly bastards!' grumbled H. to me, as we watched them. 'They're damned lucky to be alive.'

'No, they don't look surly to me,' I answered him. I indicated the convoy, forging ahead to England, as compact and as strong as ever. 'I think they're surprised. In fact, probably they can hardly believe their eyes.'

East Coast Corvette

1 CHANGING OVER

THE EXPECTED SIGNAL WAS WAITING FOR ME WHEN WE GOT IN, after another fourteen days' flurry in the North Atlantic; and something in the leading signalman's eye as he handed it to me made me ask:

'What's the big news?'

'Your draft-chit, sir.'

I read it with extreme satisfaction; it was far better than I had hoped for. 'Lieutenant Monsarrat appointed to H.M.S. *Dipper* as First Lieutenant on relief joining.'

'You're lucky,' said M. when I passed it over to him. 'They're damned good ships—like small destroyers: twin-screw, all the refinements. Of course, they don't stay afloat for very long.'

'Why not?'

'They're on the East Coast—at least, some of them are—and you know what that means: Hitler's front doorstep. A bomb every five seconds. E-boats for tea, mines in your soup. Have a big gin.'

'It'll be a change from this side.'

'It certainly will. Like hail after rain.'

But I refused to be daunted. It was a change that I wanted, above all things: a corvette in the Western Approaches is fine for a year, a trial for eighteen months, and a matter of staying-power thereafter; I wouldn't mind coming back to it in the end, but at the moment I wanted something different from the interminable fourteen-day runs, the foul weather, the startling crudity of the past two years. It wasn't that I felt I'd earned it—you don't *earn* anything in war-time except the privilege of a tougher assignment; it was just that I was ready to welcome the second course of a meal which had so far been all wind and gristle, piled rather high on the plate.

And, as readers of earlier pages may guess, I wanted the job of First Lieutenant. Two years as dogsbody, seeing only the blunt end of the ship, the second choice of leave, the drum-sticks of the chicken, give you a healthy ambition for higher things.

Leaving a ship is usually sad, no matter how good a job you are going to, and this one was no exception.

I had served nearly two years in her, joining ten days before she commissioned, up in the Clyde: her crew had been virtually unchanged throughout that time: together we had endured the Atlantic at its worst, the malice of the enemy, the few triumphs that had been our share of the Atlantic battle. There were men on board whom I would trust with my life, no matter how critical or violent the circumstances: the wardroom had a history of good parties, fierce poker sessions, talk that had often spanned an entire middle watch in harbour. The ship had been my home throughout a memorable slice of my life: she had taught me nearly all I knew of the Navy; she and her crew were a happy and successful entity of which I had long been part. To leave her now, even for a job I had been looking forward to so much, was hard.

But certainly there was a lot to do before I was clear: books to be handed back, loan-clothing to be turned in, stores to be accounted for or smoothly explained away, correspondence to be gone into with my relief. He was (as is always the case) a cautious man, a man much slower to sign for things than I had been myself (I fully expect to receive, after the war, a huge bill for paint, soap, and soda consumed by the upper-deck department): he wanted to see everything, to feel it over carefully for snags or flaws, and only then—slowly and reluctantly —could he be brought to admit its actual existence and sign for it on the dotted line. The trouble I had, for example, in persuading him that the wardroom sugar-bowl was a Bowl, Sugar, Pattern 615E, and not (as he maintained) a Basin, Slop, Pattern 921, was really past belief.

There was also the difficulty of getting the other officers to sign the audit of the Contingency Fund, which was another thing I had to get rid of. I had expected a certain caution in this respect, and I was ready to meet all reasonable queries; but it did not seem to me that the lengthy rearguard action they fought over it was a suitable tribute to our two years as messmates.

If I had not been confronted by the stuff itself, I would never have believed it possible that so much assorted junk could have been collected in one small cabin, and remained unnoticed until the time came to pack. It seemed as if I had never thrown a single thing away during the whole time I had been on board. I had originally joined the ship with two suitcases: I left it with four of them, plus a naval kitbag, a wooden chest, and my seaboots done up in brown paper. The total freight, assembled on deck by an awed quartermaster, excited suspicions which were freely voiced by everyone from the Captain downwards.

The petty officers gathered in the wardroom: the beer was sent round: the coxswain cleared his throat and began: 'I'd just like to say, sir . . .'

Farewell speeches look silly on paper, but they are moving under such circumstances as these. All the men round me had shared the excitement and the boredom and the testing-times of the past two years: they had proved themselves loyal, dependable in crisis, good to be alongside when things were happening. Now I was moving on, breaking up a pattern on which I had come to rely: my new ship might be of the same quality—it was odds that she *would* be—but I was leaving behind me a known company of friends, a guaranteed circle, and the fine feel of comradeship in action.

That was why, when the coxswain, holding his glass of beer like a hymn-book in church, cleared his throat and began a hesitating and audibly prompted speech, it was a moment of feeling and tension. But presently, the formalities done with, we were able to relax: the beer went round again as quick as a lasso, and there were jokes—about bad weather and rolling, about our U-boat, about the book I was supposed to be writing on corvettes. ('I hope you'll keep me out of it, sir,' said one Stoker Petty Officer: 'My old woman thinks this is a Boom Defence Vessel.') There was speculation as to what it would be like on the East Coast—speculation not wholly concerned with raising my spirits. Above all, there was, for me, a feeling that this was a good send-off, the right sort of ending to my stay in the ship: an ending clinched, a little later on, by a return visit to the Petty Officers' Mess, where their traditional generosity with farewell tots of rum went far towards wafting me over the gangway and along the dock-side in a state of unconcerned bliss.

The dock, when I left it, was full of destroyers and corvettes of our own and other escort-groups: some just in from sea, with upper decks still wet and the hands still in duffle-coats, others standing by ready to go out on the tide. Their masts and signal halyards made a patterned forest against the sky: there were ships with strong reputations, ships with odd or spectacular characters on board, ships with individual foibles which we had learned to respect. It was curious to think that a large part of the Battle of the Atlantic was fought from this small corner: that if you wiped out this dock and what it had done since the war started, the answer might be a starving Britain.

There is no boasting or self-satisfaction in that last sentence—one single corvette is less than a cog in the works. But she isn't a spanner in them either, and in saying farewell to that dock and all it stood for, one could draw pride and pleasure from having been a working part of it during the burden and heat of the day. It was going to be something to tell one's grandchildren about, if one could catch them in a listening mood.

A slow (and even stately) departure was offset by a quick-fire arrival. When I got to my new base, and reported, I was met by a positive whirlwind of information and instruction which swept me out into the roadway again almost before I had time to salute.

'Your ship's lying out in the stream,' I was told, 'and she's sailing in about ten minutes' time. You'll just make it if you start now. You'll probably have to leave your gear ashore, unless it's all ready for collection. Better get moving straight away: I'll have a signal sent for a boat, if they haven't hoisted it already. Down the road, first right, and then ask for the pontoon. Her pendant-numbers are ———, in case you have to scrounge a lift from someone else. Good-bye and good luck.'

I had travelled all night, and I climbed aboard, with a couple of minutes to spare, feeling like the tail-end of a hurricane. Said the retiring First Lieutenant, who met me on the quarter-deck:

'We were betting on whether you'd make it before we sailed. That's about the only sort of excitement we get on this coast, these days.'

2 THE SHIP AND THE JOB

Extract from the Captain's Standing Orders:

'The First Lieutenant is the Executive Officer, responsible to me for the cleanliness and efficiency of the ship, and the discipline and welfare of the ship's company.

'He is to maintain the ship's armament in an efficient working condition, paying particular regard to the instant readiness of the anti-aircraft armament both at sea and in harbour.

'Authority to award punishment is delegated to him under the appropriate article of King's Regulations and Admiralty Instructions.

'In addition to his duties as First Lieutenant, he is Divisional Officer for seamen, responsible for their training: Anti-Submarine Control Officer: Sports Officer: President of the Canteen Committee: President of the Wardroom Mess.

'He should always remember that he may be required to assume command of the ship at a moment's notice, and should therefore acquaint himself as far as possible with the problems involved.'

It looked like being a full day. . . . But what a grand ship she was, to have the run of. Listed in *Jane*'s as a 'patrol vessel' reclassified since the outbreak of war as a corvette, she was really, in looks and performance, a small destroyer, with all sorts of additions and refinements that put my last ship right back into the trawler class, by comparison. She had been built in the spacious days of peace-time, when things like aluminium and well-picked wood and non-austerity furniture were still available: she had twin-screws, big mess-decks, a wardroom on the upper deck, and a bridge far better designed than *Flower*'s cramped cat-walk. She was elegant, she was fast. In personnel, too, she was much better off, with a Warrant Gunner and Warrant Engineer, and Chief Petty Officers in all departments instead of Petty Officers: together they made up a strong team of experts never likely to be caught off the top line. . . . Finally she had an R.N. Captain, later to command a Fleet destroyer and exhibiting already the humanity and the absolute competence appropriate to that job.

The Naval Base from which we operated was small and self-contained, a sort of feudal village, graded in rank and consequence, where everyone knew everyone else; and, like other villages, it had its odd characters, its oldest inhabitants, its scandal-mongers, and its essential unity and comradeship. There were people who had been stationed there since the war started, who had grown old and mellow in such jobs as the stamping of passes and the prevention of waste; a walk along the quay might bring you greetings from a dozen such old stagers, always robustly cheerful, always glad to see a new face or recognize an old one. It gave the changing struggle at sea a homely background, a matey nucleus round which the rough war revolved.

But it led, sometimes, to an outlook which might with justice be described as restricted. I well remember once visiting an officer, of the worthiest character but not renowned for his energy or application, and finding his whole office in a turmoil. Reference books littered the desk, papers were scattered on the floor, a filing-cabinet, half-rifled, was in drunken disorder.

'Good heavens!' I said, startled. 'You're pretty busy this morning.'

'Busy?' He exploded, banging his fist on an open volume in front of him. 'Busy? I'm *furious*! By God, I'll have the skin off their backs for this!'

'What's gone wrong?'

'Everything! It's criminal! They've spelt my name wrong in the new Debrett!'

On another occasion, when I was talking to one of the secretaries whose department had recently changed its Senior Officer:

'It doesn't make much difference to you, does it?' I asked. 'I mean, won't he just carry on where the other one left off?'

He shook his head with great emphasis. 'Oh, no! Nothing like that at all. In fact, there've been some big changes already.' He pointed. 'That desk-lamp is new. *And both those book-cases.*'

But these were odd backwaters and eccentricities, by no means the general rule. The place was justly renowned as being one of the best Naval Bases in Great Britain; it had about it, both ashore and afloat, an air of unruffled solidity and comradeship which is the only sure foundation for successful sea warfare.

Back to the ship again, now the absorbing centre of my interest.

She had been on this section of the coast from the very beginning, escorting those coastal convoys which, every day of every week since September, 1939, have carried the life-blood of Britain to and from its heart: two and a half years, that was, of up-and-down and down-and-up, with an occasional patrol or a bit of mine-laying as a picnic treat. It had been, and still was, a lively assignment: this was the quick-trigger corner of the war, where things happened without warning—there were enemy air-bases within a long biscuit-toss, there were nests of E-boats lying in wait, there were sneak mine-layers who could set a deadly snare under cover of darkness, and then slide back unobserved. Danger seemed to go in cycles—a quick flare-up of activity, a period of calm, another stroke of luck or skill which sent ships on either side to the bottom, an armed truce again. . . . It was very different from what I had been used to, in the past: the Atlantic had been a matter of long drudgery and sustained tension, this was a lively three-round affair with the chance of a surprise knock-out any and every minute.

Of course (as was speedily pointed out to me when I mentioned an odd scrap or two in the Western Approaches, adding a pinch of salt and thirty per cent colouring matter to everything), things weren't what they *had* been on this coast, not by a long chalk. . . . That seemed to be the current watchword, at the time I joined the ship: things were quiet enough now, but you should have been here a year ago.

'Of course, there's absolutely nothing doing *now*,' remarked the Captain one evening, when we had been talking of the after-Dunkirk days, and the extreme burden laid on the Navy and the Air Force at that time. 'Anything could happen *then*, from hell to breakfast, but now. . . .'

He waved his hand negligently. 'A few E-boats. Aircraft now and then—torpedo-bombers: they seem to have given up dive-bombing. Mines occasionally. Things like that.'

'Otherwise nothing?'

'Damn all. But they have a Wrens' dance every fortnight or so, if you're looking for action.'

I found I had enough to do, however, without seeking action in any quarter.

The First Lieutenant, as the saying goes, is married to the ship; and it is not a marriage which can be left to take care of itself or which flourishes on neglect. First, the ship has to be kept clean. *Dipper* was, when I took her over, by far the cleanest ship in the flotilla, and my ambition to keep her like that meant a constant struggle with a variety of enemies. Lying out in the stream at a buoy gave plenty of opportunity for painting the ship's side: it also gave plenty of opportunity to liberty- and provision-boats which, ringed round with oil-stained motor-tyres (long overdue for the salvage dump) and the filthiest fenders imaginable, seldom left one in doubt that they had been alongside and had taken a clinging departure. One such chance visitor, expertly handled, could undo a whole morning's work with the greatest ease in a couple of minutes.

Another, minor, hostile element was the quayside dogs and cats which, unless watched, would multiply aboard as permanent residents. They had to be kept severely rationed; and luckily I was backed up in this by the Chief Bosun's Mate, who had (or professed to have) his own sinister method of dealing with the menace.

Once, when I saw him eyeing a small rat-like mongrel that had crept aboard and was being given half a seaman's dinner (by a generous stoker):

'Will you make arrangements to get rid of that one?' I said. 'You can hardly classify it as a dog, and we've got our full quota already.'

'If we can take it to sea tonight we'll be all right, sir,' he answered. Then, lowering his voice, he added, 'Those little ones sink lovely.'

My insistence on cleanliness of paintwork also brought me into occasional conflict with the Gunner, whose ambition was to have everything in his department 'working'—i.e. covered by a generous film of grease and oil. This latter state naturally included the ratings in the Gunner's party, men only too inclined to make their mark in every compartment they visited. Here, too, the age-old argument—whether you can legitimately take hands off cleaning guns and set them to stowing potatoes in the vegetable locker—was waged unceasingly. But it was, of course, a matter of adjustment, and we gradually worked out an effective compromise.

In any case the ship had to be efficient as well as clean: things had to work as well as to shine, guns had to impress both the ear and the eye. I don't think I was ever really caught out over this, though there was one occasion when the ship's bell, never ordinarily used but polished and repolished as a brilliant ornament for the quarter-deck, was found to be minus its clapper five seconds before a church service attended by a very senior (and fairly devout) officer. It was run to earth just in time, and a glad peal announced the fact; but the search for it was a splendid illustration of the phrase: 'No stone was left unturned'.

Coming up harbour and securing to a buoy is a good example of a First Lieutenant's routine which must go like clockwork if it is to be effective: it entails some preparation beforehand, attention to detail, and, at the end, a busy quarter of an hour during which a lot of ground is covered.

By the time the ship passes the harbour entrance the bridle by which she will be secured must be shackled on and made ready, together with the various wires and heaving-lines: the hands must be piped into their No. 3 rig if the weather allows, the duty boats' crews warned, the postman rounded up and held in readiness for his 'pony-express' dash ashore. The hands are then piped to 'Stations for entering Harbour', and the coxswain takes the wheel; and then the whaler and the motor-boat are both manned and turned out, the Gunner supervising, while I have a quick look round the anchorage to see which ships are in harbour—they all have to be piped as we pass them or (if they are junior) answered when they pipe us.

In the whaler is the postman, and any hands who may be required to land in a hurry—ratings taking examinations ashore, for instance; and in the motor-boat is the buoy-jumper, the athletic hand who, wearing a life-jacket and his third-best suit, balances on the buoy and waits to hook on the picking-up rope when we come up to him.

All this time we are passing destroyers at their moorings, and I am moving from side to side of the bridge seeing that they are correctly piped. Then, at a certain point on our way up harbour, I sing out 'Lower to the water-line!' and both boats go down evenly till their keels are about a foot above the water: this state of suspended animation lasts till we are about a hundred yards from our buoy. Thereafter we produce a final flourish of pipes for the Senior Officer's ship, and then, right opposite him so that he can see the full beauty of the manœuvre, I give the order 'Slip!' and both boats hit the water an almighty smack as they are freed. The whaler curves away towards the shore, the motor-boat heads for our mooring-buoy, the First Lieutenant gives a deep sigh of relief and goes down on to the fo'c'sle.

There. all is ready for the last part of the exercise; and by now, ahead of us, the buoy-jumper is waiting, doing his usual acrobatics as the buoy spins round. We come up very slowly, stemming the tide a foot at a time, while I signal the direction and distance off to the bridge: a heaving-line is thrown, the buoy-jumper catches it and hauls down the picking-up rope, and makes the clip-hook fast to the ring on the buoy. I sing out: 'Hooked on, sir!' and we heave away on the windlass till the bows of the ship overhang the buoy itself; and then the bridle is lowered—a length of cable with a mooring shackle at the end—and is in turn secured to the ring. 'Shackle on, sir!' tells the bridge that their troubles are over, and there we are—we can with safety ring off engines, rig the ladder, and lay aft for the first cup of tea of the day, and the mail from home.

In good weather, of course, it's as easy as it sounds—it can all be done in slow time, and the Captain can lay the ship with its nose dead on the buoy, like a well-trained dog bringing back a rabbit; but if there's a sea to flick the buoy about, and a cross-wind to take the ship's head off, it becomes a ticklish operation. Buoy-jumpers, by standing orders, always wear life-jackets, and they often need them—I have seen a destroyer, in a high wind, drift sideways right *over* the buoy, with the buoy-jumper going down slowly like a scuttled ship and then coming up the other side, as good as new but not nearly as enthusiastic.

As the quartermaster who was watching with me said, that sort of thing isn't what you volunteer for.

When I took over, the ship had a ready-made routine which she had been following for two and a half years: a very different matter from commissioning a ship as First Lieutenant and inventing the whole thing yourself, from scratch. It simplified my work enormously, though of course it still left day-to-day jobs and problems which had to be adequately dealt with. She was strictly run, and consequently happy; and my task of applying and maintaining discipline on board—of 'tempering harshness with severity', as the Captain put it one day—did not call for the constant nagging that is sometimes necessary.

Of course there were defaulters—leave-breakers, losers of property by negligence, ratings who (in the coxswain's magic phrase) 'tried to poke bravado at their superiors'; but they were never a daily routine,

and only on very rare occasions did the full force of the First
Lieutenant's Gestapo have to function.

Notwithstanding what I believe was a widespread view to the
contrary on board, I was not disappointed by this lack of opportunity.

Apart from special emergencies and exercises, a typical morning's
work in harbour might be stretched to cover the following:

Seeing hands fall in at 07.45, and detailing work for the day;

Scouring the upper decks for odd corners that may need a
washdown or a lick of paint;

Arranging a football match, and picking the team;

Inventing (with the help of the Chief Bosun's Mate) a new kind of
live-saving line, and having a couple of experimental ones made up;

Entertaining the guests who creep aboard with various excuses,
and remain there without any;

Seeing requestmen and defaulters;

Presiding at a meeting of the Canteen Committee;

Demonstrating a new fire-fighting appliance to all hands, with real
flames and no expense spared;

Inspecting a side of beef which the ship's butcher maintains has got
'right outside my jurisprudence, sir';

Making out and signing various demands for stores, lost-by-
accident forms, travel warrants, monthly and quarterly returns,
watch and duty bills, clothing lists, and other oddments;

Nipping ashore to the Pay Office to battle for somebody's rights;

Having a conference with the Engineer on our forthcoming defect
list;

Duplicate all this during the afternoon, add the piping of passing
ships, the arranging of boats for working parties and officers, a
couple of air-raid warnings, and a possible shift of berth just when
painting-stages have been rigged all round the ship's side, and it may
explain the confidence with which First Lieutenants maintain that
their allowance of one and sixpence a day is well earned.

Now and again, to wake us up, we have General Drill—the Captain's
delight, the First Lieutenant's nightmare: it consists of a morning given
over to exercising any and every department of the ship, simultaneously
or in series, to the accompaniment of any kind of diversion or crisis the
Captain can devise.

It starts with the Captain coming out on to the quarter-deck rather
too soon after breakfast, drawing on his gloves, and saying with a
strange relish:

'All right, Number One, let's make a start with something straightforward. Port Watch of seamen lower both anchors to the water-line, and heave them in by hand: rig the sounding boom at the same time and take a sounding. Starboard Watch of seamen rig a dan-buoy ready for dropping, and get out hawsers ready to tow aft. Stokers shore up the lower mess-deck; pull the main fuse there, and have the Torpedo Party fix up emergency lighting. Signalmen dismantle the main aerial and rig a temporary one—one that works, too. First Aid Party removed injured man from the bridge by stretcher, and get him below. Now let me see. . . . Ah, yes——' as an afterthought, 'Pipe "Fire in the steering-compartment!" using smoke-helmets, have the stokers' gun's-crew man the gun and clear it away for action, send away the motor-boat to pick up survivors, and give the emergency gas-alarm in five minutes' time. Right—get going. Midshipman!'

'Sir?'

'Get a note-book and a stop-watch. We'll time all this, and see what the record is.'

That is, perhaps, enough about the actual job: enough to indicate its scope and variety, and above all its interest. But it leaves out the most vital part of all. Though there was no moment of the day that did not bring its problem, there was, equally, no moment, from the very beginning, when I was not immensely proud of having been given the appointment. The ship buttressed that pride: to be her First Lieutenant was to have won a worthy accolade; and reporting the ship's company present and correct to the Captain at Sunday Divisions, I felt once again the sense of power and the access of confidence which had been mine when I stood my first watch alone at sea, back in my old ship.

There was humility in this sense of power; but there was all the pride in the world, too.

We could hardly have had a better wardroom—in its comradeship and joint enthusiasm, and also in its variety.

First the Captain—R.N., almost the naval officer of fiction: correct, resourceful, unfoolable, his handling of the ship a perpetual delight to watch. It was my first close-up of the Royal Navy at work, and I sometimes felt as if I were back at the kindergarten stage, assimilating knowledge in open-mouthed admiration.

Then myself—R.N.V.R., of course. 'I like a few amateurs about the place,' said the Captain once. 'It reminds you that there is an outside world, after all. . . .' As long as that was all it reminded him of, I felt I could be satisfied.

The Pilot was R.N.R.—a professional seaman with the customary formidable skill in navigation. He had a sixth sense as to the ship's whereabouts, at any hour of the day or night, which I for one found most comforting: it seemed as if he only had to come up on deck, look round once, sniff the air, and then point to a dot on the chart, for everything to fall into line.

Back to the R.N. again with the Warrant Engineer—a typical 'Chief', right on top of his job, full of technicalities and gadgets. He once, with the aid of a thermometer and a saucer of water, conducted what he called a 'cosiness test' in the wardroom. The fire was banked up: all doors and ports were shut fast: after twenty minutes, he reported, ninety per cent cosiness was achieved. . . . No one present was inclined to quarrel with the report.

And lastly the Gunner—another 'regular', and our oldest inhabitant. He could hardly have known more about his complicated job, or been keener on passing on what he knew; he had been all through the last war and was as much-travelled as most naval officers of his length of service—India, China, the Mediterranean, the Near East. He was very good company: full of stories, and small oddments which he volunteered on the spur of the moment. ('Do you know how to time the five-second interval for a twenty-one gun Royal Salute?' he would ask suddenly. 'You walk backwards and forwards across the fo'c'sle, saying to yourself: "If I wasn't a Gunner I wouldn't be here—Fire ONE: If I wasn't a Gunner I wouldn't be here—Fire TWO: If I wasn't a Gunner . . .".')

That was the total, for the greater part of my time in the ship: though later on we had an eighteen-year-old Midshipman to complete the pack, to do all the odd jobs, and (personally) to remind me that I was once young and sprightly, and the terror of the dance-floor.

As I said at the beginning, we could not have had a better wardroom. It kept us all perpetually enlivened, and was the strongest possible background for what proved an exacting job.

3 WORKING

Going to sea really starts with this entry in my Night Orders of the previous night:

'Ship is under sailing orders from 09.00.
All ratings proceeding ashore to be reported to me.

Mail will close on board at 10.30.
11.00. Secure for sea.
11.45 (approx.). Slip.'

The entry sets in train a whole routine, well-tried and absolutely foolproof, which will send us down river with no ends, human or otherwise, hanging out.

It means testing the steering-gear, the engine-room telegraphs, the revolution-counter, and all the electrical circuits controlled from the bridge. It means trying out all the noises we can make—sirens, bells, alarm-gongs, buzzers. It means taking off the bridle, and substituting a slip-rope, which releases us from the buoy in a second or two: it means keeping a check on all ratings going ashore, landing and collecting the last mail, closing all scuttles and watertight doors, taking in the ladder and the quarter-boom, stowing loose deck-gear, and finally hoisting the motor-boat.

It means, five minutes before sailing-time, piping the hands to their stations, and special sea-duty men to the bridge, and then going up there to find the following assembly awaiting the fall of the flag: the coxswain at the wheel, two quartermasters manning the telegraphs, four signalmen, a bridge messenger, and the Navigating Officer. It means looking down on the fo'c'sle, and seeing there the fo'c'sle-party, not yet fallen in, clearing up wires and fenders or just waiting about: the Chief Bosun's Mate with a hammer in his hand, ready to knock off the slip; and the immaculate Midshipman standing in the eyes of the ship, ready for anything and very likely to get it.

The Captain comes up on the bridge, takes a quick look round, judging the tide, the strength of the wind, the position of other ships in the vicinity. We hoist 'Request permission to proceed', and when it is answered by the Senior Officer of the flotilla the signal 'Obey Telegraphs' goes down to the engine-room. Then comes the final order: 'Slip!': there is a single hammer-stroke, a pause, and then the answer: 'All gone, all clear forrard!' As we move clear of the buoy I sing out: 'Fo'c'sle-party, fall in!', and then I cross over to the wing of the bridge, to take a final look round, to control the piping of other ships, and to make sure that our exit is, in every way, a good one.

Since it is done in the full glare of publicity, surrounded by a ring of hungry destroyers only awaiting the chance to give us a pair of pendants,[1] it *has* to be good.

---

[1] A ship's pendants, hoisted at the dip, signify: 'You have done something wrong and have not yet corrected it.'

Properly speaking, my station is on the bridge until we have cleared harbour; but when the hands have been piped to Defence Stations, and we are past the main anchorage, I usually take a walk round the upper deck and then go below to change into sea-going rig.

My new and beautiful suit makes this a pleasure. . . . It is only a glorified pair of overalls—but how glorified: lined with kapok throughout, neatly zip-fastened, water-proof, wind-proof, very warm; and guaranteed to keep me and two other men (not obligatory) afloat for half a day in case of necessity. A pair of sheepskin-lined flying-boots rounds it off below, and keeps me firmly anchored to the deck in the strongest wind.

Attached to the suit is a safety-lamp of the plug-in type, also for use in the water; and in the pockets I carry a flask, a ration of chocolate, my identity card, money, cheque-book, keys, Post Office bank book, and Savings Certificates. . . . All I have to do, if torpedoed, is to swim ashore and buy a cottage.

At one point, which need not be specified, on our outward journey, we pass a lightship. She dips her ensign, of course, as we go by, and we return the salute; but we usually embroider the ceremony on the loud-hailer if we have time. A plain 'Good morning' is answered by a wave: comments on the morning's news or the course of the war call forth some philosophic rejoinder; to the remark 'Did they lay any mines round here last night?' they once answered: 'We'll know in a minute. You're the first ship out.'

Seeing her anchored there, month in and month out, prompts the usual speculations as to what the other chap's job is really like. Since war broke out this lightship's crew have seen thousands of ships go past; some of them to engage the enemy and catch the headlines later, others on their way to be sunk. But as this fleeting contact, on our passage out and in, is the only one we have with them, we never know if this idea of the changes and chances of mortal life strikes a bell.

Before taking up our station in the convoy-escort, we usually close up to the leading destroyer and receive written orders from her, using the line-throwing rifle to make the necessary contact.

This is, of course, fundamentally a weapon of peace, but it has its possibilities. The 'bullet' which it fires is a metal rod with the line attached to one end of it; and given a calm day and a leading-seaman who knows his job, it is often possible to hit some quite senior officer with the missile. I know of no finer tonic at the start of a convoy than to send a gold-peaked cap spinning down into the drink, secure in the knowledge that it has all been done in the strict course of duty.

When we've got our orders we take up our appointed station on the screen. Sometimes we go about it easily, just drifting into place, sometimes we make an evolution out of it—going astern between the columns. for instance, and then darting out between a couple of close-spaced ships, turning in a flurry of foam, and settling down as if butter wouldn't melt in our turbines. It makes it interesting for us; and (as hoarse voices on megaphones indicate) it makes it interesting for the convoy too.

Most of the ships are old friends: some of them I've seen in earlier days, making the long Atlantic trip, others have been scuttling up and down Hitler's doorstep since war broke out. They are sometimes of peculiar shape and design, drawn right from the bottom of the bag to meet the emergency of war, and they often have pretty odd names; but ever since, on a rough party, we escorted a ship with the really extraordinary name of *Jolly Nights*, I have ceased to be surprised by these. . . . They are mostly heavily laden, and we hope that their cargoes are worth while. 'Looks like a benzine tanker,' said the Gunner once, of a big ship in company. 'But you never know—it's probably two thousand tons of Woolton Pie.' But whatever the filling, on this tricky and varied coast they need, and get, the most faithful shepherding during the time they are under our charge.

Over on the other side navigation was naturally all deep-water stuff—sight-taking, waiting for a glimpse of the sun or a favourite star, broad estimates of the course made good, and lashings of arithmetic. Here, close inshore, there is no occasion for using a sextant, and no room for guesswork either: to the ordinary hazards of coastal navigation the war has added its own refinement.

We have at our disposal a narrow swept channel, cared for by the mine-sweepers, provisionally fool-proof: it is marked by buoys at certain intervals, buoys which must be carefully checked as we pass them—if you lose count, and fail to turn a corner, you may find yourself taking soundings with the keel. In rough weather, at night, it is correspondingly difficult to count the flashes correctly; the buoys bob up and down and are hidden by wave-tops, and if you miss one set of flashes and take 'Three-every-ten' for 'Three-every-twenty', the mistake may be a crucial one and you may finish up on the putty or (more probably) in a minefield.

Those are the first hazards—the long shoals, the mined areas, the mines which may have been dropped long ago and lain dormant ever since; and there are others.

It is a wreck-strewn coast: the green wreck-buoys wink all round you at night, the masts and spars of many ships stick out above the water close to the channel—ships mined or torpedoed or bombed or burnt out, ships driven ashore by stress of weather: all pointing the same moral of carelessness or inaccuracy or bad luck. They have to be carefully avoided; a cross-current will often start to sweep you towards one, and when you try to edge away from it the convoy on your beam bears down on you, leaving you no room to manœuvre, squeezing you between a ship too big to hit and a wreck too shallow to miss. At night, agonized cries go up on the loud-hailer as the green lights loom nearer. . . . I once heard a destroyer on the opposite side of the convoy sing out: 'If you don't give me a bit more room, this wreck-buoy is going to refer to me as well.' That is what it feels like—an inexorable weight pushing you to disaster, and not giving a damn about the outcome.

Sometimes, if the pressure becomes intolerable, you can slip between two ships and get inside the convoy; but at night this needs very careful judgement, and there isn't always enough room. And if the manœuvre fails, it leaves you with an awful lot of explaining to do.

Thought-provoking remark by deep-sea diver, encountered ashore:
'There's a funny thing about that wreck. It's got a skeleton with its head and shoulders half-way out of one of the port-holes.'

The mine-sweepers are always with us, and God bless them for it.

Wherever you go on this coast, there is sure to be one somewhere within view: ranging in size from a tough-looking Fleet sweeper to a glorified drifter trailing a hank of grass rope aft. What a job it must be! Perhaps someone, after the war, will compute the number of man-hours spent on mine-sweeping: on plugging up and down the same bit of channel or stretch of coast-line, navigating with painstaking accuracy, never skimping or cutting corners, running risks all the time, going first down the line every day as groundbait, to keep the sea-lanes open; a job combining extreme danger with the most intolerable boredom.

Meet them ashore, and you won't be specially impressed: R.N.R. skippers, most of them foremost at the bar and red-hot at darts, but certainly not smart-looking nor particularly quiet. But see them on the job—going out in clumps in the early morning, scraping past the buoys so as to leave no bit of the channel unswept—and you'll know why such men were invented.

Now and again, at sea, you hear a 'WHOOMF!' You look round, and there is a small surprised ship scuttling away from a patch of boiling foam. That is a sweeper, having touched one off. . . . We once saw one of them almost overwhelmed by a gigantic explosion close astern of it: a huge column of water shot into the air, hiding the ship from us. When she emerged we called her up (feeling rather shaken ourselves) and said, a trifle patronizingly: 'That was a big one.' Her reply: 'What was?' put us in our place exactly.

But mostly it is boredom, and boredom again. Mine-sweeping crews have a song, exceptionally unquotable, which starts:

> 'Sweeping, sweeping, sweeping:
> Always bloody well sweeping!'

It goes to a well-known hymn-tune, and they sing it on the job. I can't say I'm very much surprised by the fact. If I had their life, I should do more than sing about it. I should scream.

The weather conditions we meet are what you would expect on this coast: cold winds, the perpetual likelihood of fog, short steep seas when it comes on to blow, an absolute cracker in the way of a gale now and then, and a sluicing tide nearly all the time. In rough weather, of course, you feel the lack of sea-room more than ever: if things get too bad out in the Atlantic you can always heave-to and drift gently for as long as you like, but here half an hour off your course might mean shipwreck. Nor can you afford bad steering or careless handling, when ships are so close together and the margin of safety on both sides is so narrow. To coastal convoys, rough weather is a challenge which must be met by ceaseless vigilance and attention to detail, at a time when physically and mentally you may be near exhaustion.

Dipper didn't roll half as badly as my old ship, but she was far less robust. You felt, all the time, that she would smash up if driven too hard: that she balanced her good looks by a certain frailty. Women may do this attractively: ships never.

Scene: A violent storm at sea.

Enter a signalman, bearing a weather report from the Admiralty reading 'Sea slight, visibility good, wind fresh, moderating: further outlook, settled.'

Signalman: 'How do they work these things out, sir?'

Self: 'They've got all sorts of instruments and things.'

Signalman: 'Don't they ever look out of the window?'

Having the Midshipman on watch with me is a real refinement, turning watch-keeping into a luxury operation. He does all the odd jobs which I find irksome—keeping the log up to date, noting the distance run each hour, checking the buoys, changing the charts as we go along. It leaves me free to survey the bridge like an eagle, to make the big decisions and the broad strokes of policy. . . . It is also pleasant to have company, particularly at night, when a companion who is prepared to make either strong cocoa or refined conversation, according to the mood, is a real asset.

His cocoa is very strong, and his conversation is improving gradually.

Sometimes, when the weather is suitable and nothing at all is happening, or likely to, I hand over the watch to the Midshipman and take the wheel from the quartermaster. I happen to enjoy steering the ship, but I seem to be in a minority here, judging from the spectators' faces. The Midshipman, with a worried look, keeps glancing from the compass to me, and back again: then he takes a quick look round the nearest ships, and then once more bends over the compass, with a 'Can-we-survive?' expression enough to disconcert the most able helmsman.

The quartermaster is different. He stands stolidly by, watching the steering-compass, saying nothing: occasionally he sucks his teeth or draws in his breath sharply. Sometimes his fingers twitch. That is all. Discipline is a wonderful thing.

Fog always seems to be lying in wait for us on this coast, no matter what the time of the year; and sometimes, when the visibility gets too bad, the convoy has to anchor in a body and wait for things to improve.

The signal 'Anchor instantly' is given by whatever means is most practicable; and the manœuvre goes all right as long as everyone plays fair and acts on it straight away. But the degree of emergency implied tends to be given a very free interpretation: some ships are inclined to wait for the sound of the other fellow's cable rattling out before coming to a stop themselves, and others, even more mistrustful, haul out of line altogether to try and find a clear space away from the convoy. As that space contains an escort, the latter manœuvre is not popular.

When the fog clears away, all is laid bare: the majority of the convoy will be lying in their proper places with haloes round them, but here and there a lone ship, which has wandered off into a corner, now stands convicted of disobedience. She will have a whole range of excuses for this, varying from 'Didn't receive the signal' to 'Must have dragged anchor in the tideway', and you won't get any joy at all if you try to make something of it.

The first time we were bombed in fog was an occasion not difficult to recall in detail.

It was early in the morning, and visibility was, at the most, fifty yards: the convoy was going very slowly, nose to tail like cattle at dusk, with the possibility of having to anchor until the fog lifted; and all our attention was being given to navigation and to trying to sort out the different sirens, which seemed to be coming at us from all round the compass.

We felt our way along, sniffing the woolly blanket which enveloped the ship, hating every moment of that muffled progress: the puzzling sirens, the drifts of fog swirling past the bridge, the rawness of the air—all added to the feeling of helplessness which fog at sea brings. We had quite enough to think about, without any complications; and when one of the look-outs cocked his head sharply and sang out: 'Sound of aircraft overhead, sir!' we found ourselves beginning to take a Job-like view of the situation.

The noise, quickly confirmed, grew louder: the aircraft seemed to be circling round just above our heads; and there, a glimpse of blue sky among the curling wisps of vapour indicated that there was perfect visibility a little higher up. It was obvious that the fog was low-lying, not much more than a sea-level blanket, and that though we had not yet sighted the aircraft, its pilot could probably see the mast of every ship in the convoy sticking out above the fog-bank, and could choose his target at leisure.

It is really extraordinary how naked you feel at such a moment—as if you were sleeping with your feet out of the window on a freezing night. The guns' crews, piped to Action Stations, looked up hopefully, but they might have been peering through frosted glass at a bird outside, for all the good it did. Then, while they were still peering, things began to happen. The noise was suddenly very near: through a gap overhead I had a second's glimpse of the aircraft peeling off for its dive, another of it half-way down, and then a view, startlingly clear, of four bombs leaving the rack and starting towards us.

They fell wide, but that's not to say they didn't touch our hearts. . . . We got off a few rounds, but—like the bombs—they only scared the target, and the plane was out of sight again in a matter of seconds. Of the various choice remarks passed on the incident, I will quote only one, made by a signalman on the bridge who muttered: 'That's the first time I've ever seen a stick of bombs end on, and lived to be called a liar.'

Another experience in fog, a bit more conclusive, came our way when we received a signal on R/T that one of the ships in convoy had been damaged in collision, and we were to find her and take her in tow.

That seemed to us to be a very easy signal to make. . . . Finding her meant abandoning our comparatively safe position on the escort screen, approaching within hailing distance of the convoy, and then feeling our way through the murk up and down the columns, calling out: 'Are you the damaged merchant ship?' to anyone we saw looming up. This seemingly reasonable question received so many odd answers that in the end we got quite selfconscious about asking it. One stentorian voice shouted back: 'No, but by God I will be, if you come any closer!' and another one, with something fairly weighty on its conscience, called out: 'It wasn't me, sir,' and scuttled off into the gloom again.

We found the one we were looking for in the end—a small merchant ship holed squarely amidships and playing a kind of drifting Blind Man's Buff among the rest of the convoy; but the difficulty we had in locating her was nothing to the job of passing the tow.

This is not simple at the best of times: half a shackle of cable, a length of eight-inch manila, sixty fathoms of towing hawser, eighty fathoms of grass rope—all this has to be flaked out on deck, with no kinks and no mistakes, so that it will run out smoothly when the towed ship heaves in. And on this occasion most of the heaving-in had to be done by shouts and guesswork: sending out the first line was all right, but by the time a quarter of the tow had been passed the damaged ship was out of sight again in the fog. We *had* to keep moving slow ahead, to avoid getting the wire round our screw; and we could only guess at her position and find out, by shouting at the blank wall astern of us, if the other end of the tow was secure.

From the bridge nothing could be seen of the operation at all: from my position on the quarter-deck aft I had to describe what was happening over the telephone, give an estimate of our distance apart, and judge when we should stop engines to avoid pulling up with a jerk and parting the tow. For if this happened, we would have to start finding the ship all over again. . . . In addition, there was always the likelihood of another ship drifting in between us and getting caught up in the wire: perhaps two ships, perhaps a buoy as well.

It was something of an anti-climax that none of these things happened. We were able to take the weight pretty smoothly, thanks chiefly to some ship-handling by the Captain which put all his previous efforts in the shade; and shortly afterwards the fog lifted and we towed her out into the sunlight—a good moment, that, like leaving a dark wood where you have been terrified all day and finding the pleasant world again. But while the uncertainty and the guesswork lasted, it was a formidable responsibility.

Look-out: 'Aircraft bearing Green 10. Angle of sight 30. Approaching the ship.'

Self (improving the occasion over the loudspeaker for the benefit of the watch on deck): 'The aircraft on the starboard bow is a Hudson belonging to Coastal Command. You can recognize it easily by the twin-fins and the thick fuselage. As it passes overhead———'

Look-out (respectfully): 'Stick of bombs coming down, sir.'

Another snatch of dialogue, warranted true.

Destroyer, to German aircraft circling convoy out of effective range: 'You are making me dizzy. Go round the other way.'

German aircraft: 'With pleasure.'

And it did.

On one convoy, one very persistent straggler resisted all our efforts to make him catch up: all orders and entreaties, if they were answered at all, were met by the declaration: 'I am going my utmost speed already,' and he continued to lag astern till the late dusk.

Came a chance single enemy aircraft which dropped a bomb fairly close to him. That got results. Within fifteen seconds clouds of smoke started to pour from his funnel: then he increased speed till he had a bow wave as big as a destroyer's, passed like an arrow right through the convoy, and came out on the other side. Still pouring smoke, he vanished into the gloom ahead of us. . . .

Said the Captain: 'There's a lot in this auto-suggestion, you know.'

We once had to stand by a damaged merchant ship all night, in filthy weather, waiting until daylight so that she could complete rough repairs and make harbour; and I remember the occasion as being the only one, in my experience so far, when the expression 'Came the dawn' has attained its full significance.

It was too rough to take her in tow, or we would have had a crack at getting her in as she was; so while she lay at anchor, dragging slowly but managing to keep out of trouble, we went round and round a nearby buoy and made what we could of the situation—shoving our nose under whenever we headed into the wind, rolling like mad when we turned into the wave-troughs, dodging the spray and getting wet through and freezing on the bridge.

For twelve hours we went lop-sidedly round that miserable little light, which flashed feebly every twenty seconds like a drunkard opening a bleary eye, with the rest of the view as black as sin, with occasional dirty waves slopping over the bridge, and howling wind-driven rain whipping us all the time. There was really no cure for the two watches I stood that night: cocoa, chocolate, sandwiches, kapok suit, fur-lined flying-boots—they all ceased to charm long before the end. The sole relief was in passing and receiving occasional signals from the merchant ship: a contact with humanity in the wilderness which enlivened both our spirits. We took to asking each other riddles in the end: waiting for daylight in the wild darkness, we needed company.

They were very bad riddles, however. Here is a sample one, which originated in a childhood Christmas cracker and should have been long since buried by the merciful years.

Q. 'Why can't a deaf and dumb man tickle nine girls?'

A. 'Because he can only gesticulate (just tickle eight).'

Their signalman took a long time to get that one.

Occasionally we are detailed for night-patrol duty—that is, keeping a certain area under observation, guarding any shipping that may be passing through, and looking for trouble on our own account.

We like patrols, as a change from routine escorting of convoys—there is something individual, almost romantic, about them, and one has a freer hand than when one is tied by station-keeping and the speed of other ships. There are several advantages peculiar to this freedom. You can make all the noise you want to, or you can lie in wait like a cat at a mouse-hole: if you feel like going full astern, or chasing a shoal of fish for practice, you can do so, without any snarling rebukes from the Senior Officer to burn your ears off. And of course, there is always a chance that you will bump into something really juicy—aircraft on a mine-laying job, for example, or a big E-boat raid on a convoy. Those are the nights when you feel you are earning your keep, and sometimes they seem a long time coming.

Nor are they handed to you on a plate, with an invitation to wade in and have your fill: at this stage of the war, on this coast, there aren't enough battles to go round. Tantalizing occasions arise when there is obviously a party going on on a neighbouring patrol, and we try to think of a good excuse for edging into it. It is annoying in the extreme to see, as we sometimes do, star-shells going up just this side of the horizon, and tracer-bullets making neat red arcs in the sky, and to know that someone is getting beaten up and that it's none of our business. If only we could saunter over carelessly and cut ourselves a slice. . . . But we've got to play fair, if only from the efficiency point of view: if we abandon our allotted patrol and go skimming off in search of excitement, that leaves a whole section unprotected, in which anything might happen.

Poaching of this sort is not popular with anyone, and least of all with the corvette or destroyer involved, who has got his teeth into a nice piece of meat and intends to hang on to it, against all comers.

This last point was once well illustrated by signals which we exchanged with a sister corvette on returning to harbour, after a night's tantalizing inaction on the edge of what had looked like Guy Fawkes's birthday party.

They: 'Any luck last night?'

We: 'No. It was on X's patrol, and they hogged it all.'

They: 'Did you expect them to make an R.P.C.?'[1]

No, poaching is not at all popular: that sort of private enterprise is heavily frowned on: you may not even stand on the outskirts of the party making chirruping noises to attract attention. But the spectacle of a frustrated corvette trying to edge its way into a destroyer-*versus*-E-boat action, like a small boy crawling between people's legs at a football match, has its pathetic side, which I hope the appropriate authorities recognize.

One dark night when we were patrolling in the vicinity of a convoy, faithful and true and doing no harm to anyone, we suddenly found ourselves the centre of a blaze of light: one of the escorting destroyers had fired a star-shell directly above us, to make sure of our identity (or, more probably, simply to make us jump). I had not realized before just how powerful a star-shell is. . . . The ship sat there, brilliantly illuminated, cold and naked under scrutiny, while they looked their fill; and on the bridge we waited for the follow-up, whatever it was to be, in some tension. It seemed possible that this was after all a serious investigation, and that they were saying: 'Can't make her out for certain. Let's chance a couple of four-inch bricks.'

When the bombers go out on '1,000-plane' nights or other big operations, some of them go over us, in an almost continuous stream which does the heart good to see and hear. At least, it does that to *my*

---

[1] 'Request the Pleasure of your Company'—the usual abbreviation for inter-ship hospitality.

heart. In such matters as air-raids and reprisals, my 'turn-the-other-cheek' Christianity turns a blind eye instead: my last ship was stuck in a dock during a seven-night blitz in 1941, and I am willing for our side to balance that account in any way they choose. And since many of this present crew come from Portsmouth and Plymouth, and have returned there on leave to find their homes razed to the ground, I don't suppose they've got much objection either.

The bombers pass over our heads in the early dusk, heading the right way: they go in line ahead, in little groups of three or four, or sometimes singly: they look enormous. At such a time they are sharply outlined against the sky: there may be the after-glow of a brilliant sunset, and across this background—pale blue and gold—moves a dark tide of aircraft seeping towards their targets. They fade out of sight and into silence, like a lovely and sinister flight of birds attending a far-off battle. When they are gone, the evening air is restored: quiet returns: there is no evidence.

Then, towards dawn, we hear them coming back; and now the occasion and the feeling are subtly different—more informal, more relaxed. Many of the aircraft are unscathed and triumphant; others are stumbling home, obviously damaged—there are spluttering engines, odd bits hanging down, pieces missing from wings and fuselage. Once we saw a Stirling with one of its engines on fire, limping alone with a little plume of flame and a tail of smoke behind it. Looking up at it, we willed it to survive its travail and make its landing-ground. . . . But whatever the state of their aircraft may be, we know how the crews must be feeling as they come within sight of home—relieved, thankful, perhaps surprised. Where they have been, all guarantees must have lapsed for a space in their minds, leaving only nerve and brain to carry the weight from second to second.

Occasionally we get a signal that there is a plane reported down in the sea, or a dinghy adrift with a bomber's crew in it. If they are anywhere near our area, we double our look-outs and do our very best to find them. After such a journey into chance—to Kiel, to Hamburg, perhaps across the Alps—they deserve our utmost effort.

We took an R.A.F. bomber-pilot along with us for one trip, and he was very good company: bringing all our slang up to date and (without too intensive an effort at line-shooting) convincing us that we were in the safe service, by comparison. But it was unfortunate that the convoy chose this occasion to open up, with every available gun, at an inoffensive Lancaster which rashly appeared out of the sunset and flew rather low over our heads.

We tried to explain to our guest that this touchiness was excusable (and even praiseworthy), but he did not seem disposed to view the affair from anything but a narrow R.A.F. angle.

We see a lot more of the Air Force on this side than I used to out in the Atlantic: they are always either covering us directly, or playing leap-frog nearby with one eye on the convoy. Sometimes we see the fighters going out on a sweep, beating hell out of the wave-tops, with outriders weaving about like eels' tails in a swift stream. Within a minute or so the whole cavalcade is over the horizon, and we return to the dull domestic grind, feeling rather like Cinderella on the night of the party. But if we miss the glamour, at least we are spared the hang-over.

'You've got to hand it to them,' the Gunner summed it up once. 'They're not all brilliantine and gremlins.'

We were detailed to escort a mine-layer while she was busy 'on the job', and it wasn't the most popular assignment of the week.

The programme was, in theory, simple enough: take her out, hang about while she dropped her mines, and bring her back again. But it had strings attached to it, and they were long and curly ones, liable to catch in anything. Firstly, the navigation had to be exact to the nearest yard: we were either filling in some gaps in our own minefield or else passing through it to make a new one (I hardly cared to look at the chart), and any mistakes we made wouldn't need to be repeated. Secondly, a ship full of mines—big black juicy ones: we'd watched them being loaded up, with shadowed eyes—is always an uncomfortable neighbour; if someone pressed the wrong button on board we might find ourselves airborne at the same time. And lastly, the excursion was in broad daylight and would take us, to put it mildly and discreetly, farther from our own coast than usual.

There were other ships in company, of course, and we left harbour in reassuring strength: once outside, we took up our pre-determined formation, and set off. The mine-layer itself, as was only natural, had the final say in navigation, but many signals flashed to and fro before the course to steer was finally approved of, and all anxieties quietened: we didn't mind them leading us if they knew what they were doing, but there was no harm in checking up on this latter point. . . . For a long time it was simply a matter of follow-my-leader, on a course which took us (we could not help realizing) a little farther from cover with every turn of the screw; and by and by a certain wariness began to show itself on board, and ratings having no conceivable connection with look-out duties—such as coders and stewards—might be observed scanning the horizon or the sky with professional zeal.

But there was certainly no harm in a little margin of safety, and towards the end of the outward run we made the precaution official and doubled the aircraft look-outs all round the ship.

When he had given his order for this last:

'Go round gun-quarters, Number One,' said the Captain; 'explain the position, and tell everyone I want the best possible look-out kept. Make one of your rabble-rousing speeches, if you like, and lay it on as thick as you can—we're in the Indians' country now.'

By and by we reached the assigned position, and presently the actual mine-laying began, after (one hoped) a last bout of estimating and arithmetic to put the matter beyond doubt. We had nothing to do during the final operation, except keep station and watch the regular splash of the mines as they were let go: they bobbed astern of the mine-layer for a couple of minutes, a trail of sinister black shapes, and then sank slowly beneath the surface, wallowing out of sight with hardly a ripple. No doubt they would make up for this peaceful descent on their return journey.

The job seemed to take ages: we hung about, conscious of tension, feeling like burglars kept waiting by a finicky accomplice who insists on putting the room tidy again before leaving. Half-way through, to add point to the occasion, an aircraft made its appearance and flew round and round us in a wide circle: one of those unidentifiable aircraft that don't appear in the manual, with two to four engines, thick-thin fuselage, and roundish-squarish wing-tips. It really might have been anything: it seemed to be going through the motions of an air escort, but they would have done equally well for hostile reconnaissance. . . . By the time the mine-layer had brought its job to a leisurely finish, we were quite ready to go home.

Said the Captain, as we turned away and got our nose towards land:

'I suppose some people like this sort of trip. To me it seems one hundred per cent morbid.'

A ship—particularly a warship—blown up by a mine can look peculiarly horrible, with an air of drunken disorder about her that is distressing in all its aspects.

When you look at her you are looking at a ruin: the decks are buckled, the bridge smashed in, the guns pointing at all angles or hanging over the side. Perhaps the worst part of it is that she looks so utterly *disorganized*: in a moment of time she has been transformed

from an efficient unit into a shambles. Here was a good ship, the pride of
her company: here is a deserted wreck, a section of scrap-iron, untidy
and shapeless and dead.

And when you pass her even a few days later, she seems to have been
dead for a hundred years already, claimed by the weed and the fish.

Swift illustration of a wrong helm-order:
'Starboard ten! . . . Where the hell are you going to?'

'Now this time *last* Christmas,' said the Captain—and I knew that
something interesting and not necessarily accurate was coming: 'this
time last Christmas—or it may have been the Christmas before, or even
Easter, but it was a religious occasion of some sort—things were
happening, and we were really in the thick of it.

'It was somewhere round here, too.' He pointed towards a nearby
wreck-buoy, which had just given us a lot of trouble. 'In fact, I think that
one is part of the hang-over. Something went wrong, anyway, and the
convoy got off the channel and ran slap through a mined area. By God,
there were mines going off like bubbles in soda-water! It was more like a
dream than anything else: you hardly had time to look at one ship
before another one bought it.

'I remember what a horrible contrast it seemed to make—Christmas
Eve, peace on earth, and ships blowing up all round us, without any
warning, and we standing by, quite helpless and liable to do the same
thing ourselves. Mining is a sneaking sort of trick at any time, and
Christmas made it seem especially treacherous. When we saw those
ships blowing up and sinking, and men swimming about in the water, it
didn't seem as if peace on earth was much of a wish, or much of a
weapon either.'

The ship comes in for all sorts of odd jobs, and so do I: anything from
boarding a doubtful character on the high seas to answering income tax
queries is the First Lieutenant's assignment, and must be dealt with in
short order and with equal ruthlessness.

I remember one 3 a.m. excursion to rescue the whaler which some
miscalculation of the Captain's had stranded on the mud during a
sailing-race earlier in the day: the salvage-operation—setting off at
dead of night with waders, heaving-lines, tow-ropes, and a dozen bottles
of beer—had an odd piratical flavour about it, and its successful
conclusion, at dawn, seemed a memorable triumph. Another time, when
we were returning from patrol, we saw a bomb floating in the sea—at
least, it was shaped like a bomb, with fins and tail complete.

'I'd like to have a look at that,' said the Captain. 'You never know—it might be a new secret weapon. Are you interested?'

I said no, not very, but after the words 'Bomb Disposal Officer' had been freely bandied about on the bridge, I was naturally involved, five minutes later, in leading the recovery operations. I approached it gingerly in the motor-boat, while the Captain, his mind possibly elsewhere, edged the ship away from the immediate vicinity and watched through binoculars.

When I lifted it out of the water it was *exactly* bomb-shaped, the kind of thing you see in photographs being loaded on to a Flying Fortress, under the caption: 'More headaches for Hitler.' I held it at arm's length while we returned to the ship: as we drew near an encouraging voice from the bridge called out: 'Don't look so worried, Number One. Even if it goes off, you'll never know a thing about it.' The fact that it turned out to be some kind of aircraft smoke-float, pro-British and harmless, was rather an anti-climax. But (as I pointed out in the wardroom later) the heroic quality of the deed was there all the same, surely?

One has, in fact, to be ready to deal with anything, even with an apparent lack of zeal on the part of the Captain. On one occasion we chanced upon a very bedraggled corpse in the water. After looking at it closely for some moments, the Captain said:

'Number One, pick all that up, will you? I'm going aft for a bit.'

It is in some way significant that I had already answered 'Aye, aye, sir,' and given the first helm-order, before the Captain interrupted in a rather hurt voice: 'That was a *joke*, Number One. I'm not *really* going aft, you know.'

And there was another, more elevating occasion, when by some caprice of the coding-department we received the odd signal: 'Commence hostilities against Japan forthwith.'

'Number One!'

'Sir?'

'Commence hostilities against Japan.'

'Aye, aye, sir. . . . Starboard ten!'

Caught out, and running southward for shelter before the worst storm on this coast for many years, the convoy laboured all through the night to stay in formation and hold its course on the safe channel.

We ourselves were lucky to be stationed astern of the main body, with a certain freedom of movement; but even so it was hard to keep at a safe distance in the darkness, and harder still to control the wild motion of the ship. The following seas, short and steep, made steering tremendously difficult: standing aft on the quarter-deck one saw them hang above the stern, then lift it up and force it to one side or the other, threatening to pin the ship in the trough of a wave and roll it over. Sometimes the waves jumped and broke, instead of surging underneath, and toppled over on to the after-deck with a blow like a giant aimless fist: as the spray cleared and the water poured outboard again, the ship lifted slowly like a dazed fighter recovering from a knock-down blow.

Out in the Atlantic the convoy would have played for safety long before, and turned in a body to meet the storm; but here there was no room to turn, and no remedy save vigilant steering and an exactly-judged speed. If we went too fast, nothing would have stopped the stern swinging round and over: and too slow would mean a sluggish ship, a target for every wave that overtook us. Somewhere between the narrow margin of the two, side-slipping, rolling crazily, we dodged and fled the enemy.

It was very black all round us, and bitterly cold: occasionally a scud of snow frosted the deck, to be wiped roughly away next moment by wind or sea water. The gale tugged at the ship and at one's clothes, the stern lifted, shuddered, settled down again in a rhythm which seemed unending. The buoys we were searching for hid themselves in the murk until we were almost on top of them: there was always the danger that a straggler, unseen in the blackness, would show herself too late to avoid disaster; and without respite, astern of us, like a vicious hue and cry, the waves smashed and snapped and chased us onwards.

It was a night of tension and waiting, twelve hours' endurance of winter's malice: dawn came up like a blessing, and showed the decks glistening, the coxswain at the wheel (after a six-hour trick) as intent as a hanging judge, and the brave convoy still together.

There's nothing more heartening, at sea, than the turn of the year, when the nights begin to pull out of winter and dusk is delayed each evening for a few minutes longer. You begin to notice the change during the dog-watches just after Christmas: gradually the first dog-watch becomes a daylight one, and when, by the middle of February, you can take over the last dog-watch (six to eight p.m.) in complete daylight, spring and hope are on the way.

It's been a long wait: ever since the previous October. But how quickly all that is forgotten.

It was odd to see the coast of France again, for the first time since 1939; the sight aroused the same sort of speculative attention as might a working-party of Dartmoor convicts, seen from the main road nearby. It looked extraordinarily near to us: the high ground inland showed greyish-white under the full moon, and the loom of the shore-lights, as they came up and faded out again, seemed like a secret signal from the prisoners within.

This distant prospect of the enemy was with us for about an hour. At one point a searchlight swept the sea, looking for strangers. Said a rating, as the beam came round: 'There's the old bastard flashing his eyes at us.' And a little later, pursuing the same train of thought: 'Get the tea up, Nobby. My patience is exhausted.'

The destroyer which had been torpedoed and sunk during the night was an old friend: we had heard the explosion from a long way off, and it was a relief, after the ensuing action and alarm, to be detailed to leave the convoy and look for survivors.

To us, knowing some of the men in the water on that bitterly cold night, this seemed the most important thing we could do, but it needed doing quickly if any good was to come of it: the strong tide meant that the survivors would be widely scattered, the speed of the ship's sinking made it unlikely that any boats had been launched, and the extreme cold would not let them last long in the water.

It was very dark, and the smell of fuel-oil was the first indication we had that we were near them: that, and a single dim light which was burning on an empty Carley raft. Making sure that the latter *was* empty wasted a lot of time—precious time, each minute of which might be snuffing out another life. But presently, taking a wide sweep round the oil patch, we heard distant shouting, and altered course towards it, as near as we could judge; and after a couple of minutes one of the look-outs made out a tiny black smudge in the sea ahead. This was an old routine, with nearly three years' nagging familiarity behind it. . . . As we closed the speck I looked at it through my binoculars, trying to distinguish its outline and see if it was worth salvaging.

'Two men,' I said, as soon as we were close enough. 'And they're alive all right—waving. But I can't see a raft or anything. In fact,' I hesitated, 'they seem to be standing in the water.'

'Stop both!' said the Captain. The telegraphs rang down, and were answered. 'I'll go right up to them,' he went on. 'We don't want to waste time lowering a boat if we can help it.' Then he raised his binoculars again, for a long look. 'You're right, Number One,' he agreed, 'they *are* in a funny position. They're either wearing their life-belts round their knees, or doing the Indian Rope Trick.'

But there was another, surprise explanation, and it was the men themselves who gave it us, with admirable presence of mind. For while we were still thirty yards off, creeping slowly towards them with the way almost off the ship, one of them called out, in a voice strident with cold but still forceful:

'Don't come any closer, sir! We're standing on the stern of the ship.'

That seemed to me to be bravery of a very special quality. Those two men had been standing up to their waists in icy water for over two hours: they were perched on the stern of a destroyer which was balanced vertically with its bows on the bottom but which might at any moment sink altogether. They saw rescue close at hand, the promise of survival from what must have seemed a miserable and hopeless position, and yet the first thing they thought about was the danger to *us* if we came too close to them. Men such as these were worth rescuing ten times over.

We laid off to a safe distance, lowered the motor-boat, and picked them up: a signalman and a stoker, both cold to the bone, their legs nearly paralysed. They could not have lasted very much longer, even if the sunk ship had kept its position. I talked to them while they were warming through again in the galley, but they knew very little of what had happened: both had been out on the upper deck when the ship went down, had swum around in darkness for a bit, and then suddenly grounded on the miraculous haven where we found them. They had not seen anyone else for a long time, though earlier on there had been a Carley raft nearby with about twenty men on it. They did not think any boats had been lowered: there had not been time.

I left them in the warmth of the galley—their blue, pinched legs and still chattering teeth a reminder of peril—and went back on to the bridge. There had been no development during the quarter of an hour I had been away: nothing more had been sighted, though they had heard some men shouting for a bit, too weakly or too far away to gauge the direction. There had been silence now for quite a long time.

'Depressing about that,' remarked the Captain suddenly: 'you know so exactly the sort of men who are in the water.' That was in all our minds, I think—that not very far away, but out of effective reach, a virtual duplicate of our own ship's company, with the same trustworthy hands and humorists and rogues, was perishing man by man.

It was now getting towards dawn, and we had been sweeping round the patch of oil in widening circles, as far as we could judge them, for four hours without any result. When daylight came we would probably see the Carley raft, but that might be too late to save the people on it.

This was something which did not need impressing on the look-outs; probably every seaman in the ship kept a perfect watch for the rest of that night. But whatever their degree of concentration, it was no use: when dawn came up we were still only two hands to the good, not much better than failure and a wretched answer to our hopes of earlier on.

Then, at full daylight, we finally sighted the raft, and made for it at speed. This must have been the main direction of the tidal set, for on the way we passed successive little groups of bodies, all lifeless, washing about in the oily sea among oddments of wreckage. Sometimes a lolling head jerked to the lift of the swell, giving an illusion of life, raising hopes which died at a second glance. This was the crew we had been looking for, but it seemed that we had spent too long in the search: we and they had both been defeated, by time and the sea.

There remained the raft: an unforgettable picture as, in the fresh sunlight of a lovely morning, we drew near it. Upright on it sat a handful of black-faced, oil-soaked men, surrounded by prone figures, sprawling in the lazy attitudes of the dead. One man, who raised a feeble arm in greeting as we came alongside, had a shipmate's head pillowed in his lap, his hand resting on the staring face with a cherishing touch which told the night's story in a single gesture. Another, whose filthy face split into a grin as we reached down for him, must have been in agony from his shattered leg. Of the others, some stared up at the ship as at a miracle: one might have been singing but, heard close to, was in fact groaning softly: all were in an extremity of cold.

We set to work as carefully as we could, putting into our handling of them the overflow of compassion which the past night and the present sight of them called forth. All the time that we were lifting them inboard, a Spitfire flew round and round the ship, close to the water, as guard, spectator, and mourner, all in one; and it was a moment that bit into the memory—the few upright figures in the raft, the ungainly dead, the aircraft circling us continually, the lovely sunlight that could warm so few. We had to rig a tackle for the dead men: their bodies dangled like hung criminals as they were hoisted up, their heads fell forwards and sideways and forwards again in a cycle of supreme ugliness. The hands detailed for the job had faces of stone as they worked the tackle. These men were themselves.

We collected many bodies, all through that morning: they were laid out on the quarter-deck, their clothes smothered in oil but with the familiar badges—the leading-seaman's anchor, the signalman's crossed flags—showing here and there. It was the sight of these last, perhaps, which brought home to us with piercing clarity that they were fellow-sailors who had met their death, who were now (in that most explicit and final of phrases) marked 'Discharged Dead' on the books. I remember the Chief looking down at one of them, and muttering: 'Three badges—that's thirteen years in the Service, at least—and now this. . . .' It summed up the continuity of the Navy, its sense of one-ness, its family pride. It was the deep feeling of a mourner who mourned, not a brother but a part of himself: the same feeling which prompts the messmates of a dead man to bid generously for all the oddments of his kit when it is disposed of. Ten shillings for a cap-ribbon, fifteen shillings for an old clasp knife—it is the measure of their comradeship, which includes his wife and family.

Since many of the destroyer's crew were still unaccounted for, and it was believed that at least two other rafts had got clear of the ship, we intended to carry on with the search. Up on the bridge I let the ship idle along at dead-slow, circling the nearest buoy, while down below in the chart-house the Captain and the Navigator pored over charts and tide-tables, trying to work out exactly where the remainder of the crew might have drifted to since their ship was sunk. Presently our signal asking permission to continue looking for survivors was answered, and we began a series of careful sweeps to cover the probable area.

That day was a memorable exercise in frustration. We crossed and recrossed the hunting-ground, we took every conceivable care and precaution, but all to no purpose: nothing was sighted save odd bits of wreckage, and not very much of that. It was maddening: the men were there, life was ebbing from them, and (it seemed) only our stupidity prevented us from rescuing them. The thought could not be put aside: we were conscious all the time of a closing gap, conscious of the race between the cold, the margin of human endurance, the hours of daylight remaining, and the square miles we had to cover. And there was one other potent item to be allowed for, in this account. The weather was growing worse with every watch; and by evening it was getting to the point where men adrift for so long could hardly be alive. They were there still, in the rising sea and the bleak dusk; there we would have to leave them; and as this fact sharpened and established itself, hope foundered on it, rage grew, sadness and pity deepened.

At nightfall we turned for home. In the wardroom, off watch, I talked with the two surviving officers: it was difficult not to feel guilty at the enjoyment of warmth and shelter, and when I told them that we were giving up, and leaving the search-area, I felt a rat. What they felt, I did not care to conjecture. One of them said: 'Well, you certainly did your best for us,' but the remark was a cover for feeling, not an expression of

it. As the revolutions mounted on the way home, the rags of satisfaction
at our efforts blew away, and were left astern with the rest.

One of the survivors, talking as men talk when they would rather
keep silent but cannot, said:

'I'd heard before that after you've spent a bit of time in the water, you
just don't care whether you live or die. I didn't think that could ever be
true in my case, as I've got a wife back home, and two children just
growing up. But it is true: after a bit, you're too cold and tired to care
what you're leaving behind you: all you want is to fall asleep and cut the
whole thing. That's the most dangerous part about being in the drink:
however much you've got to live for, if it's cold and miserable enough,
you just don't want to live any longer.'

We entered harbour well after dark, going dead-slow ahead, picking
our way among the shipping and the buoys with deliberate precision.
Lowering the whaler and hooking on to the buoy, by the light of a
shaded torch, was a complicated exercise on which it was a relief to
concentrate. But everyone on board was very quiet: today, on that
particular job, we had failed.

4   SWINGING ROUND THE BUOY

The fact that, when we are in harbour, we usually lie out at a buoy, gives
us an enclosed life on board, of a rather special sort. Though within
sight of land, the ship's isolation is complete. We can of course regulate
our contacts with the shore by running trips in, in the motor-boat; but
once you settle down to it, life in the ship can be complete and self-
contained in a rather satisfying way.

She is an individual unit, running on her own resources; and all the
odd activities which go on, apart from normal working hours—the
reading, letter-writing, card-playing, tombola, washing and mending
clothes, cooking of meals, music-making—all tend to emphasize the
ship's self-reliance and self-sufficiency. We feel that we can do
everything on board, dealing not only with all emergencies but with
every unlikely or frivolous impulse. Apart from fulfilling the ship's
normal requirements, for such things as rope-ladders or wire-splicing,
we are not taken aback by any of the following tasks: engraving a beer
tankard, silver-plating a cigarette-case (by an illegal method which I will

not describe): manufacturing a complete cigarette-lighter that works:
making an inlaid napkin-ring, a toy engine, a bookcase, a pair of rope-
soled shoes, or a canvas cover for a typewriter.

For a small ship, her resources seem almost limitless. Even a new
balance-wheel for your wrist-watch only needs a word to the engine-
room department. Or, at least, so they maintain. I'm waiting for
someone else to try it out first.

With this variety of talent to draw on, together with the necessary
amount of cleaning, painting, gun-drill, and harbour exercises, we need
not be bored however long we swing round the buoy. And sometimes,
owing to bad weather or a minor defect, we do spend quite considerable
periods out there. Time flows on, tides ebb and flood and ebb again,
while extraordinary rumours spread round the flotilla: that a special
weed is growing on the ship's bottom, not healthy sea-green but some
noxious harbour growth: that we are aground on our own empty
bottles: that the cable is rusted on to the buoy, and acetylene-cutters will
be necessary before we can put to sea. . . . It doesn't demoralize us in
the least, but it tends to demoralize other ships. They seem to think that
we are getting away with something.

There are other periods to balance this, however, when owing to
'operational requirements' (as they say) or to blasted corvettes that *will*
keep running into each other, we hardly ever see harbour at all: we poke
our nose in, oil, and go out again, on a sort of shuttle-service that cuts
sleep and recuperation down to nil.

The buoy waits for our return, surrounded by half-starved seagulls.
Ashore, the girls forget us, and transfer everything to destroyers.

Example of a spoilt afternoon nap:
Signal received at 3 p.m.: 'To *Dipper* from Flag-Officer-in-Charge:
Away whaler, row round Nos. 6 and 10 buoys, report when whaler
hoisted again.'

That seemed to me, toiling to get a bung-eyed whaler's crew away in
quick time, to be the naval version of an offensive sweep.

Sometimes we have an inspection, of that informal kind which
necessitates everyone looking exceptionally clean and tidy, and a
certain number of hands detailed to stand about in attitudes of work,
complete with brooms and brass-rags. (It is a curious fact on board ship
that men actually working in the most conscientious fashion always
look as if they are loafing, and vice versa.) After one such occasion I had
an amusing report on it from a friend of mine, Number One of a

destroyer, who had been entertained by a bird's eye view of the affair through his binoculars.

He had been able to watch the procession going round the ship—Flag-Officer-in-Charge, Captain, First Lieutenant ('never seen you wearing gloves before'), four other officers, coxswain, messenger, ship's dog, and ship's cat. 'I honestly thought the head would catch up with the tail, now and then,' he said: 'it looked like a lot of performing elephants in a ring a bit too small for them, though when the head of the procession stopped the rest of you telescoped like a goods train. But you've certainly got some resourceful ratings on board. We watched one of them, who'd been busy painting on the starboard side when the Admiral passed him, nip across to port and start splicing a rope for the return journey. Or was that a put-up job?'

I said no, it had been strictly private enterprise, and I would look into it.

'He was taking a chance, anyway, because the Admiral spoke to him the second time. We thought he must have noticed the change-over.'

It seemed to me rather likely, too. In fact it still does.

Every now and again the Gunner has a fundamental and mysterious drive on the 4-inch ammunition: emptying the entire magazine, marshalling the contents on the upper deck, and then walking round and round it with a note-book, muttering and scribbling. It is then all put back again, by ratings with expressionless faces.

Some of the shells are marked 'TO HELL WITH HITLER' in block capitals, but whether they are of special calibre I do not know.

We have a decorated gun on board which usually excites comment, as well it might: its shield is marked by a pair of swastikas labelled 'H.E. 111' and 'M.E. 110' respectively, and a small drawing of an E-boat adorns the centre. Now these three items (which are official) happen to be the ship's total bag to date; and the fact that an enterprising gun-layer has put them all on one gun, his own, which he then practically charges money to see, has been a fruitful source of argument among the Gunner's Party.

It has been agreed that, in case of doubt and to avoid an unfair distribution of the limelight, it should always be made clear that the credit-markings refer to the ship and not to the individual gun-layer; but I have not yet seen the latter looking especially modest as he answers questions about it. Some day I must stand out of sight, but within earshot, and listen to the sales-talk.

Quartermaster's humour:
  'Hands to dinner! C.W. ratings[1] to lunch!'

Good example of how bad blood between two departments on board
may start:
  I was demonstrating a tear-gas bomb to a party of newly-joined
seamen on the upper deck. Unfortunately I had placed myself, without
noticing, just under the lee of a large engine-room ventilator, and when
the bomb went off a compact cloud of gas, never deviating or losing
consistency, moved across towards the cowling and was sucked down
in one deep breath. . . . There was a short pause—one of those pauses
when you know that something's *got* to happen: then the entire engine-
room personnel started to pour out of the hatchway, fighting for breath,
their eyes streaming.
  I might have been able to explain it away smoothly as an unfortunate
accident, had not a rather intelligent-looking ordinary seaman
remarked:
  'That was a good example of a concentrated attack, sir. Can we see
one in the open air now?'
  A memorable footnote to this affair was given me later in the day, by
an engine-room artificer who had received the full charge.
  'We thought it was one of your cigars at first, sir,' he said, 'but we
soon noticed the difference.'
  I felt obliged to take this as a compliment.

Challenge of nervous young gangway-sentry:
  'Halt! There he goes!'

  It's not easy for a First Lieutenant to have a book about corvettes
published and circulating freely on board, and still retain an aloof
disciplinary air.
  By methods which I do not inquire into (though I should like my
publishers to copy them) an ex-bookseller able seaman sold two
hundred and sixty-two copies of *H.M. Corvette* to members of the ship's
company: which was fine from an author's point of view, but not so
good otherwise. It altered too many things altogether. It wasn't just the
fact of seeing dozens of hands all over the ship reading the darned thing,
though this was sufficiently distracting: it was, somehow, that everyone
had now established a claim to my favour, on a cash basis, and this had

[1] C.W. ratings are those recommended for commissions.

to be allowed for (or rather, *not* allowed for) in my dealings with them.

Stripped of its incidental humours, it seemed to boil down to the rhetorical question: how can you deal severely with a man who has just asked you for your autograph? This is something which does not normally arise in a writer's life: or, if it does, he is so completely disarmed that severity melts like snow in the sun.

It happens that the only radio we have in the wardroom comes *via* loudspeaker relayed from the stokers' messdeck, and we thus have to take what they give us, or else . . . Without naming individual items, I can certainly say that during the past year I have listened to programmes I would not otherwise have heard: I had a fair idea before (and considerable appreciation) of how high the B.B.C. aimed, but this was my first glimpse of their alternative target, and their marksmanship was stunning.

If I were Director of Programmes for the B.B.C. (and I shall be looking for a job after the war), I think I should admit that a seventeen-hour day is too long to be filled with first or even second-rate material; and I should ration the good stuff at my disposal and stay off the air for the rest of the time, instead of trying to eke it out with trash. Better to preserve an hour's silence, better (if you must have a noise) to hand over to the B.B.C. signal, rather than spread alarm and despondency by giving a free rein to the entertainment world.

The objection isn't only artistic, or even mainly so: it is directly geared to the war. If you pump this stuff out, if you fill up the minds of soldiers, for example, with thoughts of yearning and burning, and blue-birds-over-Dover, you don't get fighting men as a result: you get a lot of long-faced goons who want to go home instead of finishing the job.

These tea-time comedians and boo-hooing young women are only fill-ups, I know; but there's many a good hole in the ground that wants filling first.

Morale in the wardroom occasionally sustains a shock, too. Sales of a certain brand of gin, formerly popular, have now dropped to zero, following the receipt of a letter from the suppliers, in answer to one of ours saying that their product was becoming progressively more revolting. Part of their reply, a long apology, read:

'You will appreciate the difficulties under which the gin-trade is working when we tell you that our supplies are now imported in galvanized-iron drums which have contained lubricating oil, paraffin, and crude petroleum.'

Overheard in the wardroom:
'I believe in looking after number one—and I *don't* mean the First Lieutenant.'

There is a Fighting French destroyer which comes into the Base now and then, and sometimes we are tied up alongside her: which, if only because I am very fond of *Caporal* cigarettes, is satisfactory. But apart from this native bait she is an interesting ship to go aboard, being even more of a self-contained unit than we ourselves are: and she is, of course, an Idea as well as a ship—for the great majority of her company she is all that is left to them of France, taking the place of their homes and families and lost circle of friends, constituting the only world they can now depend on.

Her officers and crew are a curious mixture—some purely adventurous, drawn to the Fighting French cause by a natural taste for excitement, others more serious and determined only that their ship shall make a worthy contribution to the strength of the Allied Navies. But whatever the background, all their stories of escape from France have the same quality of desperate endeavour about them: and all of them on board are concerned with the outcome of the war in the special sense that they are fighting their way back home again. To some of them, this home-coming can only be a sad one: others are sustained in spirit by the meagre news which comes through, at agonizing intervals, telling them that their homes still stand and their families still live.

There are others who have had no news for a year, for two years. Putting ourselves in their place, we can understand their disgust at the loathsome farce that has been played on the French stage, and their impatience to set it to rights and reclaim their heritage.

It may be added, as an unimportant footnote, that at dances ashore the French ratings enjoy a formidable popularity, which is confined strictly to one sex.

Here is a snatch of dialogue, warranted true, from a Canadian corvette:
Captain (unable to remember the right command for falling-out the fo'c'sle-party on leaving harbour): 'All right—break it up, boys!'
Resourceful Petty Officer: 'On the command "Break it up, boys," hands will spring smartly to attention, turn forrard, and dismiss.'

There is one unvarying sentence in my night-orders which is almost part of tradition: 'Call me if it comes on to blow.' But sometimes it leaves the realm of tradition and is translated into fact by a determined quartermaster: which means getting up, usually in the pitch dark and pouring rain, to hoist the whaler and put out another bridle.

You spend the best part of an hour over this: stumbling about on the fo'c'sle in streaming oilskins, surrounded by hard breathing and unidentified bad language. The quartermaster has very likely left the call too late, and getting the whaler alongside and hoisted without smashing it up calls for a mixture of quickness and luck. All the time the wind howls as if it had a personal fury against you for the way you are trying to cheat it.

Then, when all is secured and the watch have gone below again, you come aft once more and stand in the wardroom lobby with the water dripping off you, cold to the bone: the clock says half past three, the glass is still dropping, and from down below comes a chorus of snores blended into one smug undisturbed anthem.

'Angels guard you while you sleep,' you think, with a far from angelic intensity. 'You lucky people!'

The ship's dance was a very superior affair—two hundred and forty empties, excluding soft drinks, and only three broken glasses. It was our chance to repay some of the widespread hospitality we had received in the neighbourhood, and the invitations covered the three main women's services, the V.A.D., the W.V.S., the marines, the local regiment, all corvettes in harbour, selected destroyer entries, and the Base Staff.

The Signal Branch had decorated the hall with every flag in the locker, and the party soon warmed up. Perhaps the greatest source of entertainment, for me, was seeing members of the ship's company in unaccustomed and unsuspected roles: a normally quiet Able Seaman blossomed out as Master of Ceremonies, the Chief Bosun's Mate made a remarkably good bar-tender with strong ideas on credit, the coxswain constituted himself a sort of combined chaperon and chucker-out, and made a rousing success of both. Some of the crew turned out to be expert dancers, of the kind that coil themselves and their partners up into a sort of taut spring and then release the whole thing suddenly, to the peril and confusion of their neighbours. Others turned out not to be dancers at all.

The evening was further remarkable for the Midshipman's efforts to tangle me with a rather attractive Wren officer—or 'commissioned popsy', as he described her alluringly. Judging from her puzzled and perhaps relieved air as we circled the room sedately, I could only imagine that he had given me a romantic build-up of the most lurid sort.

Tail-piece:
'We thought of a new nickname for you after reading your last article in the *Telegraph*.'
'Yes?'
'Yes. "Schermuly".'
Rather wounding, I thought. The Schermuly Pistol is a powerful line-shooting apparatus.

5 NIGHT SHOOT

From far ahead of us, the leading destroyer made the signal:
'E-boats now seem to be moving towards the stern of the convoy.'
That was our corner, and about time too. Starting with a dusk torpedo-attack on the leading ships, it had been an eventful night, in which everyone seemed to have been involved but us; and we hadn't suffered the waiting gladly. Guns had flashed, star-shells burst all round the sky, tracer-bullets advertised a crowded meeting; but it had all been outside our range and we had no excuse for interfering, our job that night being to cover the rear of the convoy. Now, with a bright chance of action, the ship woke up and clicked into place as one of the party.

The change from Defence Stations to First-degree Action Stations meant that I had to leave the bridge and go aft, to take over fire-control of the smaller guns. I always find this change-over annoying: up on the bridge they know everything and see it all happening, aft on the quarter-deck news filters through in driblets or not at all, rumours fly around, guesswork reigns. Each time, before leaving the bridge, I ask them to be sure to tell me what's going on: each time they promise that they will: each time the heat of battle puts a Ministry of Information blight on the news. The ship might be ramming the *Tirpitz*, for all one can tell aft: nothing gets through. Tonight was no exception, save that we had our own share of action handed to us on a plate, and weren't right out of the fun; and thus some of this account depends on the post-mortem afterwards, when the bridge-personnel, relaxing, found time to fill in some of the blanks and bring my record up to date.

It was a fine night, almost flat calm, with a glowing three-quarter moon making our camouflage nearly perfect and giving us just the visibility we wanted. But while we were waiting, a signal came through: 'Believed to be four or five E-boats operating.' Shortly after this there was some brisk gun-fire to starboard, and then another signal: 'Two E-boats engaged and damaged.' Said the Captain morosely: 'There'll be none of them left by the time they get to us'—a depressing thought which for some reason they took pains to pass aft to me. . . . The whole night now seemed to be in suspense: the ship moved forward very slowly, the look-outs stared out over the water, their binoculars moving in careful regulated arcs; up near the head of the convoy another star-shell, behind a cloud, gleamed like the sunset. We could still do nothing but wait for our chance.

Then, when we were beginning to doubt whether our luck was changing after all, we heard some shouting coming faintly down-wind towards us.

Now this was not unexpected, since a ship had been sunk a little earlier and the picking up of survivors might have been left to us. The only odd thing was the location of the sound—a good way off the track of the convoy, and in the opposite direction from where boats or men swimming would normally have drifted. That needed explaining, and the explanation (or half of it) came up pretty soon: for about a minute after the shooting was heard, an E-boat was sighted crossing the track of the moon about two miles away. And that was where the noise had been coming from.

'That's odd,' said the Captain. 'In fact, more than odd: almost sinister. We'll stalk that monkey and see what he's up to.'

By now the E-boat, having crossed the moon-track, was invisible again, but we had a rough idea of his course and we laid ours so as to converge at an acute angle. Fore and aft, we were ready to blaze away with all we'd got; and presently we saw him again, about a mile away. This time he seemed to be stopped, waiting. We weren't going to disappoint him, either.

We turned towards him, and the distance shortened. But now, as usual, the after-part dropped back into its Cinderella role: our alteration of course meant that we could no longer see him from aft, and there ensued a maddening few minutes when we had no idea what was happening and had nothing to look at except a blank sea. Once again, we might have been ramming a pocket-battleship. . . . Then the bridge, relenting, came through with the news we wanted:

'First Lieutenant from Captain: He's about half a mile off, dead ahead, and still stopped. In another minute I will turn to starboard so that your guns will bear. Open fire when I do.'

Nothing could be fairer than that. I crossed the quarter-deck and stood close by the gun aft, my hand touching the open-fire and check-fire gongs: at my side the gun's crew, steelhelmeted, were crouching behind their gun-shield, their fingers crooked round the laying- and training-wheels, their eyes peering out on the bearing where we *knew* the E-boat would appear. In the charged silence their breathing sounded forced and unnaturally loud: the moment had a freezing tension about it, and I felt my skin prickling as we waited, within a few seconds of action.

When the ship was about a hundred yards off, the shouting started again, and this time we could distinguish the words quite easily. They were not what we were expecting, and they were not pleasant: hoping for easy meat in the form of a rescue-ship off its guard, that E-boat's crew were calling out: 'Help! Help! We're English!'

By my side, the gun-layer drew in his breath.

'Bastards!' he said softly. 'Sinking one ship, and then using that to trap another. . . . We'll give you some help, all right.'

We began our promised turn to starboard—I felt the after-part of the ship tremble as the wheel was put hard over: she heeled slightly, and the stern swung round; and then the E-boat came into view—fifty yards away, its engines stopped, half a dozen figures roughly silhouetted on the upper deck, and someone on board shouting in a cracked voice: 'Rescue! English sailors!'

That last treacherous effort marked zero hour for both sides, and immediately afterwards three things happened very quickly. The gun forrard let fly with a tremendous crack, scoring a hit directly amidships on the water-line: all the guns aft loosed off, pouring stream after stream of tracer bullets right into the target; and a look-out on the blind side suddenly yelled out above the din:

'Another E-boat to starboard!'

I whipped round. A hundred yards away on our beam was a second E-boat, bows on to us, in a perfect position to run a torpedo. For continuing to cover his proper arc instead of being drawn to the excitement of the main action, that look-out deserved a medal.

They must have seen the newcomer from the bridge at the same moment, for immediately the telegraph clanged and the ship seemed to gather herself up and leap forward as we went to Full Ahead. We passed the E-boat we had hit, still motionless and silent: there was no answering fire, no one trying out their English, and she seemed to be settling by the stern. Then a grey-white cloud of artificial smoke, made by the second E-boat, drifted down-wind between us, and she was quickly lost to view.

There ensued a crowded and confused three minutes, of the sort easier to indicate by asterisks than to describe in detail. There were at least two other E-boats in the vicinity, and they began to make high-speed smoke-rings round us, with considerable skill: our guns kept blazing away, the arcs of tracer fanning out at odd glimpses here and there or at the sound of engines: and throughout it all, everyone on board was coughing and spluttering at the effects of the chemical smoke. Then we came under fire ourselves: a spatter of machine-gun bullets hit the upper works, and the repair parties aft ducked for cover as the noise rang out and the chips of metal began to fly. We could see the tracer coming towards us, and we fired back on the same bearing: the targets were hidden in the smoke, but certainly they were there, playing a grown-up brand of tip-and-run, with us as the ball.

It was at this point that a tracer-bullet went between my legs. I saw it coming towards me, getting bigger and bigger: I should like to say that I then turned round and watched it going away again, getting smaller and smaller. But to claim that amount of detachment wouldn't be true: I did not follow its course beyond the point where, with a business-like hum, it disappeared between my knees—a piece of calculated terrorism which discouraged further observation, as far as I was concerned.

Then suddenly we were alone, in the middle of drifting smoke, with no sound anywhere near us: the players had dispersed, without settling the score. We began a circular sweep, looking for the first E-boat, and meantime clearing up ready for the next round, if there should be one. Aft, the guns' crews were bringing up more ammunition and counting empties; and when this had been seen to and we were ready to open up again, I looked round for signs of damage. There was very little, in spite of the noise and the activity of the past quarter of an hour. One of the bullets had gone down a ventilator cowling and (it was said) chased one of the stokers all round the engine-room; but the only actual casualty was a steward who, having no business to be on the upper deck at all, had stuck his head out to see the fun and had been nicked on the forehead just above one eye. He was all right, though indignant in a general way.

We never found that E-boat, nor any trace of it: judging by the way she had been hit, we didn't really expect to. But she was officially credited to us, by a scrupulous Admiralty: which was the next best thing to collecting the bits ourselves. And as you know, the credit was duly endorsed on the after-gun-layer's shield, for all to see and for him to tell the tale about.

We gave a party to celebrate the kill, and at one end of the wardroom we hung a Nazi ensign, borrowed from the Signal Department. By way of adding point to the occasion, we then shot an imperial line to the assembled company, to the effect that the flag had been taken from the E-boat just before it went down.

How exactly did we get it? We passed so close to the sinking E-boat, we said, that a seaman standing in the stern of the ship had been able to reach out and tear it off. But why wasn't the flag itself torn? The halyard must have given way: the seaman was very strong. How did we happen to have a man standing ready? Well (here the Captain, in danger of flagging, nudged me), in our First-degree Action Stations there was always a man told off for this duty. He was armed with a boat-hook and grappling iron. He got threepence a day trophy-money.

And so on: Finally:

'Germany must be getting extremely short of raw materials,' said the most distinguished visitor present, fingering the exhibit. 'This stuff is of very poor quality—it can't compare with our own.'

After that it was too late to tell the truth.

Behind it all, of course, was a more serious and more genuine feeling of pride. The credit was to the ship: it came as a reward for months (stretching to years) of up-and-down and down-and-up, of unrelieved boredom, of bad news and bad weather. It had a score of contributing factors, including luck; but luck is something you have to be ready for. and the main core of this readiness, and of the rest, can be simplified down to this:

Being a good ship, she was four things: clean, dependable, alert, and happy. All these things, which have to be worked for, spring from people.

'Clean' inside and out: that is the coxswain—efficient, bleak of eye, helpful—and the Chief Bosun's Mate, whose grouchy exterior never conceals the extreme pride he takes in the ship's looks.

'Dependable,' is the Chief and his engine-room and stoker branches. To put it shortly, and with suitable arrogance, things go wrong with *other* ships.

'Alert' is divided between the Gunner's Party: quick on the trigger, checking and re-checking the assembly of the guns, leaving nothing to chance; and the Signal Department, led by a Yeoman of Signals, who knows all the answers to all the questions.

'Happy' is all of us. It grows out of innumerable small things. It is as potent as love. Multiplied, it explains the Royal Navy.

6 WHAT SAILORS THINK AND SAY

The great majority of the letters I received, both from home and from America, when *H.M. Corvette* was published, concerned my remarks about petrol-wasters and what sailors think about them—that is, they concerned a subject not absolutely relevant to a book of action, but not ignored or resented on that account.

That is why this section has crept into the present book: because I thought people might be interested. But it seems to me to be legitimate to include it: what sailors think and talk about affects the ship all the time, colours our corner of the war, and, matched and duplicated in the other Services, mighty profoundly affect the peace.

A great deal of it may seem intolerably naïve, but there is a reason for that, and a good one. Sailors, more than anyone, tend to get out of touch with things. They see newspapers at irregular intervals, and not always the ones they prefer: they may be sealed from the outside world for weeks at a time. What they read, and hear talked about, when they come back again sometimes surprises them: perhaps because they see only half or a quarter of the whole picture, and cannot tell that the emphasis presented to them is faulty or the view only a partial one.

But that doesn't stop them thinking and talking a lot: indeed, like most spectators, they talk the more for being out of the centre of activity; there is certainly no lack of material from which to quote. Here then, simplified and no doubt 'conditioned' by the eye and ear of one observer, is what they think and say.

1. *The War.* We are, of course, winning it: that has never been in doubt at any time. But it is tremendously difficult to see the war as a whole, and the amount of leeway we have to make up—in the Far East, for example—is barely appreciated. This makes our progress seem very slow, and particularly so at such times as the New Year or the anniversary of the ship's commissioning, when the previous year's hopes are recalled. Somehow the situation always looks very much the same, the end not much nearer, and home as distant and as hazy as ever.

Events and successes at sea naturally get the most attention, and things like the *Bismarck* sinking or the Malta convoy battle are a first-rate tonic. Our big bombing raids and sweeps are rather taken for granted, though the R.A.F. is O.K. (We have entertained some of them on board, with notable cordiality on both sides.) Army successes, until the finale of the North African campaign, were always somehow mistrusted, or at least accepted with reserve: it cannot be ignored (except by sunshine students of affairs) that the Army seemed a rather backward lot till the Battle of Alamein, and only now is it beginning to be realized that they were up against a crushing superiority of equipment in the earlier days, and that the man-versus-steel excuse is, of all excuses, the most valid one.

No blame is attached to anyone for this inequality of weapons: it is how Britain has always fought her wars, and you can't recriminate against such a national characteristic as lack of foresight.

Of our Allies, the Russians make the greatest impression: they are terrific, without qualification, and the effect of this is noted later under the heading 'The Peace'.

One does not meet any expressed *hatred* of the Germans: atrocity stories ring no bell, and the word 'Hun' is newspaper currency only. But such things as the bombing of a home town, or actual contact with some piece of treachery or ruthlessness, make for anger; and behind it all is the determination, taken as much for granted as the water under our keel, that we must win or perish. 'Roll on the peace' is a recurring and favourite catch-word, but it will have to be *our* peace: nothing sooner, and nothing less.

2. *Strikes.* I've not been able to explain to questioners why, of two men fighting the same war for the same clear stake of survival, one of them, enjoying home life, comparative security, and high-level wages, can refuse outright to work unless he is paid more: and the other, conscripted at a meagre wage and sent far from home and into danger, would be shot out of hand if he tried the same tactic.

To sailors, working like blacks under sub-human conditions for four shillings a day, war-time strikes seem a mixture of blackmail and pure treason. A country desperate for production, like a man desperate for food, is easily held to ransom: suppose the Services applied the same 'bargaining weapon' in their own sphere? 'What would happen to the country and the war if we tried the same thing?' is a frequent query; and I have heard the idea amusingly and bitterly elaborated in the mess-decks: the ship refusing to escort a convoy the last hundred miles except for a bonus of £10 a man, or the Army in Libya demanding so much a mile for advances, with time-and-a-half for retreats, and Sundays free.

What did the Russians before Stalingrad think of such manœuvres? 'I saw "STRIKE NOW IN THE WEST" chalked up on a factory wall at home,' said one Petty Officer to me when we were discussing this aspect, 'and by God! that's just what the chaps inside were doing. They'd struck all right—for an extra two bob a shift. I reckon Hitler would be in Buckingham Palace right now if we all tried it on.'

Illogical? A flaw somewhere? Write and point it out to me: having, politically, all the sympathy possible, I'd be glad to pass the explanation on.

3. *Food-wasters, petrol-wanglers.* This is where I have *my* say—as a sailor, of course.

We bring the stuff in, sometimes at cost to ourselves, nearly always at some sacrifice on the part of the ships we escort. Often, now and in the past, that cost has been tremendous: out in the Atlantic ship after ship has gone down, men have drowned or burned to death, survivors have gasped and shivered, the life-line has seemed as thin as thread. But there has always been one thing to balance all this, offsetting the horror and the pity: the idea that what we were bringing in was vital, that it goes straight to fill some threatening gap, that no part of it is wasted or diverted. To bring it home safely rubs out all other entries in the log. It has been worth while.

And then we read the newspapers.

The cases are fewer now, but still they come: food-wasters, black-market buyers and thieves, people wangling goods in excess of quota, people taking God knows what profit on the sale and re-sale of things they had hardly heard of in peace-time. Imagine what bloody fools we feel, knowing that a convoy of what we thought vital supplies has really gone to the comfort and profit of such people: the comfort of stupid folk who cannot visualize the price in blood of what they are wasting, the profit of assorted vermin who see, in a shipload of necessaries, only the chance of a squeeze.

I once overheard, at a restaurant table next to mine, one favoured citizen say to another:

'I'd have cleaned up another clear thousand quid if I'd held on till the end of the month.'

Held on to what? Not to a section of front-line trench, I'll bet. . . . It was almost certainly some necessary or other, delivered to his doorstep by the valour and endurance of brave men. Back from a rough convoy, it makes the food stick in your throat. Is such a man concentrating on

winning the war? Who is he trying to beat? It doesn't sound like Hitler.
And yet the game goes on—checked at one point, slopping over at
another: the goods are passed from hand to hand, the margin grows, the
money involved gets bigger and dirtier. If ever men should be singled
out and shot for looting, these are the prime candidates.

You can understand how it looks to sailors: these men are rats, and
we are the saps who keep them alive. And ten such men are not worth
the right arm of a Merchant Navy survivor picked off a raft in mid-
Atlantic.

Petrol-wanglers, like traitors, merit a special hell. Probably enough
has been written about the hazards of bringing an oil-tanker across the
Atlantic, and the fate of the ones that don't make it, to establish the
background and impress it on the dullest mind. None of it has been
exaggerated: tankers are dynamite, and their crews are heroes of a
particular quality.

What, then, is one to make of people who license their private cars as
taxis, in order to get extra coupons: who obtain additional petrol to
attend church on Sunday, and then don't go: who play golf by taxi (an
isolated bit of lunacy, this): who drive hundreds of miles to a race-
meeting already served by special trains: who treat petrol as if it could
be got from a tap? What sort of men are they? Stupid? Incurably
selfish? Traitorous? Do they feel clever when they've got their extra
whack? Does it give them a sense of power to know that men, foolishly
valorous, have fought and perished in hundreds, just to keep their cars
ticking over sweetly? Once again, ten such are not worth the skin of the
man who dies for them; and one sometimes wishes they could be
individually flayed, just to prove it in simple terms.

If there is bitterness in this last section, it is probably my own. I once
saw some men failing to escape from a sinking tanker. Ever since then,
that has been what I mean by 'petrol coupons'. Each coupon is
alive—to start with.

Footnote to the above. I see that it has now been declared *legal* to put
down one's place of business as 'Tattersall's Ring, So-and-so
Racecourse', and that a journey there (in the capacity of bookmaker)
counts as work sufficiently vital to warrant an extra issue of petrol. I
wish I had heard of this earlier: I am sure that many a merchant seaman
we have fished out of the water would have died the easier for knowing
it.

4. *Politics.* Virtually nothing to report here: there is no time and, in
effect, no occasion for political interest. The 'Hostilities only' ratings
have shed or put in the background whatever convictions they had

previously; and among the Active Service hands, the meagre interest they took in pre-war party politics seems to have evaporated, since the main issues—low pay and slow promotion—have largely disappeared in war-time or have been overshadowed by events.

It is perhaps worth noting, as an indication of their outlook, that a film showing Trafalgar Square speakers (mostly professional politicians) demanding a 'Second Front' received a positive barrage of laughter and cat-calls when shown at the local R.N. cinema. The feeling behind the demonstration was crystal-clear: it was the expressed attitude of the people who would be at the landing-beaches towards the people who wouldn't.

They were ready for the second front at any time, but the time was to be signalled by the competent authorities only, and no others need apply.

5. *Girls*. Sailors enjoy their reputation for gallantry, but they seldom seem to exploit it beyond the limits of good order and public decorum.

In the course of three years, I have only had to deal with one affiliation case; and that one was contested with an air of such injured purity and detachment that I felt it in doubtful taste to raise the matter at all. One case, in three years, is not large-scale debauchery, or indeed debauchery of any sort. To offset the figures, you could say that luck comes into it; but these things, if they exist at all, usually show on the record, and here they certainly do not—the record is excellent.

Of course, as is natural when men are cooped up together at close quarters, the tone of conversation does not exactly reflect a humble worship at the shrine of womanhood: there is a lot of loose talk (some of it exceptionally loose) about 'torpedoing' and other inelegant exploits, and a chance listener might reasonably suppose that he had to deal with a nest of old-fashioned rogues of the 'Yield-or-else' type. And when several ratings are together ashore they are inclined to behave badly, chi-iking girls and generally embarrassing them. But separate one of them, and put him on his own with exactly the same girl, and he usually becomes a model of deference and attention. It is only when he is with a crowd that he lacks the courage or the initiative to treat women as normal human beings.

Incidentally, there seems to be, in the Navy, a special affection for Wrens—by which I mean that they are looked on, not as fair game but as part of the Service and thus to be protected and preserved from outsiders. And what could be nicer than that?

6. *Home*. If sailors are not the most sentimental of men, then I'd like to know who are. More than half the crew of this ship are married, but

all of them, married or not, seem to have a love of home grafted deep inside them, to a degree which a cynic might not credit. It is complementary to the ship, as the inner centre of their world: it stands behind everything: when the mail, for instance, is delivered on board and distributed to the various messes, the atmosphere in the ship is a quite distinctive one, compounded of sentiment and a sort of unassailable concentration.

Furthermore, their plans for the future all seem to centre, not round jobs or a steady income, but on a house, a family, a private world which, no matter how cramped or poor it may be, will give them peace against all comers. That is what they are fighting for—the sure welcome, the bride, the old woman, the sprogs: their day-dreams are the least ambitious and the gentlest of any I know.

This is probably as vital a source of strength and endurance as could be found anywhere. Worldly success may fade out of sight or be given up as hopeless, but this inner aim is not to be quenched. Men who fight with the heart, *for* the heart, are unbeatable.

7. *The Peace*. What sailors think and say about life after the war is probably more vague and unformed than in any other service.

All the things peculiar to life afloat contribute to this: the 'closed-circuit' of the ship, the absence of outside contacts, the irregularity of communications—all these put a curtain between us and the shore. It is sometimes barely possible to keep up to date with the current war news, much less with trends of opinion and 'planning' generally.

To take a concrete example, singled out for ease of illustration irrespective of its relative importance: this ship was at sea when the Beveridge Report was published in the newspapers: as a result, not one rating in ten has any idea of its scope, not one in fifty a detailed knowledge of its provisions. (It is on chances such as this that a vote and even a lifelong attitude of mind may depend.) Roughly speaking, the plan is thought to be 'insurance for all'—'taking over the insurance from the big companies'—or even 'instead of the dole': and this is all the impression it has made and all the hope it has raised.

A copy of the Report, which I later made available to anyone interested, had a minute circulation on board. Its interest, as 'news', had by then vanished; and it did not seem to arouse any *other* interest.

As well as this enforced vagueness (and in some cases, complete indifference) as regards current projects, there is a definite 'Win-the-war-first' attitude which contributes to the same hiatus. All things considered, 'take no thought for the morrow' is a reasonable summing-up in this section; and the outline of opinion aboard which follows must be taken as lacking either directive force or indeed very much force of any sort.

What will it be like after the war? It is still felt to be mostly guesswork. Perhaps things will be much the same, possibly a little better: there is sure to be unemployment and uncertainty still, but the readiness with which enormous grants for war expenditure are authorized gives some promise that money may be found (or rather, credit furnished) for peace-time schemes to relieve this sort of distress. There will be more education available—'more of an equal chance for everybody'. I've not talked with anyone professing fear of the future: equally one does not hear of any active *determination* to make things better; there is a simple belief that they will be so, and that we have learned from war economics enough to revitalize the peace.

It seems to be accepted that money will still be the mainspring of effort and the measure of success. When I brought back from home some of my son's christening cake for distribution to the Petty Officers' mess, one of them asked me: 'What do you reckon he'll be when he grows up?' I said I hoped he'd be something like a surgeon or an architect or a musician: to which the reply was, 'Plenty of money in all of them, if you get to the top.' I said I also hoped that he would not feel that 'plenty of money' was the answer to everything, and that he would contrive to lead a full and happy life without it. This simply did not register: nor the idea (which I probably made to sound priggish and ineffective) that my son might be content to put things into the world instead of taking them out. This Petty Officer (neither an ambitious nor a selfish man) did not visualize a world in which this would be possible without a complete sacrifice of comfort and the probable starvation of whoever practised it.

There remains this pointer towards the future, which has cropped up so often that it cannot be dismissed as worthless. The heroism and endurance of the Russians frequently provoke the remark: 'They must have something really worth fighting for,' and the idea, current before the war, that they were the slaves of a soulless and hated State is now dismissed as bunk. 'It [Communism] wouldn't do for us, but something of the same sort might, if we could get it without a mess-up,' is another remark indicating the kind of impression which the Russians' resistance and readiness to die for their country and way of life, has made. There must be something in a system which produces such extreme valour, not in isolated cases here and there, but as a national characteristic: they must feel that their country, their soil, is their very own, and that no force, either of reaction or the reverse, can betray their victory.

This is not the book, nor is it the time in our history, to discuss the implications of this feeling. I am simply recording that sailors have been struck by it, as no doubt many other people have; and that, when the time comes to organize our peace-time way of life, Russia's loving and jealous defence of her own will be remembered.

Corvette Command

1 'ON ASSUMING COMMAND . . .'

IT IS ODD, AND FAINTLY IRONIC, THAT THE CROWNING PIECE OF news, for which you have been waiting ever since you joined the Navy, comes to you in a phrase of matchless insignificance. All you get—the sole spark for the tinder—is a slip of paper headed 'APPOINTMENTS': underneath is your name, and alongside that the single phrase 'WINGER in cd.'

You have to look twice at that 'cd.' before you take in the fact that it means 'Command': you have to look three times at the name before you realize that it is in truth your own. But when you have finally got the size of it, light breaks through like one of those story-book dawns. . . .

For the R.N.V.R., commands do not grow on trees—or at least, not on any tree that flourished down our way at that time. Of course, even in March, 1943, it had already been rather a long war: the supply of ready-made experts—R.N. and R.N.R.—was beginning to run out: the Admiralty were now getting down to the bottom of the bag, turning it this way and that to admit the light and see what there was to be had. Occasionally, as now, they brought up some doubtful-looking article and decided that, at a pinch, it would do. . . . But still there was a prejudice—or perhaps, more exactly, a reservation—about the R.N.V.R.: it was thought unlikely that they could successfully command His Majesty's ships of war, chiefly because there was really no reason why, as amateurs, they *should* be able to.

That was why the appointment came as a surprise, and my biggest and best so far. I was a Lieutenant with two and a half years' seniority: I had been dogsbody of my first ship, First Lieutenant of my second: now I was to command my third. As well as realizing a particular personal ambition, it was a blow for my side which I was very glad to strike.

But certainly it was a surprise. At one moment I was an old and cynical First Lieutenant, wondering why everyone else had all the luck, deciding that after all it wasn't worth ordering a new suit—the present one, shiny and paint-stricken, would last out the war, since I wasn't going any higher (nor along the Mall to Buckingham Palace, either). And then suddenly came this swift change, and the absolute necessity not only of a new suit but of a new pair of gloves as well, and an expensive and theatrical cap, rather like a German general's, all peak and prestige. . . . Having been accorded this most singular honour, I wasn't going to carry it off at cut prices.

To me, it *was* most singular: I knew the vacancy was coming up, but I hadn't cast myself for the part. *Winger* was a sister ship of *Dipper*, my present one—in fact she was a replica of her in every respect: in the same flotilla, doing the same job: a twin-screw corvette, agile, elegant, a joy to handle and a triumph to own. A year ago, to this very day, I had received the appointment as *Dipper*'s First Lieutenant. I remembered now my pride and pleasure when that appointment came through, and I tried to produce an adequate reaction to the fact that I now commanded her twin. That reaction was a long time coming: in fact, it was still being built up, from day to day and trip to trip, till the very end—a long honeymoon with an enduring bride.

Leaving *Dipper* would have been mortally sad if I had not been going to take over one of my own: as it was, the last day had its share of regret which no anticipation could lessen. I had a tremendous affection for her; the year I had spent aboard her had been by far the happiest of the war. As her Number One I had had an unusually free hand under two captains, both of whom I had liked, and that had given me a feeling about her, jealously personal, which was at its most potent when I said good-bye. What sort of chap was this new First Lieutenant? Would he keep her clean? Was he to be trusted with the uncertain galley funnel, the temperamental motor-boat, the glory of the quarter-deck brass-work? . . . He looked all right, it was true, and (most important of all) he looked as pleased as I had been when I first came aboard—but you never could tell for certain. He might have been an actor in peace-time.

I should be seeing her again, though, and that would take the sting out of the farewell. 'I'll give you hell when we're doing manœuvres,' said my late Captain, who had six months' seniority in hand. 'You'll be out of station whatever you do. . . .' There was great pleasure to be had from the idea that I would be coming back to the family, to our compact flotilla wherein I had met such good comradeship, to the base whose chief amenity—the Naval Club—was so exactly what I liked. It rounded off the whole thing in the most satisfactory way possible.

In one, minor, matter connected with the change-over I had been severely stung. *Dipper* was about to proceed on her annual refit, *Winger* had just finished hers: which meant that I would now do a second year without any leave longer than the routine boiler-cleaning periods. I had been looking forward to that leave: a year of East Coast convoying, a son six months old—they both seemed to merit a rest and a break in the routine. But if it *had* to be exchanged for another year's sea-going, then my new job was giving me the best of the bargain. Command cancelled everything.

On my way down to the dockyard where *Winger* was lying, I went home for half a day—a piece of truancy which I was prepared to justify to Their Lordships on the ground that it was my total annual leave, which it was. When I told E. what they had given me:

'Oh!' she said. 'That's much better than you expected, isn't it? How lovely.' She was very pleased. Then: 'Darling, I think the son and heir is starting a rash.'

First things first. You know how it is.

With only one day to go before the completion of her refit, *Winger* was in the usual state of uninhibited chaos when I arrived. That air of disorganization which every ship wears after a period in dockyard hands was apparent everywhere: she was hopelessly untidy, only half-painted, blotched with red lead, lacking her whaler and motor-boat (still in the boat-sheds), and littered with every conceivable sort of spare part, packing-case, tin can, rope's end, and dockyard matey. There were the inevitable riveters letting loose their private hell on the bridge superstructure: there was a small well-organized pontoon school on the gun-platform: there were lots of people slapping paint on: there was a man up the mast, with a mallet and a rapt expression, apparently enjoying the view into the Wrens' quarters nearby. Aft, on the quarter-deck, a cluster of nodding bowler hats indicated that the superintending officials were having a last intensive session before finally chucking their hands in. I looked around me, remembering *Dipper*'s polished elegance, and thought: Hell, I'll have to start all over again from zero. And then I remembered also that I wasn't the First Lieutenant any more, and wouldn't have to do anything of the sort. All I *would* have to do was complain. . . .

In contrast with the upper deck, my cabin—unlocked for me by a young steward with a wary eye—was a model of order and cleanliness: it was in fact ready for me in every respect, from the clean towel to the fresh blotting-paper. A good mark for someone; probably the First Lieutenant. There were a few letters waiting for me, and some immediate signals; and after dealing with these I saw all the officers in turn—First Lieutenant, Sub., Gunner, Engineer Officer, and Midshipman. That wariness which had shown itself in the steward's face was reflected, to a greater or less degree, in all of theirs: remembering my own reactions when greeting a new Captain I was not surprised. It was always a chancy and unpredictable moment. And after all, I was a new animal altogether; an R.N.V.R. captain, and a Lieutenant as well. What next, indeed? . . .

From Number One I had a detailed account of the ship's progress during her refit, and another report—covering the engineering side, and triumphantly technical—from the Chief. The Gunner was loud (or at least fully audible) in his praise of the ship's armament: the Sub. assured me that every chart under his care was guaranteed to be absolutely on the top line. (They always are—guaranteed, that is.) So far, so good: things seemed to be in fair working order. Then the Midshipman (the Captain's secretary) came into my cabin with what was virtually a crate full of papers, and the shadows began to fall thick and fast.

It was not his fault—nor anyone's—that there was so much outstanding, so many loose ends: it was due to the fact that the previous Captain had left at short notice a fortnight earlier, and that thus I would not get a direct turn-over from him—almost an essential of a smooth start. The fatal gap—with the ship just completing an extensive refit, with stores astray, with correspondence in arrears and musters overlooked—was at least a fifty per cent additional complication to the job of taking over. Zest and enthusiasim evaporated as I waded through those cloying files: there were weeks of work here before I could be even level with the daily quota, and that would be formidable enough in any case.

I looked up and caught the Midshipman's eye. It was entirely noncommittal. 'I am only the humble instrument,' it seemed to say. 'This mess is all yours.'

There was no impression to be made on it there and then, in any case. I roughed out a list of things which had to be done—hardly the same thing as doing them, but quite wearing enough. . . . Much later, considerably depressed, I went ashore to Operations, to make my number and find out the details of our programme. The man I had to see was an old friend, and the re-encounter was a pleasant one: but his congratulations hardly balanced the state of affairs on board, nor the news that we were due to come out of dock the following morning. I felt very strongly that I needed a breathing space: it seemed that I might have to take a long run at this job. After he had outlined a programme—oiling and storing, taking in ammunition, adjusting compasses, full-power trials—which would keep us busy till the end of our stay there:

'I'm damned glad you got the command,' he concluded. 'It's about time they tried some amateur talent. I suppose you're pretty pleased about it?'

'Well, I *was*, about five hours ago,' I said, 'and somewhere in the background I still am, very. But it has a sting or two attached to it.' I gave him an outline of the state of affairs on board, with some of the more exotic details by way of illustration, and finished, 'I'm not exactly taking over a going concern.'

He stared. 'Why should you expect to? You're meant to make it go yourself. What do you think you draw all that money for?' He was even slightly indignant. 'You've got enough jam on it already falling into a job like this, without complaining about the ...'

'All right, all right,' I interrupted. 'I just thought I'd mention it.'

We went and had a drink, and presently I felt better. What he had said was quite true. I had been given a first-rate job, whatever its temporary drawbacks, and nothing could alter its attraction or spoil its quality. And as for taking over a going concern—a good dinner and some better talk made such an idea seem almost boring.

Sitting in my cabin that night—the night before we were due out of dock—with a last brew of coffee and one of the wardroom cigars (an unexpected dividend) going well, I gave final thought to what I had taken on.

I felt confident about it, but somehow it was a near thing. . . . If anyone had told me on the day I joined the Navy that within three years I would be entrusted with the sole charge of a ship costing many thousands of pounds, and with the lives of the eighty-eight men in her, I would not only have disbelieved him—I would have voted against it. It would have seemed too far out of my line altogether: my peace-time way of life—writing, travelling all over Europe, but living and working quite alone—had not fitted me for that sort of responsibility (though I suppose that, back in 1925, Winchester faintly had). It was not that I had been shirking the world between the wars—only a personal and political lunatic could have done that with any success: it was simply that living in a crowd, and having people dependent on me, had been counter to my choice. I felt I was better off on my own, and I had made it so. . . . I had been interested in politics, but as a study rather than a practice: and my sympathies—even at their most violently radical stage—had remained sympathies and nothing much more, save for one spell of electioneering where, inevitably, the candidate of my choice had forfeited his deposit.

Presumably the Navy had taught me, and taught me quickly, that the individual, self-sufficient, self-regarding life is not commendable when it ignores strife and suffering all round it, and that responsibility, even in an alien sphere, should be welcomed as a test of personal fitness. It had, further, trained me to survive successive tests—tests of endurance, good temper, patience—and to emerge now in a position where men and equipment, both infinitely valuable, were dependent on my nerve and judgement for their survival. And more than this: the lesson, with its varied and often curious results, had been worth while from any angle, war or peace, for I had found in the Navy an opportunity for service in that exact tradition which I had thought essential between the wars, but had not really exercised with any degree of competence.

This is not the patriotic illusion that it may seem: it is a plain fact which sprang directly from my initial luck in being drafted to corvettes. The particular defensive job which my part of the Navy undertook—convoying foodstuffs, keeping people alive and healthy, collecting and caring for survivors—seemed to bear a direct relationship to my vague pre-war desire to 'help', to work for more than money, to be personally effective without personal ambition. War made the task one of supreme national importance, but, even discounting that, the enduring human values on which it was based remained clear and encouraging all the time. On these lines I had been working for the best part of three years: mostly in a minor, almost anonymous capacity, but now at last with some degree of individual distinction, with a label attached.

It was impossible not to be pleased and proud about the latter development. The job itself was mundane, unspectacular without an atom of glamour: I was glad it did not mean dispensing with pride.

Here I was in the Captain's cabin, anyway: cigar, coffee, slippers, and all. . . . During the last few minutes I found I had been fingering a small rubber stamp on my desk: one of half a dozen in an imposing rack. Now I pressed it on to the inking pad, stamped down on the signal-form in front of me, and examined the result.

It said, 'LIEUTENANT-IN-COMMAND.'

It was my favourite rubber stamp so far.

2   *WINGER* IN COMPANY

I had breakfast alone in my cabin next morning: the first time I had been able to start the day in this civilized fashion since the war began.

(Breakfast is something to which all ideas of human adjustment are inapplicable. It is like love: conversation impedes and spectators ruin it.) At half past nine I saw the current signal-log, covering the previous day's activities, and then I sent for the coxswain—mainly to discuss helm-orders and manœuvring in harbour generally. This class of corvette is fortunate in having the wheel sited on the upper bridge a few feet from the Officer-of-the-Watch, with a clear view ahead: the coxswain can thus take the ship in and out of harbour, or alongside another ship, without any orders except a general one to begin with. But the understanding between coxswain and Captain must be exact and crystal-clear for this kind of manœuvring in closed waters to be foolproof: otherwise it is really no more than a dangerous attempt at saving yourself trouble—a short cut that may lead to somewhere quite different after all.

These after-breakfast interviews, incidentally, became much more elaborate later on, when I had a proper routine worked out. Zero hour, in the future, was nine o'clock: at eight forty-five I had a second cup of coffee and finished the newspaper, at eight fifty-five I put my socks on, and at nine the rush started. The First Lieutenant with his arrangements for the day. Pilot with the latest local navigating information. Chief wanting to know the orders for steam. The Gunner with a piece of gun which had somehow disgraced itself. The Midshipman with a ton of mail. The rating who set the clocks right. The Steward who was going shopping ashore. The First Lieutenant again, with a new set of arrangements and a list of thirteen requestmen. . . . I sometimes felt that if they *all* started coming in again, in the same sequence, I might never notice.

This morning we were to leave the dry dock at eleven o'clock and go round, in tow, to the main basin. I put in an hour's paper-work—a determined nibble at it whenever possible seemed the best way of clearing off the arrears—and then walked round the upper deck with the First Lieutenant, for a preliminary survey. I knew these ships by heart already, but now I had a different pair of eyes. . . . Only in minor ways could she be distinguished from *Dipper*, but she had a better bridge, with a very large slice of the roof hinging back and making it almost an open one, and a Captain's chair which reminded me so strongly of the ones to be seen in film studios that I later had 'SHIRLEY TEMPLE' painted on the back—to the disgust of the Signal Branch, who favoured Rita Hayworth. . . . The ship had also a most distinctive camouflage, of which I thoroughly approved: when painting was finished she would challenge *Dipper* for looks (and of course *Dipper*'s looks were bound to deteriorate now). I noticed with satisfaction that the four-inch gun, now being groomed by an intent and industrious sweeper, was very well kept, and seemed to have survived the docking period unscathed. Appearance was a lot but working efficiency was all.

Already, on this pleasant sunny morning, the ship was looking much tidier—hands had turned to at seven o'clock, and clearly they had not been wasting their time. Many of them now working on the upper deck I knew by sight, from a year's visiting within the flotilla: they included one immense Able Seaman who had competed against me at putting-the-shot during the recent Corvette sports—with complete success, it may be said. The ship was now free of all but a few dockyard workers: their necessary encroachment was over, and the tide was now running strongly the other way. Stretches of the upper deck were beginning to emerge, relieved of the usual eccentricities of refitting—the derelict cups, the newspapers, the raincoats hanging on the Lewis guns. Soon it would be possible to criticize and to appraise on a normal basis.

At about half past ten the Chief, the busiest man aboard that morning, came to me with a sheaf of papers to be signed, certifying that we were ready to be floated off, that there were no inlets left open, and that we had not knowingly shifted any ballast such as might disturb our trim: and very soon after that they started to run the water in. This was, if not an anxious moment, at least a thoughtful one. I have never yet seen or even heard of a ship keeling over and sinking when the bath is filled, but that's not to say that it *couldn't* happen, and I didn't want to be the first victim. . . . Leaning over the guard-rail I watched the water running in, restoring *Winger* to her natural element. As the last wedge fell free the ship gave a barely perceptible lurch, and was released. I waited for bad news, but there was none: she had taken the water just as the makers intended.

'Dry as a bone, sir,' said the Chief in confirmation, coming up suddenly out of some rare compartment below. 'We're ready to go anywhere.'

Now there was a burst of activity ashore: bowler hats sprang up from nowhere, multiple shouting set in, the dock gates opened slowly (impelled by some very old men straining away at a hand capstan, in the authentic Egyptian slave manner), and we were in the hands of God and the tug *Gripper*. The journey, though short, took us round a lot of corners, many of them sharp, none of them roomy: from up on the bridge I could see the First Lieutenant harrying his fender-parties from one side to the other and back again, as the knuckles of the jetty loomed up to sabotage his paint-work. I was glad to see that he had his nervous reaction developed to a high degree, as I had myself. . . . But the towing and warping, as usual in a naval dockyard, were flawless, and by midday, with no greater mishap than the loss of one seaman's cap (neatly removed by a heaving line), we were secure alongside again in our new berth.

We were only in the basin, it was true: land-locked still: but we *were* afloat.

Good use was made of the rest of that day in every department: the painting was finished off, most of the stores embarked, and oiling completed. Fresh (or fairly fresh) from a generous slice of leave, both watches turned to with a will. Down in my cabin I toiled away with the Midshipman, mustering and checking the fifty-odd confidential books, the two-hundred-and-something secret publications, the charge documents, the hush-hush letters, the special keys. We got the right answer in the end, but it was a long time coming and it cost a lot in conscientious determination: everything had to be sighted, by my own dazed eyes, from the 'Notes on Oiling at Sea' to the 'Handbook on Street Fighting for Junior Officers': from 'How to Invade' to 'How to Repel Invasion': from the key of the safe to the key of the Captain's private bar—both of them on one key-ring labelled, unexpectedly but quite rightly, 'VITAL'.

This was all what might be called the dreary side of being Captain: the finicky oddments which, totally uninteresting in themselves, were yet of paramount importance, and might trip one up (to say nothing of the wider results) as surely as would a piece of bad navigation, if anything went adrift. It happens that I have a conscience about 'security' generally: the sight of, say, a secret signal left in the wardroom instead of being in its proper locked file is as good as a poke in the eye any day: I don't like pokes in the eye. The efficient custody of secret matter means endless care and trouble, often when you are tired after a hard trip: there is nothing more boring, but in many respects there is nothing more important, from any naval angle whatsoever.

At all events we had the whole thing sewn up by the end of the day—a sizeable weight off the mind, as well as one more section of undergrowth cleared away. At this rate the arrears would be worked off much earlier than I had hoped when I first struck the balance.

Next morning we really took to the ocean. Our sailing instructions came aboard, couched in that fragrant English which so endears the Signal Branch to us: '*Winger* will unbasin at 10.00 and proceed to No. 4 Buoy under own steam.' 'Unbasin' . . . I ask you. . . . Punctually at five

minutes to ten the Chief made his 'Ready to move' report, followed by
the First Lieutenant with his, and we cast off in good order. Our
berthing-position made it necessary for us to go out of the dock
backwards, meeting and turning against a strong stream as soon as we
cleared the entrance. I had no objection to this manœuvre, provided
everything functioned correctly and quick action was forthcoming from
the engine-room if the need arose. But a new and untried intermediate
shaft made it possible that we would have to stop engines without notice
in the middle; and as it turned out this was exactly what happened, the
Chief naturally choosing the most critical moment of all to report by
telephone to the bridge, in a voice almost annoyingly unemotional:
'Starboard engine out of action.'

As our 'Not under control' signal went up to the yard-arm, a rating
on the fo'c'sle was heard to say: 'My turn for leave, chum!' . . . This was
not the piece of blinding optimism it may sound: for when that message
from the engine-room came through, we were in the middle of a two-
knot tideway and going astern rapidly towards the opposite shore,
preparatory to turning: that is, we were caught on the hop. With one
engine out of action, we could only turn very slowly, backing and filling
a few degrees at a time: the tide was gradually taking us down on to a
line of mooring-buoys, and two merchant ships which were coming
upstream would shortly complicate the situation. What does A.
do?—apart from dropping the pick and going aft for a cup of tea. The
chances of leave for the Port Watch were excellent.

But I had reckoned without my friend ashore, poised like a benign
Providence for just this occasion. 'Tug coming out to us, sir!' said the
Yeoman of Signals suddenly, and there, unflatteringly prompt, was the
tug *Gripper* making for us with a bow wave like the Severn Bore. She
must have been waiting behind the pier, ready to pounce. . . . Pricked to
action by this obvious piece of nurse-maiding, I took an oath to
straighten the thing out myself, and semaphored her to lay off while I
tried it: but we were too slow in coming round, and, as I had expected,
the merchant ships did not notice my hoist and showed no sign of giving
me the extra room I needed. In the end I had to climb down, and it was
under a firm fore-and-aft tow that *Winger* hooked on to her first
mooring-buoy. Nothing could have been farther from my intentions
than this spoon-fed progress, and I was quite sure that my friend in the
Operations Room (which commanded an extensive view of the
harbour) extracted the last ounce of pleasure from seeing his prudent
forethought thus justified.

There had been other eyes watching me, too. It was impossible to be ignorant of the fact that all the time upon the bridge during that manœuvre I had been under the very closest scrutiny—by the other officers, by the coxswain, the signalman, the telegraph-hands, and that down in the engine-room they had also been observing me, trying to judge from the orders transmitted to them how firm, or otherwise, was the hand up-top. (Those engine-room dials can register far more than what is printed on them: they can reflect confidence, economy of movement, uncertainty, contradiction, flurry, almost as clearly as does the spoken word.) It was the first time that I had felt myself to be on public trial in that way, a trial impossible to evade, allowing no cover or subterfuge—and felt, moreover, that a cool reaction was essential, both now and for the future. I had known beforehand that it would be like that: I had known also that I would find all those observant eyes either a stimulant or a profound embarrassment, but I had not known which. The fact that they had been the former, under rather trying circumstances, was a matter for relief and a hopeful pointer for whatever lay ahead.

At all events we were now one stage farther on, slowly forging our way towards completion and the open sea.

Our ammunition was brought out to us by an old-fashioned sprit-sail barge—an odd fact, entirely appropriate to a topsy-turvy world. Unloading and stowing it in the magazines was a job for all hands, and took most of the afternoon: both the shells and the depth-charges had to be man-handled nearly all the way—as regards up-to-date slings and derricks, the sprit-sail barge could give us points and a comfortable beating any day of the week. Then, our engine defect (a broken oil-pump) being made good, and this time guaranteed dependable, it was time to adjust compasses: a two-hour job, and a mortally boring one at that. For the benefit of the uninitiated, the operation consists of going round and round in slow circles while a mathematical wizard (in the inevitable bowler hat) takes bearings of some conspicuous object ashore and makes out a list of them. If you go too fast, he will complain or sulk: if you go too slow you yourself will probably be driven mad by the monotony. A tug stands by all the time to see fair play: in this case the inescapable *Gripper*, all readiness and knowing smile. But for once we didn't need him.

Finally, the job was completed, and that was the end of that day's work, and about time too. Dinner in the wardroom later, topped off with a glass of orange curaçao and the slight clinching formality of 'The King', was a most pleasant reward and relaxation.

The next day—our last, by the schedule—was given over to the full-power trials, which might have been complicated and were actually the simplest and most straightforward operation so far. Machinery of the intricacy of a triple-expansion turbine is a closed book to me: it will always remain so, no matter how long the war continues: and though I encouraged the Chief to go into details of our past defects and current efficiency, it was with the guilty knowledge that if he told me that the thrust-block was cushioned on hard-boiled eggs I would hesitate to challenge the statement for fear of betraying my ignorance. But certainly the ship travelled well, that fine morning, bearing out his eulogy of her present condition. We went for a quick run up the coast, turned, manœuvred, went astern in a hurry—all smoothly and without fuss. She did everything that was asked of her. I took the opportunity of trying out her turning-circle under various degrees of helm, as well as her quickness to gather sternway when changing from 'half ahead' to 'half astern': this latter varied so much from ship to ship that it was one of the first things I wanted to fix in my mind. The different operations furnished no surprises: a slight variation of top-weight made her more tender than *Dipper* when turning, but otherwise I was at ease, on familiar ground, from the start.

As well as showing off the ship's paces and redeeming her reputation, that day's trip was of notable significance and value for me personally. For when I brought her back at the end of it, and secured to the buoy, I felt a sudden surge of self-confidence, as if I had now made sure of something that I had doubted before. The outing had done me a power of good: I knew where I was with this ship, and with myself too—and that was the first gain on a road which would have to show me plenty more, to give me the cast-iron grip I wanted.

But it *was* a notable gain. I had been wrong in hoping to step into a ready-made job, but right in believing that the job, ready-made or not, was no tougher than the determination I could bring to it.

The trouble, of course (and it was a trouble which was to recur constantly later on) was that I had no one with whom to share this sort of self-examination and self-questioning: in fact I hardly knew if it was legal, from the Service angle, and certainly it could not be expressed or implied with the rest of the wardroom. Reassurance, courage, must be from within: I was on my own and I had to look pleased about it. It happens that to find a cure for this isolation, this occasional failure of the spirit, was one of the minor reasons why I had got married: the cure had worked—had always worked, from the beginning—but now it was out of reach, and it was the only one on which I could have called with any certainty of relief. And if this seems too personal a subject for a book on corvettes, I can certify that it is yet highly relevant to the command of one. The Navy and the course of the war make constant demands on one's patience and endurance. I happen to be quite certain where mine come from.

The morning we should have started back for home found us still at our mooring in one of the thickest fogs I have ever encountered. To be at anchor in fog is several degrees better than being loose at sea in one, but it is still a mournful and lowering occasion, not easily dispelled. The ship lay as if in a cocoon, the bridge invisible from the quarter-deck, the masthead lost in the raw grey blanket which pressed round and over us. There was still a certain amount of river-traffic on the move, as the contrasting sirens showed: our bell rang out every minute or so, beating thinly against the wall all round, trying to interpose a margin of safety between us and the menace of other ships. We were lying out of the main channel, naturally, but this carried no particular guarantee: occasionally a tug or a picket-boat, nosing its way upstream from buoy to buoy, would sight us: its look-out would give a shout, the rating in charge of our bell would produce a sudden energetic solo, and the intruder would feel its way past and sheer off into nothingness again. The hands at work on deck kept looking up and staring out into the fog, unable to concentrate or take our security for granted, trying with the instinct of sailors to add their care to the sum total of watchfulness.

I had this instinct myself, and it was difficult to give attention to anything else except our present circumstances: but there was work to be done. The First Lieutenant was permanently on the upper deck, and I therefore spent most of the morning in my cabin, where the gloom rivalled the fog outside as I tackled the intricacies of the wardroom wine-books. (I am no mathematician, and a natural sucker for a dummy prospectus, but a fatherly eye had to be kept on individual wine-bills which, quite apart from the preservation of decorum, were subject to official limitations as well.) Now and again, unable to withstand the spur of a siren nearer than usual, I would climb up on deck, staying for a minute or two to peer out and sniff the thick woolly air before admitting that everything was under control, and going below again. Clearly, the time when I could delegate responsibility with an entirely quiet mind was still somewhere in the future: and as far as fog was concerned, it would probably remain there indefinitely.

The weather cleared at midday, and we started off. We had been detailed to act as additional escort for a coastal convoy as far as our base (seldom in these days does the Navy 'waste' an escort ship by sending it on passage by itself) and this meant a certain amount of hanging about at the assembly point, chasing up stragglers and running errands generally. It was good to get to work again, even at this well-known routine. It happened that there was an alteration of the normal convoy route that day, which had to be passed to each ship individually by loud-hailer: there were thirty-three ships altogether, not all of them British, not all of them bright, not all of them (it seemed) even awake. The job was naturally pushed on to us in its entirety (destroyers are not angels with wings when it comes to this sort of thing), and it took a long time and a lot of shouting: each ship had to be approached, hailed and instructed: and it had to be established beyond doubt that the diversion was absolutely clear to them before another one could be tackled. Since each separate approach involved a score of orders—minor alterations of our course and revolutions—and each detailing of the route meant repeating a long signal at least twice at dictation speed, I was both tired and hoarse by the time I had finished. I was also rather cross, but (for the first time on any stage) I had full freedom to show this, which helped considerably.

Then, a few minutes before we were due to leave the convoy and proceed home independently, the fog came down again, in a rolling bank which gave us hardly any warning. As I rang 'SLOW BOTH' and edged away from the nearest column of ships, I thought: 'This isn't fair. I'm only a writer, really. . . .' I have always loathed fog, ever since my first ship was in collision during a thick night in the North Atlantic; but this was the first occasion when loathing was a totally inadequate— even a harmful—reaction. Always, up till now, there had been someone to take the weight, always the Captain had been there, stepping in automatically and shouldering the unique responsibility of a ship moving blindly among other ships equally blind. Now (ludicrous and oppressive thought) there was no Captain—there was only me. . . .

That sudden and characteristic twinge of helplessness, of being—in technical competence—unequal to a searching occasion, did not last more than a few moments: action cured it, as it always does. I took the ship from Number One, I leant over the dodger and started peering out ahead, I gave the right orders (that original 'SLOW BOTH' had been over-cautious, a mistake induced by nervousness, and I returned to the former convoy-speed), I plotted in my head the sirens of the nearest ships and got a grip of the shadowy picture. But the sweating and the tenseness remained, appropriate and inescapable adjuncts to the moment. There we were, thirty-odd ships in company, trusting each other to do nothing foolish or unusual, rolling along in a close body but in touch only by uncertain sound. I was better off than the rest, being clear of the columns, but this was true only if the picture remained the same shape: if it altered, if it overlapped, if somebody broke loose, the whole fabric would be destroyed and we would in truth be running blind. Fog is always like that—a tenuous hold on safety which a single false step can shatter, and nothing can regain: there is no cure for it except to trust and to deserve the trust of others, in continuous unbroken loyalty.

In the gay and informal days of peace, when for instance I had drunk a jugful of Black Velvet in extraordinary surroundings, or suffered some amorous setback in the least dignified circumstances, I would usually end by saying, 'Well, that was a new experience, anyway'; and I found myself thinking it three-quarters of an hour later, when we came out of the fogbank and into sunshine again. Nothing had gone wrong, and the convoy was as good as new: but the short spell of blindfold action, backed as it was by the knowledge that I had no one on whose nerve or judgement I could lean, had been like a sudden icy shower which reached new and unrealized corners of one's body. And, like a cold shower, it had been exhilarating, with a keen edge of invigoration which lasted far beyond the immediate moment. Once more, the operation had shown a profit. 'That's fog, that was,' I thought, and knew that I had conquered one more personal doubt. There had been an initial moment of uncertainty, and I had made one minor mistake; but if it was never worse than that, even if it went on for very much longer, I reckoned that I had it taped.

To be certain of that, where before there had been nothing but an unpleasant conviction of helplessness, was certainly a gain.

I enjoyed coming up harbour on return to our base, for a variety of reasons no doubt deeply rooted in personal vanity. But to come home with virtually a brand-new ship as my first command—what, in truth, could be better than that? We took no chances with our entrance that afternoon; the hands were in their No. 3 rig in good time, the motor-boat went down like a well-conducted lift, and our piping as we passed the many destroyers and corvettes at anchor was a model of elegance and harmony. As we went at slow speed (and rather closer than was necessary) past *Dipper*, which had the buoy next to ours, there was much stirring on her upper deck: critical eyes followed us, the Officer-of-the-Day darted out with unusual promptness, and from the porthole of the Captain's cabin an inquisitive head, intent on our progress, very nearly poked out. . . . Under such circumstances, our manoeuvring up to the buoy just *had* to be good. (I noticed, incidentally, that for use on such occasions the First Lieutenant had a model phrase: 'Plenty of way on, sir!'—meaning, clearly, 'If you crack up to the buoy at this pace, you'll knock off the buoy-jumper.') It was the sort of lime-lit moment when some public blunder is almost certain to occur, and I waited for whatever it was to be—a swamped motor-boat, a man over-board—with fatalistic calm. But this time everything chose to go right: within two minutes the bridle was secured, and *Winger* was in company.

I signalled 'Greetings' to *Dipper*, who replied, 'Likewise'. Strong men waste no words.

3   THE STEP UP

To have one's First Lieutenant salute and report: 'Divisions correct, sir!' on a fine Sunday morning on the quarter-deck may seem a small thing to have waited two and a half years for. I did not find it so. Nor, as I went down the starboard side to inspect the Seamen's Division, did I feel that I was wasting my time or going through a mere rubber-stamp formality. Sunday morning is always something special on board: the ship is at her tidiest, everyone is in his smartest rig, and everyone (except for the few hands who cannot possibly be spared) presents himself at Divisions, gold badges and all, ready to meet the Captain's eye, and to survive and justify its scrutiny. For me, this first Sunday morning was the most special of all so far: it was impossible not to feel immense pride that my ship's company was waiting for me (as other ship's companies, all over the harbour and indeed in every quarter of the globe, were waiting for their Captains), and that I was playing this role in an ancient and honoured ceremony.

If pride is the deadliest of sins, it is superior in a good many other respects as well.

Very young, most of those seamen looked, as I walked slowly down their lines: young, but self-reliant and self-confident, in the manner of British seamen since the first one put to sea. Nothing has been demonstrated with more clarity in this war than that we *are* a seafaring nation, in the special sense that we breed sailors without knowing it: the sea is in the blood, and the blood proves true time and time again in countless ways. Here, for instance, were a score and more of young

men, picked haphazard from thousands of others, taken from the most
diverse jobs or from no jobs at all: they are set to work in a ship, almost
'from cold', with a minimum of previous training ashore, and in a little
while they are as much a part of that ship as her own engines, and seem
just as surely designed for the job. I don't say that no other nation can
do it—that would be to deny much of recent sea-history, and the
staunch allies we have found there: but I *do* say that this nation does it
superbly and unfailingly, as a national art that never seems to flag.

So much for *Winger*'s seamen, anyway. . . . Farther ahead of them,
on the same side, was the Communications and Miscellaneous
Division—a rather mixed collection, but a lot smarter than it sounds.
All the signalmen I knew by name already, from their work up on the
bridge, and the wardroom stewards as well: the Sick Berth Attendant
was another rating I had 'memorized', by reason of a piece of smart
salesmanship he had worked on me the previous day. I had enlisted his
professional help. 'This is just what you need, sir,' he had said, holding
out a grisly-looking bottle: '*Parafinum liquidum*.' 'Good heavens!' I
said. 'That's liquid paraffin.' 'Oh, no, sir,' he answered readily. 'This is
much more refined.' I suppose there was some sort of ambiguous truth
in the answer: it was good enough to fool me, anyway.

When I had finished with this division I crossed over to the port waist,
where the engine-room and stoker ratings were fallen in. For a ship of
her size, *Winger* carried a large complement of these: and here again,
especially among the stokers, youth was the most striking factor. War
teaches quickly, of course, but it did seem almost unreasonable to
expect some of these young lads to treat machinery properly. . . .
Beyond them was a small compact body of engine-room artificers and
stoker petty officers: older men, some of them pensioners, and the very
stuff of the Navy—as the sprinkling of Long Service and Good
Conduct medal-ribbons showed. With such a strong and experienced
team to call upon, it did not seem that *Winger* need ever stop running;
and I thought I saw in the Chief's eye as he reported them correct, the
same sort of pride as I myself felt in the whole ship. It made an
appropriate and heartening end of Divisions.

For a variety of reasons I did not speak to the ship's company on that
first Sunday morning, although I knew it was customary for a new
Captain to take the first opportunity of saying something to his crew,
'even if,' as someone at the club said, 'it is only threats and abuse.' . . . I
felt, myself, that it was too early in my command for it to mean
anything, and that whatever I said would have more reality in it when I
knew them better, and more solid effect when they knew me. A speech

from a stranger means nothing compared with one from someone you know and understand: and I did not want to start off with platitudes or a stereotyped pep-talk, for lack of material which I knew would be forthcoming later.

'Noël Coward killed that sort of thing stone dead, anyway,' said a fellow destroyer-captain feelingly, when I mentioned the subject later. 'Nowadays the troops expect too much glamour altogether....'

In any case, I let the opportunity go, that first Sunday morning. Instead, I read prayers, and the twenty-third Psalm, and between us we managed a hymn, more notable for carrying power than for harmony. And then the First Lieutenant dismissed the ship's company, and 'Pipe down' was sounded; and after I had inspected and signed the small collection of nineteen books, ranging from 'Gyro Compass Log' to 'Registered Letter Book', which came up for my attention weekly and lay solid and inescapable on my desk till they were dealt with, I myself was free to lean back and enjoy a Sunday breathing-space.

I felt I had earned it, if only by the fatiguing nature of the rounds I had gone the previous day. Captain's Rounds are what you make them—that is, anything from a negligent formality to a searching and critical examination of the whole ship: for my first occasion, I chose to make them the latter, to my own satisfaction and the surprise and exhaustion of my officers. Not only the mess-decks, but the store-rooms and magazines were all faithfully covered: it meant nearly two hours of climbing up and down ladders, squeezing through watertight hatches, bending double to get into the cable-locker and the forepeak: being roasted in the boiler-room, stifled in the paint-shop, dazzled by the bright-work in the Chief Petty Officers' mess: a prolonged and acrobatic session which gave me a lot of information and, incidentally, a formidable thirst. I saw much to commend—the bathrooms (always a difficult item) were exceptionally clean, and the engine-room positively fit to eat and sleep in—and one or two things I disliked: hammocks badly stowed, and an oven whose savoury smell came from layer upon layer of ingrained gravy-drippings. But I would have disliked it even more if there had been nothing for me to criticize. Perfection is no fun at all—unless it is prompted by one's own ideas or produced by one's own efforts.

That afternoon I made my way up to Operations, to lay my zeal and devotion at their disposal and (more seriously) to call formally upon the Admiral. The Senior Staff Officer Operations was out: his henchman, a friend of mine, was holding the fort (a deep armchair) with the utmost tenacity. When I entered the room:

'Local boy makes good,' he said amiably. 'Congratulations to you.'

'Thanks,' I answered.

'How's the ship?'

'Fine.'

'Have they cleared off the whole of your defect list?'

'Yes.'

'Did you have a good trip up?'

'Not bad.'

He looked at me. 'You used to be more talkative.'

'I used to be a First Lieutenant,' I said with simple dignity.

'All right, all right. Do you want to see the Admiral today?'

'If he wants to see me.'

'Unfortunately he is rather at the mercy of convention. New commanding officers—*very* new commanding officers—have the *entrée*. I'll go and fix it for you.' He locked all the drawers in his desk, rather ostentatiously, and then went out, while I was left to contemplate a wall-map which showed, in full colour and horrid detail, the local hazards of navigation. They were many.

Interviews with Admirals are something special and don't get into this kind of book. In any case an account of my reactions would undoubtedly make foolish reading, and especially so after the war, when very senior officers will no doubt be lumped together once more as 'brass hats' and revive their public status as ignorant figures of fun. But I will record, for the honour of truth and the mockery of posterity, that I came out of that room ready to go into action with anything, under any odds.

A number of other things cheered me up, too, less authoritatively but with a pleasant sense of goodwill near at hand. There were signals from other ships, many so robustly humorous that I might have feared for the moral welfare of the younger signalmen if they had been anything but signalmen—the unshockable branch of the Navy. There were letters from stray friends ashore, some of them betraying an unfamiliarity with naval rank which always erred on the flattering side. ('Captain Monsarrat, Royal Navy', was the mode of address used by my mother—a boy's best friend, by a long way.) It became, for a space, even easier than usual to stand drinks to people at the Naval Club ashore, people whose approach seemed disinterested enough but whose congratulations could hardly be countered with a mere acknowledgement. Nor were they all entirely disinterested, it seemed. 'I always said you'd get the job,' said someone I had never seen before in my life. 'Mine's a whisky. . . .' But this bogus phase, not without its amusing side (even at fifteen shillings a round of drinks), soon passed: normality was restored, and with it freedom to concentrate on earning the goodwill on a more official basis.

To H., a friend from my first days in the Navy, who wrote inquiring (with an eye to my peace-time interests) whether true democracy reigned on board:

'Certainly it does,' I replied, 'and not only democracy but fully centralized democracy at that. No decision is too small to evade official scrutiny. A select committee sits at the back of the bridge, debating my helm orders and countermanding any of them which appear to conflict with public welfare. Whether we go to sea or not is determined by popular vote, and I often have an uneasy time canvassing support before we can get under way. The younger seamen, of course, are organized into a Guild of Youth, with fully accredited fraternal delegates from all branches: their banners, boldly inscribed with such slogans as 'DOWN WITH THE ANCHOR', 'UP SPIRITS!', etc., make a brave sight, and hardly interfere at all with my own flag signals. I can assure you that my ship has a most distinctive air, and is certain to make her mark sooner or later, probably on the dock-wall.'

But the job allowed, basically, no such delegation of authority, interesting though the experiment might have been: and since this is an account of a job as well as of a ship, its essentials may be worth enumerating in detail. The 'step up' brought with it so many changes of habit and outlook, even within the small framework of life on board, that it was almost like entering a different branch of the service, and learning the whole thing over again.

First, and most notable, is the Captain's separation from the wardroom: this is no longer one's home and only the smallest amount of time can be spent in it. Apart from anything else, the separation is dictated by the simple demands of work: upon the Captain devolves the largest share of the ship's paper-work, in one form or another, and there are hours to be spent daily at his desk before he is free to indulge any taste for companionship he may have. Nor, once being free, *can* he indulge it as he might like: for there are other considerations even more compelling. Between a Captain and his officers there must be a gap: it is pleasant to mix freely with them without formality, on level terms, and after three years of having the wardroom as a centre of interest and activity, it is extraordinarily difficult to change one's habits: but this freedom of intercourse simply does not work. The better friends you are with your officers, the worse Captain. You may enjoy yourself, you may even seem to extend your influence, but in fact you are evading your job, which is command and nothing else.

This is a hard lesson to learn, and for someone like myself, with a personal and ingrained bias against formality and the more stifling brands of social humbug (to say nothing of a liking for parties on the heroic scale) it is a most depressing one. But learnt it must be if you are to have, when the necessity arises, absolute trust and absolute obedience. If you have bought the sort of trust which springs from being a 'good fellow', if you have swapped obedience for popularity, then God help you when the time comes to cash them to the full. You will almost certainly find yourself bankrupt, and it is a bankruptcy which only the expenditure of human life may be able to redeem.

Another, and not a minor point in this division between Captain and officers is that the wardroom is *their* home, not his, the First Lieutenant being president of the mess and the Captain only a guest there. They should be absolutely free to relax and to entertain their friends, without interference or overlooking of any sort. To cut loose under Father's eye, however benign, isn't the same thing at all. I know; I've tried it and failed consistently.

In the same way, you are now farther away from the crew and much slower to get to know them. With the exception of two or three of them—the coxswain, the signalman of the watch—they never come under your direct orders, you are not a great deal on the upper deck in any case, and only very gradually do personalities emerge and labels stick. The fact that you no longer give orders directly is sometimes tantalizing, after being accustomed as First Lieutenant, to going into action under the slightest provocation or none at all. If you see something going or already gone wrong, it is difficult not to jump into the gap and set people working directly. But this is not now the way: a fender left hanging over the side, or a bucketful of waste carelessly tipped to windward, is not the Captain's pigeon. You have to ring for the quartermaster, who fetches the Officer-of-the-Day, who is then told to deal with it: while all the time words and phrases, exquisitely rich, gloriously appropriate, struggle for utterance on your lips. . . .

For the Captain, boredom at sea is inevitable; it goes with the job, like the hard and useless shell of a nut. As a watch-keeping officer, I always had a minimum of two watches a day—eight hours—on the bridge: now it is all short spells of piecework and (especially in summer) not much of that either. I take the ship for all the difficult bits—entering and leaving harbour, manœuvring through the convoy, taking part in a club run or a shoot with destroyers or other corvettes, closing another escort for orders; and of course I have all the time to know exactly where the ship is, and to make sure that we do our escort job properly—supervision which, at the beginning of my command, kept me on the bridge far longer than was actually necessary.

But, a routine having been established, and my initial over-carefulness dispelled by a period of complete freedom from crises, mostly it is waiting: waiting in my sea-cabin directly underneath the bridge, reading, smoking, memorizing orders or manœuvring signals, eating meals, going up on the bridge for a blitz on the station-keeping: writing letters, thinking, and waiting again.

Now and then information or signals or queries come down the voice-pipe from the bridge. It is odd to be at the other end of that voice-pipe, which for so long was the focus of my attention, and to acknowledge the 'Captain, sir!' by which they call me. It was the other way about, for scores of convoys and hundreds of watches. I must have said 'Captain, sir!' a thousand times in this war, under a thousand different circumstances, and then paused, eyeing the unidentified plane, the torpedoed ship, the floating mine, and waited for an answer from the heart of the ship. Now I am it: on call to meet any emergency: the end-of-the-voice-pipe answer which must always be the right one.

Of course, if something happens, all this suspended activity is reversed. Waiting is finished with, and short spells on the bridge as well: a set four-hour watch becomes a picnic beside the long stretches which may then be necessary. A gale, a fog, a breakdown, an action—all these keep me up on the bridge until they are at an end, six hours, eight hours, ten hours later; they are all, in a greater or less degree, tests of endurance as well as skill. Waiting at the end of the voice-pipe, you know that, sooner or later, whatever reserve of strength you have will be fully tried: that is the certainty which justifies your position. It is your job to have a reserve, by the way: no excuses on this point are acceptable, or, indeed, thinkable.

And when you *are* up on the bridge you have a part to play which must be nothing less than flawless. Up there, you must, to begin and end with, be a centre of absolute calm, but in such a *positive* way that the calm—automatic, inviolable, taken for granted—extends all round you. Among the dozen or so on the bridge there is silence except for the minimum exchanges—the helmsman repeating courses, the Yeoman of Signals reading a message, the Pilot answering a query, his head bent over the chart-table. Into that silence your orders, never above a conversational tone, should drop like stones: crisp, direct, final. If you show signs of excitement, the chances are that the order you give will be carried out more hurriedly than the rating concerned can properly manage; and an order bungled for that reason is no one's fault but your own. And because mistakes like this can always be covered up and shifted to someone else, they must never be made. . . . I said at the beginning that it was a part to be played, and so it is: an elaborate masquerade which must hide almost all your normal feelings and reactions, and leave only stillness and a level voice. But it pays an incomparable dividend, this kind of restraint—for yourself as much as for the ship. Schooled down and confined to the essentials, you become, in the end, the instrument of precision that you yourself need.

Certainly you have need of the best you can get in that line, since—and here is the last aspect of command which is worth recounting—there is absolutely no one else to do your job if it seems to be growing too big for you. This is something entirely novel, and it means reversing a habit of mind which has been yours ever since you joined the Navy and went to sea. On every single occasion up to now, in any matter concerning the ships you have served in, there has always been someone to lean on: behind every decision, every development or crisis, there has always been the Captain, taking the weight and the final responsibility. The fact does not destroy initiative, but it qualifies it: whatever you do, you know you have at hand a judge and a friend—the one to satisfy, the other to turn to if need be.

All that is now ended. All trails now lead to you yourself: you are it—the focus of other people's eyes, the heart and brain of the ship. You are quite alone: you can dodge no issue, you can shelve no burden or decision of any sort. It is a moment which surprises you—it had surprised me, when we ran into fog the first day: the Navy has been training you for this moment for months and years, but only the moment itself can teach, and you are in luck if you have a comfortable space to learn it in.

For it is not something which clicks into place when the bell strikes, and thereafter stays there. It takes a little time, and now and again your instinct tries to retreat from it, and back comes the initial astonishment. That is where your self-discipline must be at hand to help you. Astonishment won't do—or it won't do on the surface at least; somehow it must be translated into cool reaction and the usual level voice, if it is not to spread fatally to those around you. And somehow it *is* translated, and the effort itself is the cure, and presently you find that you are as fully in control as you were pretending to be, a little while ago. . . .

That is the value of the masquerade: it develops until it takes charge altogether: the character-part becomes the reality and the reality is priceless.

For once you have the central idea fixed in your brain, you know where you are, and a firm grip follows. The grip—the absolute confidence—is helped all the time by pride, in the ship and in the size of the job: probably the most sustaining thing of all.

You need something to sustain you: once again, this is it.

4   EARNING IT

I took over in the spring—a final blessing on the appointment. Ahead of us lay a long summer, nights shortening to nothing, and fair weather: only in the far distance was the trial and turmoil of winter in view. There was also, as an additional item on the credit side, the possibility of decisive action in our particular corner of the war: 'First up the Seine', was a current corvette catchword: we felt we were waiting and preparing for something, and we hoped that the flotilla wouldn't be left out of it when it came. I remember the speculation on that point at the time: on the possibility that we might actually be present at a landing on the European coast—our shallow draught and extreme manœuvrability seemed to make this a reasonable bet—or (more likely) that we would be convoying men and material on a cross-Channel shuttle service as soon as a bridgehead was fairly established. The further alternative, a grisly one, was that we would be left out of things altogether and would be kept on at our old East Coast convoy assignment while the destroyers stole the limelight and the fun. . . . In the meantime, all through that spring and early summer, we went on with the job—in and out on patrol, up and down on convoy-escort, training, exercising, sharpening up (we hoped) for the real party which was to come. The ship looked a daisy, incidentally—though the fact is neither relevant nor strictly concerned with war.

If, at first, I found the job of taking *Winger* to sea a wearing one, it was probably my own fault. There seemed so much to remember, so many precautions to take, such a slender margin of things one could safely leave to other people. . . . I expect there *are* Captains who don't worry at sea, who can keep off the bridge for hours at a stretch, who are not nagged all the time by a thousand possibilities, a thousand doubts: but I was not one in those early days—nor am I yet, to the extent I should like. It isn't a question of trusting one's officers, it is a matter of balancing chances and making sure of the right verdict: absolute responsibility needs absolute certainty, and how can you obtain that otherwise than by unending personal supervision?

Something *might* go wrong, even during the simplest operations. Number One *might* miss a buoy. Pilot *might* get out of station. Guns *might* steer north instead of south. Up you go on to the bridge to make quite sure. It was a habit of mind, a nervous reaction that only time could cure: things got better, naturally, as I came to know each officer's capabilities and to trust his judgement in a sudden crisis: but at the beginning, for the first few weeks, every trip was a continuous and wakeful ordeal which left me unhappily doubtful of my own staying power. At this pace, winter with its sixteen hours of darkness could finish me off. Indeed, at this pace I would never see winter at all.

In point of fact I was well served in the matter of watch-keeping officers. *Winger*'s wardroom compared very favourably with some other ships, where the 'dilution' of wartime had left the mixture a bit weak. The First Lieutenant had been a long time on the coast, and had the whole thing sewn up tight: the Pilot (Sub., R.N.R.) was as competent as I could wish, the Gunner (the least experienced) was conscientious and painstaking, and the Midshipman was a valiant and independent young man who was ready to take over my job any day of the week and hold it down against all comers.

But I still wanted to be told every single thing that went on. ... One of the more helpful attributes of a good Officer-of-the-Watch is that he knows when to call the Captain and when to contend with a situation himself: a watch-keeper whose judgement is really trustworthy in this respect is an enormous asset as far as the Captain's peace of mind is concerned. It is helpful also if this ability to estimate crisis is roughly the same among all one's officers: too often it is not, and whereas one of them, over-zealous, will sing out if he as much passes a floating log, another (usually the least accomplished) will proceed with such sturdy independence that, when finally you are summoned to the bridge, the entire world seems to be compounded of ships bearing down on you from all angles, hoarse cries out of the darkness, and a line of hungry breakers just over the port rail. When, later (often much later) you ask for an explanation, you will be told that 'things looked all right, but they got worse suddenly'—an account transparently and desperately true, but giving you neither satisfaction with the past nor confidence in the future.

Since there is nothing more ageing than this kind of uncertainty, I laid down in my Standing Orders a list of directions designed to cover every eventuality, as far as could be foreseen, for all our operations on this coast: the text of the relevant paragraph was as follows:

'The Officer-of-the-Watch is to call me, without fail, in the following circumstances:

(*a*) On sighting or hearing an aircraft not identified as friendly.

(*b*) On obtaining an Asdic contact.

(*c*) On sighting any vessel which is either (1) suspicious or (2) likely to interfere with our intended course (e.g. a destroyer on patrol or a mine-sweeper on our own side of the channel).

(*d*) On sighting flares or star-shell at night.

(*e*) On a change in the weather or visibility.

(*f*) If a buoy or light-vessel is not sighted at the expected time.

(*g*) On an escort or ship in convoy leaving its proper station.

(*h*) On any ship (escort or merchant ship) joining the convoy.

(*i*) If the presence of other ships nearby seems likely to force us off the swept channel, or on the wrong side of a wreck buoy or other dangerous obstruction.

(*j*) In any doubt or emergency.'

It might be thought that these left no loophole for surprises: but even this list did not prevent an occasional jolt. There it was, anyway, as full as I could make it: designed to keep the ship out of trouble, and myself awake, for most of the twenty-four hours.

We started the season with a nautical oddment of the sort which, for no real reason, is a first-rate tonic for a ship and which I myself found distinctly heartening: the interception and bringing in of a couple of fishing-drifters with a number of refugees aboard.

The meeting was entirely a matter of chance. Our convoy that morning had taken us rather farther north than usual, and I was stooging about to seaward of it, wondering if the dropping of a practice depth-charge would (*a*) escape the attention of the Senior Officer, who didn't like that sort of thing round his convoys, and (*b*) stun enough fish to make it worth while lowering the whaler, when the look-out suddenly reported 'Objects to starboard'. Visibility was very good, and within a few moments they were identified as a pair of small drifters, south-bound, farther out than those generally are but still harmless enough. I decided to close them, nevertheless: nominally to 'establish identity beyond doubt', actually to see if I could save the expense of that depth-charge. The crews of the drifters working on this coast are

extraordinarily generous with their catches whenever we encounter
them. . . .

There was, however, soon to be another factor: for when we were still
about two miles off the signalman of the watch suddenly called out:

'I don't think they're British, sir!' He was wrinkling his eyes as he
stared at them through his binoculars. 'Some sort of foreign
ensign—and they've got colours painted on their sides as well. Blue and
red. There's some lettering, too. Looks like Norwegian, sir.'

That was something quite different. I increased speed, altered course
to intercept them and, as a precaution, went to Action Stations. It might
be any sort of a ruse, from a Q-ship to a disguised submarine, and I did
not want to be caught out. As the distance lessened, and it was clear that
they were both flying Norwegian ensigns, every one on the upper deck
who was not manning a gun crowded to the rails to examine them: the
first visitors from 'over there' that we had ever seen. There was one big
and one small boat, both with large flags painted on their sides, and both
apparently unarmed. The people on board were staring back at us, and
some of them waved energetically; but of course it wouldn't do to be
taken in by such a simple trick as that. I hoisted the International Code
signal for 'Stop instantly', and when this was obeyed, and I had circled
them once in silence, I stopped engines and called the First Lieutenant
to the bridge.

'Boarding party ready, Number One,' I told him. 'Yourself and four
good hands. Revolvers. I'll get these chaps to come alongside one at a
time: we'll take the big one first. When you get on board, see the captain,
and then search the boat throughout, whatever sort of yarn he tells. The
Norwegian for "Hands up!" is . . .' I thought rapidly, without avail, '. . .
is probably "Hands up!" I don't suppose that sort of language difficulty
will arise, anyway. But look out for surprises.' And then, over the loud-
hailer (which reached all parts of the upper deck): 'Train all guns to
starboard and cover those two,' I said. 'Make it as obvious as you can.
If they start anything, open fire.'

Last of all, still through the loud-hailer, 'Train on the big drifter.'

'Speaker trained, sir!'

I mustered the most basic English I could think of. 'Come alongside,'
I called out. 'Slowly. One of you only. We will throw a rope.'

An arm waved acknowledgement from the window of the deck-
house, and obediently the larger drifter edged alongside. It was here that
things got slightly out of hand. As I have indicated, we were prepared
for surprises, but their next move was scarcely foreseeable. For the
instant that the two ships touched, half a dozen of the drifter's crew

started to shovel fish on to our upper deck from their own: enormous fish, in glistening cascades. The First Lieutenant, as he jumped across, boarded under a positive barrage of them. I thought furiously for a moment, my mind running on explosive cod. . . . Then I relaxed: after all, they *were* neutral ships, and this was a damned good visiting card—in fact, it was the best one they could have produced.

After a few moments of this, during which the piles of fish grew to huge proportions and some of the more astute mess-cooks were already staking their claims, the First Lieutenant poked his head out of the deck-house.

'It's all right, sir,' he called out. 'They're all friendly.'

'They'd better be,' I answered in a thunderous voice over the loud-hailer. Then, 'Have a good look round, and then come back aboard and tell him to lay off while we take a look at the other one. And for goodness' sake stop them slinging that fish over. We've got far more than we need, and we've developed a five-degree list already.'

Number One's search revealed nothing except a lot more fish below decks, and a great many talkative and happy passengers. ('Some of them kissed me,' he said in the wardroom later, with no particular expression in his voice), and when the second boat had been searched he came back aboard to report. Both skippers told the same story (a slight odour which I recognized enviously as Schnapps floated round the bridge as he gave me the details). They had been ten days at sea, making for England, had lost their way (having no sextant, and only the most inadequate charts), had been bombed and gunned by German aircraft, and were now overjoyed to be free once more, after months of planning. I sent off a signal, outlining the incident and asking permission to take them in: and meanwhile I tried to circle round and round them, to keep them under general observation. (We had no means of checking their story and all the passengers might have been just so many quislings or spies, for all we knew to the contrary. But that was a shoreside worry—my job was to see that they didn't step out of line while they were afloat.) Keeping them under observation from a proper distance, however, proved almost impossible: it seemed that having found a friend they were going to hang on to him, for they attached themselves to my stern like a couple of porpoises following a whale, clinging one to each quarter as I circled. No matter what I did, they followed me as if I were towing them on a short elastic hawser. . . . It was something of a relief when my signal was approved and I could put an end to the circus parade by setting course for our destination. I didn't want to hurt their feelings: not after all that fish (already there was a most pungent odour of frying cod permeating the whole ship): but there is a limit to what one can suffer in the cause of politeness, even under those condtions.

We were to hand them over to a trio of patrol-trawlers coming out to meet us, and when we reached the rendezvous an affectionate farewell was taken, with much cheering and waving on both sides. The leading patrol-trawler signalled (rather foolishly): 'Are they dangerous?' to which I replied, 'Yes. Beware flying fish.' In spite of interrogatives I didn't elaborate the signal for him. It would keep him up to the mark, and he'd find out, anyway, as soon as he got anywhere within throwing distance.

This was, as I have said, a chance oddment, which might have been specially planned to enliven us: the backbone of our job—patrolling and escorting—was much more mundane, with a minimum of variation and no Schnapps at all. Here, in illustration, is a sample week, of no special significance, but fairly representative of our work, elaborated from the deck-log some time during June.

No frenzied signalling preceded it: the week's work started, in fact, at the R.N. cinema on the quay, and was formally covered by the log-entry: 'Leave to the Starboard Watch from 13.00 to 18.00. Canteen Cinema leave, 19.30.' When the ship was under sailing orders before a patrol, leave expired four hours before sailing time—four hours being the time calculated as sufficient to dissipate the fog of love in a rating's eye or any other sort of fog anywhere else. But I usually extended this leave till the end of the performance at the quayside cinema since no one could come to any harm there, and if all liberty-men were in one definite place together they could be recalled very simply—the main consideration. Thus we generally went along in a body: the whole wardroom (except the Officer-of-the-Day) and half the ship's company. It was almost an official exercise: indeed, in the case of some films it was a collective endurance test in itself.

Surfeited on this occasion by Dorothy Lamour (if such a statement is not ungallant or actionable) we strolled along the quay towards the pontoon where the liberty-boat was waiting for us: half a ship's company, relaxed, at ease in the sunlight, enjoying a last spell of freedom preparatory to tightening up again. There was five minutes to spare before the boat left, so I called in at the mine-sweeping office to get the latest report of our patrol area, and find out if there were any special sections to be avoided. Mines—treacherous and unpredictable—are something I specially loathe: my friend in charge of the M/S office seemed to have a correspondingly tender affection for them. At any rate it was with obvious satisfaction that he produced his sweeping chart and pointed out the current pitfalls and queries.

'Now this,' he said, tapping with his pencil an area thick with sinister black crosses, 'this is a *lovely* corner. It's been giving us no end of trouble, and it's not finished with yet, by a long chalk. The sweepers put up two *there*, yesterday, and another one *there* this morning. That's the lot so far, but I shouldn't be surprised if there was another clump of them *there*.'

It's me that'll be surprised, not you, I thought. But I nodded.

'What about my actual patrol area tonight?'

He shook his head, almost as if he were sorry to disappoint me. 'It looks pretty well clear,' he answered. 'Has been for weeks, in fact. But you never know, do you? I shouldn't go wandering off very far to the eastward round about K Buoy, if I were you.'

'I promise faithfully I won't.'

'The channel itself will be swept as usual, anyway, before you get there, and you'll pick up all the signals if anything turns up.'

Disregarding the fact (of which he was well aware) that the first signal about a mine is often a bang and an enormous column of water just astern of you, I bade him good night and crossed the quay to the waiting boat.

Dinner was ready when we got back on board—a rather austere meal, as usual on such occasions, without any alcohol before, during, or after. There is no special rule about drinking either before sailing or when we are actually at sea; but my own feeling, which the wardroom shares, is that it is giving away a definite chance to fortune if you are anything but absolutely normal and unexhilarated when afloat. Drink always stimulates, in a greater or less degree: a stimulated judgement is an unsound one; and (taking the gloomy view which may always jump into reality at any moment) if the ship is sunk, and you are in the water, you are a dead duck from the start unless you can stay awake and aware indefinitely. At such times, a single shot of whisky, taken earlier on, might give you a comfortable glow, lulling you into that carelessness which is the equivalent of an obituary notice, any day of the week. So that evening, as on other evenings before sailing, we all drank water, and even contrived to give the impression of liking it.

After dinner, according to our custom, I walked up and down the length of the quarter-deck with Number One. We were not due to leave for our patrol until ten o'clock—summer had turned night-patrolling into a short operation, with an agreeably late start; and tonight the cool air, the evening sunshine, the quiet isolation of our berth at the buoy, all made the interval an exceptionally pleasant prelude to sea-going. There were, as usual, others walking up and down in the same fashion as ourselves, in different parts of the ship: the coxswain and the Chief E.R.A., earnestly conferring: a couple of young telegraphists up on the fo'c'sle: a lone hand with bent head, arms folded, and something weighty on his mind, who strode up and down the iron deck as if it were a deserted country lane. There were people washing out clothes at the entrance to the mess-deck passageway: there was a gramophone playing somewhere forward: there was a rating in the port waist, under the ordeal of having his hair cut by a stoker, and not pretending he was in the least satisfied with the operation. Summer evening in harbour: all of it familiar and all of it good. At such times we seemed more than a ship's company, almost a family, with the family's varied interests and closely binding ties—Number One said, suddenly: 'About that proposed alteration to the flag-locker . . .' and I was recalled to a nearer reality. But still the surrounding peace remained with us, securely settled and comfortingly strong.

As I half-turned towards him, I noticed the quartermaster standing nearby wrinkling up his nose at a drift of my cigar-smoke, with an expression which seemed to indicate pleasure but which may have been a long way from it. Whatever it was, it vanished instantly, as if sponged off, when he became aware of my glance, and with a look of enormous concentration he bent down and began to polish the butt of his revolver. Yes, there was nothing wrong with this evening, or with this ship either.

An hour later saw us intensely active, and almost ready to go. I was down in my cabin then, first collecting and laying out the small pile of secret signal logs and Operational Orders which the Midshipman would take up to the bridge, and later changing into sea-going rig: but I could follow the exact progress of work both down below and on the upper deck, so clear and assignable were the various noises as the Chief ran through his tests and the First Lieutenant secured the ship for sea. A faint humming noise was main engines being tried, at twenty or thirty revolutions, a tremble was the wheel being put from full-over to full-over: the engine-room telegraph bells and the revolution-counter spoke for themselves, even at this distance: and the 'Action Stations' bell (preceded by the pipe, 'Warning: alarm gongs testing!' so as to avoid confusion) rang through the cabin flat with the shrill and startling persistence which made it recognizable above a hundred other noises.

Earlier, there had been a faraway clanking up forward—the cable passing through the windlass as the bridle was changed for a slip-rope: a vile clattering just over my head had been the Mediterranean ladder coming in, a final thunder of feet was the motor-boat being hoisted. Now, with five minutes to go before sailing time, the Chief reported, 'Ready to move'; the First Lieutenant, 'Ready to proceed' (some subtle difference there), and the rest of it was mine.

Up on the bridge, just before slipping, the exchange of information and orders follows an automatic, almost a blindfold routine: it is like some simple tune in which a wrong note sticks out a mile, and a phrase missed out makes every one look up in surprise. Solemnly contrapuntal, it makes its way from stage to stage:

Coxswain: 'Special sea-duty-men closed up, sir.'

Self: 'Very good.'

Coxswain: 'Main engines rung on, sir.'

Self: 'Very good.'

Yeoman of Signals: 'Approved to proceed, sir.'

Self: 'Very good.'

Sub. (calling from fo'c'sle): 'Ready to slip, sir.'

Self: 'Where's the buoy?'

Sub.: Close under the port bow, sir.'

Self: 'Right. Stand by to slip. .... Anything moving in the harbour?'

Midshipman: 'Nothing, sir,' or 'Seventeen trawlers coming upstream,' as the case may be.

Self: 'Slip!'

There is a chunk! as the hammer knocks off the slip and we are free of the buoy.

Turning a ship in a narrow stream is not complicated when you have two screws to play with, and plenty of power in reserve: it simply needs controlling so that the ship never moves more than a few yards ahead or astern until she is heading the right way—downstream. For students of the drama, the necessary orders go like this:

'Slow astern port.'

'Slow ahead starboard.'

'Hard aport.'

'Half ahead starboard.'

'Half astern port.'

'Slow ahead starboard.'

'Wheel amidships.'

'Slow astern port.'

'Stop port.'

'Hard aport.'

'Slow ahead together.'

'Half ahead together.'

That is an example of an absolutely straightforward and continuous turn, with no crises and no cross-traffic to interrupt it. Tonight we waited, after our half-circle, with both engines stopped while a destroyer at a lower berth who was also due on patrol went through the same manœuvre. There was no other traffic on the move. Drifting very gently downstream with the ebb tide, I watched her carefully, on the look-out for mistakes: but as usual she gave a perfect performance. When she was round we fell into line astern of her, and left harbour in company. Since it was after sunset we did not pipe the other ships at anchor, but slipped out anonymously.

Once clear of the harbour, and with the destroyer drawing ahead and away from us at a stately twenty-five knots (I had dined with her Captain the previous evening, and to my parting signal, 'No red wine tonight,' he answered grimly, 'Blood will do . . .') we went to Action Stations as usual. The Gunner gave his gun's crew a quick run-through at loading and aiming (using a startled M.L. as a target), and then we tested all our close-range guns, firing quick bursts of tracer on a safe bearing. This was the time for guns to jam, if jam they must: later wouldn't do. There was now a certain amount of traffic about, which kept me on the bridge till we were well on our way: mine-sweepers coming in or out, small independent coasters punching the tide as they tried to get in before nightfall, a trio of motor-torpedo-boats snarling away towards the dusk and the opposite coast. I flashed to their leader, 'Good luck!' to which he replied, 'Thanks. Actually we rely on skill.' Then presently we were clear of the approaches, with nothing to do but plug along till we reached our patrol area, and after checking Pilot's estimate of the speed we wanted to make good I handed over to Number One and went below for a smoke.

We had an official engagement that night, as it happened, and since nothing occurred to sabotage it, we spent the early part of our patrol playing cops-and-robbers with a flotilla of motor-gunboats—or, in the more austere service phraseology, 'taking part in Night Encounter Exercise with light coastal forces'. This was the first one I had done, and I enjoyed it a lot: after a preliminary conference the gunboats withdrew out of range, split up and then came in to attack at various angles. We took 'evasive action', plotted their courses, and tried to work out and forestall their tactics: and in the meantime I practised a running commentary on the loud-hailer for the benefit of the guns' crews.

The agreed routine was that when we spotted the gunboats, and 'opened fire', we were to flash a lamp in their direction: and when they got near enough to run a torpedo, they were to do the same. It says something for the vigour of the exercise that before it was completed the whole horizon was nothing but winking lights, with our own playing a furious solo in the middle.... But it was good fun, as I have said, besides being moderately instructive; and I was sorry when the time came to call off the battle, tot up the score, and turn to something a bit more serious.

Not that it was really anything of the sort: our patrol that night was one of the patrols that don't pay for their oil-fuel—except, I suppose, as a preventive measure. We had one query on the way up—something which might have been a mine-laying aircraft, but which positively dissolved into correct recognition signals when it saw what it was running into—and that was really all. For the rest of the time we just ploughed up and down, faithful and dumb as spaniels. Once, at the top of our run, we met the destroyer who had gone out with us that evening. Equally bored with nothing to do, she challenged us fiercely, but we were ready for that one. I felt wideawake after the motor-gunboat game, and having no other work to do, I spent most of the time up on the bridge, talking to the First Lieutenant (who shared the middle watch with the Midshipman) and coming in for a noble share of the latter's recurrent brews of cocoa.

Towards dawn we had a long convoy passing through our area, during which operation we drew aside respectfully—and wisely: our camouflage was too good to get involved with fifty-odd determined merchantmen, since we looked like a vague blur at night and that was just what they preferred to open fire at. Then, when they were clear, and we were ready to sink back into boredom again, we got a signal giving us a definite job—to go and look for an R.A.F. dinghy reported adrift, with survivors, to the eastwards of our patrol. (A lot of our bombers had gone out earlier: this was presumably one of the unlucky ones.) When we reached the estimated position we went through our usual routine in such cases—a box-search of the area, in gradually widening squares; there was a Walrus joining in the hunt, stolid and unwieldy, making slow circles round the same spot, and occasionally coming down to sea-level to inspect something which had caught its eye. Neither of us had any luck: but shortly afterwards we had a second signal to say that the dinghy had been picked up farther north by a rescue motor-launch, with all its crew safe. We were glad to get that signal: to have to leave a bomber-crew adrift somewhere on this coast, knowing (or guessing) what they endure on their own job quite apart from this sort of ordeal, is one of the least cheering things that come our way.

By now it was near daylight, a pale flush to the eastwards, a lightening of the sea from black to cold grey, a subtle and welcome change. South of us some night mine-sweepers came up, vague shapes, invisible and unsuspected a few moments before, each of them suddenly knitting together a patch of darkness until it thickened into the outline of a ship: they also must be glad of daylight and an end to their task. The light, creeping over the wave-tops and spreading towards the land. seemed to answer all the night's questions with a comforting and absolute wisdom.

At sea, every dawn is a thrill: that is something which has never changed and never lessened, throughout years of sea-going. no matter how grisly the occasion. It may not be beautiful: it may indeed be actively ugly: but, by God, it is a relief! It solves so many problems—of station-keeping, of avoiding traffic and trouble: it gives you certainty instead of guesswork: it is safety after hazard.

It was also, this time, rather cold, with a bleak wind blowing offshore and slapping the waves roughly against our bows as we turned for home. Satisfied that there was nothing more to be done (an easy decision to arrive at, under the circumstances), I went below for the journey back, leaving Pilot, who knew this bit blindfolded, to overtake the sweepers and bring her in.

An hour's sleep was cut short by his cautious, 'Rather a lot of traffic ahead, sir,' down the voice-pipe: and when I climbed up to the bridge again I found that we were now close inshore, and faced by a familiar problem which turned up at the end of nine patrols out of ten. The harbour was closed, as an unchallengeable signal on the lightship proclaimed: it would not be opened till the approach-channel had been swept, at some time (beyond prediction) ahead. In front of us, as we covered the last mile, was a milling collection of sweepers and coastal craft, also waiting to go in: some of them anchored, others jockeying for position in case the 'Port Closed' signal came down earlier than usual. Our problem was whether to anchor or not ourselves, and it was governed by three factors: that we had to oil when we got in: that there were only two berths available at the oiler, owing to some diving operations nearby: and that just astern of us two destroyers, also coming in from patrol, were waiting to nip in front at short notice and enormous speed. If we anchored, and they didn't, we should be right out of the picture: if we turned slow circles round the lightship (it might be for an hour or more) while they lost patience and dropped their picks, we might have time to get in front of them and stake a claim.

Both of them oiling ahead of us, and keeping us hanging about in the offing, would mean a great waste of time, cutting into our very short spell in harbour. There were quite a lot of things to be seen to, and we were due to go out again, on convoy, at eleven o'clock.

This time I waited around, champing, talking to the Captain of a Dutch minesweeper (gravely introduced to me the previous night as 'the originator of the Dutch treat') and being jostled by all and sundry, until I finally got bored with it, left the main mob, and dropped anchor nearby. It was still quite early. Hardly had the riding-slip been put on, hardly had I stirred my tea, when the lightship's flag came down with a run. The assembled fleet sprang into life: the destroyers pressed the button and roared past. Unfair to corvettes, I thought, as I sped up to the bridge again and let loose a torrent of orders—to the engine-room, the cable party, the First Lieutenant. It was a waste of time, really, since whatever speed we made we couldn't catch them up, but it went some way towards relieving the feelings.

As it happened, something else relieved them too, rather more effectively. When we neared the harbour entrance the usual hoists went up aboard the destroyers (now a long way ahead of us) indicating which berth they were making for. I called to the Yeoman:

'Both going to the oiler, I suppose?'

He shook his head. 'No, sir. One's a single number. Looks like Number Three Buoy.'

It *was* Number Three Buoy, which left a vacant berth for us at the oiler and saved us a lot of time. The position was retrieved: breakfast would be tolerable after all. Within a few minutes the First Lieutenant had piped the hands to their stations and the wires and fenders were ready for securing to the oiler.

I had already had, even then, plenty of practice at coming alongside, but conditions varied so much from day to day that I never felt entirely sure that a perfect manœuvre would be forthcoming. Both wind and tide dead ahead of you, of course, are the ideal conditions: they ensure that you can keep the screws turning until the very last moment, and render the ship far more manœuvrable. At the other end of the scale—with the tide under your stern and the wind blowing the ship away from the oiler or the quay—anything may happen, from loss of paint to a docking-job. On one such occasion I had first failed entirely to come alongside the oiler—our relative positions took on a closer and closer resemblance to a T-bone steak, until after three tries I had to give up altogether—and then, trying to secure up to the Senior Officer's ship, I had put the fluke of my anchor through his bow-plating, causing a neat and unmendable tear. ('I wish we could do this sort of thing to Jerry,' said a rating below me, not quite quietly enough, as we backed away from the target area.)

But that had been a really bad day—the tail-end of a gale and of a very tiring convoy. Usually it is less spectacular and relatively inexpensive. And when it is neatly done (as on this present occasion it chanced to be) it has a satisfying style and finish about it. If the moment to go 'Half astern both' has been properly judged the ship stops dead, exactly parallel and exactly in the right spot, with the oiler's hose overhanging the ship's fuel-pipe connection: the heaving lines fore and aft whip across together, the headrope goes to the windlass and is heaved in slowly. Between the ship and the oiler the water is imprisoned, squeezed together: it seethes with a sudden spite, and the jumbled waves slop to and fro, criss-crosssing between the two ships like echoes caught in a cavern: but foot by foot it is compressed and conquered, until suddenly it vanishes altogether, the ships' sides touch and part and touch again, and the trip—good or bad—futile or satisfactory—is over.

This morning, when oiling had been completed (concurrently with a bath and shave for myself) we went the short distance up harbour to our buoy. It was still rather early, and I took care to draw attention to the fact by unnecessary (or perhaps over-scrupulous) use of the siren: nothing is more tempting, when you have been out all night, than a harbour full of smug and sleeping corvettes. (Destroyers, of course, never sleep.) The boat which we had sent ashore from the oiler was already alongside with the mail and the morning papers: breakfast, backed by these, was practically civilized and certainly refreshing, even counting the fake-egg-omelette. But the breathing-space did not last long: there was just time for Number One to wash down the upper deck and for myself to answer two official letters, before our sailing-orders arrived by the signal-boat. We were to start straight away. The mail was landed in a hurry, the mess-caterers ashore at the canteen were rounded up and brought back: then once more it was 'Secure for sea', 'Ready to proceed', 'Slip!' and off we went again.

We were due to join up with a north-bound convoy, taking out a small parcel of ships ourselves to add to the collection—a sort of nautical bottle-party. I had a trawler to help me, nominally under my orders but by nature independent (and incidentally senior to me in rank). Rounding up our contingent, getting them in formation, and adjusting their speed so that they neither hung about at the rendezvous nor panted ten miles astern of the main body—all this devolved on me, while the trawler, belching smoke of hideous density and hue, trundled on ahead to show us how. (I might have objected to this display of individuality, but a natural reluctance to raise hell was intensified, in this case, by the conviction that I was probably better off doing the thing myself in my own way. Trawlers have a lot to commend them, but they are not exactly the greyhounds of the ocean. And—though I know there are many people who disagree—one war at a time is really enough.) At any rate we got the flock out to the interception point at the proper time, and after the usual bout of 'After you, Cecil; after you, Claude', they tacked themselves on to the stern of the convoy, while I closed the Senior Officer of the escort (a destroyer) to collect the convoy papers, and any last-minute orders he might have for me.

I was rather fond of this operation, which consisted of keeping pace with the other ship on a parallel course while the papers were transferred by hand-line: it could be done in any number of ways, from creeping alongside like a sick mongrel to dashing up at speed and dropping dead on the doorstep: I usually favoured the latter method, though that was probably more than the Senior Officer did. It was generally enlivened—as now—by a cross-talk on the loud hailer, wherein a robust wit was tempered hardly at all by the knowledge that every word of what one was saying was fully audible over a range of about two miles.

Having collected the packet of papers, a rather good story about an Indian prisoner-of-war, and a compliment on my camouflage, I dropped astern between the long lines of ships to muster them and then take up my station on the escort-screen. Like everyone else serving in corvettes or destroyers, I had seen hundreds of convoys in this war; and if they did not always impress with the same pride and the same admiration as at the beginning, that was simply because of the human inability to hold an impression, however strong or vivid, indefinitely. Certainly the sea and the ships were the same: the proof was Britain itself still fighting.

When this is all over, someone will—someone *must*—write an adequate history of the Merchant Service in action, free from armchair heroics about 'forgotten men', but not too shy to dwell upon the spirit and the flame. I wouldn't be able to do it, if only because (as I have said) I took them so much for granted already: they had been for so long in the centre of the picture, a picture bound, for that reason, to lose its force—just as a photograph, even of someone deeply loved, comes in the end to mean no more than any other ornament, because of its familiarity. But the feeling did return at odd times, such as this convoy-muster, with its significance undiminished and in all its old intensity.

In this present collection of ships, for example, which now moved past me in their slow disciplined columns as I checked names and numbers, there was probably enough of the recent history of courage to form an imperishable chronicle, if it could be faithfully transcribed. There were ships that had seen scores of long-drawn-out actions, and still came back cheerfully for more: there were men—British and Allied sailors—who dared all, not as a job for money but simply as a chosen habit, who returned to the same task and the same run after two or even three hideous ordeals as survivors, who stuck to oil-tankers as other people stick to one brand of bottled beer. Even apart from action with the enemy, the men in these ships—some of them, old friends, were waving as I passed them now—had seen their job transformed by war into something a hundred times more difficult and more hazardous: they had accepted loyally the irksome compulsion of convoys, of never moving except in crowded company—a discipline quite alien to sailors, whose foremost instinct is to beat it in the opposite direction when another ship comes over the horizon: they had accepted the necessity of wallowing along for hundreds of miles at the speed of the slowest, and of keeping close station in weather like a dirty blanket hanging all around them.

They had accepted strange companions on their journeys. In this very convoy there were new tankers moving like fortresses, powerful American freighters, coastal scuttlers rolling, their decks awash, dead-beat tramps flogging worn-out engines for the extra revs needed to keep up even this crawling speed. (One Master, when we told him to hurry up and close a gap, shouted back: 'Can't do it. The Chief will give me hell if I ask for more revs.') Under the necessity of keeping coastwise traffic moving, and of other ships reaching their rendezvous in time to join trans-ocean convoys, there was really no alternative to chucking them all together and telling them to get on with it. War conditions had made this kind of bran-tub inevitable: but the disadvantages—inequality of speed and manœuvrability, the dependable keeping station on the unpredictable—were obvious, and they could only be countered by seamanship of a high order, a blend of skill and vigilance beyond belief and beyond praise.

That these qualities had been forthcoming, in continuous and unstinting measure, since the first day of the war, was fortunate: without the valour of her merchant seamen Britain could not have survived. One could only feel proud to share a job with such men. Nominally we were in charge of them, on all their undertakings: but it was really a more complex relationship, in which admiration had its full share and a brotherly regard seasoned all the discipline we had to enforce. If an occasional blast was necessary, it was a blast delivered in the full knowledge that, were the positions reversed, we should be at the receiving end just as often and for just the same reasons.

Men like these had died in their hundreds: I had seen them dying, had picked them up or failed to find them, had mourned their passing, wondered at their courage, and cursed their executioners. But however lonely or cruel their end, a part of them lived always, indestructible as the sea itself, to the glory of their race and calling, and the certain doom of the enemy.

When we had said hello to another destroyer, taken up our station astern of the convoy and dealt out one or two hints to potential stragglers, I went below for lunch and my afternoon nap. The convoy was progressing slowly, butting into a head wind and a rising sea: through a ventilator above my berth the wind whistled on a high, discouraging note, and the patter and drift of spray against the forward bulkhead told its story of water freely shipped and bows buried, now and then, under a flurry of foam and green sea. But this was an accustomed lullaby, and, as usual, I dozed off, while the convoy crept northwards and the Officer-of-the-Watch kept distance and station at the tail of the columns. Occasionally signals came down the voice-pipe—weather forecasts, movements of other convoys in the area—but this also was a routine chorus in the background, which penetrated only deep enough to establish its unimportance. The change of the watch, and tea-time, came round with a good two hours' sleep stored up, in reserve for any emergency later on.

Then there was a more definite interruption, delivered by the Sub-Lieutenant *via* the voice-pipe:

'Captain, sir!'

I rolled over. 'What is it?'

'Signal from the leading destroyer, sir: "Are there any stragglers?"'

'Are there?'

'One starting to drop back a bit, sir. The small one with the funnel aft.'

'What revs are we doing?'

He told me.

'Slow enough. . . . All right, I'll come up.'

I put on my sea-boots and stepped out into the wind and the spray, and up to the bridge. The convoy was now spread out over several miles, and though visibility was still good we were only just in signalling-touch with the leading destroyer. Tailing on to the starboard column, a good mile astern of it, was the first straggler, whom I had actually marked down as a possibility as soon as we joined up: a very small, very old-fashioned packet liberally daubed with red lead, the after-part hung with cleanish washing which had little chance of emerging as such from the billows of smoke pouring out of her funnel. She was making heavy weather of it, stubbing her nose into every second wave, shaking herself free of water in a listless fashion, as if she knew she was doing the wrong thing and did not greatly care either way. After watching her for a few minutes I called to the signalman:

'Signal to the leader: "One dumb chum. I will turn on the heat." All right, Pilot—put her alongside, and we'll do some talking.'

We increased speed and closed to within comfortable hailing distance. As we drew near our quarry an old man wearing, of all things, a bowler hat, walked to the side of the bridge and peered over the rail, prepared to give battle. That was probably all he was going to give: he knew what I had come for, well enough, and looked quite ready to swear he hadn't got it in stock.

I began mildly. 'Can you do anything about this gap in front of you?'

He waved his hand in a gesture which might have conveyed any one of half a dozen different meanings: despair, indifference, promise, leave-me-alone-blast-you. . . . But he said nothing.

'Can you go any faster?'

Faintly across the water came the answer, through a megaphone:

'Doing the best I can.'

'Well, you want to close this gap somehow, or I'll have to send you in.'

The megaphone was shaken furiously heavenwards. 'The commodore's going too fast.'

'He's going very slowly. Now what about a few extra revs to make up?'

'I can't do it, I tell you. Chief's sitting on the bloody safety-valve as it is.'

I made an appropriate comment, which was well received. Then: 'Well, do your best for the next hour, and we'll see what happens.'

Another wave of the megaphone, less energetic, told me that the message had got through. We sheered off and regained our station, while from the straggler's funnel a slight thickening of the smoke gave promise of an extra effort. I called to the signalman again.

'Make to the leader: "Straggler is doing his best to close one-mile gap. Will report in an hour's time." Let me know what happens, Pilot. If he drops back any more he'll have to go in.'

'Aye, aye, sir.'

At the end of an hour the position was much the same: he was no farther astern, but the gap was still there. (That extra cloud of smoke had probably been the cook disposing of the tea-leaves.) I signalled: 'Straggler is holding his own, but cannot close the gap at present convoy speed,' to which the reply presently came back: 'Don't want to reduce speed. Remain with him and report position at dusk.' After another bout of prompting over the loud-hailer, during which the old man remained obstinately dumb, acknowledging my remarks by a subtle variety of megaphone waves, we settled down astern to await the outcome.

At dusk the gap was still there, and it was now slowly increasing. In the old days it would have mattered rather a lot; we would probably have been bombed already or, more likely still, the gap in the escort-screen astern would have been noticed by reconnaissance aircraft, and the ships ahead attacked while we were still a mile beyond effective range. But now, with enemy air activity against shipping reduced virtually to nothing and with almost continuous air-cover provided by the R.A.F., the straggler was more of a nuisance than a danger. It was too rough for E-boats to come over—the only thing that could have menaced the position. Of course we were wasted where we were, toiling along astern with this funny little crate: but as it happened we weren't likely to be needed anywhere else, and could afford to play nursemaid to the problem child in the bowler hat.

The provision of air-cover over these East Coast convoys had simplified our job, during the past year or so, to a very great degree, and we were always glad to see the R.A.F. around, whether they were Spitfires wave-hopping at speed, Walruses hovering like mid-Victorian buzzards, or some unidentifiable American machine using his own—his very own—recognition-signals. Out in the Atlantic they were proving invaluable as U-boat spotters and strikers: here they were a steel umbrella over our heads and a most effective deterrent to hit-and-run raids on coastwise shipping.

In short, we wanted their help, we were glad to get it, and we were not ashamed to say so. Need anyone else have been ashamed on our behalf? The question occurs because the fact that the Navy had to have air-cover at many points had latterly been used to promote inter-Service *rivalry*, highly partisan, often ill-natured, and indeed (in some quarters) not rising above the 'I-told-you-so' of the triumphant schoolboy. The wrangle did not affect the men on the job, it was true: it started (and finished) ashore, among people with no better occupation than that of scoring off each other in the correspondence columns of *The Times*: but if it was really the fact that there were in the background persons *of influence* dissipating their energies in such struggles, then the sailors who sailed and the airmen who flew might well feel alarmed and despondent.

When I had made my dusk report the Senior Officer had answered: 'Not worth sending straggler in now. Not an E-boat night, anyway. Stay with him and report position in the morning, by R/T if necessary. Good night.' I had a last interview with the culprit, who was now about two miles astern but not (it seemed) correspondingly repentant, and then settled down to the probable boredom of the dark hours. It turned out a depressing sort of night: the wind and the sea eased off, but the rain made the visibility very poor, and it was difficult to keep in proper touch with this exceptionally sluggish companion. We made our way north yard by yard: the buoys seemed to crawl past, the rain flogged the bridge windows continuously, the straggler yawed and loitered and occasionally went off on some inexplicable course of his own choosing, from which he had to be retrieved, straightened up and started off again. At about midnight there was a short-lived scare: somewhere to seaward of us a trawler opened up at a low-flying aircraft, and the tracer-bullets, passing across our bows not far ahead, were a stimulating reminder of the real thing. Later still a patrol destroyer, cruising southwards rather fast, came close enough to cause two minutes' slightly hectic activity on the bridge. I imagine that, having passed the main body of the convoy ahead of us, they thought the channel would be clear of shipping and had relaxed their look-out somewhat: at any rate the switching on of our navigation-lights resulted in their turning sharply with an impressive wash, and sliding between us and our charge. In full daylight it would have made a pretty picture—'Destroyer manœuvring at speed': in a rain-squall on a dark night it failed to charm.

(At such a moment, thoughts of a deplorable irrelevance present themselves. Though aware, at the critical point, that she would have to alter course within the next five seconds to avoid cutting us in half, I found myself recalling that I had not answered an invitation from this destroyer's Captain to attend a 'select party, with actresses' on the following Saturday night. I decided that I would do, if spared: and would certainly balance the present scare by stinging them for an extra gin—or actress.)

But soon it was daylight again: another dawn, another letting up of tension, as good as ever. When full light came, the last ships of the convoy could only just be seen, hull down ahead of us; and having reported this on R/T I was told to route the straggler independently and then rejoin the convoy as soon as possible. It seemed slightly fatuous to tell my charge to 'proceed independently' when he had been doing little else for the past twenty-four hours, and when I closed him and passed the formal order by loud-hailer it was received with a most expressive smile, and a lifting of the bowler hat which I think demonstrated the victorious rather than the courteous spirit. But at least we had discharged our responsibility and were quit of a trying job: nursing a straggler can never be anything else, whether you are left alone or not.

After taking the most dignified farewell I could muster under the circumstances, and tendering some good advice which probably had as much effect as a blast on the bagpipes, we cracked on speed and presently caught up the convoy: and until the late afternoon we made good progress northward, the weather moderating all the time. There was little to do except maintain station and apply the whip occasionally, so as to keep the tail of the convoy neatly tucked in, and I spent most of the day sleeping or working on the monthly returns which would be due as soon as we got back to harbour. Then ships were reported ahead of us, and identified as the south-bound convoy which we were to take in: and having got permission to leave we crossed over to make the change.

It was, for once, a very small convoy. ('Too many for bridge, not enough for tombola,' I signalled to the Senior Officer of the escort, who considered the remark in silence before replying, 'Take up your correct station.') Once more we steamed down the middle, collecting names and numbers; once more we exchanged greetings with another escort: then we fell in astern, as before, to complete the screen and seal off the rear of the convoy from without and from within.

When we turned south, to start our homeward journey, we had a light wind astern of us and the sun hot on our faces: the sort of perfect cruising weather which, ironically, war seemed to bring far more often than peace. There was, on that lovely afternoon, a sensual pleasure in sea-going, in being afloat on a dark blue-green sea which was now our ally: the ship seemed, for that short spell, to lose its warlike character and to be concerned only with giving us a gentle and effortless passage. I lay at ease on the roof of the bridge, the iron plates hot under my hand when I stretched out my arms: I watched in turn the water slipping past below, the clean line of our bow wave, spreading in infinite creamy ripples, the slow-moving ships ahead, the pale sky which the mast was lazily probing. The sun warmed my whole body through and through, the following breeze took all thrusting out of our forward movement: only an occasional gentle roll, only the ship deep beneath me stirring and lifting to the swell, confirmed that we were held in balance on free and friendly water.

All afternoon and evening we progressed thus, burnished by the sun, blessed by a cool sea, lulled to an absolute security. Nothing obtruded, though sometimes stray movements from inside the dream would touch the surface for a moment—a helm-order louder than usual, a sea-gull enclosed, as if by enchantment, in a triangle of mast, shroud and yard-arm, a look-out's call: then the sun would flow over everything again and the woven peace would be restored. Hours slid by, with a smooth sameness like the water sliding past our keel: the watch was relieved; down below in the waist the hands sunbathed till the light declined, and it was time to darken ship and return to the war again. The bosun's pipe which finally broke the stillness seemed, as it cut the air, to be the first insistent sound within the memory.

Night came like any other night, with its last persuasive hints to the slow movers, its dimmed exchange of signals between escort and escort, its final bedding-down. The head of the convoy faded gradually to nothing, and our view was bounded by a circle of black water, a green-flashing wreck-buoy, and five dark smudges in the gloom ahead. To these we clung, as they clung to each other: straining the eye to preserve an exact distance, watching for the fading-in of a too sharp outline or the fading-out of everything: altering course as the main body altered, but keeping a separate check on our navigation, in case someone ahead slipped up. (A whole convoy had been led astray before now, through playing follow-my-leader with an inexperienced Commodore—five ships aground in half an hour, and the rest backing away like rabbits from the wrong hole. It took a lot of explaining: for all I know it is still being explained.)

By now it was intensely cold. Going up on the bridge at midnight, I was glad of my duffle-coat and of the brew of cocoa which I had been counting on as the watch changed. But already, after no more than two hours of darkness, the night had brought a query.

'No. 25 Buoy should be in sight by now,' said the Gunner, as he prepared to go off watch. 'In fact we really ought to be up to it already. But perhaps it's not working. I don't think the convoy can have missed it; their course has been O.K. That's the position, anyway,' he added, with the cheerfulness of the man to whom the position will, in thirty seconds' time, mean less than nothing.

'The ship may be anywhere, in fact,' said the First Lieutenant, who was taking over the watch. 'Fry's cocoa, and all's to hell. I suppose you'll be turning in quite comfortably just the same?'

'Yes,' said the Gunner. 'Good night.'

'Good night, Quisling.'

Listening in the darkness, on one wing of the bridge, I smiled to myself. That end-of-the-watch feeling was familiar, and unalterable.

The Gunner tramped off below, to his camp-bed under the wardroom table: the First Lieutenant received and acknowledged the routine report from the Petty Officer of the watch—'Guns' crews and look-outs correct: galley fire burning low.' The Midshipman, his head under the chart-table screen, answered my questions about our course and the tidal set affecting it. Time passed, and No. 25 Buoy still did not appear. Since, in this particular corner, we would have to go a long way before we ran into serious trouble, I was not worried—yet: but I was curious to know what had happened and how we had come to miss the buoy, as I believed we had. Visibility was inclined to be patchy, but not as patchy as all that, and if the light were extinguished (which seemed the most likely explanation), I should have to report it to the shore authority.

Presently: 'I thought I saw it a moment ago,' said the First Lieutenant. 'But it's gone again. Probably a ship showing a light by mistake. This is just about the time they make up the galley fire.'

The signalman joined in suddenly. 'Flashing light ahead, sir . . . right among the port column. It seems to be irregular, though.'

'We'll see in a minute. It may have been damaged earlier on.'

But we didn't see in a minute. Fifteen of them passed, and still we were not up to the light nor, apparently, any nearer to it. Now and then I thought I saw it, now and then the sighting was confirmed by someone else on the bridge: but uncannily, we didn't seem to be catching it up. Then, very slowly, a ship ahead of us drew out of its column and turned to port, crossing our bows. She looked as if she were in trouble of some sort, and she appeared to be signalling to us: single flashes, curiously low down, came in our direction, though they didn't make any sense—they were simply spaced at regular ten-second intervals. It was the Midshipman who, when we were about five cables off and still wondering, jumped to the right conclusion.

'That's the buoy flashing, sir!' he exclaimed suddenly. 'It's caught up amidships—you can see the shape of it against the hull. They must have been pulling it along with them all the time.'

This was the correct answer, as the ship herself confirmed when we got within hailing distance. It had just been one of those things. . . . Miscalculating the strength of the tide at one turn of the channel, she had got foul of the buoy and for the past hour had been towing it down the fairway, flashing industriously all the time. Number 25 Buoy had been taken for a ride.

When I asked the ship why she had not stopped immediately the buoy became attached, instead of plugging away until she was firmly tethered, back came the reply, 'I thought I could shake it off if I steamed hard enough'—an answer which seemed to contain, deep within it, some of the elements of a nightmare. Now, however, she was stopped, a few yards from us. Her dark grey shape overtopped our bridge, and the flashing light alongside advertised her indifferent navigation every ten seconds, with what must have been mortifying persistence. An unwise but habitual flippancy made me call out to her: 'Well, you're certainly right on the swept channel now.' This uproarious sally was coldly received and shortly afterwards a man climbed down and tied a sack over the lamp. I felt tacitly rebuked by this manœuvre—as was no doubt the intention when the order was given.

Meanwhile the convoy felt its way slowly past us, while I got in touch with the leading destroyer and explained the situation. I suggested that the ship be taken in tow then and there (part of the buoy-cable had now become entangled with her rudder) and presently I received an answering signal: 'Instruct the tug to take her in tow, and remain as close escort yourself.' Finding the tug (which had wandered off, as usual, to a safe night-position well clear of the convoy), passing the order, guiding her to the derelict, standing by while the tow was passed, and leading them both back to the channel and the next buoy—all this took time: we must have been a good ten miles astern of the main body when we finally made our start in the right direction, and the speed of towing, with a ship of this size, was very slow. After a session in the chart-house, I had just made the mournful calculation that we were unlikely to get home by the following night, even if the tow held until the end, when we had an unexpected respite in the form of another signal from the leader: 'Make contact with the trawler, tell her to take over escort, and rejoin the convoy.'

Why the Senior Officer had changed his mind I didn't know, though certainly we were better occupied escorting the convoy than looking after a single ship, and the trawler could more easily be spared. At any rate it was good news, once the complications were accepted. These were the normal ones attending this sort of manœuvre at night, but they meant a certain amount of extra care: the time was now 2 a.m.. the night at its blackest, and to catch up the convoy, overtake half of it, and find the trawler (which might or might not be in its assigned position) was less easy than a lot of other things. But we cracked on speed with a

will—anything was better than seeping along at nought knots at the tail
of a towing-party—and set out to chase the main body.

It took us a hard-running hour to catch them, and in the end they
came up with startling suddenness—an untidy cluster of ships, no more
than blurred smudges, ahead of us, where a second before had been a
blank horizon and safe sea-room. I stared at them through my glasses,
trying to determine which column was which and to work out the angle
I was approaching at; but there was really no satisfactory answer to be
had—they had lost their strict daytime formation, and to overtake at
speed we would have to dodge and trust to luck. At the moment they
almost seemed to be coming towards us, darkening outlines on a pale
sea. I swung wide to starboard, to give them a safe clearance, and
straight away another one came up dead ahead, a low-built straggler (of
the type we called a 'flat-iron', almost impossible to see in the dark)
nowhere near his proper column and steering no particular course
either. It seemed a good moment to reduce speed: clearly the ships at the
tail of the convoy were jogging along independently, safe from father's
eye, and their various positions were quite unpredictable. We eased
down to two or three knots more than the convoy speed, and then
began to feel our way past, ship by ship, looking for the trawler.

We found her in the end, though I don't really know why. On a
dark night a trawler looks like any other ship until you are close
up to her, and we must have sighted and examined a dozen likely
candidates—approaching them gently so as not to alarm them into
ramming tactics, keeping careful watch for other ships nearby,
extricating ourselves again when the current choice turned out to be
something quite different—before we finally got the right one. But when
we *did* find her, her indignation at being disturbed, and her clamorous
disbelief of the orders which would send her back at least fifteen miles
and keep her at sea for an extra night, almost made up for our trouble.
At one point I thought she would crack the diaphragm of her loud-
hailer. But she sheered off in the end, turning round very slowly like a
child doing something it dislikes but doesn't dare to refuse; and soon
afterwards it was dawn again, and time to whip in the stragglers, before
a fine sunrise brought some warmth to the bridge and made breakfast
sound good and taste better. It had been a long night, but taking it
altogether we had got off lightly, from a situation which might well have
become the extreme of boredom.

We carried a strong tide with us all that morning, and by late
afternoon we were near enough to our base for me to ask permission to
leave the convoy and go home independently. There were no ships to be

taken in, and (this time) no tug or trawler to accompany us, which made it very different from the usual end-of-convoy manœuvre. For generally there was a merchant ship or two due to break off with us, which of course had to be escorted the whole way in; and for this purpose the tug and trawler came under my orders. It was here that the fun would start.

In theory the three of us should emerge as a separate flotilla, whose constituent units I could move about like pawns on a chess-board, and which would respond to my touch like a restive horse; but it was never as straightforward as that, and 'restive' remained the only operative word. It was their natural ambition, when we were nearing home, to slip away at speed and leave me holding the baby; and to this end every artifice was employed, with a diligence which, used against the enemy, might well have shortened the war. Since early morning they would have been hiding themselves behind other ships, dodging my signals, and generally playing stupid in the hope that I would give up and do the job myself. But it was nearer home, when we were actually preparing to leave, that the more active and less scrupulous part of the operation would begin, and close supervision became vital.

Possibly I might go below for a few minutes, for a cup of tea and a change into harbour rig. Without fail, when I returned to the bridge, the trawler would be edging away towards home, and the tug increasing speed as discreetly as its vast billows of smoke allowed. After a sharp word to the tug, designed to discourage any such initiative, we would call up the trawler, intending to signal: 'Take up your proper station and remain with our portion of convoy.' Visibility, at this point, unaccountably deteriorated. For a long time no answer would be forthcoming: then they would start giving us a succession of 'W's" (code-letter for 'Train your light properly'); and then, our signal being spelt out with immense care and precision by a hard-breathing Yeoman, they would begin to read it very slowly—missing words, asking for them to be repeated, sprinkling 'W's' here and there like coarse interjections. All the time, of course, they were slowly fading out of sight, contriving to lay a smoke-screen between the two ships which further complicated the signalling. Finally we would crack on speed, and come too close for them not to acknowledge the signal and to act on it: then, cursing all individualists, we would turn about and go back to the merchant ships. And then we would start looking round for the tug.

Occasionally, in the street, one sees a harassed-looking woman trying to take half a dozen dogs, of assorted breeds and sizes, for a walk in a given direction. It is a grim and discouraging spectacle: often she will age ten years between two lamp-posts.

Getting four merchant ships, a trawler and a tug to go the way you want them to, at a level speed, was sometimes rather like that.

This time, however, we had no one but ourselves to think about, and there were no complications to delay us. Increasing to the maximum permissible speed, we darted off homewards, cutting corners, whipping round buoys, passing everything on the road. An hour later we were tied up to the oiler, and looking forward to all-night leave; in the wardroom the mail was being distributed, in the rough proportion of the more junior the officer the greater the number of his letters. I myself had a couple of bills, and the Midshipman, as usual, a positive mound of assorted envelopes, all to himself. Then the quartermaster knocked on the door, looking for the Officer-of-the-Day.

'Signal boat coming alongside, sir.'

I opened the sealed envelope when it was handed to me and then looked round a wardroom which had suddenly become attentive.

'Not so bad,' I said, when I had glanced over the pink slip. 'We've got tonight in, anyway. All-night leave tonight, convoy again tomorrow morning. We'll have to start about ten o'clock.'

'It's like going to the office every morning,' said the First Lieutenant, after a pause. 'Backwards and forwards. One of these days I'm going to put in for a bowler hat and a season ticket.'

That was one routine convoy trip, with nothing special to it. It could be (and was) multiplied *ad infinitum* with only the smallest variations. Obviously, as Number One implied, the job had an element of boredom in it: you could be interested in the first twenty times or so, but after that. . . . If anyone, reading this far, has not already asked, 'But where is the enemy?' he may ask it now, as we ourselves did every time we came back from a featureless trip. Broadly speaking, it could be said that the enemy simply was not there. The East Coast used to be a hot assignment, earning all its reputation and most of its lurid nicknames, but that was quite a long time ago: for the past year or more it had been extraordinarily quiet, and the very occasional air-raids, E-boat sorties, and attempts at mine-laying only served to show up the general flatness of the whole. Of course that did not alter the sea-going part of it, which demanded the same care and the same endurance whatever was or was not going on besides; but it was a let-up as far as one kind of attention was concerned, and from my point of view it cut, by half, the worry and strain that necessarily went with the job.

There *were* occasional variations, however. Certain things claimed the attention and stayed in the memory, adding subtlety or shadow or some fresh and vivid significance to the old picture. There was the dark

night when some enemy aircraft overhead started looking for the
convoy, dropping flares with a leisurely Teutonic thoroughness which,
it seemed, *must* be successful. The flares started quite far out to sea:
they crossed ahead of us, they went step by step round the stern, and
then out to seawards again, but they never quite landed in the middle,
and the convoy slipped by anonymously after all. Up on the bridge,
aware—in myself and in the people close round me—of the constraint
and tension of Action Stations, aware of the coxswain craning his neck
for a quick look skywards when he had the ship steady on her course, I
had found myself privately betting against that piece of good fortune.

For the crews of the merchant-ships on our beam it was a test of
nerve which one could feel going on all the time. Up and down those
long lines there must have been scores of fingers ready on the trigger,
scores of minds speculating as to whether it wouldn't be better to open
up now instead of waiting for the aircraft mechanically crossing and
weaving overhead to start their bombing. One urge of impatience or of
fear, one single tracer-bullet loosed off for luck, would have given us all
away. Afterwards, it seemed natural that no single gunner in forty-odd
ships had failed in the test or had played his own hand: at the time, the
temptation and the likelihood had seemed inhumanly strong.

There were occasional bouts of vile weather, that spring and summer,
as unpleasant (if not as long-lasting) as anything I had met in the
Atlantic. There were many times when, from a convoy labouring hours
late against wind and tide, we would come driving in for home, rolling,
side-slipping, the glistening decks shaking themselves free of water and
then falling away again for another sluicing plunge. There was,
especially, one very heavy gale in a harbour crowded with ships:
normally the shelter was perfect, but this was not normal, and things
started to go wrong. A destroyer broke adrift, and crowded down on
top of another: the tug sent to extricate her was crushed between the two
of them, and put completely out of action: the second destroyer began
to drag her own moorings and menaced a third which only just
managed, by superb seamanship, to slip out before it was too late, and
to keep clear of the *crescendo* of trouble which was developing.

It was distressing to watch the gradual deterioration of this scene,
from order to disorder, until at the height of the gale the harbour
seemed to be verging on irreparable chaos: the three destroyers in a
perilous tangle, the wrecked tug caught in between, two other tugs
cruising up and down trying to get to grips with the situation, a ship's
whaler adrift and battered to pieces against the pier, a cluster of small
craft which had nosed upstream into a creek for shelter: and all the time

this incredible screaming wind which seemed to be scooping up whole sheets of the surface of the water and tossing them bodily against the quay.

Out at a midstream buoy, in the very centre of the fury, we were ready for anything—steam up, coxswain at the wheel, myself on the bridge waiting for the cable to part or the buoy to break adrift from its moorings. For more than an hour—the worst hour—we steamed slow ahead against the weight and thrust of the wind, taking the strain off the buoy which, barely visible in the spray-filled air, was tugged and battered without a moment's respite. Both the moorings and our own cable held: towards evening the wind veered and dropped, and the harbour returned to normal again, in an almost shame-faced way. But the afternoon remained in the memory, a reminder that ships, no matter how securely berthed, are never quite beyond the reach of the sea.

There were other occasional crises: unfair strokes of fortune, things that went wrong for ourselves or for other people. There was the time that the gyro-compass went haywire, not suddenly but by a treacherous creeping action which deceived the Quartermaster and the Officer-of-the-Watch into steering, in the end, not less than sixty degrees off our proper course. Only the unexpected appearance of a very rare buoy, which I myself had never seen before and indeed had only heard about vaguely, gave us a clue as to where the ship had wandered in the meantime. There was the night the steering-gear broke down, and we kept our course and station for several hours by the tiresome operation known as 'steering by main engines'—that is, keeping one screw turning at a fixed rate and adjusting the speed of the other so as to control the swing of the ship. It was interesting to begin with—like threading needle after needle for someone you love. But in the end . . .

I remember, too, once surveying the violent aftermath of a collision between a corvette and a destroyer, and being shown over the corvette's damage in detail—the mess-deck cut in half, the torn plates, the wires hanging like entrails. She really was a horrifying sight: the destroyer's bows had gone deep into her, and almost out the other side. Only the presence of mind of the Officer-of-the-Watch, who had pressed the alarm-bell half a minute before the crash, had prevented a startling loss of life. The mess-deck had been crammed with sleeping men when that alarm-bell went. Easy to remember, also, was the dejected face of her Captain, as he told me how it happened. He was blameless: it was just one of those things: but that was the least important part of it. I touched wood when I saw that corvette: having one of my own to lose, equally vulnerable and equally loved.

One thing didn't change in this corner of the war or in any other: perhaps it is worth remarking on it in passing and letting it go at that. Now and then, up and down the coast, ships were sunk and survivors had to be collected. It was hard to find any variety here, at this stage of the war, and, as I have said, it need not be enlarged on in detail: but here and there some superb or pitiful act, some exceptional ugliness or some odd warping of the horror, would strike a new note and prove that the theme was not yet exhausted.

There were plenty of things on the tonic side, too. A clutch of E-boats getting thoroughly beaten up, or a succession of really big convoys coming in, as good as when they left the other side, crammed with food or war materials. There was an occasional glorious circus of a night-action, with mine-sweepers, patrol-trawlers, corvettes, destroyers, M.L.s, and motor-gunboats, all having a smack at the same wilting bunch of E-boats, while an R.A.F. rescue launch, somewhere on the outer fringe, tried to squeeze between people's legs and sneak the prey for their own branch.

One very satisfying (and more orthodox) show which the R.A.F. laid on for us, one afternoon, was the shooting down of a high-flying reconnaissance 'plane almost over the convoy. It had come in from seaward, so high as to be almost invisible, but betrayed by a lengthening streak of vapour astern of it. As it crossed the coast another pair of streaks—British fighters—came hurtling in from the westward to intercept. The enemy 'plane turned sharply, the fighters set a course to cut him off, their trails thickening as they increased speed: the three streaks converged, and blended into one, and then there was a sudden burst of orange flame from the very tip of the vapour-trail, and the enemy 'plane fell, twisting and turning, growing larger, taking on the hard outlines of the Dornier, until it finally dropped into the sea ahead of us and became smoke and vapour once more.

There were a few other departures from the normal, which served to give the job a saving degree of variation. Sometimes, when nothing special promised, we would take passengers on a trip with us—R.A.F. officers, for instance, whose nearly incomprehensible slang would gain currency in the wardroom, so that for a few days we would all talk freely of 'blacks' and 'binds' and 'pranging'. (The Midshipman, handing over the watch, was once heard to say, 'Just keep on stooging around at nought feet.' I did not really object to this, but his later use of the expression 'Glamour-pants' to describe an attractive young woman of my acquaintance was *not* approved.) Possibly, for further variety, our guests would be officers from the Intelligence Division, whom we christened 'Warrant Spies', and filled up with careless and colourful information which they would have no difficulty in proving false as soon as they returned home. But whoever they were, we enjoyed having them: a new face and voice was always a welcome diversion, in the cramped and limited world on board.

Ocasionally, we were given a short holiday between trips, at a rarely visited Northern port: a five-day respite which we would fill in by painting ship throughout, polishing every conceivable metal surface or object, and emerging at the end like a newly hatched butterfly, to dazzle the flotilla and provoke jealous signals when we came up harbour again. At other times, when there was nothing 'operational' to do, we would go out on a shoot with the destroyers—a humble role, this, consisting of following in their wake like a well-trained terrier and getting in an occasional shot at a half-demolished target. More fun were our own flotilla manœuvres, when five or six corvettes would proceed to sea in company and perform prodigies of evolution, some of them in the Fleet Signal Book, others (as the Yeoman would patiently explain) not, and never likely to be either. But at least it was a family affair, and the signal '*Winger* astern of station', which the Senior Officer appeared to keep bent on to the halyard, ready for immediate use, was no more than a paternal scolding administered in sorrow rather than in anger, and received by everyone on the bridge in the same spirit.

Lastly, among the things designed to keep us on our toes and out of the nuthouse, there were such unclassifiable oddments as the bomb that near-missed us, one dark night in the middle watch. It happened without any warning. There was a loud metallic clang, a golden rain of sparks, a lot of dirty water, and finally the First Lieutenant's brooding voice as he wrote in the deck-log: 'Near-missed by medium-weight bomb, thirty yards off starboard bow.' But whose bomb? The sky was full of friendly aircraft at the time, and when the convoy, incensed, opened fire in a vaguely vertical direction, it became full of correct recognition-flares as well, with hardly a second's delay. Suspicious? I suppose it *might* have been an enemy intruder-'plane mixing in with our out-going bombers, but somehow I doubt it—a doubt shared by the ship's company, who seemed to be convinced that it was one of ours jettisoning its bombs (or, as one able-seaman put it tersely: 'Too bloody lazy to fly to Berlin.') But we were none the worse for it, since there were no casualties and no damage—'if' (in the words of my report) 'a slight and temporary cooling of inter-Service relations be excepted.'

It was not, by the way, a very big bomb—to start with. But (defying the laws of perspective) it tended to grow bigger the farther away it got.

About a fortnight later someone at the Naval Club said to me: 'I hear you were near-missed by an eight-thousand-pounder.'

It is never easy to scotch that kind of rumour: in fact, hardly worth trying.

I returned an evasive answer. It was not too evasive either way, however.[1]

But mostly, as I have said, the job was purely a routine one, without variations even as mild as the foregoing: a series of blank patrols and uneventful coastal convoys which, for me, boiled down to taking the ship out, bringing the ship in, waiting for something to happen and keeping out of trouble in the meantime.

None of us could really complain: we had volunteered for boredom as well as for action, and as far as I was concerned the actual *sea-going* part of it was an incomparable way of passing the war. I am not warlike, though if chance had placed me, for example, in my younger brother's job—Royal Artillery, till his death in North Africa—I would no doubt have made some kind of a soldier, though not as good a one as he. But luck put me in the Navy: the rest followed: and it was impossible to deny that there were some parts of my job I should be sorry to lose, when it was all over. If, for instance, our peace-time way of life promoted half the comradeship, laughter, and self-respecting pride of endeavour which going to sea in corvettes had done, I should be very lucky—and so would Great Britain. This feeling and this experience (however widespread they may be) of course do not go an inch of the way towards 'justifying' war—i.e. making it worth while for its own sake; but they certainly affect, in a vital degree, the day-to-day business of hanging on until the war is won.

I loathe war and all its works, with my whole heart: it is wasteful, confused, lying, and often futile; but the Naval side of it was none of these things, and since the war has to be got through somehow, this was by far the best way of getting through it.

It seemed, also, to be one of the fastest. At this job, the time flew by so fast that when one tried to recall a certain month, even in the recent past, it might have been missed out altogether, so swiftly had it vanished from the memory. I had taken over the ship in the early spring: a few times up and down the coast, a few spells of leave, a fully established confidence, and winter was round again—the fifth of the war, my fourth at sea, and a most familiar testing-time for ships and for men.

[1] Further example of a baseless rumour: 'I hear that unless your requestmen can produce a copy of *East Coast Corvette* you won't even see them at the table.'

But as a final sweetener before it started, I was promoted to Lieutenant-Commander. Since I had the job and the ship I wanted, I had not been worrying overmuch about my slow progress up the scale; but it was pleasant to leave, at last, the ranks of the Dead End Kids (there are an awful lot of Lieutenants, R.N.V.R., in the Navy) and to get once more within striking distance of my friends, all of whom seemed to be either Wing-Commanders or Colonels.

5 PEOPLE

To start with a very small person.

I saw my son at intervals just long enough for him to record a perceptible change on each occasion. Leave—in short and fleeting spells—came fairly regularly, and each time I was home was marked by another stage in his progress: sleeping, rolling over, sitting up, crawling, steaming round on all fours, standing unaided, walking, sucking his teeth like a disgruntled A.B. Other people's children are always boring, and there is no reason why mine should be an exception, so I will not enlarge further on the details of the growing-up process, and not at all on what I felt about him. But I found him absorbing to watch, apart from anything else. He was yet another reason why it was, each time, good to come home and sad to leave it.

It sometimes seems that this whole war is nothing but saying good-bye, usually in grisly circumstances—on black winter mornings, at railway stations, outside dock gates in the rain: circumstances rendered more grisly still by one's knowledge of what waits close ahead—the cold, the exhaustion, the boredom. But it is easy to forget all these things during leave, if you are helped. Women are remarkable in this respect—in their bravery, their disguise of emotion, their studious ignoring of time; they can fashion a centre of warmth and peace, giving it their whole care although they know it can be enjoyed only for a little space, and this they maintain secure, under the very shadow of dispersal. They spend themselves to the utmost limit when one is there, knowing that zero hour—the end of one's leave—means a kind of bankrupt solitude, a total loneliness, for themselves.

Or is this only one woman? I hope not.

Indeed I hope not. I was married four days after the war broke out: a war which (particularly when I was on long Atlantic convoys) I do not think I could have supported without a personal background of an exceptional quality. Innumerable other people must find, at home, the same source of strength, and must be sustained in the same way by a security and a happiness they can count on in every conceivable circumstance. What really beats me is how anyone, in this bloody war, can do without it. It is, of course, a matter of individual capacity and inclination. Some people, naturally self-sufficient, seem to prefer a leave-period consisting of a few days' full-calibre racketing followed by a recuperative trip to sea—and indeed, thirty years ago (or ten, anyway) it might even have suited me: but now it would be quite inadequate, from any point of view whatsoever. As far as I am concerned, war can be made tolerable by a background of love and sanity: anything else would bring the machine to a dead stop.

I have said that I hope other people, who may need this sort of help, are able to count on it in their home life. This is probably true for the majority, though from personal knowledge I know it is not the universal rule. Now and again I have to see someone 'privately'—that is, a rating requests an interview alone with me, free from witnesses and the formality of the quarter-deck, and almost always it is something gone wrong with a marriage which prompts the request. The unfaithful wife, the bastard child, sexual maladjustment, the wife who 'turns funny' after a child is born—these are all sad variants of the same theme. Much of the trouble is due to sheer ignorance, much more to lack of imagination. But war-time separation is itself a potent factor, working (as it were) against our side, and sailors, determinedly sentimental about women, are sometimes let down.

'When I went home last time, sir,' said a young rating who had asked me about a legal separation, 'I found the wife sitting about in one of those hotel lounges, drinking port with some chaps she'd never seen before.' I saw the whole woman in that single phrase—blast her.

'Blast her,' because so much depended on her—as on all women at home. Individual morale falls to nothing if there is a doubt of that kind nagging away all the time, and for me to answer such a story by saying that there is 'probably nothing in it' is a foolish evasion. From the only important angle—the *instinct* (as against the physical fact) of faithfulness—there is everything in it.

Morale is made up of odd things, some of them trivial to a degree, some of them paradoxical in the way they manifest themselves. The *general* level of morale in the Navy is so high that it is something no one worries about; but—here is the paradox—it is high because the average sailor is often more of an individual than a member of a unit, however happy and efficient that unit may be: he keeps intact his prejudices, his humours, his stubborn self-respect, and he makes it blessedly clear that when he does his best he expects due recognition of the fact, and a parallel effort, from his superiors.

Here is a very short snatch of dialogue which I think illustrates this high individual morale perfectly—though it is only fair to say that so far everyone I have told it to says that it illustrates gross insubordination and nothing else at all.

The scene is the bridge on a very unpleasant night, with the spray washing over and everyone, from the Officer-of-the-Watch down to bridge-messenger, inclined to be rather sick of the sea.

> *Look-out* (reporting some lights seen with extreme difficulty through the scud): 'Ship on the port beam, sir!'
> *Bad-tempered Officer-of-the-Watch* (very crossly): 'How do you know it's a ship?'
> *Look-out* (fed-up at last): 'Too near to be a horse and cart, sir.'

Does anyone else agree that this classic back-answer indicates an admirable spirit of independence? I may be on the wrong lines entirely, but that is what it demonstrates to me. The man knew that he would be punished for it—that is the whole point: but he had established the fact that when he was doing his job under trying circumstances (it was a *very* black and dirty night), he wasn't going to be mucked about by a harassed officer looking for someone on whom to work off his bad temper. To establish that personal integrity, to prove himself a man and not a spiritless and unresisting block of wood, was judged to be worth the punishment, whatever it was: and I am prepared to bet that that seaman would be a better man to have at one's side in a tight corner than any yes-man accustomed to turn away wrath by producing a smile and a soft answer on every single occasion.

(*Note.* These are unorthodox views, I know, and I may well be the only officer in the Navy to hold them; but there it is. It may be added that they do not indicate the general level of discipline on board H.M.S. *Winger*, which was not the ship it happened in. Nor, incidentally, should they be taken as a reliable guide for the future behaviour of look-outs, in any ship under my command.)

Here is another short exchange, funny in itself, and demonstrating the same sort of independence on a less provocative plane:

> *Captain* (to defaulter): 'The evidence is that you got drunk when ashore, went to the local Y.M.C.A., got into bed while still smoking a

cigarette, fell asleep, and set your bed on fire. What have you to say?'
Defaulter: 'It's a lie, sir! The bed was on fire when I got into it.'

It seems to me that enshrined in that answer is the same refusal to
accept defeat, against all the odds, as has stood this country in such
very good stead for threequarters of the war so far. I think it is a native
product. For instance, I cannot imagine a German soldier or sailor
thinking up an excuse like that, or not being practically crucified for
producing it. That may sound like patriotism of a provincial sort, but I
believe it to be true. In any case, as long as we have that kind of
humorous self-reliance to draw upon in case of need, we can leave most
aspects of morale to take care of themselves. They will not suffer.

The Royal Navy produces 'types', as does every other walk of life: it
also produces remarkable *men*, who, while conforming to these types
bring along their own special brand of loyalty and devotion to
illuminate and adorn their respective jobs. They are not machines: they
are complete individuals, reliable to an infinite degree, and often
prompted by loyalty to the Navy, and love of the ship they are serving
in, to work and fight and endure beyond all reasonable expectation.
Much of it is training, of course, but there must always be something
else—a spark, a continuous thread of inspiration; and it seems that
there always is.

One can appraise and admire the types as well as the men, knowing
that one is reasonably certain of meeting them in any ship one serves in.
Take, for example, the coxswain of a small ship, a corvette or a
destroyer. A good coxswain is a jewel: most of them *are* jewels: they
have been rigorously trained as such, and they have undertaken to play
the part themselves as well. The coxswain can make all the difference on
board. As the senior rating in the ship, responsible for much of its
discipline and administration, he has a profound effect in producing a
happy and efficient ship's company. Usually he is a 'character', to use
an overworked but explicit word: that is, a strong personality who
would make himself felt in any surroundings, and who is, in his present
world, a man of exceptional weight and influence. He keeps an eye on
everything, from the rum issue to the cleanliness of hammocks, from the
chocolate ration to the length of the side-whiskers of the second-class
stokers. It is his duty to find things out, however obscure or
camouflaged they may be—a case of bullying, a case of smuggled beer,
a case of 'mechanized dandruff' in the seamen's mess—and either set
them right or else report them forthwith to a higher authority. In the

majority of cases, as might be expected, he is fully competent to set them right himself, and can be trusted to do so.

He is the friend of everyone on board, and a good friend too—if they want him to be, and if they deserve it: failing that, he makes a very bad enemy. He knows the regulations off by heart: he knows when to cite them, and when to turn the page quickly. He is above all, a jealous guardian—of naval tradition, of the ship's good name, of the Captain's reputation and his peace of mind as well.

He is always an unmistakable figure on board: a purely naval product, and one of its very best.

Somewhere at the other end of the scale—in one sense—you have that legendary character, the Three Badge A.B. 'Three Badge' because he has three good-conduct badges, denoting at least thirteen years in the Navy: and 'A.B.' because—well, either he hasn't the brain and energy to pass for Leading Seaman, or he doesn't welcome responsibility, or he 'likes it where he is', or for any other reason which can keep a man an able seaman and nothing more till the end of his days in the Service. He may sound dull and stupid, but he is rarely that; more often than not he knows it all, like the coxswain—but from a different angle.

The 'angle' is something between laziness, lack of ambition and a self-respect inseparable from long service and patiently acquired seamanship. Give him a job and he will work his way through it: not with any flash display of energy, like one of those jumped-up young Petty Officers, but at a careful and steady pace, which escapes both commendation and criticism. He can go on all day like that: he often has to, thanks to the First Lieutenant, so why should he break his heart trying? And (assuming that time doesn't matter) you will be able to rely on the job when it is finished. If it is a bit of painting it will be smooth and economical, if it is a wire splice it will hold till doomsday. That's because, lagging astern or not, he is still a seaman, with the seaman's contempt for a botched job. No length of service, disfigured conduct-sheet or lack of promotion can alter that.

As might be expected, he 'knows it all' in the other sense too, habitually steering within an inch of the law with the straightest of faces and an absolute confidence that, one way or another, he will always get away with it. He can return on board time after time, not strictly sober but not drunk enough to attract attention. He knows his rights, and the way to get them: at the table (i.e. when appearing as a requestman or defaulter) he can extract the utmost advantage from every stage of the proceedings, and if the reporting officer makes any sort of a slip he will give him hell—in a respectfully injured way, of course, but hell all the same. In that sense he needs careful watching, though that is not really a drawback. It is, in fact, the reverse: by rendering necessary a strict attention to procedure and the letter of the law, he keeps everyone up to the mark. He is, in his own way, a guardian of naval tradition just as much as a senior rating, safeguarding the proprieties from mixed motives, but safeguarding them none the less.

He is certainly an engaging type, but of course there *are* others, just as engaging, who don't need watching like a hawk the whole time. If you want an example of alert intelligence in the Navy, a young signalman, interested in his job and keen to get ahead, is probably the best specimen. From the very nature of his work, he knows more about the ship and her movements than any other rating; and he has the opportunity of learning much more besides. He sees almost every signal that comes in, on a very wide variety of subjects ranging from the First Lord's anniversary greetings to the provision of tropical underwear for Wrens. He spends long hours up on the bridge, in the centre of things, where he has the best opportunity of talking to his officers and of picking up fresh ideas. He learns flotilla routines, the types and names and movements of other ships. The job of signalling itself enlarges his vocabulary—he deals in words, and they are the currency of intelligence. He can often acquire, too, a formidable knowledge of navigation: the charts are always there for him to study, and if, as is usual, he has an inquiring mind, he makes good use of the chance, aided by an officer who is probably only too glad to find someone interested—someone, moreover, who can often be most helpful in supplying information quickly and accurately at an awkward moment.

Watch-keeping is a boring job. Signalmen are usually talkative, retailing (among other things) the cream of the crop of rumours put out by the galley-wireless: their talk makes the time pass a bit quicker, and that, God knows, is something on the credit side at sea. When I was in a corvette doing Atlantic escort duty, burdened with a standing middle watch for nearly eighteen months on end, their companionship often made all the difference between a spell of rank boredom and a tolerable watch. I have had something of an affection for the Signal Branch ever since.

If I have singled out these—coxswain, able seaman, and signalman—for special mention, let no one think that they are the first and the rest are nowhere. This is no place for a catalogue or a List of Complement, but certainly a lot of people go to the running of a ship: not least the engine-room ratings and stokers, who attract less attention but whose vigilance is essential and who can take as much pride in their work as any seaman. It leaves out, too, the Telegraphist and Coding branches: unobtrusive, also, working out of sight at a job largely routine and often intolerably boring, but vital to the efficient working of the ship, both in action and otherwise. And when reckoning up these 'out-of-sight' ratings and their value to a smooth-running whole, the contribution of the wardroom stewards should not be left out of account: a good steward can make or mar a wardroom and, consequently, the life on board of any officer, whose exacting job does need a certain minimum of comfort and service if he is to be free to concentrate on his own specialized duty to the ship.

I have met people who are ready to argue this latter point, on 'privileged-class', 'life-of-luxury' lines: but I think it can be fairly said that an officer who has the immense responsibility of a ship on his hands for eight hours a day should be relieved of *all* other worries, as far as is humanly possible.

Speaking from the personal angle, I certainly found it essential in my own case, and I was very lucky in this respect. My servant made an enormous difference to my comfort and well-being at sea—always on hand at the right moment, producing cups of tea or extra scarves when they were most needed, fashioning by his personal care and loyalty something like a separate home for me, where I could be at ease whenever I wanted. His efforts, in harbour, even included an embarrassed search for a special brand of infants' food, at a time of local shortage at home: which, since he was a bachelor and a rather shy sort of man in any case, was devotion of a high order.

If anyone thinks that to be a naval steward is not a man's job, let him think again. Better still, let him come to sea and try serving a hot meal to six officers in the middle of a gale of wind, struggling against his own seasickness in a rolling, tossing, over-heated pantry, and still finding the strength to administer to their needs and to make them comfortable on and off watch. It needs a man to do all that: stewards take it in their stride.

These are some of the men who go to sea in corvettes. They are all sailors: they and the Merchant Navy are the same breed. In this war they have done work not to be measured in terms of earning money or medals: they have done their utmost, and left it at that.

When the war is over the vast majority of them will be returning to civil life. Of the Royal Navy 'regulars', also, some are certain to be axed from the Service and will have to fit into the same framework. They have deserved a lot in this war; they will be entitled to present the bill at the end of it. Are they going to get a fair settlement, or are they going on the scrap-heap again?

Let us start by forgetting fairness and straight-dealing, and reducing the question to its lowest level, in terms of pure national self-interest. These men may one day be needed again; but whether they are needed or not, their continued loyalty and love of country is a national asset, to be prized above very many other things. It is worth keeping that loyalty: that is to say, a fair deal will pay a dividend which one day we may want to cash, and it will be as well to make sure that we have it at our disposal.

If we default, if we cheat, if we just forget and turn our backs, we may be caught short when the wheel comes round again.

We are learning that now, to our cost and embarrassment. Strikes—in the coal-mines, the engineering shops, among the dockers—are part of that cost: absenteeism and slacking are others. I abhor war-time strikes: it is, to me, ridiculous that the strike-weapon should be taken away from one section of the community—the Services—and left for free use in the hands of the rest; but, by God, you can understand how strikes come about! The dictum 'As ye sow, so shall ye reap', covers them exactly, and it is idle to look beyond that. Many of these men who strike now were treated like dirt for years before the war: almost literally like dirt—they were tipped and shovelled out of the way and on to a sort of slag-heap of unemployed and unemployables. They didn't learn love of country from that. . . .

Now they have power, almost paramount power, and they use it to square up the account. It isn't patriotism, certainly (the system which pauperized them wasn't patriotism either): it is not in the end even common sense; but it is assuredly human nature. The argument seems, to them, crystal clear: why should they listen to appeals to their better feelings now, when they wore their hearts sick *making* those appeals—futile and neglected ones—in the lean and seedy years between the wars?

Why indeed should they *have* any better feelings? They are working at the same jobs as in peace-time, jobs which present no challenge to their courage, no real incentive to selfless endurance: naturally they fall back on peace-time tactics whenever a chance of 'improvement' comes their way.

Incidentally, it is the merchant seamen especially who have risen above the peace-time grudge they might well bear, and have glorified their calling by an unmerited generosity. Their valour and spirit have heaped coals of fire: no class in Britain was treated worse, or was more brutally disregarded, than merchant seamen in the early nineteen-thirties, and no class forgot it more quickly and completely when the call to action came.

Are we going to do better this time? Are we going to improve on that sort of world, where competing forces, individual and national, snap and snarl at each other like so many hyenas, enforcing a cut-throat competition in which the real loser is the common man: where human values are disdained: where the weakest goes to the wall—and even there is charged a luxury price for standing-room? There are signs of hope, I know, but there are other signs too: indeed, one current pointer indicates that we are *not* going to improve on it at all, except to make the competition fiercer and the fate of the losers more permanently miserable.

The pointer is, shortly, that there are still people, of consequence (or at least of financial standing) whom the war has not affected at all, except that it has served to enrich them at a prodigious rate. They are not contributing to the national effort: they are playing a lone hand, with some very familiar cards in it. Sailors have to fight and endure for *them*, as well as for their true countrymen. . . . After the war, clearly, these people expect Britain to pick up exactly where she left off: and the fact that this means the dying and futile nineteen-thirties again, with their masses of dying and futile victims, doesn't seem to have penetrated at all, except as a clarion call to plunder.

For instance: anyone with an eye for detail and a retentive memory can give you the names of half a dozen firms who are doing nothing in this war except buying and storing second-hand motor-cars, in the certainty of making enormous profits out of them during the first scarce days of peace. Often, with loathsome effrontery, the operation is covered up by some such phrase as, 'Sell your car and help the war effort'—which, to put it at its most polite, is all eyewash and hot swill. The firms involved are *not* helping the war effort in the remotest degree: they are simply buying for a rise, creating scarcity under privileged conditions with an eye to a future squeeze, when the gallant lads in the Forces (God bless 'em) have finished the job and cleared the ground.

Now these people may be high-class rodents, but they are rats for all that. Nor are they alone: there are others playing a similar game with other classes of goods which are certain to be in short supply at the end of the war—second-hand furniture is one example: and there have been some fragrant deals in building-plots and 'bomb sites', deals which will stultify any intelligent town-planning except at enormous cost, deals which tell the same story of predatory ambition in its most selfish and cynical form.

Is this the sort of world we are coming back to? Is this the noble future? We might as well chuck in here and now if it is.

We might as well chuck in because it means that all the jokes we make in the wardroom about life after the war—about match-selling, about hawking trays of carbon-paper and india-rubbers, about buying chicken-farms and selling vacuum-cleaners—all those grim fancies, products of a sense of insecurity, aren't going to be jokes at all. They are going to come true: there *will* be millions of unemployed, medals pawned, Welsh miners in the gutters of London: there *will* be barrel-organs again, with men as the flea-bitten monkeys in attendance.

Unless we improve on that grisly progress, we can all forecast its exact course and its gross and pitiful details. A blue-print of misery exists already—the one we used last time. Some people are acting as if we are going to use it again: as if, indeed, there was no other sort to be had, and no real need for a different one either.

There *is* a different one: there must be: and of course we *won't* chuck in because we are hopeful—and, it may be said, determined. Perhaps only some of us, perhaps only a few, but enough for the spark—for such ideas spread easily, backed by the stimulus to co-operation which war furnishes, and the plain *success* of comradeship which it demonstrates.

We are going to improve on last time, because we clearly have the collective will, spread all through the Forces—the young men. An army does not fight the breadth of Africa and then allow itself to be sold down the river when it gets home: sailors develop qualities of determination which are useful in any sphere: the 'few to whom the many owe so much' can easily decide to collect their debt.

It need not demand money as the mainspring, this new world, but it will certainly require generosity and understanding, and continued service, too. It will need, most important of all, a social conscience working continuously all through the social scale. With a few blind spots, the war has produced evidence of all these things, in abundance. If we can carry them over to peace-time, we have high hopes of the future.

6 PERHAPS NEXT TIME

I had intended this chapter to record the past winter in *Winger*, with (I had hoped) a certain amount of action and some really phenomenal line-shooting as regards the weather. But in this intention I was forestalled by the Admiralty, who in the early autumn took *Winger* away from me and gave me a frigate instead.

It was a surprise, after only seven months in command, and a bigger job and ship than I had ever hoped to get: and it brought my time in corvettes to an end, after three and a quarter years. They had been full and varied years, and I had grown to love the ships and admire the men who served in them: but I could not help looking forward to the North Atlantic again, and to a ship bigger, faster and more powerful than any I had yet sailed in.

The book, therefore, remains as it stands now, with an almost total lack of incident; recounting only the privilege and the test of command, and the dead-level of convoy escort: the record of a ship plugging away at a routine job but engaging the enemy more remotely every day. I must acknowledge that this lack of explosions, screaming Stukas, and Indians biting the iron-deck is a serious flaw; as someone reading the first draft for me said, 'Don't you think the cheese is grated a bit fine this time?' But I'm prepared to take a chance on it, in the hope that perhaps next time (if there *is* a next time) I will be able to reach the required standard of violence. Command of a frigate in the North Atlantic might well provide an adequate background.

But whatever the future, I won't forget *Winger*—my first command, and a very happy one. The small model of her which the ship's company gave me on leaving (at a presentation ceremony which left me quite speechless with embarrassment, shyness and pride) will recall a grand ship and a first-rate crew.

As I wrote in a letter to the coxswain, over the first drink of my leave in the only hotel in London:

'This place is a lot more comfortable than *Winger*'s bridge on a wet night, but I don't like the people half as much.'

Even after the last drink, I still thought that.

I Was There

S HE WAS A LOVELY BOAT, AND A THOUSAND TIMES DURING THAT long trip across the Channel and up the French coast, from Southampton to Flushing, I found myself wishing she were mine. But country lawyers in a small way of business don't own sixty-ton diesel-powered yawls like the *Ariadne*: if they are lucky, they get the job of delivering them from their builders to other, more fortunate people. That was what I was doing, that June evening, and not hurrying the job either; we had a fortnight to make the trip, ironing out the snarls on the way, and none of us wanted to cut that fortnight short.

'Us' was three people altogether: myself, on holiday from the dry-as-dust legal business of an English market town; George Wainwright, about whom I knew nothing save that he was on the fringe of London's theatrical world, and an excellent small-boat navigator; and Ginger, who tripled as steward, deck-hand, and running commentator. 'Call me Ginger!' he said, in a cheerful Cockney voice, as soon as we met on the dockside: 'My mother was scared by a carrot!'

I had left it at 'Ginger'; he was the kind of man who didn't need a second name.

This was the sort of holiday I took every year, signing on with a yacht-delivery service and pulling strings to wangle the best boat and the best trip I could. It was the only way I could get to sea nowadays; the war had taken my own boat, and the post-war my bank balance. George Wainwright told me, airily, that he was 'resting between shows', though I fancy he was glad enough to pick up free quarters, and twenty pounds, for making what was virtually a pleasure cruise. He was a big man, sinewy and tough. I had the impression that he had done a lot of ocean-racing at one time, in other people's boats, though I couldn't imagine him in any conceivable part in any West End play.

Ginger, the steward, didn't volunteer anything about himself. He never stopped talking, for all that.

The crew on these 'builder's delivery' jobs was usually a scratch lot, though it struck me that this time we were remarkably assorted. Middle-aged lawyer, forty-year-old actor, a red-headed Cockney who might have been fresh out of jail—the crew of the *Ariadne* seemed to have been picked at random from the Yellow Pages. But we had made her sail like a champion, all the same.

We had made her sail to such good purpose that now, with two days in hand, we were loafing along on the last hundred miles of the journey. Earlier, we had come smoking up the Channel before a Force 6 gale; *Ariadne*, handling beautifully, had logged a steady ten knots under her storm canvas. But then the wind had fallen light, and the leg from Dover to Calais had become a gentle drifting under hazy sunshine, while the decks and the sails dried out, and we made what small repairs were necessary. Nothing had gone wrong that didn't always go wrong in a boat fresh from the builders—a leaking skylight, some chafed rigging, a cupboard door that wouldn't stay shut in a seaway. By and large, she went like a dream—as far as I was concerned, an envious dream of ownership that I would never live in reality.

George Wainwright and I had taken turn-about at the wheel, with Ginger filling in for an odd trick or two, to give us an extra margin of sleep. We had lived on tea, corned beef, beans, and something which Ginger called 'cheesy-hammy-eggy', and which, for cold, hungry, and tired men, was a banquet in itself. Rum, twice a day, completed our paradise.

Now, towards the end of that paradise, we were punching eastwards against the ebb tide, at six o'clock of a magic evening. *Ariadne*, under all plain sail, could not make much of the light air; we were barely holding our own, creeping up the flat coastline with the sun warm on our backs. I had the wheel, letting the spokes slide through my fingers with a sensual joy. Ginger, standing with his head poking out of the cabin top, was drying cups and saucers. George Wainwright, his elbows planted on the chart, stared landwards through his binoculars.

'We're not making any headway,' he said presently. 'Barely a knot, I should say.'

'Suits me,' said Ginger irrepressibly. He could never resist a comment on anything, from U.N. politics to juvenile delinquency. 'I've got all year.'

The water gurgled at the bow. The sail slatted, empty of wind.

'We might as well anchor,' I said. 'The tide will be against us for another four hours. What's the depth here?'

George Wainwright glanced at the chart. 'About four fathoms. Sandy bottom. She'll hold all right.'

'We'll anchor till the flood,' I decided. 'Give us a chance to catch up on our sleep.' I eased *Ariadne* up into the wind, and our way fell off. Ginger went forward to see to the windlass. 'How far are we off shore?' I asked George.

'About a mile,' he answered. 'The tide sets us inwards.'

'And where, exactly?'

'Off Dunkirk.'

Dunkirk. . . . As the anchor-chain rattled down through the leads, and *Ariadne* swung and settled to her cable, I was conscious of an odd foreboding. It was true that we were a mile off Dunkirk: I recognized, as if from a hundred photographs, the oily swell, the sloping beaches, the flat mainland enclosing a loose-knit grey town. Here were the waters, full of ghosts, full of sunken ships and dead men, which a decade earlier—no, it was now nearly *two* decades—had resounded to a murderous uproar. In my mind's eye I saw them all again; the straggling lines of men wading through the shallows, crying out for rescue or waiting in dull stupor to be picked up: the burning town behind, the Stukas overhead, and the small boats darting in and out—going in light, coming out laden to the gunwales—on an errand of mercy and salvage that went on hour after hour, day after day. That was what Dunkirk would always mean to me—a name at once grisly and proud, a symbol, a haunting from the past. I was curious to know what it meant to the other two, and I did not have to wait long to find out.

Ginger, having secured the anchor, came aft again; George Wainwright looked up from his chart, where *Ariadne*'s observed position was now marked by a neatly pencilled cross. There was no need to wonder which of them would speak first. It would have been an easy bet to win.

'Good old Dunkirk!' said Ginger jauntily. He wiped his hands, greasy from the windlass, on a bunch of cotton-waste, and looked round him at *Ariadne*'s benevolent anchorage. 'Makes you think a bit, don't it?'

'How do you mean, Ginger?' asked George Wainwright.

'All this. . . .' Ginger waved his hand round vaguely. 'It's nineteen years ago now, but by cripes it's like yesterday! . . . The bombers coming over as thick as bloody fleas, the lads waiting. . . . I'll never forget it, not as long as I live. By cripes, skipper!' he turned to me, his creased leathery face alight, 'I could tell you a yarn that would curl your hair! A yarn——'

. . . a yarn which, as the sun sank to the westwards, and *Ariadne*'s wavering shadow lengthened and faded on the tranquil waters off Dunkirk, recalled all the horrors, terrors, and triumphs of those mortal days. Ginger told it well; I knew that he must have had many audiences, many chances to polish and perfect.

The lads, he said (and we could all see them as lads, beefy Lancashire lads from the mills, grey-faced lads from the Yorkshire coal pits, likely lads from Bermondsey and Bow)—the lads were fed-up. The officer had promised them they'd be taken off that night, and they'd been content with that, after a week's dodging the bombers on their way back to the coast, and they'd settled down on the beach to wait. But they hadn't been taken off, not that night, nor the next, nor the next. That was the Army for you—waiting about, nobody knowing what was happening, all a lot of bull, put that bloody light out! . . . First they had waited on the beach; then at the water's edge; then chest-high in the water itself.

The straggling line inched its way outwards from the shallows to the deep water. 'Link arms, there!' said the officer; so they linked arms, and with the other hand held their rifles safely above water. 'Because you'll be using those rifles tomorrow,' said the officer. 'Keep them dry, keep them ready for instant action!' ''Ark at 'im,' said the lads. . . .

They waited in the shallows and the deeps. It was cold at night; then it was hot; behind them the town was burning, and the perimeter force kept blazing away with everything they'd got, and the Stukas circled, and swooped, and roared away again, leaving behind them a salty human flotsam—men mixed with sand, men mixed with water, seaweed, other men, all draining slowly away as the tide ebbed. 'Where's the bloody Air Force?' asked the lads, scanning the alien sky between waves of noise and pain. 'Tucked up in bed with anyone they can get hold of' . . . 'Heard from your missus lately? . . .'

It was cold at night, then it was burning hot. Men were hit, and dropped out; men got cramp, and floated away; men went mad, and tried to hide beneath the waves. There were other straggling lines within sight, like feelers weaving and groping towards home. Their own line grew thinner; sometimes part of it disappeared altogether, as if by weight of noise and pressure. 'Close up!' said the officer. 'And no smoking there! Might give away our position.'

The officer was the last to go. He was one of the lads himself, only a bit lah-di-dah. . . . When it was their turn to be taken off, the boat from the destroyer, bobbing inshore after a stick of bombs had straddled the shallows, drew alongside the wavering line.

'Look lively!' said the sailor at the helm, as cool as fresh salad, and they looked lively—as lively as they could after three days of it. There was one lad going off his head with the noise and the sun, and he tried to clamber on board, suddenly screaming with mingled pain and joy, and the officer came up behind and gave him a heave into the boat, and then himself crumpled up like a sodden newspaper and disappeared without a trace.

They fished around for him, couldn't find him, suddenly abandoned the idea and drew swiftly away. Better to save twenty lives, they reassured themselves. . . . But it was funny how surprised he had looked, after three such days, just before he faded out.

Dusk came down like a blessing. *Ariadne* rode to her anchor proudly; she was gleaming new, and the white of her doused sails seemed to hold the sunlight long after it had dipped below the horizon. I would have needed a lot of things—a lot of luck, a lot of horse-sense, a lot of drive I had never had—to possess a boat like this. But somehow, sitting relaxed in the cockpit, nursing a rum-and-water, I found it easy to imagine that it had all happened, and that she was mine.

The lights of Dunkirk were coming on one by one. George Wainwright took an anchor-bearing from them, satisfied himself that we were not dragging, and sat down by my side again. He raised his voice, against the lap and gurgle of the tideway.

'That was a good yarn of yours, Ginger,' he said. 'I know exactly how you must have felt. . . . But it was just as bad for the little ships that had to come close inshore and take the troops off. If you want to hear a story. . . .'

. . . a story about a big man in a small boat (and looking at George Wainwright's broad shoulders as he lounged at the after-end of the cockpit, we both knew that it was *his* story). Hundreds of little ships played their part in the evacuation of Dunkirk; everything from old paddle-wheel ferries to ship's lifeboats, nursed across the Channel by a man and a boy. Their job was to run a shuttle service—to come close inshore, load up with troops, and bring them out to deeper water, where the bigger boats and the destroyers were waiting.

Some of the little ships kept it up for three or four days. The two-and-a-half-ton sloop *Tantivvy* was one of these.

Tantivvy (said George Wainwright) was nothing to look at, though she was the owner's pride and joy. She'd sailed across from Dover with the rest of the mob, following a call on the radio which asked for every small ship that could stay afloat to report for emergency duty. The motley fleet fanned out like a crazy Armada, then converged on Dunkirk. Dunkirk, with its pall of smoke, its mass of shipping, its hurricane of gunfire, was something you couldn't miss.

Tantivvy, drawing less than four feet, could get within half a mile of the shore; and there she anchored, and presently launched from her upper deck a small pram-dinghy, propelled by a large man whose bulk left room for, at the very most, two other passengers. . . . All day, and most of the night, the dinghy plied to and fro, taking off two soldiers at a time from the waiting hordes, loading them on to the deck of *Tantivvy*, and then going back for more.

There came a time, towards dawn, when *Tantivvy* had fifty passengers. They sprawled in the tiny cabin, grey-faced, dead to the world; they lay about on the upper deck, soiling it with their blood; they sat with their backs to the mast, staring at nothing, waiting for peace. After his twenty-fifth trip, the big man looked at them, and said: 'Not many more, I'm afraid.'

One of the soldiers, still awake and still able to talk, waited for a lull in the bombing, and called out: 'Let's get going, for God's sake!'

'We might manage two more,' said the big man, resting his swollen, aching arms on the oars.

'Don't be a bloody fool!' said the soldier, in a cracked voice. 'You'll lose the lot of us if you do. We're damn' near sinking already.'

A bomb fell with a screaming crump! and a shower of dirty water, close beside them.

'Well . . .' said the big man. His face was deadly tired, his eyes puffy and discoloured.

He climbed on board, secured the dinghy to the stern post, and started up the tiny motor.

'Help me with the anchor,' he said to the soldier.

The two of them shambled forwards, picking their way between half-dead men who, even when kicked out of the way, could not spare them a glance. They heaved on the anchor, and finally brought it home. The big man stood upright, and then suddenly stiffened.

'You stupid bastard!' he said to the soldier.

'What?' said the soldier, in amazement.

There was an enormous explosion ashore, and the small boat, gathering way, rocked as the hot shock-wave reached them.

'*Don't you know better,*' asked the big man, with murderous sarcasm, '*than to walk on a wooden deck in those blasted hobnailed boots?*'

There was a breeze coming up from the southward, sending the small ripples slap-slapping against *Ariadne*'s shapely hull. An hour before moonrise, it was now very dark; Dunkirk's glow was reflected in the sky overhead, but between the town and the boat there was a waste of inky black water, deserted, featureless. It was as if the soldiers had all been picked up, and we were free to go. . . .

In the glow from the binnacle, Ginger's perky face was sombre. Perhaps, for him as well, the ghosts were still thick around us. If only for our comfort, I knew that I had to tell them about the triumphant part, the end of the story. . . .

. . . the end of the story, which I could see now, as clearly as the others had seen theirs.

She was an old destroyer, a bit cranky in her ways (which were the ways of 1916, not 1940) and bringing her alongside at Dover, feverishly crammed with shipping, was not easy. Not if you'd been on the bridge for thirty-six hours, and made two trips to Dunkirk, and dodged the bombers all the way there and all the way back, and waited offshore, sweating, while eight hundred and sixty-two men scrambled, clawed, and bullocked their way on board. Not if you had to go back, as soon as this lot was landed, and do the whole thing over and over again till there were no more soldiers showing above water.

The old destroyer slipped between two trawlers leaving for a routine mine-sweep, stopped in her tracks with a sudden boiling of foam aft, and edged sideways towards the quay. The lines went snaking ashore, the windlasses took in the slack; presently she was berthed, and the hum of the main engines ceased. The captain walked to the back of the bridge, and looked aft along the length of his ship.

This was the dividend, this is what the excursion had been for. . . . There wasn't an inch of the deck that was not covered with men—men in khaki. On the trip home, they had lain there as though stunned or dead; now they were stirring, moving towards the gangway and peering down at the Dover dockside as if they could scarcely believe their eyes. Their uniforms were filthy, their faces unshaven, their many bandages bloodstained; they looked like a wretched scarecrow army in some hollow Shakespearian comedy. About half of them had rifles. There was no other equipment.

The destroyer captain thought: if this is what's left of the British Army, then God help us. . . .

They began to disembark, shambling down the gang-plank like men sleepwalking in a dream of death. They collected in groups, and then in ragged lines, filling the whole quayside. There was a bunch of them directly below the bridge, standing as if in a shattered trance.

Then suddenly one of them, a small lance-corporal, looked up at the bridge, and then directly at the destroyer captain himself. For a moment they held each other's eyes, as if they were seeking some rare, unheard-of element that could bridge the ground between a stunted Cockney soldier and a tall, beribboned Royal Navy captain; and then the small lance-corporal grinned, and looked round at his weary comrades, and shouted, on a cracked note of energy:

'Come on, lads! Three cheers for the bleedin' Navy!'

They could hardly be called three cheers; they were like the thin rise and fall of a groan, or a spectral sighing from an army of ghosts. But they did emanate from those bedraggled ranks, and they did reach the gaunt, teak-faced destroyer captain on the bridge.

The captain, when he went ashore, was the elder son of an earl; and, when afloat, an unbending disciplinarian who had been known to deal out exemplary punishment for a sloppy salute. It was a difficult moment, covered by no textbook, no family code, and indeed no war so far. But he also had something important to express, and he did the best he could. He leant over the wing of his bridge, stiff as a rod in spite of his weariness, and enunciated very clearly:

'My compliments to *you*, gentlemen—my *best* compliments.'

They liked my story, I could tell that; it reminded them that the Dunkirk disaster could be read two ways. In the binnacle glow, Ginger's face grew cheerful again, and George Wainwright took a swig of his rum as if toasting Victory herself. The night breeze, from landwards, brought a warm homely smell of Flanders fields. At anchor off Dunkirk, we had mourned long enough; for the tragedy had a happy ending after all.

'That's what we tend to forget,' said George, echoing my thoughts. 'We *did* take off more than three hundred thousand of them, and they *did* get back again, in the end.'

Looking up after the long spell of talking, I became aware that the lights of Dunkirk were no longer on *Ariadne*'s starboard beam, but traversing slowly round astern of her. The Channel tide was flooding.

'We're swinging, skipper,' said George Wainwright, noticing at the same moment. 'The tide's with us now. The wind's got some weight in it, too.'

I clicked the switch of the navigation lights, and the friendly red and green eyes brought *Ariadne* to life.

'Let's get under way,' I said.

'Now you're talking!' said Ginger. 'This place gives me the creeps.'

We were all standing up, ready to go about our tasks—hoisting the foresail and the main, getting up the anchor, putting ourselves and *Ariadne* to work again.

'Of course Dunkirk is haunted,' said George Wainwright, suddenly. 'But it gave us something to be proud of, all the same.'

Some quality of wistfulness in his voice prompted me to ask a question which had been in my mind ever since the three of us started talking.

'Tell me something,' I said. '*Were* you at Dunkirk?'

It was light enough to see him grin. 'Not actually, old boy,' he answered. Suddenly he *did* sound like an actor, rather a good one. 'I was touring with ENSA at the time. *Private Lives*—eight shows a week. I wasn't actually *at* Dunkirk.'

It seemed right that he did not sound sheepish. . . . I turned towards the slight figure clambering up to the fo'c'sle deck.

'Ginger? Were you?'

'Not me!' I might have been charging him with picking pockets. '1940, wasn't it?—I was in the glasshouse already! Asleep on sentry-go, the man said. What a —— liberty!'

I knew what was coming next.

'Were *you* there?' George Wainwright asked me.

I didn't want to embarrass either of them; in any case, I couldn't be sure that, even now, they were telling the truth. One of them was an actor, the other a liar; they lived, congenitally, in opposite corners of the same dream-world. And I myself led such a dull life nowadays. . . .

'Afraid not,' I answered. 'Bad heart, you know. . . . I was doing civil defence work in London, all that summer. I wasn't at Dunkirk either.'

But the moment of revelation did not make us ashamed among ourselves, nor were we truly liars, whether we were lying or not. For our last three answers had been all wrong. Every Englishman was at Dunkirk.

A Ship to Remember

WRITING OF THE EVACUATION OF BRITISH TROOPS AFTER Dunkirk and the fall of France in 1940, Sir Winston Churchill recalled:

'One frightful incident occurred on 17 June at St Nazaire. The liner *Lancastria*, with 5,000 men on board, was bombed and set on fire just as she was about to leave . . . Upwards of 3,000 men perished. . . .

'When this news came to me in the quiet Cabinet Room during the afternoon I forbade its publication, saying: "The newspapers have got quite enough disaster for today at least." I had intended to release the news a few days later, but events crowded upon us so black and so quickly that I forgot to lift the ban, and it was some years before the knowledge of this horror became public.'

The phrase 'I forgot to lift the ban' is so un-Churchillian that one feels entitled to wonder at it. Churchill did not forget things, as his wartime colleagues were only too ready to attest.

In the next ten days alone, in addition to masterminding the total war-strategy, he remembered to fire off minutes on such subjects as smoke-screens for war factories, the *Hood* and the *Ark Royal* 'lolling about' in Gibraltar, German prisoner pilots, American destroyers, steel imports, arming Palestine Jews for self-defence, and what to do if the French Navy took against us.

How could a British troopship going down with 3,000 dead possibly slip his mind? More important still: how could a troopship sinking in shallow water in a crowded anchorage lose 3,000 men?

There were plenty of rumours at the time, and not very attractive ones; they centred on the twin themes of panic on board the *Lancastria*, and the bashfulness of nearby ships in coming to the rescue.

Perhaps the record can never be set straight; too many of the witnesses were dead men before the tragedy was half completed. But enough has emerged to establish that what Churchill forgot, or was trying to forget, or wished to conceal from a public already shattered by

the news of Dunkirk, was perhaps the worst maritime disaster in sea
history.

Its focus—the name of the graveyard—was the French port of St
Nazaire on the Bay of Biscay; and the time, two weeks after the
Dunkirk evacuation. The German grip was now tightening round one of
the few escape routes left; a troop-train had been bombed before it
reached the docks; and St Nazaire, continuously hit, beset by raging
fires, was already half in ruins.

Into this battered enclave, this murderous little box of a town, all
sorts and conditions of men hurried or drifted, to take their chance of
rescue from the sea.

Some were fighting men, most were 'Lines of Communication'
troops, the back-up boys who kept the aircraft flying, the front-line
troops fed, and the guns loaded. But, as units, they were already in bits,
the flotsam of an army on the run.

There were signallers, and engineers, and searchlight men: Red Cross
personnel, Church Army sisters, ambulance drivers, ground-crew
airmen with no more planes to service; NAAFI people, Army truck
mechanics, French and Belgian refugees, women, children, and dogs.

There were about 90,000 of them in St Nazaire, hoping for escape.
Among them was Major C. V. Petit, an ex-sailor (Boy Seaman, 1914),
and now with an RASC outfit running NAAFI canteens. His 'unit', if
the word could be applied to a loose, shambling collection of men
making hopefully for the sea, had trekked all the way from Reims (350
miles as the lucky crow flies), with most of their stores and several
million francs, all faithfully accounted for later.

Major Petit was to live the story of the *Lancastria* for the next forty-
eight hours, and has lived it ever since. But for his eyes and ears and
memory, much of this account would have drowned with the ship and
the men.

There was a prime, reassuring collection of transports waiting for the
wanderers (and between all the ships, they *did* take off 57,000 men).
They were anchored ten miles up the coast in Quiberon Bay, where,
only 181 years earlier, Admiral Lord Hawke had defeated the French in
what the history books called 'one of the few total victories in the
history of maritime war'.

Forgetting the French (somebody has to lose), the omens were good,
and the ships were all that exhausted footslogging men could pray for.

There was a frieze of good-looking liners (*Georgic, Duchess of York,
John Holt, Oronsay, Batory, Sobieski, Franconia, Teiresias.*) There
was a clutch of destroyers (*Havelock, Wolverine, Beagle, Highlander,*

Vanoc, Punjabi). There was the Irish packet *Ulster Prince*, and the armed trawler *Cambridgeshire*. There were French tugs, and fishing-boats by the dozen, and launches, and skiffs.

There was the Cunard liner *Lancastria*, 16,000 tons, Captain Rudolph Sharp in command.

She was not the finest ship in the world. A rather ugly-looking one-funnel job, her keel was twenty-six years old that summer; launched just after the First World War as the *Tyrrhenia*, she had been (travel agents reported) unpopular with everyone. She had been renamed *Lancastria* in 1924, and she had been plodding around on 'medium-priced cruises' and the North Atlantic run, at her maximum speed of 17 knots, ever since.

But she was just the ship for just this moment. Having served as a troopship since 1939, voyaging to and from Canada, Norway, and Iceland, she had lots of room: lots of room for everyone.

Everyone began to come on board, ferried out by anything that floated. Destroyers took 600 at a time: tugs 300. Major Petit's lot (329 of them) arrived in a French Railways tender. Like many other boats, it had been making for the *Oronsay*, but when they saw the *Oronsay* bombed, and her bridge and upper-works smashed to bits, they headed for the *Lancastria* instead.

On board the *Lancastria*, there was not exactly chaos. But there was, understandably, a bit of a mess. Men were clambering up from half a dozen boats, big and small, all at the same time; and for that reason it was never established exactly how many she embarked.

Officially, it was 5,800 (*History of the Second World War*: H.M. Stationery Office). Captain Sharp said he ordered a halt at 5,000, but 'hundreds more got on after that'. A sergeant, talking to an officer, was overheard reporting the figure as 8,020.

Captain F. E. Griggs, a Royal Engineer 'press-ganged' as acting Ship's Adjutant, took 4,000 names; having knocked off for lunch, he then came back to find many of the spaces he had checked occupied by entirely new characters. Griggs estimated that the final total was 9,000.

Thus the later tally of the dead varied considerably. But at this, the first moment of hope, no tally of the dead was in view. It would have seemed ridiculous. *Lancastria* was a fine big ship. She was a Cunard liner, still run in Cunard style.

Stewards handed out cards with cabin numbers on them. Breakfast was announced. The barber's shop was thronged with men looking for an overdue hair-cut. There was a four-course lunch, with stewards again in attendance. The bar, open until the very moment the bombs began to fall, did the best trade of all.

Meanwhile, though already full to bursting, *Lancastria* remained at anchor. It was Captain Sharp's decision, and his to make, without question. Various factors weighed heavily with him. He had been forbidden by the French Port Admiral to sail at night. The Loire Estuary was a tricky one, with strong tides: there was a minefield offshore, buoyed but not lit. His charts of this were not up to date: he would need some help with it, even in daytime.

He preferred to wait for a planned convoy of all the other ships, with the destroyers as escorts. At the moment this could not be organized, nor could any destroyers be detached for a lone sailing.

It was 17 June, the day that France accepted Hitler's terms of surrender. *Lancastria* swung to her anchor, crammed with men above and below decks. During their long wait they heard plenty of stories about other ships being bombed.

The *Franconia* had been put out of action completely; the *Teiresias* sunk. They had been able to watch *Oronsay* being severely mangled. Then, without warning, at 3.50 p.m., it was their own turn.

Lancastria, armed with a few World War One guns ('The fault of Baldwin & Co.', a politically-minded survivor charged), could offer no real resistance, and she was hit at close range by four bombs altogether. It was enough, even for this solid ship, which 'jumped in the water' as the last one fell.

One bomb set her on fire; two or three went straight down into her holds, one of which held, or had held, 800 Air Force men. They had no means of escape; an R.A.F. padre went *down* on a rope, to lead the living in 'O God Our Help in Ages Past', just as Major Petit, who had been asleep in his cabin, came on deck.

He found fires all round him, but the worst damage was out of sight, and it was mortal. The bombs had ripped out most of the port side of the ship, as well as the bulkheads in between, so that *Lancastria* was virtually open to the sea. She took a tremendous list to port, righted herself as the men on deck climbed up to the other side, and then began to settle down. Already it was clear that she was going.

She went down in less than twenty minutes. Only four life-boats were launched, mostly by soldiers and other amateurs; a lot of the crew had been caught below or on the foc's'le, and could not get through to the boat-deck. Of the four boats, the first one, full of women and children, capsized half-way down because an enthusiatic soldier cut the falls with a jack-knife.

The second, under the guard of a ship's officer armed with a revolver which he did not have to use, was sent down empty to pick up the survivors from the first. The third boat was lowered so quickly, and crashed into the sea with such force, that its bottom was stove in.

The fourth, sent away by an engineer officer, came to no harm. But that was all. Davits jamming, boats' falls sticking, the impossible angle of the sinking ship, made all other efforts fruitless. Now it was 'every man for himself', on the command from the bridge. There were, Captain Griggs estimated, life-belts for only one in ten of the passengers.

Men, clambering along decks already unbearably hot from the fire below, and then over the ship's side, began to jump into the sea. From the stern, now high out of the water, some plummeted down sixty or seventy feet; others, fearful or sensible, waited until the last moment and then walked out on to the water.

Non-swimmers found they could swim; others drowned immediately in oil, which was beginning to gush out from the ship's side; others again were hit by falling debris as the deck canted, or by falling rifles and steel helmets as these were cast away, or by other men jumping on top of them, or by breaking their own necks as the old-fashioned cork life-belts smashed into their chins when they hit the water.

Living and dead, the sluicing tide began to disperse them all.

If *Lancastria* had sunk upright, in shallow water, most of the upperworks would have been clear, and many more might have been saved. But she settled on her side; only the wing of the bridge was above water, and on this collected a small cluster of men singing (wouldn't you know it?) 'Roll Out the Barrel'. The last men waiting to swim for their lives thronged the stern round the bared propellers. It was 'black with men' before it went under.

Major Petit, giving up his life-jacket to a scared non-swimmer, stripped, took to the sea sedately, and began to paddle away. He found a solid deck chair ('Thank' God for Cunard teak furniture') and had leisure to survey the scene. It was appalling.

He was one of thousands of men, adrift on water now polluted by all the debris of a dead ship—corpses, deck-gear, smashed boats, rafts, and the great gouts of oil welling up from *Lancastria*, which had just taken on 1,600 tons of it.

Some of this oil was set on fire, not by incendiary bombs (as a few survivors claimed) but by the calcium flares attached to the life-belts, which automatically ignited as they made contact with the sea.

But many men *were* machine-gunned in the water, and had their lungs collapsed by nearby falling bombs, and were fried to death, and drowned in mundane fashion, or grew tired of swimming after four hours, or swallowed corrosive fuel oil and, while trying to get rid of it, rid themselves of life as well.

Men died, women died, dogs died. *Fish* died, stunned by the explosions: Captain Griggs, swimming around in this muck, found himself noting: we've got oil, and sardines: all we need is the tins. A Hurricane pilot overhead dropped his Mae West life-jacket into the sea, to save at least one life. Major Petit was picked up by a destroyer's whaleboat. A mother and child lived, a fat old woman lost heart and sank between snatches of prayer.

The anti-submarine trawler *Cambridgeshire*, of Grimsby (Skipper W. G. Easton), was hero of that day, and of many days after. Under continuous bombing, she picked up 1,100 survivors; she was so deep-laden that, when she discharged them to the waiting ship *John Holt*, her draught rose from 23 feet to 16.

No wonder her Captain, edging this monstrous, top-heavy cargo towards safety, called out: 'Don't anybody sneeze!'

How many died altogether was and is a matter of gruesome conjecture. The *Official History* recorded 3,000. Sir Winston Churchill said 'Upwards of 3,000'. The *Guinness Book of Records* says 'About 4,000'—which is only 120 short of the worst sea disaster of all time.

This is where the question-marks start. Why was there such an appalling loss, from a ship sinking, not too fast, among a lot of other ships? The *Cambridgeshire* performed valiant miracles of rescue. Did anyone else?

The evidence is hard to come by. The *Official History*, once again, phrased it tactfully: 'Why more of the small ships did not follow [*Cambridgeshire*'s example] is obscure': and went on to suggest that they may have been so busy defending themselves against continuous bombing that they did not notice *Lancastria*'s plight.

It is possible. Perhaps one is left with the question, 'What *else* went wrong, besides the normal horrors of this sort of sinking?'

Apart from the ferociously accurate bombing which killed so many men outright, the fires, the swirling tide, the lack of life-belts, the trouble with the life-boats, the machine-gunning in the water, and the gross amount of oil which was a natural killer, was there anything else, man-made or man-induced? Is there, somewhere, an ugly face peeping out?

A general ragbag of rumour and suspicion hung, and still hangs, over this disaster; and what follows now is not evidence, but hearsay, conjecture, canteen gossip, and the sad talk of men in mourning for their friends, men who feel the need to blame somebody or something.

It was said that rescue ships held off, or made one trip and then beat it for safety. (But many of them were full of troops from on shore already.)

That other ships were slow in launching their boats. That French fishing-boats were seen hooking up kit-bags, instead of men, in search of loot. (How much loot is there in a sodden kitbag?) That there was panic on board. (Captain Sharp said No, definitively.)

One survivor, Staff Sergeant Percy Fairfax, who seemed to see or hear all the bad news, afterwards wrote of: 'An officer at the head of a staircase driving men below, not realizing we were sinking so fast': 'Men jumping onto each other in the sea': 'A man in the water taking a revolver from a string round his neck, shooting his pal and then himself': 'Another officer in a full rowing-boat shooting a man who tried to get on board. The officer was then shot himself': 'Frenchmen in search of loot pushing survivors away with oars.'

Against that must be set stories of individual courage and self-sacrifice, enough to balance many a shameful story. Major Petit gave up his life-belt. So did Church Army Sister Gladys Trott: she threw it to a soldier hanging on to *Lancastria*'s rail, and remarked afterwards: 'I'm glad he caught it. You know how bad women are at aiming.'

Lancastria lost 55 of her own crew. *Cambridgeshire* collected enough survivors to bring herself near to sinking. So did *Ulster Prince* (licensed accommodation, 500) which carried 2,650 home. 'I'm glad I didn't know,' said her master afterwards, 'or I'd have been up the wall.'

The 'carriers-home' were valiant indeed; the convoy for which *Lancastria* had been waiting finally delivered 23,000 men to Plymouth. Perhaps the paragon among this pride of ships was the shattered *Oronsay*, minus her bridge and steered by muscle-power from aft, whose human cargo was 10,000 men, dressed in anything from pyjamas to a butcher's apron.

On board the destroyer *Highlander*, which had picked up a Belgian woman and her child, Steward Bell washed and ironed their oil-soaked clothes, muttering: 'These bloody frills!' On the crowded beaches of Plymouth, sunbathing holiday-makers waved cheerfully as the jolly sailor-boys went by. They, it was generally felt, would find out before long.

It is all old history now. Less than full-fathom-five thy father lies, but he has lain there for thirty years, and will lie forever. Yet Major Petit, at seventy-two, still keeps in touch with 'Lancastrians'.

Himself rescued by *Highlander* and brought home by *Oronsay*, he founded an association of survivors in Berlin in 1946; it still numbers 700, and they hold a yearly reunion. They even have their own hand-woven tie: exclusive men's wear indeed.

In a small London church, St Katharine Cree in Leadenhall Street, a stained-glass window commemorates their story, and the ship, and the dead. Among them now is Captain Rudolph Sharp, the man in the middle on that day, a 'survivor' for a short two years, who died heroically on board another shattered troopship, the *Laconia*, in 1942.

Without doubt there were brave men, and cowards, in that evil hour when *Lancastria* went down. Under the fearful terrors of shipwreck, as old as *The Tempest*, or as St Paul himself, both these masks of fear would certainly be there, plain for all to see. Perhaps it is enough to say, by way of epitaph: *Toll for the brave, the brave that are no more*. The rest don't matter.

Note: *Major C. V. Petit, the essential historian of this disaster, died one year after this writing, on 31 May 1971, at the age of seventy-three.*

'H.M.S. *Marlborough* Will Enter Harbour'

I

THE SLOOP 'MARLBOROUGH,' 1,200 TONS, COMPLEMENT 8 officers and 130 men, was torpedoed at dusk on the last day of 1942 while on independent passage from Iceland to the Clyde. She was on her way home for refit, and for the leave that went with it, after a fourteen-month stretch of North Atlantic convoy escort with no break, except for routine boiler-cleaning. Three weeks' leave to each watch—that had been the buzz going round the ship's company when they left Reykjavik after taking in the last convoy; but many of them never found out how much truth there was in that buzz, for the torpedo struck at the worst moment, with two-thirds of the ship's company having tea below decks, and when it exploded under the forward mess-deck at least sixty of them were killed outright.

H.M.S. *Marlborough* was an old ship, seventeen years old, and she took the outrage as an old lady of breeding should. At the noise and jar of the explosion a delicate shudder went all through her: then as her speed fell off there was stillness, while she seemed to be making an effort to ignore the whole thing: and then, brought face to face with the fury of this mortal attack, gradually and disdainfully she conceded the victory.

The deck plating of the fo'c'sle buckled and sagged, pulled downwards by the weight of the anchors and cables: all this deck, indeed, crumpled as far as the four-inch gun-mounting, which toppled forwards until the gun-muzzles were pointing foolishly to the sea; a big lurch tore loose many of the ammunition lockers and sent them cascading over the side. Until the way of her 16 knots fell off, there were crunching noises as successive bulkheads took the weight of water, butted at it for a moment, and then gave in: and thus, after a space, she lay—motionless, cruelly hit, two hundred miles south-west of the Faeroes and five hundred miles from home.

So far it had been an affair of metal: now swiftly it became an affair of men. From forward came muffled shouting—screaming, some of it—borne on the wind down the whole length of the ship, to advertise the shambles buried below. The dazed gun's crew from 'A' gun, which had been directly over the explosion, climbed down from their sagging platform and drew off aft. There was a noise of trampling running feet from all over the ship: along alley-ways, up ladders leading from the untouched spaces aft: confused voices, tossed to and fro by the wind, called as men tried to find out how bad the damage was, what the orders were, whether their friends had been caught or not.

On the upper deck, near the boats and at the foot of the bridge-ladders, the clatter and slur of feet and voices reached its climax. In the few moments before a firm hand was taken, with every light in the ship out and only the shock of the explosion as a guide to what had happened, there was confusion, noisy and urgent: the paramount need to move quickly clashed with indecision and doubt as to where that move could best be made. The dusk, the rising sea, the bitterly cold wind, which carried an acrid smell in sharp eddying puffs, were all part of this discordant aftermath: the iron trampling of those racing feet all over the ship bound it together, co-ordinating fear into a vast uneasy whole, a spur for panic if panic ever showed itself.

It never did show itself. The first disciplined reaction, one of many such small reassurances, to reach the bridge was the quartermaster's voice, admirably matter-of-fact, coming up the wheel-house voice-pipe: 'Gyro compass gone dead, sir!' The Midshipman, who shared the watch with the First Lieutenant and was at that moment licking a lip split open on the edge of the glass dodger, looked round uncertainly, found he was the only officer on the bridge, and answered: 'Very good. Steer by magnetic,' before he realized the futility of this automatic order. Then he jerked his head sideways, level with another voice-pipe, the one leading to the Captain's cabin, and called: 'Captain, sir!'

There was no answer. Probably the Captain was on his way up already. God, suppose he'd been killed, though. . . . The Midshipman called again: 'Captain, sir!' and a voice behind him said: 'All right, Mid. I heard it.'

He turned round, to find the comforting bulk of the Captain's duffle coat outlined against the dusk. It was not light enough to see the expression on his face, nor was there anything in his voice to give a clue to it. It did not occur to the Midshipman to speculate about this, in any case: for him, this was simply the Captain, the man he had been waiting for, the man on whom every burden could now be squarely placed.

'Torpedo, sir.'

'Yes.'

The Captain, moving with purpose but without hurry, stepped up on to the central compass platform, glanced once round him—and sat down. There was something special in that act of sitting down, there in the middle of the noise and movement reaching the bridge from all over the ship, and everyone near him caught it. The Captain, on the bridge, sitting in the Captain's chair. Of course: that was what they had been waiting for. . . . It was the beginning, the tiny tough centre, of control and order. Soon it would spread outwards.

'Which side was it from?'

'Port, sir. Just under "A" gun.'

'Tell the engine-room what's happened. . . . Where is the First Lieutenant?'

'He must have gone down, sir. I suppose he's with the Damage Control Party.'

Up the voice-pipe came the quartermaster's voice again: 'She won't come round, sir. The wheel's hard a-starboard.'

'Never mind.' The Captain turned his head slightly. 'Pilot!'

A figure, bent over the chart table behind him, straightened up. 'Sir?'

'Work out our position, and we'll send a signal.'

'Just getting it out now.'

The Captain bent forward to the voice pipe again. 'Bosun's Mate!'

'Sir?'

'Find the First Lieutenant. He'll be forrard somewhere. Tell him to report the damage as soon as he can.'

'Aye, aye, sir.'

That, at least, was a small space cleared. . . . Under him the ship felt sluggish and helpless; on the upper deck the voices clamoured, from below the cries still welled up. He looked round him, trying in the increasing darkness to find out who was on the bridge. Not everyone he expected to see, not all the men who should have collected at such a moment, were there. The signalman and the bridge messenger. Two look-outs. Bridger, his servant, standing just behind him. Pilot and the Mid. Someone else he could not make out.

He called: 'Coxswain?'

There was a pause, and then a voice said: 'He was below, sir.'

'Who's that?'

'Adams, sir.'

Adams was the Chief Bosun's Mate, and the second senior rating on board. After a moment the Captain said:

'If he doesn't get out, you take over, Adams. . . . You'd better organize three or four of your quartermasters, for piping round the ship. I'll want you to stay by me. If there's anything to be piped you can pass it on.'

'Aye, aye, sir.'

There was too much noise on the upper deck, for a start. But perhaps it would be better if he spoke to them over the loud-hailer. Once more the Captain turned his head.

'Yeoman!'

Another pause, and then the same definitive phrase, this time from the signalman of the watch: 'He was below, sir.'

A wicked lurch, and another tearing noise from below, covered the silence after the words were spoken. But the Captain seemed to take them in his stride.

'See if the hailer's working,' he said to the signalman.

'I've got the position, sir,' said Haines, the navigating officer. 'Will you draft a signal?'

'Get on to the W/T office and see if they can send it, first.'

'The hailer's all right, sir,' said the signalman. 'Batteries still working.'

'Very good. Train the speaker aft.'

He clicked on the microphone, and from force of habit blew through it sharply. A healthy roar told him that the thing was in order. He cleared his throat.

'Attention, please! This is the Captain speaking.' His voice, magnified without distortion, overcame the wind and the shouting, which died away to nothing, 'I want to tell you what's happened. We've been torpedoed on the port side, under "A" gun. The First Lieutenant is finding out about the damage now. I want you all to keep quiet, and move about as little as possible, until I know what the position is. . . . "X" gun's crew will stand fast, the rest of the watch-on-deck clear away the boats and rafts ready for lowering. Do *not* start lowering, or do anything else, until I give the order over this hailer, or until you hear the pipe. That is all.'

The speaker clicked off, leaving silence on the bridge and all over the upper deck. Only the voices hidden below still called. He became aware that Haines was standing by his elbow, preparing to speak.

'What is it, Pilot?'

'It's the W/T office, sir. They can't transmit.'

'Who's down there?'

'The leading tel., sir. The P.O. tel. was below.' (That damned phrase again. If those two messes, the Chiefs' and the Petty Officers', were both written off, it was going to play hell with organizing the next move, whatever it was.) 'But he knows what he's doing, sir,' Haines went on. 'The dynamo's been thrown off the board, but the set's had a terrible knock anyway.'

'Go down yourself and make sure.' Haines, as well as being navigating officer, was an electrical expert, and this was in fact his department.

'Aye, aye, sir.'

'Midshipman!'

'Sir?'

'Pass the word to the Gunnery Officer——'

'I'm here, sir.' Guns' tall figure loomed up behind him. 'I've been looking at "A" gun.'

'Well?'

'It's finished, I'm afraid, sir.'

Guns knew his job, and the Captain did not ask him to elaborate. Instead he said:

'I think we'll try a little offensive action while we're waiting, in case those —— come up to take a look at us.' He considered. 'Close up on "X" gun, go into local control, fire a spread of star-shell through this arc'—he indicated the port bow and beam—'and let fly if you see anything. I'll leave the details to you.'

'Aye, aye, sir.'

Guns clumped off down the ladder on his way aft. It was one of his idiosyncrasies to wear street-cleaner's thigh boots with thick wooden soles, and his movements up and down the ship were easily traceable, earning indeed a good deal of fluent abuse from people who were trying to get to sleep below. As the heavy footfalls receded aft, the Captain stood up and leant over the port side of the bridge, staring down at the tumbling water. There was nothing to be seen of the main area of the damage, which was hidden by the outward flare of the bows; but the ship had less freedom of movement now—she was deeper, more solidly settled in the water. They must have taken tons of it in the ripped-up spaces forward: the fo'c'sle covering them looked like a slowly crumbling ruin. It was about time the First Lieutenant came through with his report. If they had to——

'What's that?' he asked suddenly.

A thin voice was calling 'Bridge, Bridge', from one of the voice-pipes. He bent down to the row nearest to him, but from none of them did the voice issue clearly. Behind him the midshipman was conducting the same search on his side. The voice went on calling 'Bridge, Bridge, Bridge', in a patient monotone. It was the Captain's servant, Bridger, who finally traced it—a voice-pipe low down on the deck, its anti-spray cover still clipped on.

The man bent down to it and snapped back the cover. 'Bridge here.'

A single murmured sentence answered him. Bridger looked up to the
Captain. 'It's the Engineer Officer, sir, speaking from the galley flat.'

The Captain bent down. A waft of bitter fume-laden air met his
nostrils. 'Yes, Chief?'

'I'm afraid Number One got caught by that last bulkhead, sir.'

'What happened? I heard it go a little while back.'

'We thought it would hold, sir.' The level voice, coming from the
heart of the ruined fo'c'sle, had an apologetic note, as if the speaker,
even in that shambles, had had the cool honesty to convict himself of an
error of judgement. 'It did look like holding for a bit, too. Number One
was with the damage control party, between the seamen's mess-deck
and the bathrooms. They'd shut the watertight door behind them, and
were just going to shore up, when the forrard bulkhead went.' Chief
paused. 'You know what it's like, sir. We can't get at them without
opening up.'

'Can't do that now, Chief.'

'No, sir.'

'Can you hear anything?'

'Not now.'

'How many were there with the First Lieutenant?'

'Fourteen, sir. Mostly stokers.' There was another pause. 'I took
charge down here, sir. We're shoring up the next one.'

'What do you think of it?'

'Not too good. It's badly strained already, and leaking down one
seam.' There was, now, a slightly sharpened note in his voice travelling
up from below. 'There's a hell of a mess down here. sir. And if this one
goes, that'll mean the whole lot.'

'Yes, I know.' The Captain thought quickly, while overhead and to
port the sea was suddenly lit up by a cold yellow glare—the first spread
of star-shell, four slowly dropping lights shadowing their spinning
parachutes against the cloud overhead. Very pretty. . . . The news from
below could hardly have been worse: it added up to fully a third of the
ship flooded, all the forward mess-decks cut off, fourteen men drowned
at one stroke, and God knows how many more caught by the original
explosion. 'Look here, Chief, I don't want any more men lost like that.
You must use your own judgement about getting out in a hurry. See
how the shoring up goes, and let me know as soon as you can if you
think it'll hold.'

'All right, sir.'

'We're firing star-shell at the moment, to see if there's anything on the
surface. "X" gun may be firing independently, any time from now on.'

'All right, sir.'

'Take care of yourself, Chief.'

He could almost hear the other man smiling at what was, from the Captain, an unexpected remark. 'I'll do that, sir.'

The voice-pipe went dead. Walking back to his chair, the Captain allowed himself a moment of profound depression and regret. The First Lieutenant had gone. A good kid, doing his first big job in the Navy and tremendously keen to do it properly. With a young wife, too—the three of them had had dinner at the Adelphi in Liverpool, not two weeks ago. There was a bad letter to be written there, later on. And the loss might make a deal of difference to the next few hours.

The star-shell soared and dropped again. Sitting in his chair, waiting for Chief's report, listening to the green seas slapping and thumping against the side as *Marlborough* sagged downwind in the wave troughs with a new, ugly motion, he was under no illusions as to what the next few hours might bring, and the chances of that 'bad letter' ever being written by himself. But that was not what he was now concentrating on: that was not in the mapped-out programme. . . . This was the moment for which the Navy had long been preparing him: for years his training and experience had had this precise occasion in view; that was why he was a commander, and the Captain of *Marlborough* when she was hit. Taking charge, gauging chances, foreseeing the next eventuality and if necessary forestalling it—none of it could take him by surprise, any more than could the chapter headings of a favourite book. When the moment had arrived he had recognized it instantly, and the sequence of his behaviour had lain before him like a familiar pattern, of which he now had to take the tenth or twentieth tracing. He had not been torpedoed before, but no matter: tucked away in his mind and brain there had always been a picture of a torpedoed ship, and of himself as, necessarily, the key figure in this picture. Now that the curtain was drawn, and the image became the reality, he simply had to play his assigned part with as much intelligence, skill, and endurance as he could muster. The loss of the First Lieutenant and over half the ship's company already was a bitter stroke, both personally and professionally: it would return in full force later; but for the moment it was only a debit item which had to be fitted into the evolving picture.

'Signalman!'

'Sir.'

'Get the Gunnery Officer on the quarter-deck telephone.'

A pause. More star-shell, reflected on a waste of cold tumbling water, dropped slowly till they were drowned in darkness again. There wasn't really much point in going on with the illumination now: the U-boat probably thought they had other ships in company ready to counter-attack, and had sheered off. She had, indeed, cause to be satisfied, without pursuing the advantage further. . . .

'Gunnery Officer on the telephone, sir.'

The Captain took the proffered receiver. 'Guns?'

'Yes, sir?'

'I'm afraid Number One has been killed. I want you to take over.'

'Oh—all right, sir.'

Hearing the shocked surprise in his voice, the Captain remembered that the two of them had been very good friends. But that, again, was something to be considered later: only the bald announcement was part of the present plan. He continued:

'I think you had better stay aft, as if we were still at full action stations. Chief is in charge of damage control forrard. Stop star-shell now—I take it you've seen nothing.'

'Nothing, sir.'

'Right. You'd better have all the depth-charges set to safe—in fact have the primers withdrawn and dropped over the side. And I want someone to have a look at our draught-marks aft.'

'I've just had them checked, sir. There's nothing to go on, I'm afraid: they're right clear of the water.'

'Are the screws out of the water too?'

'Can't see in this light, sir. The top blades, probably.'

'Right. Get going on those depth-charges.'

The Captain handed back the receiver, at the same time saying to the signalman: 'Get your confidential books in the weighted bags ready for ditching. And tell the W/T office to do the same.'

'Aye, aye, sir.'

'Bridger.'

'Yes, sir.'

'Go down and get the black hold-all, and come back here.'

'Aye, aye, sir.' Bridger's tough, unemotional expression did not alter, but his shoulders stiffened instinctively. He knew what the order meant. The black hold-all was, in his own phrase, the scram-bag: it held a bottle of brandy, morphine ampoules, a first-aid kit, some warm clothes, and a few personal papers. It had been tucked away in a corner of the skipper's cabin for nearly three years. It was as good as a ticket over the side. They'd start swimming any moment now.

The report from aft about the draught-marks had certainly quickened the tempo a little: his orders to Bridger and to the signalman were an endorsement of this. But quick tempo or slow, there was still the same number of things to be fitted into the available time, the same number of lines in the pattern to be traced. Now, in the darkness, as he turned to the next task, very little noise or movement reached the bridge from anywhere in the ship: only a sound of hammering from deep below (the damage control party busy on their shoring job), a voice calling 'Take a turn, there', as the whaler was swung out, the endless thump and surge of the waves driving downwind—only these were counter distractions in the core of heart and brain which the bridge had now become. Indeed, the Captain was much less conscious of these than of the heavy breathing of Adams, the Chief Bosun's Mate, who stood by his elbow as close and attentive as a spaniel at the butts. Adams had heard the order to Bridger, and guessed what it meant: it had aroused, not his curiosity—matters were past such a faint reaction as curiosity now—but the same tough determination as the Captain himself had felt. They were both men of the same stamp: seamen first, human beings afterwards; the kind of men whom *Marlborough*, in her extremity, most needed and most deserved.

'Mid!'

'Yes, sir?'

'Go along to the sick bay, and——'

One of the voice-pipe bells rang sharply. The Midshipman listened for a moment, and then said: 'That's the doctor now, sir.'

The Captain bent down. 'Yes, doc?'

'I wanted to report about casualties, sir.'

'What's the position?'

'I've got nine down here, sir. Burns, mostly. One stoker with a broken arm. I got a stretcher-party organized, and brought them down aft.'

'I was hoping there'd be more.'

'Afraid not, sir.'

'Do you need any hands to help you?'

'No, I'm all right, sir. I've got one sick-berth attendant—Jamieson was caught forrard, I'm afraid—and the leading steward is giving a hand.'

'Very well. But you'll have to start moving them, I'm afraid. Get them on the upper deck, on the lee side. Ask Guns to lend you some hands from "X" gun.'

There was a pause. Then the doctor's voice came through again, more hesitantly. 'They shouldn't really be moved, sir, unless——'

'That's what I meant. You understand?'

'Yes, sir.'

'Send the walking cases up to the boat-deck, and see to the others yourself. Divide them up between the two boats. I'll leave the details for you.'

'Very well, sir.'

Thank God for a good doctor, anyway—as bored, cynical, and impatient as most naval doctors were for three-quarters of their time, with nothing to do but treat warts and censor the mail: and then, on an occasion like this, summoning all the resource and skill that had been kept idle, and throwing them instantly into the breach. The doctor was going to be an asset during the next few hours. So, indeed, was every officer and man left to the ship.

He would have liked to muster the remaining hands, to see how many the explosion had caught and how many he had left to work with; but that would disrupt things too much, at a time when there must be no halting in the desperate race to save the ship or, at least, as many of the remaining lives as possible. But as he sat back in his chair, waiting for what he was now almost sure must happen, the Captain reviewed his officers one by one, swiftly tabulating their work at this moment, speculating whether they could be better employed. Number One was gone, of course. Guns in charge aft, Haines in the wireless office (time he was back, incidentally). Chief working the damage control party—that was technically his responsibility anyway, and there was a first-class Chief E.R.A. in charge of the engine-room. The Mid here on the bridge. The doctor with his hands full in the sick bay. Merrett—the Captain frowned suddenly. Where the devil was Merrett? He'd forgotten all about him—and indeed it was easy to overlook the shy, newly joined sub who had startled the wardroom on his first night by remarking: 'My father went to prison as a conscientious objector during the last war, so he's rather ashamed of me in this one,' but then had relapsed into the negative, colourless attitude which seemed natural to him. Where had he got to now?

The Captain repeated the query aloud to the Midshipman.

'I haven't seen him at all, sir,' the latter answered. 'He was in the wardroom when I came on watch. Shall I call them up?'

'Yes, do.'

After a moment at one of the voice-pipes the Midshipman came through with the answer: 'He was there a moment ago, sir. They think he's on the upper deck somewhere.'

'Send one of the bosun's mates to——' The Captain paused. No, that might not be a good move. 'See if you can find him, Mid, and ask him to come up here.'

When the Midshipman had left the bridge the Captain frowned again. Why in God's name had Merrett been in the wardroom a moment ago? What was he doing there at a time like this? Any sort of alarm or crisis meant that officers went to their action stations automatically: Merrett should have gone first to 'A' gun, where he was in charge, and then, as that was out of action, up to the bridge for orders. Now all that was known of him was that he had been in the wardroom, right aft. The Captain hoped there was a good explanation, not the attack of nerves or the breakdown of self-control he had been guessing at when he sent the Midshipman to find Merrett. He could understand such a thing happening—the boy was barely twenty, and this was his first ship—but they just could not afford it now.

His guess had been right: so much became obvious as soon as Merrett was standing in front of him. Even in the darkness, with the exact expression on his face blurred and shadowed, he seemed to manifest an almost exalted state of terror. The movements of foot and hand, the twitching shoulders, the slight, uncontrolled chattering of teeth, the shine of sweat on the forehead—all were here, a distillation of fear which would, in full daylight, have been horrible to look at. So that was it. . . . For a moment the Captain hesitated, trying to balance their present crucial danger, and his own controlled reaction to it, against the almost unknown feelings of a boy, a landsman-turned-sailor, confronted with the same ordeal; but then the overriding necessity of everyone on board doing his utmost swept away any readiness to make allowances for failure in this respect. The details, the pros and cons, the fine-drawn questions could wait; nothing but one hundred per cent effectiveness would suffice now, and that was what he must re-establish.

'Where have you been?' he asked curtly.

Merrett swallowed, looked across the shattered fo'c'sle to the wild sea, and drew no comfort or reassurance from it. He said, in a dry strained voice: 'I'm sorry, sir. I didn't know what to do, exactly.'

'Then you should come and ask me. Do you expect me to come and tell you?' It was rough: it was, in Merrett's present state, brutally so: but it was clearly dictated by the situation they were in. 'Where were you when we were hit?'

'I'd just gone up to "A" gun, sir.'

'Must have shaken you up a bit.' So much allowance, and no more, did the Captain make for what he could only guess at now—youth, uncertainty, self-distrust, perhaps an inherited horror of violence. 'But I don't want to have to send for individual officers at a time like this. You understand?'

'Yes, sir.' It was a whisper, almost a sigh. He'd been drinking whisky, too, the Captain thought. Well, that didn't matter as long as it had the right result; and this, and the tonic effect of giving him a definite job to do, could be put to the test now.

'Very well. . . . There's something I want you to do,' he went on, changing his tone in such a way as to indicate clearly that a fresh start could now be made. 'Go down to the boat-deck and see how they're getting on with the boats. They're to be swung out ready for lowering, and all the rafts cleared away as well. You'd better check up on the boats' crews, too: remember we've only got this one watch of seamen to play with, so far as we know. You'll want a coxswain, a stoker, and a bowman told off for the motor-boat, and a coxswain and a bowman for the whaler. Got that?'

'Yes, sir.'

It seemed that he had: already he was making some attempt to take a grip on his body, and his voice was more under control. Watching him turn and make for the bridge-ladder, the Captain felt ready to bet that he would make a good job of it. The few minutes had not been wasted.

But they had been no more than an odd, irrelevant delay in the main flow of the current; and now, in quick succession, as if to re-establish the ordained pace of disaster, three more stages came and were passed. Bridger appeared with the black hold-all, and with something else which he handed to the Captain almost furtively. 'Better have this, sir,' he said, as the Captain's hand closed over it. It was his safety-light, which he had forgotten to clip on to his life-jacket—one of the small watertight bulb-and-battery sets which were meant to be plugged in and switched on when in the water. The Captain took it with a grunt and fastened it on, his eyes turned instinctively to the black expanse of water washing and swirling round them. Yes, better have the light ready. . . .

Then Haines came up the ladder from below, starting to speak almost before he was on the bridge:

'I'm afraid they were right about the W/T set sir,' he began. 'It's finished. And the main switchboard has blown, too. Even if we got the dynamo back on the board——'

'All right, Pilot,' said the Captain suddenly. And then, to the figure he had discerned at the top of the ladder, the third messenger of evil, he said: 'Yes, Chief?'

The engineer officer did not speak until he was standing close by the Captain, but there was no hesitation about his opening words. 'I don't think it's any good, sir.' He spoke with a clipped intensity, which did not disguise an exhaustion of spirit. 'That bulkhead—it might go any minute, and she'll probably break in two when it happens. That means a lot more men caught, sir.'

'You've shored up completely?'

'Yes, sir. But the space is too big, and the bulkhead was warped too much before we got the shores to it. It's working badly already. I can't see it holding more than another hour, if that.'

'It's the last one worth shoring,' said the Captain, almost to himself.

'Yes, sir.' Chief hesitated. 'I've still seven or eight hands down in the engine-room, I'd like to get them out in good time. Is that all right, sir?'

Chief was looking at him. They were all looking at him—Haines, the Midshipman, the signalman, Adams, the look-outs, the hard-breathing Bridger—all waiting for the one plain order, which they now knew must come. Until that moment he had been refusing to look squarely at this order as it drew nearer and nearer; he could not believe that his loved ship must be given up, and even now, as he hesitated, and the men round him wondered, the idea still had no sort of reality about it. For this man on whom they all relied, this man to whom they attributed no feelings or qualities apart from the skill and forethought of seamanship, was not quite the stock figure, the thirty-eight-year-old R.N. commander, that they took him to be.

True, he fitted the normal mould well enough. He had always done so, from Dartmouth onwards, and the progress from midshipman to commander had followed its appointed course—twenty years of naval routine in which a mistake, a stepping-out-of-line, would have denied him his present rank. He never had stepped out of line; he had been, and still was, normal about everything except this ship; but for her he had a special feeling, a romantic conception, which would have astounded the men waiting round him. It was not the Navy, or his high sense of duty, or the fact that he commanded her, which had given him this feeling: it was love.

The old *Marlborough*. . . . The Captain was not married, and if he had been it might not have made any difference: he was profoundly and exclusively in love with this ship, and the passion, fed especially on the dangers and ordeals of the past three war years, left no room for a rival. It had started in 1926, when she was brand new and he had commissioned her: it had been his first job as First Lieutenant, and his proudest so far. She had been the very latest in ships then—a new sloop, Clyde-built, twin turbines, two four-inch guns (the twin mountings came later), and a host of gadgets and items of novel equipment which were sharp on the palate. . . . There had been other ships, of course, in the sixteen years between; his first command had been a river gunboat, his second a destroyer: but he had never forgotten *Marlborough*. He had kept an eye on her all the time, checking her movements as she transferred from the Home Fleet to the Mediterranean, thence to the China Station, then home again: looking up her officers in the Navy List and wondering if they were taking proper care of her: making a special trip up to Rosyth on one of his leaves, to have another look at her; and when, at the outbreak of war, he had been given command of her, it had been like coming home again, to someone dearly loved who was not yet past the honeymoon stage.

She was not, in point of fact, much of a command for a commander, even as the senior ship of an escort group, and he could have done better if he had wished. But he did not wish. Old-fashioned she might be, battered with much hard driving, none too comfortable, at least three knots slower than the job really demanded; but she could still show her teeth and she still ran as sweet as a sewing machine, and the last three years had been the happiest of his career. He was intensely jealous of her efficiency when contrasted with more up-to-date ships, and he went to endless trouble over this, intriguing for the fitting of new equipment 'for experimental purposes', demanding the replacement of officers or key ratings if any weak point in the team began to show itself. In three years of North Atlantic convoy work he had spared neither himself nor his ship's company any of the intense strain which the job imposed; but *Marlborough* he had nursed continuously, so that the prodigious record of hours steamed and miles covered had cost the minimum of wear.

He knew her from end to end, not only with the efficient 'technical' eye of the man who had watched the last five months of her building, but with an added, intimate regard for every part of her, a loving admiration, an eye tenderly blind to her shortcomings.

Now she was going. No wonder he could not phrase that final order, no wonder he stared back almost angrily at the Chief, delaying what he knew must happen, waiting for the miracle to forestall it.

Up to the bridge came a new, curious noise. It came from deep within the fo'c'sle, a blend of thud and iron clang which coincided with the ship's rolling. Something very solid must have broken adrift down there, either through the shock or the unusual level of their trim, and was now washing to and fro out of control. Chief, his face puckered, tried to place it; it might have been any one of a dozen bits of heavy equipment in the forward store. The big portable pump, most likely. There must be the hell of a mess down there. Men and gear smashing up together—it hardly bore thinking of. And the noise was unnerving; it sounded like the toll of a bell, half sunk, tied to a wreck and washing with the tide. A damned sight too appropriate.

The Captain said suddenly: 'I'll come down and look at that bulkhead, Chief. Haines, take over here.' He turned to Adams. 'You come with me. Bring one of the quartermasters, too.'

There might be some piping to do in a hurry.

The journey down, deck by deck, had the same element of compulsion in it as, in a nightmare, distinguishes the random lunatic journey which can only lead to some inescapable horror at its end. The boat-deck was crowded: two loaded stretchers lay near the whaler, the figures on them not more than vague impressions of pain in the gloom: Merrett was directing the unlashing of a raft near by: on the lee side of the funnel a dozen hands, staring out at the water, were singing 'Home on the Range', in low-pitched chorus. The small party—Captain, Chief, Adams, the quartermaster—made their way aft, past the figures grouped round 'X' gun, and down another ladder. At the iron-deck level, a few feet from the water, all was deserted. 'I sent the damage control party up, as soon as we'd finished, sir,' the Chief said, as he stepped through the canvas screen into the alley-way leading forward. 'There was nothing else for them to do.'

Under cover now, the four of them moved along the rocking passage: Chief's torch picking out the way, flicking from side to side of the hollow tunnel against which the water was already lapping. Under their stumbling scraping feet the slope led fatally downwards. The clanging toll seemed to advance to meet them. They passed the entrance to the engine-room: just within, feet straddled on the grating, stood a young stoker, the link with the outside world in case the bridge voice-pipe failed. To him, as they passed, the Chief said: 'No orders yet. I'll be coming back in a minute,' and the stoker drew back into the shadows to pass the message on. Then they came to a closed watertight door, and this they eased slowly open, a clip at a time, so that any pressure of water within would show immediately. But it was still dry . . . the door swung back, and they stepped inside the last watertight space that lay between floating and sinking.

It was dimly lit, by two battery lanterns clipped to overhead brackets: the light struck down on a tangle of joists and beams, heel-pieces, wedges, cross-battens—the work of the damage control party. The deck was wet underfoot, and as *Marlborough* rolled some inches of dirty water slopped from side to side, carrying with it a scummy flotsam of caps and boots and ditty-boxes. The Captain switched on his torch, ducked under a transverse beam, and stepped up close to the bulkhead. It was, as Chief had said, in bad shape; bulging towards him, strained and leaking all down one seam, responding to the ship's movements with a long-drawn-out, harsh creaking. For a single moment, as he watched it, he seemed to be looking through into the space beyond, where Number One and his fourteen damage control hands had been caught. The forbidden picture—forbidden in the strict scheme of his captaincy—gave place to another one, conjured up in its turn by the clanging which now sounded desperately loud and clear: the three flooded mess-decks underneath his feet, the sealed-off shambles of the explosion area. Then his mind swung back, guiltily, to the only part of it that mattered now, the shored-up section he was standing in, and he nodded to himself as he glanced round it once more. It confirmed what he had been expecting but had only now faced fairly and squarely: Chief had done a good job, but it just wasn't good enough.

He turned quickly. 'All right, Chief. Bring your engine-room party out on to the upper deck. Adams! Pipe "Hands to stations for——"'

The words 'Abandon ship' were cut off by a violent explosion above their heads.

For a moment the noise was so puzzling that he could not assign it to anything: it was just an interruption, almost supernatural, which had stopped him finishing that hated sentence. Then another piece of the pattern clicked into place, and he said: 'That was a shell, by God!' and made swiftly for the doorway.

Outside he called back over his shoulder: 'Chief—see to the door again!' and then started to run. His footsteps rang in the confined space: he heard Adams following close behind him down the passageway, the noise echoing and clattering all round him, urging him on. Reaching the open air at last was like escaping from a nightmare into a sweating wakefulness which must somehow be instantly co-ordinated and controlled. As he went up the ladder to the boat-deck there was a brilliant flash and another explosion up on the bridge, followed by the sharp reek of the shell-burst. Damned good shooting from somewhere . . . something shot past his head and spun into a ventilator with a loud clang. He began to run again, brushing close by a figure making for 'X' gun shouting, 'Close up again! Load star-shell!' Guns, at least, had his part of it under control.

He passed the space between the two boats. It was here, he saw, that the first shell had struck: the motor-boat was damaged, one of the stretchers overturned, and there were three separate groups of men bending over figures stretched out on deck. He wanted to stop and find out how bad the damage was, and, especially, how many men had been killed or hurt, but he could not: the bridge called him, and had the prior claim.

It was while he was climbing quickly up the ladder that he realized that the moon had now risen, low in the sky, and that *Marlborough* must be cleanly silhouetted against the horizon. If no one on the upper deck had seen the flash of the submarine's firing, the moon ought to give them a line on her position. Guns would probably work that out for himself. But it would be better to make sure.

Now he was at the top of the ladder, his eyes grown accustomed to the gloom, his nostrils assailed by the acrid stink of the explosion. The shell he had seen land when he first came out on deck had caught the bridge fair and square, going through one wing and exploding against the chart-house. Only two men were still on their feet—the signalman and one of the look-outs: the other look-out was lying, headless, against his machine-gun mounting. Adams, at his shoulder, drew in his breath sharply at the sight, but the Captain's eyes had already moved farther on, to where three other figures—who must be Haines, the Midshipman, and the messenger—had fallen in a curiously theatrical grouping round the compass platform. The light there was too dim to show any details: the dark shambles could only be guessed at. But one of the figures was still moving. It was the Midshipman, clinging to a voice-pipe and trying to hoist himself upright.

He said quickly: 'Lie still, Mid,' and then: 'Signalman, give me the hailer,' and lastly, to Adams: 'Do what you can for them.' He caught sight of the young, shocked face of the other look-out staring at him, and he called out sharply: 'Don't look in-board. Watch your proper arc. Use your glasses.' Then he switched on the microphone, and spoke into it:

'X gun, X gun—illuminate away from the moon—illuminate away from the moon.' He paused, then continued: 'Doctor or sick-berth attendant report to the bridge now—doctor or sick-berth attendant.'

Pity had inclined him to put the last order first: the instinct of command had told him otherwise. But almost before he stopped speaking, the sharp crack of 'X' gun came from aft, and the star-shell soared. Guns had had the same idea as himself.

Adams, who was kneeling down and working away at a rough tourniquet, said over his shoulder:

'Shall I carry on with that pipe, sir?'

'No. Wait.'

The U-boat coming to the surface had altered everything. The ship was now only a platform for 'X' gun, and not to be abandoned while 'X' gun still had work to do.

As the star-shell burst and hung, lighting up the grey moving sea, the

Captain raised his glasses and swept the arc of water that lay on their beam. Almost immediately he saw the U-boat, stopped on the surface, broadside on to them and not more than a mile away. Before he had time to speak over the hailer, or give any warning, there was a noise from aft as Guns shouted a fresh order and then things happened very quickly.

'X' gun roared. A spout of water, luminous under the star-shell, leapt upwards, just beyond the U-boat and dead in line—a superb sighting shot, considering the suddenness of this new crisis. There was a pause, while the Captain's mind raced over the two possibilities now open—that the U-boat, guessing she had only a badly crippled ship to deal with, would fight it out on the surface, or that she would submerge to periscope depth and fire another torpedo. Then came the next shot, to settle all his doubts.

It came from both ships, and it was almost farcically conclusive. The flash of both guns was simultaneous. The U-boat's shell exploded aft, right on 'X' gun, ripping the whole platform to pieces; but from the U-boat herself a brilliant orange flash spurted suddenly, to be succeeded by the crump of an explosion. Then she disappeared completely.

'X' gun, mortally wounded itself, had made its last shot a mortal one for the enemy.

Silence now all over the ship, save for a faint moaning from aft. The Captain reached for the hailer, and then paused. No point in saying anything at this moment: they would be looking after 'X' gun's crew, what was left of them, and there was no more enemy to deal with. He listened for a moment to Adams's heavy breathing as he bent over the Midshipman, and then turned as a figure showed itself at the top of the bridge-ladder.

'Captain, sir.'

'What is it?'

'S.B.A., sir. The doctor's gone aft to the gun.'

'All right. Bear a hand here. Who's that behind you?'

'It's me, sir,' said Bridger's voice from the top of the ladder. 'I was helping the S.B.A.'

'Were you up here when the second shell landed?'

'No, sir—just missed it.' Bridger sounded competent and unsurprised, as if he had arranged the thing that way. 'I went down to give them a hand when the first one hit the boat-deck, sir.'

'How much damage down there?'

'Killed three of the lads, sir.' The sick-berth attendant's voice breaking in was strained and rather uneven. 'Mr Merrett's gone, too. He was just by the motor-boat.'

Another officer lost. Guns had probably been killed, too. That meant—the Captain checked suddenly, running over the list in his mind. Number One, caught by that bulkhead. Haines and the Midshipman finished up here; Merrett gone, dying typically in a quiet corner, escaping his notice. Guns almost certainly killed at 'X' gun. That meant that there were no executive officers left at all: only Chief and the doctor. If they didn't abandon ship—if somehow they got her going again—it would be an almost impossible job, single-handed. . . . He put the thought on one side for the moment, and said to the sick-berth attendant:

'Take over from Petty Officer Adams. Have a look at the others first, and then get the Midshipman aft to the wardroom.'

He waited again, as the man got to work. The heavy clanging from below, which had stopped momentarily when the gun was fired, now started once more. Presently the doctor came up to the bridge, to report what he had been expecting to hear—that Guns, and the whole crew of seven, had been killed by the last shot from the U-boat. Even though he had been prepared for it, it was impossible to hear the news with indifference. But for some reason it confirmed a thought which had been growing in his mind, ever since the U-boat had been sunk. They were on their own now, and the only danger was from the sea. His loved *Marlborough* had survived so much, had produced such a brilliant last-minute counter-stroke, that he could not leave her now. Reason told him to carry on with the order he had given down below, but reason seemed to have had no part in the last few minutes: something else, some product of heart and instinct, seemed to have taken control of them all. That last shot of 'X' gun had been a miracle. Suppose there were more miracles on the way?

Adams, straightening up as the sick-berth attendant took over, once again tried, respectfully, to recall the critical moment to him:

'Carry on with that pipe, sir?'

'No.' The Captain, divining the uncertainty in the man's mind, smiled in the darkness. 'No, Adams, I hadn't forgotten. But we'll wait till daylight.'

2

There were fourteen hours till daylight: fourteen hours to review that decision, to ascribe it correctly either to emotion or to a reasonable

assessment of chance, and to foresee the outcome. What struck the
Captain most strongly about it was the professional aspect of what he
had done. Down there in the shored-up fo'c'sle, he had made a precise,
technical examination of the damage and the repairs to it, and come to a
clear decision: if the U-boat's shell had not hit them, and interrupted the
order, they would now be sitting in the boats, lying off in the darkness
and waiting for *Marlborough* to go down. But something had
intervened: not simply the absolute necessity of fighting the U-boat as
long as possible, not even second thoughts on their chances of keeping
the ship afloat, but something stronger still. It was so long since the
Captain had changed his mind about any personal or professional
decision that he hardly knew how to analyse it. But certainly the change
of mind was there.

He could find excuses for it now, though not very adequate ones.
Daylight would give them more chance to survey the damage properly.
(But he had done that already.) With the motor-boat wrecked by the
first shell-burst, there were not enough boats for the crew to take to.
(But some of them would always have to use rafts anyway, and if
Marlborough sank they would have no choice in the matter.) They had
a number of badly wounded men on board who must be sheltered for as
long as possible, if they were not to die of neglect or exposure. (But they
certainly stood more chance of surviving an orderly abandonment of
the ship, rather than a last-minute emergency retreat.) No, none of these
ideas had really any part in it. It boiled down to nothing more precise
than a surge of feeling which had attacked him as soon as the U-boat
was sunk: a foolish emotional idea, product both of the past years and
of this last tremendous stroke, that after *Marlborough* had done so
much for them they could not leave her to die. It wasn't an explanation
which would look well in the Report of Proceedings; but it was as near
the truth as he could phrase it.

The answer would come with daylight, anyway: till then he must
wait. If the bulkhead held, and the weather moderated, and Chief was
able to get things going again (that main switchboard would have to be
rewired, for a start), then they might be able to do something: creep
southwards, perhaps, till they were athwart the main convoy route and
could get help. It was the longest chance he had ever taken: sitting there
in his chair on the bridge, brooding in the darkness, he tried to visualize
its successive stages. Funnier things had happened at sea. . . . But the
final picture, the one that remained with him all that night, was of a
ship—his ship—drawing 32 feet forward and nothing aft, drifting
helplessly down-wind with little prospect of surviving till daylight.

No one ashore knew anything about them, and no one would start worrying for at least three days.

Within the ship, ignoring and somehow isolating itself against this preposterous weight of odds, there was much to do; and with no officers to call on except the doctor, who was busy with casualties, and the Chief, whom he left to make a start in the engine-room, the Captain set to work to organize it himself. He kept Bridger by him, to relay orders, and a signalman, in case something unexpected happened (there was a faint chance of an aircraft on passage being in their area, and within signalling distance): Adams was installed as a virtual First Lieutenant; and from this nucleus the control and routine of the ship was set in motion again.

The bulkhead he could do nothing about; Chief set to work on the main switchboard, the first step towards raising steam again, and the leading telegraphist was working on the wireless transmitter; the boats and rafts were left in instant readiness, and the more severe casualties taken back under cover again. (A hard decision, this; but to keep them on the upper deck in this bitter weather was a degree nearer killing them than running the risk of trapping them below.) Among the casualties was the Midshipman, still alive after a cruel lacerated wound in the chest and now in the sick bay waiting for a blood transfusion. The bodies of the other three who had been killed on the bridge—Haines, the look-out, and the bridge messenger—had been taken aft to the quarter-deck, to join the rest, from 'X' gun's crew and the party on the boat-deck, awaiting burial.

Then, after a spell of cleaning up, which included the chaos of loose gear and ammunition round 'A' gun, which had been directly over the explosion, the Captain told Adams to muster what was left of the ship's company and report the numbers. He was still in his chair on the bridge, sipping a mug of cocoa, which Bridger had cooked up in the wardroom pantry, when Adams came up with his report, and he listened to the details with an attention which he tried to rid of all personal feeling. These crude figures, which Adams, bending over the chart-table light, was reading out, were men, some of them well known and liked, some of them ship-mates of two and three years' standing, all of them sailors; but from now on they must only be numbers, only losses on a chart of activity and endurance. The dead were not to be sailors any more: just 'missing potential', 'negative assets'—some damned phrase like that.

Adams said: 'I've written it all down, sir, as well as I could.' He had, in his voice, the same matter-of-fact impersonal tone as the Captain would have used: the words 'as well as I could' might have referred to some trifling clerical inconvenience instead of the difficulty of sorting out the living, the dead, and the dying in the pitch darkness. 'There's the ones we know about, first. There's three officers and twelve ratings killed—that's the Gunnery Officer, Lieutenant Haines, and Mr Merrett, and the gun's crew and the ones on the boat-deck and the two up here. The Surgeon Lieutenant has one officer and sixteen men in the sick bay. We'll have to count most of them out, I'm afraid, sir. Nine of them were out of the fo'c'sle: Then there's'—he paused—'one officer and seventy-four men missing.' He stopped again, expecting the Captain to say something, but as no word came from the dark figure in the chair he went on: 'Then what we've got left, sir. There's yourself, and the Surgeon Lieutenant, and the engineer—that's three officers, and twenty-eight men out of the Red Watch, the one that was on duty.'

'Twenty-eight. Is that all?'

'That's all, sir. They lost seven seamen at "X" gun, three by the boats, and two here. Then there's seven of them down in the sick bay. That's forty-seven altogether.'

'How are the twenty-eight made up? How many seamen have we?'

Adams straightened up and turned round from the table. This part of it he evidently knew by heart. 'There's myself, sir, and Leading Seaman Tapper, and seven A.B.s: the quartermaster and the Bosun's Mate, that were in the wheel-house: and Bridger. That's twelve. Then there's the hands who were on watch in the W/T office: the leading tel. and two others, and two coders. That makes seventeen altogether. The signalman up here, eighteen. The S.B.A., nineteen. The leading steward, twenty.'

'Any other stewards?'

'No, sir.'

It didn't matter, thought the Captain: no officers, either.

'The rest are all engine-room branch, sir,' Adams went on. 'Eight of them altogether.'

'How are they made up?'

'It's pretty good, sir, as far as experience goes. The Chief E.R.A. and one of the younger ones, and a stoker petty officer and five stokers. If it was just one watch they'd be all right. But of course there's no reliefs for them, and they'll have to be split into two watches if it comes to steaming.' Adams paused, on the verge of a question, but the Captain, seeing it coming, interrupted him. He didn't yet feel ready to discuss their chances of getting under way again.

'Just give me those figures again, Adams,' he said, 'as I say the headings. Let's have the fit men first.'

Adams bent down to the light once more. 'Yourself and two officers and twenty-eight men, sir.'

'Killed and wounded?'

Adams added quickly: 'Four officers and twenty-eight.'

'And missing, the First Lieutenant and seventy-four.' He had no need to be reminded of that item: that 'seventy-four' would stay with him always. Not counting the accident to Number One's damage control party, there must have been sixty men killed or cut off by the first explosion. All of them still there, deep down underneath his feet. Twenty-eight left out of a hundred and thirty. Whatever he was able to do with the *Marlborough* now, the weight of those figures could never be lightened.

'Will I make some more cocoa?' said Bridger suddenly. He had been waiting in silence all this time, standing behind the Captain's chair. The numbers and details which Adams had produced, even though they concerned Bridger's own messmates, were real to him only so far as they affected the Captain: this moment, he judged instinctively, was the worst so far, and he tried to dissipate it in the only way open to him.

The Captain's figure, which had been hunched deep in the chair, straightened suddenly. He shook himself. The cold air was stiffening his legs, and he stood up. 'No, thanks, Bridger,' he answered. 'I'm going to turn in, in a minute. Bring up my sleeping-bag and a pillow, and I'll sleep in the asdic hut.'

'Aye, aye, sir.' Bridger clumped off at a solid workmanlike pace, his heavy sea-boots ringing their way down the ladder. The Captain turned to Adams again. 'We'd better work out a routine for the time between now and daylight,' he said briskly. 'We can leave the engine-room out of it for the moment: they're busy enough. You'd better arrange the seamen in two watches: the telegraphists and coders can work in with them, except for the leading tel.—he can stay on the set. Send half the hands off watch now: they can sleep in the wardroom alley-way or on the upper deck, whichever they prefer. The rest can carry on with cleaning up.'

'The doctor may want some help down there, sir.'

'Yes—see about that too. . . . Keep two look-outs on the upper deck for the rest of tonight: tell them they're listening for aircraft as well. We'll show an Aldis lamp if we hear anything, and chance it being hostile. You'd better put the signalman up here, with those instructions; and pick out the most intelligent coder, and have him work watch-and-watch with the signalman. That's about all. I think. See that I'm called if anything happens.'

'Do you want a hand to watch that bulkhead, sir?'

'No. The engine-room will cover that: they're nearest. About meals. . . .' The Captain scratched his chin. 'We'll just have to do our best with the wardroom pantry. There were some dry provisions in the after store, weren't there?'

'Corned beef and biscuits, sir, and some tinned milk, I think. And there's plenty of tea. We'll not go short.'

'Right. . . . That'll do for tonight, then. I'll see what things are like in the morning: there'll be plenty of squaring up to do. You'll have to get those bodies sewn up, too. If we do get under way again,' the Captain tried, and failed, to say in a normal voice, 'you'll have to work out a scheme of guns' crews and look-outs and quartermasters.'

'Better take the wheel myself, sir.'

The Captain smiled. 'It won't exactly be fleet manœuvres, Adams.'

The expected question came at last. 'How much chance have we got, sir?'

'Hard to say.' He answered it as unemotionally as he could. 'You saw the state that bulkhead was in. It might go any time, or it might hold indefinitely. But even very slow headway would make a big difference to the strain on it, unless the bows stay rigid where they are, and take most of the weight. Almost everything depends on the weather.'

As he said this, the arrangements he had been making with Adams receded into the background, and he became aware of the ship again, and of her sluggish motion under his feet. She was quieter now, certainly: no shock or grinding from below, no advertisement of distress. But he could feel, as if it were going on inside his own body, the strain on the whole ship, the anguish of that slow cumbersome roll downwind. Earlier she had seemed to be dying: this now was the rallying process, infinitely painful both to endure and to watch. Long after Adams had left the bridge, the Captain still stood there, suffering all that the ship suffered, aware that the only effective anæsthetic was death.

It was an idea which at any other time he would have dismissed as fanciful and ridiculous, unseamanlike as a poet talking of his soul. Now it was natural, deeply felt and deeply resented. His professional responsibility for *Marlborough* was transformed: he felt for her nothing save anger and pity.

Just before he turned in, Chief came up from below to report progress. He stood at the top of the ladder, a tired but not dispirited figure, and his voice had the old downright confidence on which the Captain had come to rely. He had been in *Marlborough* for nearly three years; as an engineering lieutenant he, too, could probably have got a better job, but he had never shown any signs of wanting one.

'We've made a good start on the switchboard, sir,' he began. 'We ought to get the fans going some time tomorrow.' There was nothing in his tone to suggest the danger, which he must have felt all the time, of working deep down below decks at a time like this. 'The boiler-room's in a bit of a mess—there's a lot of water about—but we'll clear that up as soon as we can get pressure on the pumps.'

'What about the bulkhead, Chief?'

'It's about the same, sir. I've been in once myself, and I've a hand listening all the time outside the next watertight door. There's nothing to report there.' He turned, and looked behind him down the length of the ship, and then up at the sky. 'She seems a lot easier, sir.'

'Yes, the wind's going down.' The phrase was like a blessing.

'By God, we'll do it yet!' Chief, preparing to go down again, slurred his feet along the deck and found it sticky. 'Bit of a mess here,' he commented.

'Blood,' said the Captain shortly. 'They haven't cleaned up yet.'

'We're going to be pretty short-handed,' said Chief, following a natural train of thought. 'But that's tomorrow's worry. Good night, sir.'

'Good night, Chief. Get some sleep if you can.'

But later he himself found sleep almost impossible to achieve, weary as he was after nearly nine hours on the bridge. He lay in his sleeping-bag on the hard floor of the asdic hut, feeling underneath him the trials and tremors of the ship's painful labouring. It was very cold. Poor *Marlborough*, he thought, losing between waking and sleeping the full control of his thoughts. Poor old *Marlborough*. We shouldn't do this to you. None of us should: not us, or the Germans, or those poor chaps washing about in the fo'c'sle. No ship deserved an ordeal as evil as this. Only human beings, immeasurably base, deserved such punishment.

Bridger woke him at first light, with a mug of tea and an insinuating 'Seven o'clock, sir!' so normal as to make him smile. But the smile was not much more than a momentary flicker. Under him he felt the ship very slowly rolling to and fro, without will and without protest: she seemed more a part of the sea itself than a separate burden on it. The weather must have moderated a lot, but *Marlborough* might be deeper in the water as well.

Cold and stiff, he lay for a few minutes before getting up, collecting his thoughts and remembering what was waiting for him outside the asdic hut. It would be bitterly cold, possibly wet as well: the ship would

seem deformed and ugly, the damage meeting his eyes at every turn: the
blood on the bridge would be dried black. All over the upper deck there
would be men, grey-faced and shivering, waking to face the day: not
cheerful and noisy as they usually were, but dully astonished that the
ship was still afloat and that they had survived so far; unwilling, even, to
meet each other's eye, in the embarrassment of fear and disbelief of the
future. And there were those other men down in the fo'c'sle, who would
not wake. There were the burials to see to. There was the bulkhead.

He got up.

The bulkhead first, with the Chief and Adams. The rating outside the
watertight door said: 'Haven't heard anything, sir,' in a noncommittal
way, as if he did not really believe that they were not all wasting their
time. He was a young stoker: sixteen men in his mess had been caught
forward: no hope of any sort had yet been communicated to him.
Noting this, the Captain thought: I'll have to talk to them, some time
this morning. . . . Inside, things were as before: there was a little more
water, and the atmosphere was now thick and sour: but nothing had
shifted, and with the decrease in the ship's rolling the bulkhead itself was
rigid, without sound or movement.

'I think it's even improved a bit, sir,' said the Chief. He ran his hand
down the central seam, which before had been leaking: his fingers now
came away dry. 'This seems to have worked itself watertight again. If
we could alter the trim a bit, so that even part of this space is above the
water-line, we might be able to save it.'

'That's going to be today's job,' said the Captain, 'moving everything
we can aft, so as to bring her head up a bit. I'll go into details when we
get outside.'

On his way back he visited the boiler- and engine-rooms. The boiler-
room was deserted, and already cooling fast: here again the forward
bulkhead was a tangle of shores and joists, braced against the angle-
pieces that joined the frames.

'What about this one?' he asked.

'Doesn't seem to be any strain on it, sir,' Chief answered. 'I think the
space next to it—that's the drying-room and the small bosun's
store—must still be watertight.'

The Captain nodded without saying anything. He was beginning to
feel immensely and unreasonably cheerful, but to communicate that
feeling to anyone else seemed frivolous in the extreme. There was so
little to go on: it might all be a product of what he felt about the ship
herself, and unfit to be shared with anyone.

The engine-room was very much alive. Two men—the Chief E.R.A.

and a young telegraphist—were working on the main switchboard: the telegraphist, lying flat on his back behind it, was pulling through a length of thick insulated cable and connecting it up. Two more hands were busy on one of the main steam valves. There was an air of purpose here, of men who knew clearly what the next job was to be, and how to set about it.

The Chief E.R.A., an old pensioner with a smooth bald head in odd contrast with the craggy wrinkles of his face, smiled when he saw the Captain. They came from the same Kentish village, and the Chief E.R.A.'s appointment to *Marlborough* had been the biggest wangle the Captain had ever undertaken. But it had been justified a score of times in the last two years, and obviously it was in process of being justified again now.

'Well, Chief?'

'Going on all right, sir. It won't be much to look at, but I reckon it'll serve.'

'That's all we want.' The Captain turned to the engineer officer. 'Any other troubles down here?'

'I'm a bit worried about the port engine, sir. That torpedo was a big shock. It may have knocked the shaft out.'

'It doesn't matter if we only have one screw. We couldn't go more than a few knots anyway, with that bulkhead.'

'That's what I thought, sir.'

The Chief E.R.A., presuming on their peace-time friendship in a way which the Captain had anticipated, and did not mind, said:

'Do you think we'll be able to steam, sir?'

Everyone in the engine-room stopped work to listen to the answer. The Captain hesitated a moment, and then said:

'If the weather stays like it is now, and we can correct the trim a bit, I think we ought to make a start.'

'How far to go, sir?'

'About five hundred miles.' That was as much as he wanted to talk about it and he nodded and turned to go. With his foot on the ladder he said: 'I expect we'll be able to count every one of them.'

The laughter as he began to climb was a tonic for himself as well. It hadn't been a very good joke, but it was the first one for a long time.

The sick bay next. The doctor was asleep in an arm-chair when he came in, his young sensitive face turned away from the light, his hands splayed out on the arms of the chair as if each individual finger were resting after an exhausting effort. The sick-berth attendant was bending over one of the lower cots, where a bandaged figure lay with closed, deeply circled eyes. There were eight men altogether: after the night's turmoil the room was surprisingly tidy, save for a pile of bloodstained swabs and dressings which had overflowed from the waste-basket. The tidiness and the sharp aseptic smell were reassuring.

He put his hand out, and touched the sleeping figure.

'Good morning, Doctor.'

Soundlessly the doctor woke, opened his eyes, and sat up. Even this movement seemed part of some controlled competent routine.

'Hallo, sir!'

'Busy night?'

'Very, sir. All right, though.'

'Just what you were waiting for?' The Captain smiled.

The doctor looked at the Captain, and smiled back, and said: 'I haven't felt so well for years.'

It must be odd to feel like that, about what must surely have been the goriest night of his life. But it was natural, if you were proud and confident of your professional skill, and for three years you felt you had been utterly wasted. This young man, who had barely been qualified when war broke out, must now feel, with justice, that the initials after his name had at last come to life.

The Captain looked round the sick bay. 'Where are the rest of them? Adams said you had sixteen.'

'Four died.' It was extraordinary how the simplicity of phrase and tone still conveyed an assurance that the lives had been fought for, and only surrendered in the last extremity. 'I've spread the rest over the officers' cabins, where they'll be more comfortable. There's one in yours, sir.'

'That's all right. . . . How's the Midshipman?'

'Bad. In fact going, I'm afraid, sir. That chest wound was too deep, and he lost too much blood. Do you want to take a look at him? He's in his own cabin.'

'Is he conscious?'

The doctor shook his head. 'No. I've had to dope him pretty thoroughly. That's the trouble: if I go on doping him he'll die of it, and if I let him wake up there's enough shock and pain to kill him almost immediately. That's why it's no good.' Again the simple tone seemed able to imply an infinity of skill and care, which had proved unavailing.

'I won't bother, then.' The phrase sounded callous, but he did not bother to qualify it: he was suddenly impatient to leave this antiseptic corner, and get to work on the ship. She, at least, was still among the living: no dope, no ordered death-bed for her. He had skill and care of his own sort. . . .

As he came out on the quarter-deck he checked his step, for there, arranged in neat rows, which somehow seemed a caricature of the whole idea of burial, were the sewn-up bodies which he must later commit to the deep. Nineteen of them: three officers and sixteen men. There had not been enough ensigns to cover them all, he noted: here and there three of them shared one flag, crowding under it in a pathetic, last-minute symbolism. . . . Adams, who had been waiting for him, straightened up as he emerged. He had only been bending down to adjust one of the formal canvas packages; but the Captain had a sudden ghoulish fancy that Adams had been giving it the traditional 'last stitch'—the needle and thread through the nose, by which the sailmaker used to satisfy himself that the body he was sewing up was beyond doubt that of a dead man. The Captain looked away, and up at the sky. It was full light now: a grey cold day, the veiled sun shedding the thinnest watery gleam, the waste of water round them reduced to a long flat swell. The passing of the storm, or some lull in its centre, had brought a windless day for their respite.

Chief, who had waited behind in the engine-room, now joined them, and together the three men crossed the upper deck towards the fo'c'sle. The Captain led the party, picking his way past the bloody ruin of 'X' gun, and the men who were at work cleaning up. He was conscious of them looking at him: conscious of a suppressed, heightened tension among them all: conscious, for example, that Leading Seaman Tapper, not an outstanding personality, had this morning assumed a new, almost heroic bearing. As the only leading seaman left alive, he was already rising to the challenge. . . . With the coming of daylight all these men had won back what the stokers, working and waiting below decks, still lacked: hope in the future, confidence in themselves and the ship. 'The ship is your best life-belt'—a phrase in his Standing Orders for damage control returned to him. By God, that was still true; and all the men up here trusted and believed it.

Presently they were standing on the fo'c'sle by 'A' gun. From here the deck, buckled and distorted, led steeply downwards, till the bullring in the bows was not more than three or four feet from the water: even allowing for this downward curve of the deck, *Marlborough* must be drawing about twenty-eight feet instead of her normal sixteen. Obviously, the first essential was to correct this if possible: not only to ease pressure forward when they started moving, but also to bring the screws fully under water again.

The Captain stepped forward carefully till he was standing directly over the explosion area: there he leant over the rail, staring down into the water a few feet away. From somewhere below an oily scum oozed out, trailing aft and away like some disgusting suppuration; but of the wound itself nothing could be seen. Unprofessionally, he was glad of that: it was sufficiently distressing to note the broad outlines of *Marlborough*'s plight on this cold grey morning, without being confronted with the gross details. He realized suddenly that this must now be treated as a technical problem, and nothing more, and after a quick look round the rest of the fo'c'sle he turned back to the Chief and Adams.

'I've got three ideas,' he said briskly. 'You may have some more. . . . For a start, we'll get rid of as much as possible of this'—he tapped one of the lowered barrels of 'A' gun, askew on its drooping platform. 'It wouldn't be safe to fire them anyway, so we can ditch the barrels—and even the mounting itself if we can lift it clear.'

'The derrick can deal with the barrels, sir,' said Adams. 'I don't know about the rest.'

'We'll see. . . . Then there are the anchors. We can either let them run out altogether, with their cables, or else let the anchors go by themselves, and manhandle the cable aft as a counterweight. What do you think, Chief?'

'The second idea is the best one, sir. But without steam on the windlass we can't get the cable out of the locker.'

'We'll have to do that by hand.' The Captain turned to Adams again. 'We've still got one of those weapons, haven't we?—the ratchet-and-pawl lever?'

'Yes, sir. It's a long job, though.'

'I know.' They had once had to weigh anchor by this archaic method, a long time ago, bringing in the cable link by link, half a link to each stroke of the lever, which needed four men to operate it. It had been an agonizingly slow process, taking nearly six hours and everyone's temper. Now they would have to do it to each cable in turn. . . . 'But it's worth it, to get some of the weight aft. Then there's the windlass itself. If we pull it to pieces and use a sheer-legs to lift the heavy parts, we might get rid of a lot of weight that way.'

The Engineer Officer nodded, rather abstractedly. It would be his job later to account for all this, item by item, in triplicate at least, and the whole thing was a horrid distortion of the principles of storekeeping. But he put the thought on one side, and produced an idea which must have been professionally more acceptable.

'I was wondering about the fore-peak, sir,' he began. 'You know we've kept it flooded for the last two trips, to balance the weight of those extra depth-charges aft. We can't pump it out now, because the suction-line is broken. But it we took this cover-plate off'—he pointed to the small plate screwed to the deck, right up in the bows—'and made sure the compartment was still isolated, we could pump it out by hand. That would give us some buoyancy just where we need it.'

The Captain nodded quickly. 'Good idea, Chief. You'll have to go carefully, though, in case the bulkhead's gone and it's all part of the explosion area. By the way, what's the fuel situation going to be, with all this part isolated?'

'Oh, we'll have plenty, sir, especially if we're only steaming on one boiler. We've still got the two big tanks aft.'

'Right. . . .' He looked out at the sea again, and then at his watch. It was nearly nine. 'I'll read the burial service in half an hour, Adams, if you'll have everything ready by then. Then you can make a start on the weight-lifting programme—the gun first, and then the anchors. Can you spare any stokers, Chief?'

'Maybe two, sir.'

'The fresh air will be a nice change for them. . . .'

His spirits were rising.

But there was nothing artificial, no formal assumption of mourning, in what he felt half an hour later, as he opened his prayer book, gave 'Off caps' in a low, almost gentle voice, and prepared to read the service. All that remained of his ship's company stood in a rough square on the quarter-deck: at their feet the nineteen bodies, in their canvas shrouds, seemed like some sinister carpet from which they could not take their eyes. There were altogether too many of them: barely did the living outnumber the dead, and if the men caught in the fo'c'sle were reckoned the living were only curious survivals of a vanished time. . . . That pause in the service, when he said 'We do now commit their bodies to the deep,' and then waited, as the burial party got to work and the nineteen bodies made their successive splashes, their long dive—that pause seemed to be lasting for ever.

The men in their stained sea-boots and duffle coats stood silent, their hair ruffled, watching the bodies go: flanking him, the doctor and the Chief completed the square of witnesses. The rough canvases scraped the deck as they were dragged across; the bodies splashed and vanished; the ship rolled, and all their feet shifted automatically to meet it; a seaman coughed; the silence under the cold sky was oppressive and somehow futile. He himself, with an appalling clarity of feeling, was conscious of cruel loss. These had been his own men: to see them 'discharged dead' in this perfunctory wholesale fashion only deepened the sense of personal bereavement which was in his face and his voice as he took up the reading again.

When it was done he put the book away and faced his ship's company: in their expression, too, was something of the wastage and sadness of the moment. It was not what he wished to dwell on, but he could not dismiss it without a word: that would have been as cruelly artificial as using the dead men to whip up hatred, or additional energy for the task ahead. It was no time for anything save sincerity.

'I shall never need reminding of this moment,' he began, 'and I know that is true for all of you too. We have lost good men, good shipmates, and there are many more whom we cannot even reach to give them proper burial. We can't forget them, any more than we can forget the three officers and sixteen men we've just seen over the side. But,' he raised his voice a little, 'one of the hardest things of war is that there is never any spare time to think about these things, or to mourn men like these as they deserve. That has to come later: there's always something to do; and in this case it's going to be the toughest job any of us has ever undertaken. I may as well tell you that I nearly gave the order to abandon ship last night: for the moment the weather has saved us, and we must do our utmost to profit by it. I'm not going to hold out too much hope: but if the weather holds, and the bulkhead, which is taking most of the strain, doesn't collapse, and if I can correct the trim, we stand a good chance of getting in—or at least of going far enough south to meet other ships.' He smiled. 'You can see there are a lot of "ifs" about this job. But it would be a hundred times worth trying, even if our lives didn't depend on it. I myself am going to do my utmost to get this ship in, and I'm counting on every man to back me up. Remember there are only thirty-one of us altogether, and that means a double and triple effort from each one of you. . . . We'll stand easy now, and then get to work. And keep this idea in the back of your minds: if we do get *Marlborough* in, it will be the finest thing any of us has ever done.'

He wanted to say more: affected as he had been by the burials, he wanted to dwell on this aspect of sacrifice, and on *Marlborough* as a measure of its validity and as something dear to them all. But he was afraid of sounding theatrical: better perhaps to leave it like this, a challenge to their endurance and seamanship, and look to the outcome.

When he returned to the bridge he took out the deck-log and began to make an entry concerning the death and burial of his men. It was while he was adding the nineteen names and ratings that he noticed it was the morning of New Year's Day.

3

All that day they lay there, the ship's only motion a sluggish rolling. But within her the movement and the noises were cheerful. The ditching of "A" gun barrels and the greater part of the mounting was easy: the breaking and moving of the anchor cables a long-drawn-out effort which lasted till well after dark. But the cables, hauled in sections along the upper deck and stowed right aft among the depth-charges, made an appreciable difference to their trim: so did the jettisoned windlass, which disappeared overboard bit by bit, as in some mysterious conjuring trick. (It was too heavy and unwieldy to move aft.) But the pumping out of the fore-peak (the triangular section which makes up the bows) was the most successful of all. It acted as a buoyancy chamber where it could exert the most leverage, and it brought the bows up cheerfully. Altogether, by the time the programme was fulfilled, the draught forrard had improved to twenty-four feet, and the screws aft were deep enough to get a firm grip of the water. Of course, she would steer like a mongrel waving its tail; but that wouldn't matter. There was no one watching.

One curious accident attended the lightening process. As *Marlborough*'s draught forrard began to alter decisively, two bodies, released by some chance movement of the hull, floated out from the hole in the port side. They drifted away before they could be recovered: they were both badly burned, and both sprawling in relaxed, ungainly attitudes as though glad to be quit of their burden. The Captain, looking down from the bridge, watched them with absorbed attention, obsessed by the fancy that they were a first instalment of the sacrifice which must be paid before the ship got under way. He heard a rating on the fo'c'sle say: 'The second one was Fletcher—poor bastard,' and he felt angry at the curt epitaph, as if its informality might somehow weaker the magic. He could not remember having had thoughts like that since he was a small boy. Perhaps it was the beginning of feeling really tired.

For him it had been a long day, and now at dusk, with the prospect of another night of drifting, he felt impatient to put things to the test. He had been all over the ship again: he had seen the Midshipman and two ratings who were also dying: he had looked at the radio set (from which the leading tel. had at last stood back and said: 'It's no good, sir—there's too much smashed'): he had made a third examination of the bulkhead, where they had been able to insert another shore and a felt-and-tallow patch, to take up the slack as the pressure on it relaxed. He had directed the work on the cables, Adams being busy on 'A' gun. Now he had nothing to do but wait for Chief's report from the engine-room: the hardest part of all. He had the sky to watch, and the barometer, low but steady; and that was all. The main ordeal still lay ahead.

It was nine o'clock that evening before the Engineer Officer came up with his report: the Captain was sitting in the deserted wardroom aft, eating the corned beef hash which was now their staple diet and remembering other parties which this room had witnessed, when there were eight of them, with Number One's wife and Guns' fiancée and one of the Mid.'s colourful young women to cheer them. Now the dead men and the mourning women outnumbered the living: no charm, no laughter could enliven any of the absent. . . . Impatiently he ground a half-smoked cigarette into his plate, cursing these ridiculous thoughts and fancies, unlike any he could remember, which were beginning to crowd in on him. There was no time to spare for such irrelevancies: he had one supreme task to concentrate on, and anything else was a drain on energy and attention alike.

Chief came in, shedding a pair of oily gauntlets, looking down apologetically at his stained white overalls.

'Well, Chief?'

'Pretty good, sir.' He crossed to the pantry hatch and hammered on it, demanding his supper. Then he sat down in his usual place at the foot of the table, and leant back. 'The switchboard's done, and they're working on the dynamo now: it had a bad shake-up, but I think we'll manage.' He was obviously very tired, eyelids drooping in a grey lined face. The Captain suddenly realized how much depended on this man's skill. 'I'll be flashing up when I've finished supper.'

'How long before we can steam?'

'Can't say to the nearest hour, sir. It'll be some time tomorrow, unless we run into more snags. There's the boiler-room to pump out, and a lot of cleaning up besides. It'll only be one screw, I'm afraid. The other's nearly locked: the shaft must be badly bent.'

'It doesn't matter.'

Bridger came in with the Chief's supper, and for a little while there was silence as he ate. Then, between bites, he asked:

'How's the Midshipman, sir?'

'Pretty nearly gone. God knows what keeps him alive. His chest's in an awful mess.'

Chief looked round the room, and said: 'It's funny to see this place empty.'

There was silence again till he had finished eating. They shared the same thoughts, but it was less discomforting to leave them unspoken. Bridger, coming in with the Chief's coffee, broke the silence by asking the Captain:

'Will you be sleeping down here, sir?'

'No, in the asdic hut again.'

'Will you see Petty Officer Adams, sir?'

'Yes. Tell him to come in.'

There was a whispering in the pantry, and Adams came in, cap in hand. 'Same routine tonight, sir?' he asked.

'Yes, Adams. Two look-outs, and the signalman on the bridge. I'll be in the asdic hut.'

'Aye, aye, sir.'

'Things seem to be going all right. We should get going some time tomorrow.'

Adams's severe face cracked into a grin. 'Can I tell the hands, sir?'

'Yes, do.' The Captain stood up, and began to put on his duffle coat. 'How about some sleep for you, Chief?'

The Chief nodded. 'As soon as I've finished up, sir. There'll be a bit of time to spare then.' Relaxing, with coffee-cup in hand, he looked round the wardroom. 'New Year's Day. I wish we had the radio. It feels so cut off.'

'With luck you'll have your bedtime music tomorrow.' He went out, stepping over the dozen sleeping men who crowded the alley-way, and made his way forward to the bridge again. With luck tomorrow might bring everything they were waiting for.

The sea was still calm, the glass unwaveringly steady.

He awoke suddenly at five o'clock, startled and uneasy. For a moment he puzzled over what had disturbed him: then he realized gratefully what it was. The lights had come on, and the little heater screwed to the bulkhead was glowing. It meant that the dynamos were now running properly, and the switchboard, which the Chief had been reserving for the engine-room circuit, was able to deal with the full load. With a surge of thankfulness almost light-headed, he got up and went over to the side table. On it lay a chart and a pair of dividers, ready for a job which, impelled by yet another of those queer fancies, he had sworn

not to tackle until this moment had arrived. The course for home. . . .
He took out his pencil and prepared to calculate.

The only mark on the chart was Pilot's neat cross (too damned
appropriate) marking their estimated position when the torpedo struck
them, with the time and date—1630/31/12. From this he started to
measure off. Distance to the Clyde—520 miles. Distance to the nearest
of the Faeroes—210 miles, and nothing much when you got there.
Distance to the nearest point of Britain—the Butt of Lewis, 270 miles.
And just round the corner, another 30 miles or so—Stornoway. . . .
That was the place to make for, he knew. It had no big repairing
facilities, but it would be shelter enough, and they would be able to send
tugs to bring them the rest of the way home. Stornoway—300 miles.
Say three knots. A hundred hours. Four days. Good enough.

Now for the course. The magnetic course, it must be: the master
gyro-compass had been wrecked, and they would have to depend on the
magnetic compasses, trusting that the explosion and the shifting of
ballast had not put them out. South-east would do it. South-east for four
days. Butt of Lewis was a good mark for them (he checked it on the
chart): a flashing light, visible fourteen miles. That would bring them in
all right. And what a landfall. . . .

When finally he laid down his pencil he was still in the same state of
exaltation as had possessed him when he saw the lights come on. The
desire to sleep had vanished: impelled to some sort of activity, he left the
shelter of the asdic hut and began to pace up and down outside. By God,
once they got going there would be no stopping them. . . . What did four
days matter?—they could keep going for four weeks if it meant
Marlborough making harbour at the end. There was no depression now,
no morbid brooding about sacrifices or the cost in men. It was
Marlborough against the sea and the enemy, and tomorrow would see
her cheating them both. He looked up at the sky, clear and frosty: a
night for action, for steering small, for laughing and killing at the same
time. The first night of 1943. And tomorrow they would sail into the
new year like a prizefighter going in for the finish. Nothing was going to
stop them now.

Midday found them still drifting, still powerless. A succession of
minor breakdowns involving in turn the fans and the steering-engine
held up everything during the morning: at noon a defect in one of the oil
pumps led to more delay. The suspended activity, the anti-climax after
that first rush of feeling, was a severe test of patience: it was with
difficulty that the Captain, walking the upper deck, managed to exhibit
a normal confidence. Part of the morning was taken up with the burying

of two more men who had died during the night, but for the remainder
he had little to occupy him; and as the afternoon advanced and the light
declined, a dull stupor, matching his own indolence, seemed to envelop
the ship. Stricken with the curse of immobility, she accepted the dusk as
if it were all that her languor deserved.

Then, as swiftly as that first torpedo strike, the good news came.
Chief, presenting himself in the wardroom with a cheerful grin,
announced that his repairs were complete: he used the classic formula
'Ready to proceed, sir!' and he seemed to shed ten years in saying it.
The Captain got up slowly, smiling in answer.

'Thank you, Chief. . . . A remarkable effort.'

'We're all touching wood, sir.' But he was almost boyish in his good
humour.

'I want to start very gently. Twenty or thirty revs, not more. Will you
put a reliable hand on the bulkhead?'

'I'll go myself, sir. The Chief E.R.A. can take charge in the engine-
room.'

'All right.' The Captain raised his voice. 'Pantry!'

The leading steward appeared.

'Ask Petty Officer Adams to come up to the bridge.'

'Aye, aye, sir.'

'I'll just ring "Slow ahead" when I'm ready, Chief. We can do the rest
by voice-pipe. If you hear anything at all from the bulkhead, stop
engines straightaway, of your own accord.'

Within a minute or so he was on the bridge, the signalman by his side,
Adams in the wheel-house below. Leaning across the faintly lit compass
he called down the voice-pipe:

'How's her head down there?'

'South, eighty west, sir.'

The two compasses were in agreement. 'Right. . . . Our course is
south-east, Adams. Bring her round very slowly when we begin to
move.'

'Aye, aye, sir.' Adams's voice, like the signalman's fierce breathing at
his elbow, reflected the tension that was binding them all.

The Captain took a deep breath. 'Slow ahead starboard.'

'Slow ahead starboard, sir.'

The telegraph rang. There was a pause, then a slight tremor, then the
beginning of a smooth pulsation. Very slowly *Marlborough* began to
move. A thin ripple of bow-wave stood out in the luminous twilight:
then another. In the compass bowl the floating disk stirred, edging away

to the right. The ship started her turn, a slow, barely perceptible turn, 125 degrees to port in a wide half-circle nearly a mile across.

Presently he called down the voice-pipe: 'Steering all right?'

'Yes, sir. Five degrees of port wheel on.'

The engine-room bell rang, and he bent to the voice-pipe, his throat constricted. 'What is it?'

From the background of noise below an anonymous voice said: 'Message from the engineer, sir. "Nothing to report." '

'Thank you.'

A long pause, with nothing but smooth sliding movement. Then from Adams, suddenly: 'Course—south-east, sir.'

'Very good.'

They were started. Forty-eight hours after the torpedoing: two days and two nights adrift. Course south-east.

The wind, now growing cold on his cheek, was like a caress.

That first night, those first fourteen hours of darkness on the bridge, had the intensity and the disquiet of personal dedication. It was as if he were taking hold of *Marlborough*—a sick, uncertain, but brave accomplice—and nursing her through the beginnings of a desperate convalescence. He rarely stirred from his chair, because he could see all he wanted from there—the sagging fo'c'sle, the still rigid bows—and he could hear and feel all the subtleties of her movement forward: but occasionally he stepped to the wing of the bridge and glanced aft, where their pale wake glittered and spread. Of all that his eyes could rest on, that was the most heartening. . . . Then back to his chair, and the stealthy advance of the bows, and the perpetual humming undercurrent that came from the engine-room voice-pipe, as comforting as the steady beat of an aircraft engine in mid-ocean. He was not in the least tired: sustained by love and hope, he felt ready to lend to *Marlborough* all his reserves of endurance.

At midnight the Chief came up to join him. His report was good: the engine had settled down, the bulkhead seemed unaffected by their forward movement. They discussed the idea of increasing speed, and decided against it; the log showed a steady three knots, sufficient for his plans.

'There's no point in taking bigger chances,' said the Captain finally. 'She's settled down so well that it would be stupid to fool about with the revs. I think we'll leave things as they are.'

'Suits me, sir. It'll be a lot easier, seeing how short-handed we are down there.'

'You're working watch-and-watch, I suppose?'

'Got to, sir, with only two E.R.A.s. I'd stand a watch myself, but there's all the auxiliary machinery to look after.' He yawned and stretched. 'How about you, sir? Shall I give you a spell?'

'No, I'm all right, thanks, Chief. You turn in now, and get some sleep.' The Captain smiled. 'I always seem to be saying that to you. I hope you're doing it.'

Chief smiled back. 'Trust me, sir. Good night.'

Presently, up the voice-pipe, came Adams's voice: 'All right to hand over, sir?'

'Who's taking the wheel?'

'Leading Seaman Tapper, sir.'

'All right, Adams. What does the steering feel like now?'

'A bit lumpy, sir. It takes a lot to bring her round if she starts swinging off. But it's nothing out of the way, really.'

'I don't want anyone except you or Tapper to take the wheel until daylight.'

'Aye, aye, sir.'

It meant a long trick at the wheel for both these two; but inexpert steering might put too great a strain on the hull, and he wanted its endurance to be fully demonstrated before running any risks.

A moment later he heard the confirmatory 'Course south-east—starboard engine slow ahead—Leading Seaman Tapper on the wheel,' as Adams was relieved. Then the bridge settled down to its overall watchful tranquillity again.

Indeed, his only other visitor, save for Bridger with a two-hourly relay of cocoa, was the doctor, who came up to tell him that the Midshipman was dead. It was news which he had been waiting for, news with no element of surprise in it; but coming at a time of tension and weariness, towards the dawn, when he was cold and stiff and his eyes felt rimmed with tiredness, it was profoundly depressing. The Midshipman, as captain's secretary, had spent a great deal of time with him: he was a cheerful, still irresponsible young man who had the makings of a first-class sailor. Now, at daylight, they would be burying him—and that only after alternate periods of agony and stupor, which had robbed death of every dignity. This, the latest and the most touching of the sacrifices that had been demanded of them, destroyed for the moment all the night's achievement.

Dawn restored it: a grey sunless dawn, only a lightening of the dull arch above them: but the new and blessed day for all that. As the gloom round them retreated and he was able to see, first the full outline of

Marlborough's hull, then the shades of colour in the water, and then the horizon all round them, the triumph of the moment grew and warmed within him, dissolving all other feeling. By God, he thought, we can keep going for ever like this. . . . They were forty miles to the good already: there were only 260 more—three more nights, three more heartening dawns such as this: and *Marlborough*, creeping ahead over the smooth paling sea, was as strong as ever. If they could hold on to that (he touched the wood of his chair) then they were home.

At eight o'clock, the change of the watch, he called Leading Seaman Tapper to the bridge, and told him to turn over the wheel to the regular quartermaster and to take over as officer of the watch. It was irregular (he smiled as he realized how irregular), but he had to get some rest and there was no one else available to take his place: Chief was owed many hours of sleep, the doctor had been up all night with the Midshipman, Adams had been on the wheel since four o'clock. It simply could not be helped.

He lay down at the back of the bridge, drew the hood of his duffle coat over his face, and closed his eyes against the frosty light. It was such bliss to relax at last, to sink away from care, that he found himself grinning foolishly. Fourteen hours on the bridge: and God knows how many the night before. . . . He would have to watch that. Might get the doc. to fix him up. Leading Seaman Tapper—*Acting* Leading Seaman Tapper. . . . No, it couldn't be helped. In any case there was nothing to guard, nothing to watch for, nothing for them to fight with. Now, they had simply to endure.

4

It was at midday that the wind began to freshen, from the south.

The noise, slight as it was, woke the Captain. It began as no more than an occasional wave-slap against the bows, and a gentle lifting to the increased swell; but into his deep drugged sleep it stabbed like a sliver of ice. He lay still for a moment, getting the feel of the ship again, guessing at what had happened: by the way *Marlborough* was moving, the wind was slightly off the bow, and already blowing crisply. Then he stood up, shook off his blankets, and walked to the front of the bridge.

It was as he had thought: a fresh breeze, curling the wave-tops, was now meeting them, about twenty degrees off the starboard bow. Of the two, that was the better side, as it kept the torpedoed area under shelter: but the angle was still bad, it could still impart to their progress a twisting movement which might become a severe strain. While he was considering it, Adams came up to relieve Tapper, and they all three stood in silence for a moment, watching the waves as they slapped and broke against *Marlborough*'s lowered bows.

'You'd better go back on the wheel, Adams,' said the Captain presently. 'If this gets any worse we'll have to turn directly into it, and slow down.'

It did get worse, in the next hour he spent in his chair, and when the first wave, breaking right over the bows, splashed the fo'c'sle itself, he rang the bell to the engine-room. Chief himself answered.

'I'll have to take the revs off, Chief, I'm afraid,' he said. 'It's getting too lively altogether. What are they now?'

'Thirty-five, sir.'

'Make that twenty. Have you got a hand on the bulkhead?'

'No, sir. I'll put one on.'

'Right.' He turned to the wheel-house voice-pipe. 'Steer south, twenty-five east, Adams. And tell me if she's losing steerage-way. I want to keep the wind dead ahead.'

'Aye, aye, sir.'

The alteration, and the decrease in speed, served them well for an hour: then it suddenly seemed to lose its effect, and their movements became thoroughly strained and awkward. He decreased speed again, to fifteen revolutions—bare steerage-way—but still the awkwardness and the distress persisted: it became a steady thumping as each wave hit them, a recurrent lift-and-crunch which might have been specially designed to threaten their weakest point. It was now blowing steadily and strongly from the south: he listened to the wind rising with a murderous attention. At about half past three it backed suddenly to the south-east, and he followed it: it meant they were heading for home again—the sole good point in a situation rapidly deteriorating. He looked at the seas running swiftly past them, and felt the ones breaking at the bows, and he knew that all their advantage was ebbing away from them. This was how it had been when he had been ready to abandon ship, three nights ago; it was this that was going to destroy them.

Quick steps rang on the bridge ladder, and he turned. It was the Chief: in the failing light his face looked grey and defeated.

'That bulkhead can't take this, sir,' he began immediately. 'I've been in to have a look, and it's started working again—there's the same leak down that seam. We'll have to stop.'

The Captain shook his head. 'That's no good, Chief. If we stop in this sea, we'll just bang ourselves to bits.' A big wave hit them as he spoke, breaking down on the bows, driving them under. *Marlborough* came up from it very slowly indeed. 'We've got to keep head to wind, at all costs.'

'Can we go any slower, sir?'

'No. She'll barely steer as it is.'

Another wave took them fair and square on the fo'c'sle, sweeping along the upper deck as *Marlborough* sagged into the trough. The wind tugged at them. It was as if the death-bed scene were starting all over again.

The Chief looked swiftly at the Captain. 'Could we go astern into it?'

'Probably pull the bows off, Chief.'

'Better than this, sir. This is just murder.'

'Yes. . . . All right. . . . She may not come round.' He leant over to the voice-pipe. 'Stop starboard.'

'Stop starboard, sir.' The telegraph clanged.

'Adams, I'm going astern, and up into the wind stern first. Put the wheel over hard a-starboard.'

'Hard a-starboard, sir.'

'Slow astern starboard.'

The bell clanged again. 'Starboard engine slow astern, wheel hard a-starboard, sir.'

'Very good.'

They waited. Those few minutes before *Marlborough* gathered stern-way were horrible. She seemed to be standing in the jaws of the wind and sea, mutely undergoing a wild torture. She came down upon one wave with so solid a crash that it seemed impossible that the whole bows should not be wrenched off: a second, with a cruelty and malice almost deliberate, hit them a treacherous slewing blow on the port side. Slowly *Marlborough* backed away, shaking and staggering as if from a mortal thrust. The compass faltered, and started very slowly to turn: then as the wind caught the bows she began to swing sharply. He called out: 'Watch it, Adams! Meet her! Bring her head on to north-west,' and his hands as he gripped the pedestal were as white as the compass-card. The last few moments, before *Marlborough* was safely balanced with her stern into the teeth of the wind, were like the sweating end of a nightmare.

Behind him the Chief sighed deeply. 'Thank God for that. What revs do you want, sir?'

'We'll try twenty.'

It was by now almost dark. *Marlborough* settled down to her awkward progress: both Adams and then Tapper wrestled steadily to keep her stern to the wind, while the waves mounted and steepened and broke solidly upon the quarter-deck. That whole night, which the Captain spent on the bridge, had a desperate quality of unrelieved distress. All the time the wind blew with great force from the south-east, all the time the seas ran against them as if powered by a living hate, and the vicious spray lashed the funnel and the bridge structure. At first light it began to snow: the driving clouds settled and lay thick all over them, crusting the upper deck in total icy whiteness. *Marlborough* might have been sailing backwards off a Christmas cake ... but still, with unending, hopeless persistence, she butted her way southwards.

Five days later—one hundred and twenty-one hours—she was still doing it. The snow was gone, and the gale had eased to a stiff southerly breeze; but the sea was still running too high for them to risk turning their bows into it, and so they maintained, stern first, their ludicrous progress. The whole afterpart of the ship had been drenched with water ever since they turned; the wardroom had been made uninhabitable by a leaking skylight, the alley-way in which the men slept was six inches awash with a frothy residue of spray. It was hardly to be wondered at, thought the Captain as he slopped through it on his way back to the bridge: poor old *Marlborough* hadn't been designed for this sort of thing.

He was very tired. He had hardly had two consecutive hours of sleep in the last five days: the strain had settled in his face like a tight and ugly mask. The doctor had done his best to relieve him, by taking an occasional spell on the bridge when the remaining four serious patients could be left; but even this seemed of no avail—his weariness, and the hours of concentration on *Marlborough*'s foolish movements, pursued him like a hypnosis, twitching his eyelids when he sought sleep, making his scalp prickle and the brain inside flutter. Hope of rest was destroyed by a twanging tension such as sometimes made him want to scream aloud. When he sat down in his chair on that fifth night of stern-way—the ninth since they were torpedoed—and hunched his stiff shoulders against the cold, he was conscious of nothing save an appalling lassitude. Even to stare and search ahead, in quest of those shore-lights that never showed themselves, was effort enough to make him feel sick in doing it.

He had no idea where they were. They had seen nothing—no lights at night, no aircraft, not a single smudge of smoke anywhere on the horizon. The sextant had been smashed by the shellfire, and there was no sun anyway to take sights by. Even at two knots, even at one and a half, they should have raised Butt of Lewis light by now, if their course were correct. That was the hellish, the insane part of it. Probably it wasn't correct: probably the torpedoing and the weight-shifting had put everything out, and the magnetic compasses were completely haywire. Probably they were heading straight out into the Atlantic instead of pointing for home. And Hell! he thought, this bloody cock-eyed way of steaming . . . you couldn't tell where the ship was going to. They might be anywhere. They might be going round in circles, digging their own grave.

Bridger, the admirable unassailable Bridger, appeared at his elbow. The cup of cocoa which seemed to be part of his right arm was once more tendered. While he drank it, Bridger stood in silence, looking out at the sea. Then he said:

'Easing off a bit, sir.'

'Just a little, yes.'

There was another pause: then Bridger added: 'It's a lot drier aft, sir.'

'Good.' It was impossible not to respond to this effort at raising his spirits, or to be unaffected by it; and he said suddenly: 'What do the hands think about all this?' It was the sort of question he had never before asked any rating except the coxswain.

Bridger considered. It was entirely novel to him, too; what the lower deck thought of things, and what they said about them to their officers, were two differing aspects of truth. At length:

'They're a bit sick of the corned beef, sir.'

The Captain laughed, for the first time for many days. 'Is that all?'

'Just about, sir. But we're having a sweepstake on when we get in.'

For some reason the Captain felt like crying at that one. He said, after a moment:

'Has your number come up yet?'

'No, sir. Six more days to run.'

There was much more that the Captain wanted to ask: did they really think *Marlborough* would get in: were they still confident in his judgement, after all these days and nights of blundering along: did they trust him absolutely?—questions he would never even have thought of, save in a light-headed hunger for reassurance. But suddenly Bridger said:

'They hope you're getting enough sleep, sir!'

Then he sucked in his breath, as though discovered in some appalling breach of discipline, took the cup from the top of the compass, and quickly left the bridge. Alone once more, the Captain smiled tautly at the most moving thing that had ever been said to him, and settled back in his chair to take up the watch again. He *wasn't* getting enough sleep, but the fact that the ship's company realized this, and wished him well over it, was as sustaining and comforting as a strong arm round his shoulders.

On the morning of the tenth day since they were torpedoed, he had a conference with the Chief on the bridge. They had seen little of each other during the preceding time: five days of having the reversing gear in continuous action had proved an unaccustomed strain, and the Chief has been kept busy below, nursing the one remaining engine through its ordeal. Now, at nine o'clock, he had come up with some fresh news.

'Have you noticed the fo'c'sle, sir?'

'No, Chief, I hadn't.' After yet another night on the bridge he felt no more and no less tired than usual: he seemed to be living in some nether hell of weariness which nothing could deepen. 'What's happened to it?'

'The bows have started to bend upwards again.' He pointed. 'You can just about see it from here, sir. There's a kink in the deck, like folding a bit of paper.'

'You mean the whole thing's being pulled off.'

'Something like that, sir. It's a slow process, but if it gets any worse we'll lose the buoyancy of the fore-peak, and that may bring the screws out of the water again.'

'What's the answer, technically?'

'Either slow down to nothing, or turn round and push them on again.'

The Captain gestured irritably. 'My God, it's like fooling around with a bundle of scrap-iron! "Push the bows on again"—it sounds like some blasted lid off a tin!'

'Yes, sir.' While Chief waited for the foolish spasm to spend itself, he wondered idly what the Captain *really* thought *Marlborough* should be like, after what she had gone through. 'Bundle of scrap-iron' wasn't far wide of the mark: she could float, she could lollop along backwards, and that was about all. 'Well, that's the choice, sir,' he said presently. 'I don't think we can carry on like this much longer.'

The Captain got hold of himself again: at this late hour, he wasn't going to start dramatizing the situation. It was all this damned tiredness. . . . 'We could just about turn round now,' he said slowly, looking at the sea with its long rolling swell and occasional breaking wave-tops. 'It was a lot worse than this before we turned last time.'

'About how far have we got to go, sir?'

'I don't know, Chief.' He did not make the mistake of admitting his ignorance in a totally normal voice, but he managed to imply that there was nothing to be gained either by a full discussion of it, or by surrendering to its hopeless implication. 'If we were on our proper course we should have raised Butt of Lewis a long time ago. Probably the compasses are faulty. I'm just going to keep on like this till we hit something.'

Stopping, and turning the bows into the wind again, was an even slower process than it had been five days earlier: at times it seemed that *Marlborough*, lying lumpishly off the wind and butting those fragile bows against the run of the waves, *would not* come up to her course. The Captain dared not increase speed, in order to give the rudder more leverage; and so for a full half-hour they tumbled athwart the wave-troughs, gaining a point on the compass-card, sagging back again, wavering on and off the wind like a creaking weathercock that no one trusts any longer. Down in the wheel-house, Leading Seaman Tapper leant against the wheel which he had put hard a-starboard, and waited, his eyes on the compass-card. If she wouldn't, she wouldn't: no good worrying, no good fiddling about. . . . All over the ship, during the past few days, that sort of thing had been growing: things either went right, or they didn't, and that was all there was to it. Between a deep weariness and a deeper fatalism, the whole crew accepted the situation, and were carried sluggishly along with it.

At the end of half an hour a lull allowed *Marlborough* to come round on her course. She settled down again slowly, as if she did not really believe in it, but knew she had no choice. South-east, it was, and one and a half knots. It *must* bring them home. It had to.

It did not bring them home: it did not seem to bring them anywhere. They steamed all that day, and all the next, and all the next, and all the next: four more days and nights, to add to the fantastic total of that south-easterly passage. But *was* it a south-easterly passage?—for if so, they should by now have been right through Scotland, and out the other side: eleven days steaming, it added up to, and thirteen days since they had been torpedoed. It just didn't make sense.

The weather did not help. It did not deteriorate, it did not improve: the stiff breeze held all the time, the sloppy uneven sea came running at them for hour after hour and day after day. The ship took it all with a tough determination which could not disguise a steady progressive breaking down. The bulkhead wavered and creaked, the water ran down the splitting seam, slopped about on the deck, increased in weight till it began to drag the bows down to a fatal level. The noise mounted gradually to an appalling racket: clanging, groaning, knocking, protesting—the whole hull in pain, ill-treated as an old galled horse sweating against the collar, fit only for the knacker's yard but hardly strong enough to drag itself there. Gallant, ramshackle, on her last legs, *Marlborough* bumped and rolled southwards, at a pace which was itself a wretched trial of patience.

Above all, there was now a smell—a sweetish, sickish smell seeping up the ventilators from the fo'c'sle. It penetrated to every part of the ship, it hung in the wind, it followed them till there seemed to be nothing around them in the sea or the sky but the gross stink of the dead, those seventy-odd corpses which they carried with them as their obscene ballast. It could not be escaped anywhere in the ship. Every man on board lived with it, tried to shut it out with sleep, woke with it sweet and beastly in his nostrils. It became the unmentionable horror that attended them wherever they went.

They all hated it, but there was so much more to hate. The tiredness of overstrained men working four hours on and four hours off, for day after day and night after night, lay all over the ship, a tangible weight of weariness that affected every yard of their progress. The ship's company, whether watching on the upper deck or tending the boilers and the engine-room, moved in a tired dream barely distinguishable from sleep. A grotesque fatigue assailed them all: they stayed on watch till their eyes ran raw and their bodies seemed ready to crumple: they ate like men who could scarcely move their jaws against some dry and tasteless substance: they fell asleep where they dropped, wedged against ventilators, curled up like bundles of rags in odd corners of the deck. All of them were filthy, bearded, grimed with spray and smoke: there was no water to wash with, no change of clothes, nothing to hearten them but tea and hard biscuit and corned beef, for every meal of every day of the voyage. All over the ship one met them, or stumbled over them: wild-eyed, dirty, slightly mad. And all round them, and above and below, hung that smell of death, a thick enveloping curtain, the price of sea-power translated into a squalid and disgusting currency.

And the Captain . . . he summed up, in his person, all that tiredness, all that stress and dirt, all that wild fatigue. He had had the least sleep of anyone on board, throughout the thirteen days: at the end of it he still held the whole thing in his grip, but it was a grip that had another quality besides strength—it had something cracked and desperate about it. His was the worry, his the responsibility, his the appalling doubt as to whether they were really going anywhere at all: he held on because there was no choice, because they could not give up, above all because this was *Marlborough*, his own ship, and he would not surrender her to God or man or the sea. Like a lover, light-headed and despairing, he hoped and strove and would not be forsworn.

The bridge was now his prison. . . . Wedged in his chair, chin on hand, a small thing was beginning to obsess him. On one of the instruments in front of him there was a splash of dried blood, overlooked when they cleaned up after the shell-burst. It had an odd shape, like a boot, like Italy: but the silly thing was that when he looked to one side that shape seemed to change, spinning round and round like a windmill, expanding and contracting as if the blood still lived and still moved to a pulse. He tried to catch it moving, but when he stared at it directly it became Italy again, a dirty brownish smear that no one wanted. He roared out suddenly: 'Signalman!' and then: 'For the Lord's sake clean that off—it's filthy!' and when the man, staring, set to work on the job, he watched him as if his sanity depended on it. Then he looked ahead again, scanning the horizon, the damned crystal-clear horizon. No change there: no shadow, no smudge of smoke, nothing. Where were they going to? Was there anything ahead but deep water? Was he leading *Marlborough*, and the wretched remnant of her ship's company, on a fantastic chase into the blue? And God Almighty! That smell from forrard. . . . It was like a curse, clamped down hard on their necks. Perhaps they were all going to perish of it in the end: perhaps the whole ship and her dead and dying crew, welded together in a solid mass of corruption, would one night dip soundlessly beneath the sea and touch bottom a thousand fathoms below.

At 4 a.m. on the morning of 14 January, Petty Officer Adams came up on the bridge, to see the Captain before taking over the wheel. He had a pair of binoculars slung beneath the hood of his duffle coat, and from force of habit he raised them and swept slowly round the horizon, a barely distinguishable line of shadow on that black moonless night. He did this twice: then, on the verge of lowering his glasses, he checked suddenly and stared for a long minute ahead, blinking at the rawness, the watery eye-strain, which even this slight effort induced. Then he said, in a compressed, almost croaking voice:

'There's a light dead ahead, sir.'

The words fell into the silence of the bridge like a rock in a pool. They all whipped up their glasses and stared in turn—the Captain, the signalman, Bridger, with his cocoa-cup forgotten: all of them intent, tremendously alert, checking their breathing as if afraid of losing an instant's concentration. Then Adams said again:

'There it is, sir—only the loom of it, but you can see it sweeping across.'

And the Captain, answering him, said very softly: 'Yes.'

It *was* a light—the faintest lifting of the gloom in the sky, like a spectral fan opening and closing, like a whisper—but it *was* a light. For a moment, the Captain was childishly annoyed that he had not seen it first: and then a terrific and overpowering relief seemed to rise in his throat, choking him, pricking his eyes, flooding all over his body in a shaking spasm. The soreness which he had felt round his heart all through the last few days rose to an agonizing twinge and then fell away, leaving him weak, almost gasping. He found the light again, and then dropped his binoculars and leant against his chair. The wish to cry, at the end of the fourteen days' tension, was almost insupportable.

Round him the others reacted in their own way, contributing to a moment of release so extraordinary that no extravagance of movement or word could have been out of place. The cup which Bridger had placed on a ledge fell and shattered. The signalman was whistling an imitation of a bosun's pipe, a triumphant skirl of sound. Adams, unknowing, muttered: 'Jesus Christ, Jesus Christ, Jesus Christ,' over and over again, in a voice from which everything save a sober humility had disappeared. They were men in a moment of triumph and of weakness, as vulnerable as young children, as unstable, as near to ecstasy or to weeping in the same single breath. They were men in entrancement.

It *was* a light—and soon there were others: three altogether, winking and beckoning them towards the vast promise of the horizon. The Captain took a grip of himself, the tightest grip yet, and went into the chart-house to work them out; while all over the ship men, awakened by some extraordinary urgency which ran everywhere like a licking flame, leant over the rails, and stared and whispered and laughed at what they saw. Lights ahead—land—home—they'd made it after all. Some of them stared up at the bridge, seeing nothing but feeling that they were looking at the heart of the ship, the thing that had brought them home, the man who more than anyone had worked the miracle. And then they would go back to the lights again, and count the flashes, and start singing or cursing in ragged chorus. There was no one anywhere in the ship who did not share in this moment: the hands on the upper deck shouted the news down to the engine-room, the signalman on the bridge gave a breathless running commentary to the wheel-house. The release from ordeal moved them all to the same wild exaltation.

Only the Captain, faced by the array of charts on the table, no longer shared the full measure of their relief. For he was now concentrating on something else, something he could not make out at all. They were lights all right—but what lights? The one that Adams had first seen was not Butt of Lewis: the other two did not seem to fit any part of the chart, either Lewis or the mainland round Cape Wrath, or the scattered islands centred on Scapa Flow and the Orkneys. He checked them again, he laid off the bearings on a piece of tracing-paper and then moved it here and there on the chart, hesitatingly, like a child with its first jigsaw puzzle. He even moved it up to Iceland, but the answer would not come—and it was an answer they *must* have before very long: they were running into something, closing an unknown coastline which might have any number of hazards—outlying rocks, dangerous overfalls, minefields barring any approach except by a single swept channel. Sucking his pencil, frowning at the harsh lamplight, he strove to find the answer: even at this last moment, delay might rob them of their triumph. But the answer would not come.

Presently he opened the chart-house door and came out again, ready to take fresh bearings and to make doubly certain of what the lights showed. Both the doctor and the Chief were now on the bridge, talking in low voices through which ran a strong note of satisfaction and assurance. The Chief turned as he heard the step, and then jerked his head at the lights.

'Finest sight I've seen in my life, sir.'

The Captain smiled. 'Same here, Chief.'

'Is that Butt of Lewis, sir?' asked the doctor.

'No.' He raised his glasses, checked the number of the flashes, and bent to the compass to take a fresh bearing. 'No, Doc, I haven't worked out what it is yet.'

'It's something solid, anyway.'

'Enough for me,' said the Chief. 'All I want is the good old putty, anywhere between Cape Wrath and the Longships.'

To himself the Captain thought: I wish I could guarantee that.

'Another light, sir!' exclaimed the signalman suddenly. 'Port bow—about four-oh.'

The Captain raised his glasses once more.

'There it is, sir,' said the signalman again, before the Captain had found it. 'It's a red one this time.'

'Red?'

'Yes, sir. I got it clearly then.'

Red . . . that rang a bell, by God! There was a red light at the end of Rathlin Island, off the north coast of Ireland: it was the only one he could remember, in fact. But Rathlin Island. He walked quickly into the chart-house, and moved the tracing-paper southwards. The jigsaw suddenly resolved itself. It *was* Rathlin: the light they had first seen was Inistrahull, the others were Inishowen and something else he could not check—probably an aircraft beacon. Rathlin Island—that meant that they had come all down the coast of Scotland, over two hundred miles farther than he had thought: it meant that they must have been steering at least fifteen degrees off their proper course. Those bloody compasses! But what did it matter now? Rathlin Island. They could put in at Londonderry and get patched up, and then go home. Northern Ireland instead of Butt of Lewis—that would look good in the Report. But what the hell *did* it matter? They had made their landfall.

He walked back to his chair, sat down, and said, in as level a voice as he had ever used:

'That's the north coast of Ireland. We'll be going to Derry.'

It was a peerless morning: the clean grey sky, flecked with pearly grey clouds, turned suddenly to gold as the sun climbed over the eastern horizon. There was now land ahead: a dark bluish coastline, with noble hills beyond. The Captain's stiff stubbly face warmed slowly to the sunshine: the ache across his shoulders and round his heart seemed to melt away, taking with it his desperate fatigue. Not much longer—and then sleep, and sleep, and sleep. . . . Bridger handed him the morning cup of cocoa, his face one enormous grin. But all he said was: 'Cocoa, sir.'

'Thanks . . . We made it, Bridger.'

'Yes, sir.'

'Who won that sweepstake?'

'The Buffer, sir—I mean, Petty Officer Adams.'

The Captain laughed aloud. 'Bad luck!' For the ship's company that must be the one flaw in an otherwise perfect morning. There were a lot of hands on the upper deck now, smiling and pointing. He felt bound to them as closely as one man could be to another. Later, he wanted to find some words that would give them an idea of that. And something about *Marlborough*, too, the ship he loved, the ship they had all striven for.

'Trawlers ahead, sir,' said the signalman, breaking in on his thoughts. 'Three of them. I think they're sweeping.'

Back to civilization: to lights, harbours, dawn mine-sweepers, patrolling aircraft, a guarded fairway.

'Call them up, signalman.'

But one of the trawlers was already flashing to them. The signalman acknowledged the message, and said: 'From the trawler, sir: "Can I help you?" '

'Make: "Thank you. Are you going into Londonderry?" '

A pause, while the lamps flickered. Then: 'Reply "Yes", sir!'

'Right. Make: "Will you pass a message to the Port War Signal Station for me, please?" '

Another pause. 'Reply, "Certainly", sir.'

The Captain drew a long breath, conscious deep within him of an enormous satisfaction. 'Write this down, and then send it to them. "To Flag Officer in Charge, Londonderry, v. *Marlborough.* H.M.S. *Marlborough* will enter harbour at 1300 today. Ship is severely damaged above and below water-line. Request pilot, tugs, dockyard assistance, and burial arrangements for one officer and seventy-four ratings." Got that?'

'Yes, sir.'

'Right. Send it off. . . . Bridger!'

'Sir?'

'Ask the Surgeon-Lieutenant to relieve me for an hour. I'm going to shave. And wash. And change. And then eat.'

It Was Cruel

I USED TO TALK ABOUT THE WAR AT SEA FOR A YEAR OR SO afterwards, and then it became a bore, and peacetime grew exciting and much more important. I wrote about it twenty years ago, but never again. Yet even now, a great wheeling quarter-century later, it is still vivid, still awful, still a scar of sorts, however handsomely healed. . . .

There was a catch-phrase on board our ship, 'A corvette would roll on wet grass'; and its ring of truth had swiftly turned sour indeed. Corvettes were abominable ships to live in, in any kind of weather; already cramped, wet, noisy, crowded, and starkly uncomfortable, they pitched and rolled and swung with a brutal persistence as long as any breeze blew.

To fight in, with any kind of spirit, they were worst of all. The first enemy and the last, the eternal bully, was the atrocious sea; and when we had come to terms with that, we still had to tackle the men who were trying to burn us, or maim us, or blow us up, or hunt us down, and strangle us with the sea's own noose.

Our personal shield, our own tin life-boat, was H.M.S. *Campanula*, the eighteenth corvette out of many hundreds soon to be built in a crash programme designed to meet the swift and violent threat to our convoys, the early prime thrust of the enemy.

By some ludicrous stroke of policy all corvettes bore the names of gentle and delicate flowers. But some names, it was obvious, were preferable to others; we would rather have had our own than Wallflower, or Periwinkle, or Daffodil, or Meadowsweet (their Lordships of the Admiralty, with man-of-the-world delicacy, had excluded Pansy from the list).

But the ships, however prettily named, were all the same: bare platforms for a four-inch pop-gun and a huge clutch of depth-charges, and wallowing cages for eighty-eight men condemned to a world of shock, fatigue, crude violence, and grinding anxiety.

On the job of convoy escort we simply had to point ourselves in the

right direction—due west for the New World and after that due east for
the battered Old—and then get going. Convoys, at this crucial moment
of the war, when an average of three precious ships a day were being
sunk, and yet supplies had to be brought in to keep the island fighting, to
keep the island fed, to let the island survive at all—convoys could not
wait upon the weather.

We were the smallest warships on regular convoy escort in the
North Atlantic, the armed trawlers being gradually phased out after the
wicked winter of 1940; and we were very proud of the fact. We were
also very glad to give up and go home again after our own eternal
pasting by the elements.

Because we might have to go out again in a hurry we had to be refilled
with everything we had spent on the last brave voyage. The first long
day ashore ended at 2300 (the hour of 11 p.m. had vanished with the
civilized past), when the last of the liberty-men stumbled down the quay,
stumbled up the gangway, arranged themselves in a tousled wavering
line, and were, after scrutiny, allowed to go below. This inspection was
not an item of vile slave-tyranny. Mild drunkenness did not matter; but
incapacity—i.e. falling headlong down a twelve-foot ladder and earning
a broken neck at the bottom—was too expensive to be risked, if a
searching glance could take care of it.

The Officer-of-the-Day had done his job if the ship settled down
peacefully by midnight. He had failed if someone got hurt in a fight or
hurt himself on his way to sleep. There were marginal areas, often
summed up in certain formal charges to be preferred next morning:
'Able Seaman Briginshaw did create vandalism in the galley', or 'Did
urinate in the stokers' mess-deck'. Anything like this meant that the
OOD's searching glance had not been searching enough.

But in H.M.S. *Campanula* the OOD had another hazard to put up
with.

It would come at any moment in the form of a voice which rang out
with a particular raucous prison clang:

'Monsarrat! I'm going ashore!'

Or: 'Monsarrat!' (I had never realized that my name could sound so
like the bark of an Alsatian.) 'Where's that bloody steward?'

Or: 'Monsarrat! That stern-wire's slack again! Hop to it!'

Or: 'Monsarrat! There's too much noise over my cabin!'

Or on one memorable occasion: 'Monsarrat! I've been calling you
for ten minutes!'

'Sorry, sir, I was in the lavatory.'

'Don't go to the lavatory! Bake it!'

This was our Captain, on whom my present peace of mind and future prospects entirely depended.

Just as I was in the Navy because I had raced a 14-foot dinghy from the age of fifteen, and crewed in boats as big as four tons, so I was the Correspondence Officer because I had written four novels and a play. There were other jobs assigned to me, and there was often the same kind of eerie logic to back up the choice.

I was the Censoring Officer (if I could write, I could presumably read, especially between the lines). There was no such thing as a private letter leaving any warship; they all had to be read.

One minor point of interest, as far as I was concerned, was in the choice of the code-word scribbled on the back of the envelope; among these were SWALK ('Sealed with a loving kiss'), HOLLAND ('Hope our love lasts and never dies'), BOLTOP ('Better on lips than on paper'), and the more urgent BURMA ('Be undressed and ready my angel'). Why these messages were not written out *en clair* in the letter itself I never discovered; certainly I did not need to be shielded—I had ceased to be shocked by any aspect of a sailor's yearning for home after a small incident on the bridge when I was Officer-of-the-Watch.

Through the windows of the wheelhouse I noticed the standby quartermaster opening a matchbox and showing something inside it to the man at the wheel. Since I did not want the latter's attention to be distracted (he might start 'writing his name astern,' which was our slang for bad steering), I broke up the colloquy and asked what it was all about.

The man with the matchbox, not at all abashed, exhibited his trophy again. Inside the box, enshrined in a tuft of cotton-wool, was a small—a very small—curly hair, of unmistakable origin.

'Just to remind me of home, sir,' he explained. Possibly some private remnant of innocence showed in my face, or perhaps he was certain that all officers must lead sheltered lives, for he added: 'Wilson's got *three*.' As I left the wheelhouse I heard a mumbled voice behind me: 'All different colours, I'll bet.'

As an additional duty, since I had once tried to be a BBC announcer, and must therefore have the right kind of voice, I took Divisions on Sunday (the naval version of church parade), and read the service.

This had to be prefaced by an order which was awkward to prounounce with any kind of naval precision. It was not easy to combine authority with religious tolerance in the words: 'Fall out, the

Roman Catholics!' But it had to be done; tradition, or more probably 'King's Regulations and Admiralty Instructions', had so laid it down.

Thus every Sunday, at this command, half a dozen men would turn smartly right and double away behind the funnel, leaving us to our heretical rites.

The rites were mine to choose and, with a free hand, I made up the pattern myself. We recited the Lord's Prayer together; and then I read that marvellous 23rd Psalm which could still ring a gentle carillon of bells within the most agnostic skull.

The Lord is my shepherd; I shall not want.
He maketh me to lie down in green pastures; he leadeth me beside the
   still waters. . . .

Ah, those still waters. . . . Then came the Lesson for the day; then the 'Naval prayer' which started so splendidly: 'Oh Lord God, Who alone spreadest out the heavens'; and then we sang that hymn which could still bring me near to tears, even at the age of thirty-one, even after a hundred crude scenes of slaughter; a hundred burials—'Eternal Father, strong to save.'

It ended, of course, with 'O hear us when we cry to Thee, For those in peril on the sea', and by God, we meant it!—or I meant it, and I hoped the spark might catch. But did I really believe, even in the face of fear? I didn't know then, and I don't know now.

Perhaps I was not alone in doubt or even derision. To that tune of 'Eternal Father, strong to save,' where it came to the lines 'O hear us when we cry to Thee, For those in peril on the sea' there was, I knew, a sophisticated back-row choir which sang, *sotto voce*:

> The working class can kiss my arse,
> I've got the foreman's job at last.

The trouble was, I hadn't yet made up my mind about that breach of taste, either. But discipline, or at least its public framework, could be restored by another Sunday morning traditional, the reading of half a dozen excerpts from the Articles of War, perhaps the most threatening reminder of the rules ever framed. As I rolled out the fate of the mutineer and the coward-in-the-face-of-the-enemy—'Shall suffer *Death*, or such other punishment as the Lords Commissioners of the Admiralty shall decree'—it sometimes sounded a little rough for Sunday worship. But then I thought of Nelson, and was confident again. When asked about the hanging of some mutineers on a Sunday he had snapped back, 'I would have hanged them on Christmas morning!'

After that, we all went below for the first drink of the Sabbath morning—called by some wag, the thirst after righteousness—and then I shed my ghostly cassock and got back to the paperwork.

Since my father was a surgeon, and the Captain knew this, I was also appointed the ship's Medical Officer within a few hours of reporting on board. This was the worst of all my jobs, the most moving, the most ugly, the most calculated to make me wish that I could revert to an innocent child again.

At first it meant nothing much; I landscaped a few ingrowing toenails and bandaged a few scraped elbows. But then *Campanula* went to sea, and then to war, and then to violence and bloodshed; and after that my patients were all survivors from ships torpedoed in convoy, and the worst horror-film of my life began.

Survivors, climbing on board with gasping lungs, or hauled over the side like oil-soaked fish from the scrambling nets, or hoisted up with a rope to torture anew a shattered body, could be suffering from anything, no matter how terrible. They could have swallowed mouthfuls of corrosive fuel oil, and be coughing up their guts until they died; they could be shuddering in the last bitter extremity of cold and exhaustion; they might have sustained gross wounds and the shock that went with them; they could be screaming with the pain of deep, hopeless burns, and broken limbs, and bodies half-flayed by a rough ship's side as they slid down into the water.

But good or bad, bad or unspeakable, they were all mine; and when they were brought below, or, too anguished to be moved, were propped up gently in the lee of the depth-charge rails, I had to pick up my little black bag and attend their sorrows.

I got used to it in the end, after a season of near-vomiting fear; I grew hardened to the loathsome sights and sounds, and perhaps more skilful in rough-and-ready treatment, and less guilty when, in all compassion, I hurt a writhing man until the watching ring of his shipmates, and of mine, seemed likely to break their appalled silence at this butchery, and snatch the knife or the needle or the probe from my hand and drive it into the back of my skull.

But if anyone had told me, when I answered an advertisement in *The Times* in 1940 for gentlemen with yachting experience to apply for a commission in the R.N.V.R., that as a result I would soon be stitching up a gashed throat without benefit of anaesthetics, or trying to coax a dangling eyeball back into its socket; or if I had known that a man with a deep stomach wound, spread-eagled on what seemed like the very rack of Christ, could actually *smell* so awful, like an opened drain, I might well have kept my yachting experience as secret as the grave, and settled for the Army Pay Corps or for prison or for shameful defeat itself.

First mine was butcher's work, and then, all too often, dustman's. To tidy up my medical practice, and because it was probably all my fault anyway, I was assigned to take charge of all burials and to see the bodies—noted in the log, with raw finality, as 'Discharged Dead'—tipped over the side for their long dive.

I came to know that burial service by heart. I could easily have closed the book on 'Man that is born of woman hath but a short time to live, and is full of misery', and run right on through the 'Stop engines' signal to the bridge, without a written word to help me.

But I did read from the text, for fear of making a mistake, and also because the words were so beautiful and deserved this reverence.

Just as with my crude doctoring, so with this allied task; one grew hardened to it; the most important thing was that the figures should add up correctly at the end of the voyage, and that the Coxswain's 'victualling sheets', swelled by these chance visitors, should be shown to have been diminished by the moment of this leave-taking. A tidy disposal was all.

Once—it was at the dawn of my thirty-first birthday—I buried eight men before breakfast; five we had picked up dead, and three more who had died at the end of my watch. Eight men, eight sailors, eight comrades in this fearful enterprise—I should be in tears, I should be wearing a mourning band round my very heart. . . . But all it meant was that the exercise took a little longer than usual; I still found a ready appetite for the fried bread, the powdered-egg omelette, and the thin brew of coffee essence which was our reward an hour later.

Finally, to round off the long list of things I was doing to bring the Germans to their knees, I was the Depth-Charge Control Officer: not the skilful fellow who operated our Asdic set to decide when the depth-charges should be dropped, but the man who actually rolled them over the stern or splayed them out from the throwers; and that job, at least, suited me fine.

As a lapsed pacifist I was still glad that I didn't have to fire guns, which could shed blood and were terribly noisy anyway (even our modest 4-inch peashooter, which was boldly dated 1913). Depth-charges were quite different, as all the world knew. They didn't really kill people; they just sank U-boats, metal objects which were trying to kill *us*. The convention that whereas we had submarines (noble and skilful), the hated Hun actually used U-boats (wicked and treacherous) was still a persistent gloss on history, continued from 1914.

Depth-charges exploded with satisfying violence, an almighty WHOOMP! which shattered the surface of the sea, brought the middle depths to the boil, and when adroitly used in coastal waters could supply all hands with a prime fish dinner. The D.C. Control Officer had an inevitable link with the Correspondence Officer. I had to keep an individual case-history of every single one under my charge—or, rather, of the numbered detonator-pistols which set them off: the date they were fired, the depth setting, the type, and the performance. Then the empty boxes, all of them also listed in detail, had to be returned to Naval Armaments.

It might not do any damage, I sometimes thought, as I cast my mighty missile into the sea; but at least I had its right number!

So Monsarrat—sailor, surgeon, scribe and sexton, all wrapped up in one harassed parcel tied with the tarry twine of naval discipline—so I confronted the enemy. Or, rather, all the enemies. First there was the sea, undeniably hostile. Then there were the Germans, violently and successfully so. Then—not last of all, often near the top of my private list—there were the people who were supposed to be on my side: certain of my shipmates and superiors, the small string of putrid albatross which never left my neck.

Let us start at the top and perhaps end there, for there the tune was set.

The Captain, a long-term professional sailor in the R.N.R., thought nothing—less than nothing—of us, the pink-cheeked amateurs; and the various ways in which he made this clear, not fewer than seventeen times a day, ensured that the feeling was mutual. It stemmed, without doubt, from the traditional stupid and childish feud between the Royal Naval Reserve and the Royal Naval Volunteer Reserve—and anyone who doubts that lack of one initial could make such a whale of a difference should take a parallel alphabetical rift between the R.N. and the R.N.R. and try it on for size.

The last convoy of March was one of the most terrible so far, completing the toll of an awful month which had started with the loss of twenty-nine ships *in one week*. From the atrocious weather, and then from the enemy, we took such a mauling that my private graph (Are we winning? Are we losing? How will it all end?) made its steepest nose-dive of the war, far below the horizon of hope. A scudding wind was bashing us against the pier as we began to make ready for sea; the familiar summons in the familiar accent: 'Hands to stations for leaving harbour! Special sea-duty-men—close up!' sounded like the chaplain's call for a dawn hanging.

The wind was westerly, hard westerly, as we butted our way outwards from the Bar Light Vessel into the Irish Sea, and set course for Chicken Rock, off the Isle of Man. We had twenty ships under our wing, the Liverpool portion of the west-bound convoy; and for many long hours we cherished them and chivvied them and joked with them and told them to make less smoke and crack on more speed. Then, rounding the last light of England, we turned north and began to roll and shudder in good earnest.

Very slowly we drew past places which we knew only as labels, the names of lighthouses and headlands and forbidding cliffs; places we should never visit, places we might never see again. On passage we picked up ships like anticipant girls—some of them very old girls; gradually we drew together a vast acreage of sixty-five merchantmen which, with us, was trying for the tenth or the twentieth or the fiftieth time the fearsome passage from the old world to the new.

The monstrous Cape Wrath was our last sight of land. It faded astern as we turned north-west again for Iceland and into the teeth of an Atlantic gale, enough (said our leading signalman, a noted phrase-maker) to blow the balls off a bull.

The convoy was in fighting shape now, in spite of all the elements against it: a huge blunt fortress of ships, ranged in eight columns and more than two miles wide from flank to flank: with six scurrying corvettes as outriders and an elegant old V & W destroyer to keep the whole thing in line. The fact that the convoy stayed resolutely in this pattern was something I never ceased to marvel at, and to admire.

In the next six howling days and nights, with visibility anything from poor to nothing at all, it still remained a convoy: keeping good station, preserving discipline and order, turning when it was ordered to turn, showing no lights, making no betraying smoke. These were men, it should be remembered, whose first instinct on sighting another ship was to keep as far away from it as possible: to whom collision was the ultimate disaster; who truly hated such close company.

And yet, in this awful weather, which made a big ship almost unmanageable and a small ship a wildly bucking hazard, they still agreed to crowd together and to obey the rules; and on the bridge of the Commodore's ship the man in total charge was probably a retired admiral, not less than sixty-five years old, who had left a Sussex garden or a Chelsea flat or a fireside of grandchildren to take on this grinding sea-duty again.

I could never forget that while we took pride in our little blue suits and little brass buttons and little bits of gold braid, and zigzagged about and turned on a sixpence and dashed off towards the nearest horizon, there were other sailors—thousands of them—who had to stay faithfully in convoy and keep their unwieldy ships in line, even in this wallowing turmoil; who trusted us to guard them while they plodded onwards at a speed grotesquely less than their best; whose ships were often *the* target—slow-moving, slow-turning, large, violently inflammable.

Yet when one met them ashore, elbow-to-elbow in a dockside pub, they were quiet men in quiet shabby suits, in whose quiet voices the enormous tensions of this shared ordeal could not even be guessed at.

Our battering continued, for watch after watch and day after day; *Campanula* had deteriorated to her usual ugly shambles, with water sloshing about in the mess-decks and one of the wardroom armchairs thrown against a bulkhead and smashed to splinters. The food had gone the same way as the ship; for three days we had been reduced to a changeless menu, at all meals, of tea, soup, and corned-beef sand-wiches. Nothing more ambitious could be made to stay in or on the galley stove.

There was one comforting thought, to help the eternal strain and tiredness: it was too rough for U-boats, which would have given up the hopeless task of taking aim and be comfortably riding this out in the still calm of six fathoms down.

Within sight of Iceland it was bitterly cold. The black forbidding land loomed up briefly, and was lost in the scud again. We shed a few ships for Reykjavik and wished above everything that we could have been one of them. Then we turned southwards again, groaning and labouring, for our meeting with the east-bound convoy, the one we were, at long last, to take home with us.

Luck and naval navigation and skilful planning by slide-rule men on those faraway east and western shores gave us a perfect rendezvous—correct to within five miles, in an ocean which held thirty-one million square miles of salt water, all of it in total disorder. The change-over was without dramatics: we gave them our lot, and took over theirs, and then settled down in station again.

But turning in the teeth of this gale, bringing the ship round with agonizing slowness, wallowing helplessly in a long succession of huge wave-troughs, and then starting to run before a wicked following sea which often lifted our stern higher than the top of our funnel—that set the pattern for another two long days of torture. When the wind unbelievably took on an extra edge of frenzy, the wise Commodore signalled us all to heave-to—which meant turning our raw faces into the storm again, with the same painful slowness. Sadly, despairingly, we had turned our backs on home and were going the wrong way, however slowly.

We were imprisoned thus for a day and a night, and then, at the second dawn, there came a sudden lull. Our world fell silent; the rigging and the signal halyards and the funnel-guys gave up their screaming and slatted idly in the sulky air; the waves no longer broke, but butted us, and each other, with lumpish ill-humour. While it lasted, we waited in this stillness, suspecting it, uneasy at such swift respite.

The battered convoy, seizing the chance, drew its ranks together, came quickly round, and headed eastwards with hopeful readiness; and then, with no more notice than a distant sighing, the wind itself whipped round and picked up its surging strength and began to blow savagely against us again. It was now a north-east gale, straight from Siberia.

But this, it turned out, was only a quick, two-day piece of spite; presently, after a pitch-black howling night, it really did ease off, and once more we pulled ourselves together and set a fair course for home.

It was the sixteenth day already and we were still in 25° West, a thousand miles from safety; and very soon, as if to make the point beyond doubt, the radio began to chatter, and from Commander-in-Chief, Western Approaches, using his magic box in faraway, much-loved Liverpool, the first U-boat reports began to arrive.

In the better weather they had come up for air, and for us.

It was an established sequence: the wolf-pack pattern which the Germans were now bringing to a grisly peak of efficiency. One U-boat must have spotted us (the convoy had made quite a lot of smoke when it put on speed again, and in clear weather smoke could be seen from fifty miles away). He had called up all his chums, strategically placed across a hundred miles of the known convoy tracks, and waiting for this sighting report; and within twenty-four hours, as the diligent Admiralty signalled, there were 'up to seven U-boats in your area'.

The familiar sick feeling took hold of *Campanula*—or at least it took hold of me, a good average coward, and I did not mind owning to it. The odds were rough indeed; if we had had double the number of escorts, seven U-boats could always get through the screen. All it needed was for two of them to show themselves or make some kind of diversion (firing a distress rocket was a favourite) ahead and astern of the convoy. Corvettes had to be sent away to investigate and the convoy's flanks were thus left with gaps literally a mile wide. Through these the other U-boats slid and went to work.

It was a middle watch attack, as usual, starting with an underwater thud reported by a stunned Asdic operator, and then a huge sheet of flame, topped by acrid smoke billowing black against the stars, on the far side of the convoy. It could only be an oil-tanker. . . . I pressed the alarm-bell for action stations, but already I could hear sea-boots, of men in a hurry, men in fear or expectation, drumming and echoing along the iron decks. It was not a night for sleeping.

It was in fact the start of a desperate three-day running fight with the enemy, during which we lost eleven ships and got nothing in return. I do not want to fight it again. But there were certain highlights or lowlights or moments of special ugliness and terror.

These did not always happen when 'Darken ship' was piped. One torpedo scored a hit in broad daylight on what must have been an ammunition ship; we had noticed her earlier because she carried a packed deck-cargo of armoured cars and medium tanks and aircraft with folded-back wings, stuck on to the upper deck like presents on a Christmas tree.

She went up with a great roar, disintegrating from end to end at a single stroke; and after that her place in the convoy was marked only by huge spray-filled splashes as that precious deck-cargo fell back into the sea, item by item.

The U-boats sank two more tankers, to add to the first victim. They were only small ones, but death in burning oil must always be just about the same size.

While we were collecting the aftermath of this considerable mess, just after dawn, a Sunderland flying-boat (known to us as a steam chicken) flew over on its patrol. She signalled, on her Aldis lamp: 'What happened?' The Captain was fed up, as usual, with other people's stupidities, and for once I didn't blame him. He sent back: 'Everything', and we got on with the task of tidying up a most squalid corner of the sea.

We had with us what was known as a CAM-ship, the initials standing for Catapult Aircraft Merchant; an ordinary freighter, but specially equipped to launch a Hurricane fighter-plane from a monstrous steam-catapult on the fo'c'sle. When the pilot had finished his job he ditched his aircraft and parachuted down; it was an expensive, even madcap, exercise, but it was aimed at doing something about a new breed of German reconnaissance plane called a Focke-Wulf (at least, some called them that) which was currently plaguing our convoys.

One of them was plaguing us now; the Hurricane took off in a cloud of steam and a whirl of salty spray, chased its quarry and lost it, and the R.A.F. pilot then jumped, according to the drill. But a cross-wind carried him into the middle of the convoy, which could not stop for such heroics; and while we waited astern to pick him up his parachute got entangled in the propellers of a small, intent, persevering merchant ship which also could not leave its station, nor alter course, nor slacken speed, nor cut him loose; and he was towed away to a dog's death—but slowly.

The third night was the worst; we lost five good ships, and uncounted men, and we never came to grips with a single one of the enemy. Struck with the guilt of sailors who should have done much better, who should have warded off at least some part of this slaughter, we did the only thing left to us—stopped engines and waited, dead in the water, to pick up survivors.

We were not the only dead in the water. By the light from a ship burning handily nearby we could see the usual rubbish of disaster: crates, baulks of timber, coal-dust, doors, rope-ends, a dead cat, odd bits of clothing, empty life-rafts, and wallowing corpses—all floating in inch-thick stinking oil. But presently it became the familiar seascape with figures. Men lived here. There was a life-boat coming towards us, with creaking oars; there were dozens of little lights clustered together—the small bulbs, clipped to life-jackets, which gave men still swimming their only chance of being seen in time for rescue.

We did the best we could. Among the lolling dead who drifted alongside and were hauled in with the rest there was one extraordinary object: like a dummy figure, like a caricature of a man, grossly swollen, with a great pink face which, by the light of a torch, might have been part of some obscene carnival.

Staring down at it, I had visions of a new weapon, a decoy-man which, like a decoy-duck, lured others to their doom. Still slow in the uptake, I called down to the leading seaman clinging to the foot of the scrambling net, who was trying to get a line round this bobbing balloon:

'What on earth is it?'

He looked up at me. His face in the torch-light was the colour of putty. Then he was sick. Then he called back: 'It's an old one.'

We did the best we could, on that night as on the other nights. We picked up a total of 180 survivors in the three-day action; the crowding, the stench of oil all over the ship, the groaning and the retching, the patient agony and the trembling terror gave *Campanula* a foretaste of the very marrow of hell. There were twelve Norwegians and Danes and Poles, some bare-footed, some in rags of uniform, quartered in the wardroom; 168 Malays and Chinese and Indians in the crammed mess-decks.

I was a busy man on that last night; and I was down in the mess-decks myself, seeing how the poor lived, ten feet below the waterline, ten feet from the barest chance of safety. It had been crowded enough with eighty-eight of our own crew; now, with another 168 men added, it was chaos.

There were men praying and weeping and laughing on a cracked note of hysteria, and crooning as they cradled their dead friends; and other men struck dumb but screaming with their eyes.

This was my surgery, on that busy night. Here were the men waiting to be helped, and other men waiting to be buried.

I did the best I could, with the coxswain to bear a hand, and the leading signalman to hold the first-aid kit, and a telegraphist who had once been a vet to give me a second opinion. But how did one tell a burnt man, while staring straight into his jellied eyes, that he would be feeling better soon? What did one do for the tortured lascar with the mortal oil seeping down into his gut?

Often I willed such men to die, even while I tended them: and sometimes they agreed. Yet when the longed-for silence did fall, when they became acquainted with death, that was the worst moment of all.

One of my father's odd bits of old wartime slang had been to say, when a man was killed in the trenches, that he had become 'a landowner in France'. Now, in my turn, I could greatly improve on this: the moment had come when I could confer on these lost warriors the vast freehold of the Atlantic.

But it was still the cleanest burial of all—and even in the act of committal I remembered a slightly drunken conversation, years earlier, with a man belonging to the Imperial War Graves Commission who had just come back from Flanders. He had been busy transferring World War I bodies from a small cemetery to a larger one, in the interest of economizing on real estate and to appease the French.

'There are never any coffins left, *as such*,' he had told me importantly. 'No uniforms either. Just a skeleton and some buttons, and the socks. Always the socks.'

Always the socks. . . . I put on my cap, saluted and turned away, and
climbed up to the bridge to enter my own graveyard item in the deck-
log. Then I went below to the mess-decks. There were so many things to
do, at the dawn of another day, and I had to be on watch again at noon.

But nothing lasted for ever, not even murder at sea. It was the R.A.F.
who eventually came to our rescue, not for the first time; they sent out
two of their new flyingboats, called Catalinas, and then two more on a
round-the-clock search-and-strike patrol which really worked. The
planes kept the U-boats below the surface by day and scared them
down again with flares at night; gradually the convoy was able to draw
ahead and slip out of danger. We blessed them as we made our escape,
and plodded slowly home with what we had left.

This was quite a lot of ships, in fact, though it hadn't felt like it while
the convoy was taking its thrashing; we still had fifty-four deep-laden
merchantmen on our books, and as we led the Liverpool portion up
river we began to feel happier.

The finish did not seem too tame, nor too depressing. It was even, in a
minor key, triumphant. There was still this solid array of ships; there
were our 180 survivors, now crowding the rails and looking at the
shore-line as if it were part of Eden instead of the distant prospect of
Bootle.

Then, steaming past the Bar Light Vessel, we touched off a magnetic
mine, and this could really be called a near-miss; it exploded with a
shattering bang and a huge column of dirty water, about thirty yards
astern of us. There was no damage except to our nerves; but we
reported it swiftly to the shore signal-station in case it was one of a
cluster.

Perhaps we made it sound worse than it was. Their immediate
acknowledgement came in the form of the most heartless signal ever to
reach us from Western Approaches Command. It was the simple
directive:

'Do not sink in the swept channel.'

Campanula scraped the knuckle of the dock as we came into
harbour, and it was my fault; in charge on the quarter-deck, I
misunderstood one of those mysterious whistle-blasts and held on to the
back-spring too long. The ship lost a bit of paint and I some poise.

'*Monsarrat*!' came the expected roar from the bridge. 'What the hell
are you playing at?'

2

I had got married on 7 September 1939, four days after war broke out. The enormous confusion and uncertainty dictated by war, the severance of so many accustomed ties, the massive breaking of rules, all seemed to make such a step inevitable; a loving marriage was the answer, the anchor, the rock.

We had been engaged for about six months, in the face of tepid enthusiasm on the part of her parents. I was manifestly a poor prospect, a cul-de-sac in the tunnel of love; her mother took a dim view of my inward nature ('Bolshy!') and my outward appearance, especially my only pair of shoes, which were of grey suede scuffed down to the bone. Her father was dubious about my financial prospects, candidly admitted to be nil.

But I liked him, and he was always nice to me, though I was aware all the time that he could tell a fortune-hunter at a very considerable distance, just as Eileen's mother could spot an 'actor-fellow', as I had promptly been labelled, the moment he slid his dusty boots on to the high-gloss drawing-room parquet.

However, the fearful deed had been done, at Marylebone Town Hall, and we had set up house in a tiny flat in Church Street, Kensington, conveniently sited over a grocer's shop (London flats were very easy to pick up, at that doubtful moment of history). We lived frugally on my stretcher-bearer's pay of £2 18s 5d a week, plus Eileen's dowry of £1 a week from her parents. Since my working hours were twelve on and twelve off, changing to night-duty every other month, married life was disjointed; but we were very happy, independent at last, while conducting some singularly tight housekeeping based on a black japanned money-box with seven labelled divisions: Rent, Coal, Food, Gas, Electricity, Sundries, and unbelievably, Savings (2s 6d a week).

We never went out: we didn't want to, and we couldn't afford it, and the time-schedule, with sleep to be regained, made it impossible anyway.

Marriage had seemed important when it happened, under the first impact of war. Now, one and a half years later, when I was finding out about the Battle of the Atlantic in the corvette *Campanula*, it had become essential, involving reason itself. I knew already (and it did not need blood, squalor, or the miserable pricks of authority to drive the point home), that I would never survive this particular prison sentence without her; and the debt remained, never to be repaid, long after the war was won and the magic had been swallowed by it, or destroyed by me, or lost in a post-war, duller-than-dull detergent wash.

War was inevitably a matter of saying good-bye, usually in grisly circumstances: on black winter mornings, in grimy railway stations, outside dock-gates in the rain. It was made more grisly still, for both of us, by knowing exactly what lay in store as soon as the bell tolled: I was headed for my particular menu of cold, exhaustion, boredom, and fear, while she went back to her empty lair, to find on the mat a fresh sheaf of incomprehensible directives from the Ministry of Food. But we had managed to give this whole process a lift by renting a small cottage in Gateacre, a village just outside Liverpool, and there setting up house.

It was only a bungalow, as shabby, run-down, and draughty as a bottom-of-the-garden shack; but it was the rock-cave I had to have, and Eileen swiftly fashioned it into a longed-for home. I had already invested in a motor-cycle, a $2\frac{1}{2}$ h.p. Francis Barnett, as a means of getting about when public transport was curtailed or, under threat of an air-raid, had given up altogether; and this was my home-coming chariot, my link between Albert Dock in the gruesome heart of Liverpool and the rustic solitude waiting for me outside.

It did a lot of sea-time, that motor-bike: up to the Clyde, across to Northern Ireland, and down to Gibraltar, among other brave voyages. But its best voyage of all was the seven-mile chugging run out to Gateacre, when *Campanula* came into harbour at the end of a convoy.

We did nothing at all in that funny little house, except eat and sleep and make love and, as far as I was concerned, uncoil the fearful spring which a seventeen-day convoy could tighten almost beyond endurance. . . .

Early in 1941, I went back from a treasured leave to find on board *Campanula* a superior break in the clouds. Suddenly I had an ally, someone I could talk to; instead of the zoo-like grunting and snuffling which had ruled us so far, actual sentences were now to be heard, with verbs and all.

My rescuer was a man called Jim Harmsworth—or, more correctly, Lieutenant St J. B. V. Harmsworth, whose disposition did much to dispel the gloom of *Campanula*. He had been a barrister and hoped one day to return to practise 'when all this inconvenience is over'.

Sometimes he mentioned, without emphasis, 'my cousin Esmond'. As a small ex-snob from Liverpool, I was very impressed. Cousin Esmond was Lord Rothermere of the *Daily Mail*.

Jim Harmsworth, as well as his distinguished name, had the added glamour of having been torpedoed, in an armed merchant cruiser called *Patroclus* which went to the bottom off Bloody Foreland in November 1940. 'Oh, I simply swam about,' he said, when questioned about this. 'There were various people looking after us, and they came round to me before too long. But I may say that Bloody Foreland was christened with tolerable accuracy. Quite apart from the snow, the water was *extremely* cold.'

As an officer, he was easygoing, and famous on board as an undeniably soft touch, from the disciplinary point of view. Once when an infuriated 'Hostilities Only' able seaman, hauled before him by the hard-breathing coxswain, burst out in a sudden snarl of revolt: 'Well I'm buggered if I'm going to be buggered about by a silly old bugger like this bugger here!' Jim's comment was: 'You are in some danger of becoming monotonous.'

I was glad to note, many years later, when he was a magistrate at Great Marlborough Street Magistrates' Court, and dealing with a substantial traffic in student protest that things had tightened up considerably in this area.

We enjoyed—well, I enjoyed—one occasion of singular charm, when *Campanula*, in common with the rest of our escort group, was inspected from stem to stern by a member of the C.-in-C.'s shore staff. This was Commander John Broome, who was later to bring a celebrated libel action about the PQ17 convoy to Russia.

He toured the whole ship at the head of a comet-tail of nervous officers, with the coxswain, the Chief Bosun's Mate carrying the traditional storm-lantern, and the uninvited, inquisitive ship's dog bringing up the rear. Commander Broome, equally inquisitive, asked questions about everything, from the First Lieutenant's anchor cables to my clutch of depth-charges; from the wardroom wine accounts to the state of the galley stove (indifferent, it seemed).

We were all grilled, in a thoroughly seamanlike manner. Finally came Jim Harmsworth's turn to be put on the rack. Commander Broome rounded on him suddenly. 'What's *your* job?'

Harmsworth was relieved to be on safe ground. 'Barrister, sir,' he answered promptly. 'I'd been in practice about five years when——'

'I mean your job in the ship,' Broome interrupted, with a 'Bloody clot!' look which would have stunned a less assured man.

'Signal Officer, sir.'

'Oh. How many ten-inch projectors do you carry?'

'I think they're all four-inch, sir,' said Harmsworth, courteously enough.

'*Four-inch*? Nonsense! There's no such thing. You couldn't see it at fifty yards! How many *ten*-inch projectors?'

I realized what had happened; Jim, mishearing the question or being confused, at this testing moment, over the difference between a projector, which was a signalling lamp, and a projectile, which was what came out of a gun when the button was pressed, had picked the wrong one. This was confirmed when he answered: 'I'm not sure, sir. And I'm afraid the Gunnery Officer is on leave.'

Commander Broome steered clear of this *impasse* by ignoring it; he might already have arrived at what judges called 'a certain conclusion' about my friend. We moved on, in thoughtful silence, up to the signal bridge, and there, by bad luck, came a sudden cascade of high-speed Morse transmission from inside the wireless telegraphy office.

The Commander swung round again. 'What's that?' he demanded.

'W/T office, sir.'

'I know *that*. But can you read it?'

'No, sir.' We had men on board who could read high-speed Morse, but Jim was not one of them. Nor was I.

'Pity about that. You could intercept the German broadcasts.'

The idea of Jim Harmsworth, who even then preferred to make a measured appreciation of every move, reading German Morse at the rate of about two hundred words a minute was an affecting one, and I had to turn away and stare at some nearby paintwork before I had properly mastered it. Behind me, I heard him making a last try for justice.

'I'm afraid it's rather too fast for me.'

'I thought you said you were the Signal Officer!' said Broome, as if he could scarcely believe his ears.

'Well—*faute de mieux*, sir.'

'What's that?'

'*Faute de mieux*.'

'Oh. . . .' A suspicious glance frosted the air between them. '*Faute de mal*, I should think you mean.' In spite of the wayward French, it lost very little in translation.

Yet Broome was not the kind of 'shore type' one could seriously resent, except as a professional disciplinarian in avid search of our amateur shortcomings; and in any case he was only coasting between jobs as a destroyer captain in charge of an escort group, which was a superior sailor indeed.

Jim and I had more satisfaction, however, with the other kind of shore-based sailor, who spent large amounts of time on board *Campanula*, performing such modest tasks as twiddling two small knobs on a Lewis-gun mounting, saying: 'That should be all right now' (it had been all right before), and then settling down in the wardroom to drink our gin, cadge our cigarettes, and bewail the fact that he was 'stuck ashore', instead of performing prodigies of valour on the bounding main.

A few such visitors were genuine in this ambition, and a blanket condemnation would have been unfair; a ship had to have a base, a base had to have specialists, and people so categorized had to stay where they were, and do the dull jobs instead of the exciting ones.

But there was one suspect and recurrent pest, whom we finally routed.

'You know, I really envy you chaps,' he once said, taking his ease in one of our few remaining armchairs. ('We chaps' were still thawing out our frozen toes after a winter gale which had pursued us to the very threshold of the dock.) 'Actually going out on convoy. . . . And here am I, just because I have certain specialist qualifications, assigned to the C.-in-C.'s staff for what looks like the duration. I can assure you, I would do anything—*anything*—to get to sea.'

I became aware that Jim Harmsworth, sitting quietly in one corner, drawing on a cigar, had decided to strike. He said, using an early blend of the judicial and the influential:

'That might be arranged.'

'Really?'

'I will have a word with Noble.'

Our visitor's assurance suddenly lessened. 'How do you mean, Noble?'

'Sir Percy Noble,' Jim answered. 'Commander-in-Chief, Western Approaches. He is some sort of connection of mine.' (I knew this to be a lie, but it was a lie in a very good cause.) 'He would certainly never stand in the way of any young officer who preferred to serve in corvettes rather than on his staff.'

The effect was swift. Indeed, I had never before seen a man contract hay-fever before my very eyes. He coughed, he spluttered, he lay back gasping; he wiped his streaming eyes before he managed to say: 'There *is* another reason. . . . I don't talk much about it, but there it is. . . . It's my infernal bronchial trouble. . . . That's really why they put me ashore in the first place. . . .'

We had to have a *little* fun.

But were we winning the war? It was, as we got deeper into 1941, very hard to tell.

Certainly there were nuggets of good news. We had captured a sort of joke-town called Sidi Barrani, and another called Bardia on the Libyan-Egyptian border; we had gone on to capture (or was it recapture?) a town called Tobruk, a much-disputed prize which General Wavell had wrested from Marshal Graziani, with a surrendered garrison of 100,000 Italian prisoners.

'Some of them,' a friend of mine on the spot reported, 'were the most depressed-looking little sods you ever saw, with sweaty green uniforms and crinkly cardboard jackboots and drooping cocks'-feathers on top of their helmets. They were all about five feet tall, including the dust. They said they were called the Wolves of the South.'

We had won a spectacular naval victory near Cape Matapan, off the southern tip of Greece. It was, we were presently told, the first use of radar in gunnery. Radar was then known as radio-location or R.D.F. (radio direction finding).

Putting two and two together we decided before very long that the famous R.A.F. fighter pilot, nicknamed Cat's-Eyes Cunningham, who could shoot down German planes because he could see in the dark, owed this gift to radar rather than to the six raw carrots which, according to the current fable, he always munched before he took off.

But would small escort-ships ever get this R.D.F.? Think of the difference it would make in station-keeping, in convoy, in spotting surfaced U-boats. . . . It was rumoured that one or two of our destroyers had already been blessed. Would corvettes ever get it?

'*Corvettes?*' our Captain pronounced, in scornful dismissal, 'We're sucking on the hind tit!'

Then there was news which was good and bad mixed. We sank the German battleship *Bismarck*, brand-new and hugely powerful (45,000 tons), after a tremendous sea chase; but very early in the action a fateful 15-inch shell from the *Bismarck*, forged in an evil hour, apparently bounced off the fore-deck of one of our highly-prized warriors, H.M.S. *Hood*, and went down an open magazine hatch.

The range was twelve miles, and the destruction total. It was the gambling equivalent of hitting Zero at the roulette table not within the confines of the wheel itself but from across Trafalgar Square.

It sometimes seemed that the labour and the wounds *were* going to be in vain, as the old hymn cautioned us; that we had started a job which we could not finish, and that the price of trying would bankrupt us, in blood and treasure, long before any westward sky brightened into daylight.

As if to point up this morbid doubt, Liverpool suffered the most ferocious punishment of its life, from a week-long series of raids which altered its pattern and perhaps its spirit for ever.

I recorded it in my notebook, day by day, as it all happened, because *Campanula* was in harbour, in the heart of the docks, throughout that fearful week.

Liverpool, the hub of the Western Approaches command, was a target well worth hitting. There were never less than a hundred ships in harbour, loading and unloading; plus their tugs, and the oil-storage tanks, and eleven miles of docks with their cranes and ammunition barges and ship-repair yards and warehouses and dock-gates and the whole network of rail-linkage which bound it to the rest of England. Worth hitting, it was now hit, with relentless accuracy, for eight nights on end.

The sustained, continuous bombing started huge fires, laid waste acres of the town, and killed hundreds of people. The fires, indeed, were one of the principal features; at dusk each evening there were always one or two of them still burning from the previous night's onslaught, serving as a pointer to the heart of the city from a hundred miles away.

One night the bonded warehouse alongside us was set ablaze, and we had to land a fire-party to help put it out, expecting all the time that the whole flaming structure, glowing scarlet like a runaway oven, would crash down on to the upper deck.

Since corvettes weren't built for that sort of thing, we always warped ourselves out into the middle of the dock after that; it gave us, at least, an additional twenty yards' margin of safety.

The waiting, each evening, in the absolute certainty that the raids would go on for at least another night, was the finest exercise in patience, nervous control, and the avoidance of heroics, I had ever had; it also kept the sweat-glands in admirable trim.

The war took us on three more summer convoys (though the North Atlantic had not yet been notified that it was summer), and then came a real treat: a refit, and the six weeks' lay-off that went with it. Better even than that, we were to go into dry-dock in Liverpool; and best of all, I was now the heir, despite our Captain's earlier pessimism, to the latest of a wonderful line of inventions which, starting with the motor-car and building up via the aeroplane, the telephone, the radio, the talkies, television, and the contraceptive diaphragm, had now topped off the process with the finest blessing a sailor could hope for—a radar set.

Radar was still such a Most Secret secret that, bound as I was to the blunt end of the ship, I never heard anything about its arrival until I noticed that a curious, round, opaque glass cylinder, like the top third of a lighthouse, had been hoisted up and clipped to our mainmast. It had arrived under heavy guard, I learned via the galley-wireless, the rumour-mill which mixed truth and fantasy as skilfully as it turned out our favourite cheesy-hammy-eggy, and had been unpacked in strict security below decks; two scientists *in very dark clothes* had remained closeted with the Captain for over an hour while all this was going on.

We were now told what it was, and instructed to return 'evasive replies' if asked about it. The most popular evasion was that our impenetrable new structure would be used for growing fresh tomatoes at sea. Perhaps this would have been a better idea, at least to start with, because it was a long time before we could get this embryo model to work. But presently, with the aid of an entirely new crew member, a leading radar mechanic who was also a demon bridge player, it shed its teething troubles and settled down.

It was to work wonders for us, that precious radar set. It made station-keeping at close quarters a safe and exact science. It found lost convoys, and wandering escorts, and headlands hidden in the murk of a Hebridean summer day. It could pick up channel buoys as we went down river in fog; and ship's boats whose survivors might otherwise have been left to die; and rain-squalls just over the horizon which, an hour later, would blot out everything except the vague grey hump which was our own windlass; and offshore fishing-boats careless of their riding-lights.

Best of all, it could find surfaced U-boats and, with the help of an ingenious plotting device, betray their plans. Though radar would never supplant seamanship and skill and watchful common sense, yet it aided them all so enormously that we were left wondering how we had ever survived two years of convoy-escort without it.

Among the many myths surrounding this magic instrument was one to the effect that close contact with it rendered the operator sterile—a rumour so widespread that it had to be countered by an official pronouncement that there was no ground for any such fears, and that radar operators should be assured that, no matter how long they worked on the set, it could not affect their capacity to have children. Whether this was good news or bad news, was, even then, a matter of dispute.

But before we could be equipped with this paragon, and benefit also from certain other alterations and improvements, we had to survive six weeks in a Liverpool dry-dock.

The executive order for this was 'H.M.S. *Campanula* will basin at 0800 hours' (what on earth had happened to the English language while we had been in Scotland, temporarily transferred to the Clyde Escort Force?). In due course we basined; the vast groaning gates swung shut behind us, divorcing us from the sea; finger-flipping men in bowler hats spread-eagled us dead-centre on our enseamed bed as the water-level dropped, and enormous oily baulks of timber shored us up, to preserve what was left of our poise.

Since two out of the three watches had gone on leave, and I was left in sole charge of the wardroom, the ship would have been something of an echoing iron cage in any case; with the boilers blown down (no heating) and the humming generators silent for the first time in half a year, she seemed somewhat spooky as well. When, preparing for evening rounds, I walked out on to the shadowy quarter-deck which had seen so much mortuary service in recent months, I could not help feeling that we must surely have collected quite a lot of poor drowned ghosts already.

Campanula quickly grew derelict and cold and uncomfortable; the assistant cook's meals were so terrible that I knew he must be pining for his peacetime job in the pickle factory; the necessity of using the dockside lavatory instead of our own was an awkward nuisance, with undertones of squalor.

At night, the steady drip of water into the great stone grave below did nothing to lull me into easy sleep. After-dinner drinking did not help either, though I gave it a good try.

But each morning the ship came alive again, in a way I grew to dislike even more than the night's loneliness. From 8 a.m. onwards we were invaded by an army of major and minor technicians concerned with our refit: riveters, welders, joiners, plumbers, painters, electricians, carpenters, caulkers, boiler scalers, funnel sweeps, plain crash-and-bangers, tea-makers' mates. . . . They trooped on board in a snuffling, untidy, foot-dragging, shambling throng and took over the ship; and the ship, lately so disciplined, so taut, so keyed up to its job, began to suffer from it.

Each day *Campanula* became a dirtier shambles; soon she was no longer a ship-of-war in working trim, but a kind of run-down factory hard hit by the depression, and only waiting for the rats to take over. All the decks which we had kept scoured and scrubbed since the day we commissioned became a barnyard of cigarette ends, cartons, crates,

woodshavings, oily rags, slices of metal, strips of welding, bits of wire:
bottles, cans, half-eaten sandwiches and gobs of prime Liverpool
sputum.

At first it made me angry, and then sad, and then resigned. The sight
of a filthy raincoat dangling from a gun-barrel had, on Day One, seemed
scandalous and insulting. Presently it became a natural part of the
infected scene, an item of our squalid camouflage. And common sense
told me that a major refit must inevitably turn the place upside down,
and propriety with it.

But there was another aspect of the invasion where anger did not ebb
away, nor give place to common sense. Most of these people 'concerned
with our refit' were hardly concerned at all. They were not working very
hard. Some of them, as far as I could judge, were not working at all. The
first time I came on a school of card-players snugged down in the
Captain's sea-cabin at ten o'clock in the morning, I was furious, and
showed it. I remained furious on all later occasions, but I was officially
told not to be, and above all not to 'interfere'.

There might be a strike. . . .

Our able seamen, working like galley slaves in sub-human conditions, got their keep and four shillings a day. An eighteen-year-old
fitter's mate ashore who kicked up a row about his 'conditions of
employment' was found to be earning £13 a week. These contrasting
oddments multiplied as time went on.

I reached a certain personal peak of disgust when one of our visitors,
tilting up his welder's mask with an agile thumb, offered me 'all the
petrol I liked' for my motorcycle without the formality of coupons. For
me, as for all other sailors, a petrol coupon was not a grubby slip of
paper; it was a man, an actual mother's son with frying hair, swimming
away from a burning tanker and failing to make it. It was a life. God
damn it, it was *my* life! I felt bound to tell him, sniffily, that I was all right
for petrol.

H.M.S. *Campanula* duly 'unbasined'. But the melancholy word
enshrined a cleansing process which a sailor could only welcome; after
the six weeks' ministration of our dockyard maties, the sea at last came
to our rescue, and sluiced away the grime of foreign hands, and baptized
us under the honest name of ship again.

I leant over the quarter-deck guardrail and watched as the dry-dock
crew began to run the bath-water. The incoming tide sucked and swirled
round the baulks of timber which had been cradling us for so many
days; on its way it picked up a horrid chaplet of wood and rubbish and

filth, topped by a grimy slick of coal-dust and oil, as the level rose and climbed step by step up the side of the dock. The gangs of men in waders, stationed far below us, collecting the shores and wedges as they floated free, soon began to retreat in a widening circle, leaving us to our own element.

Presently the good salty Mersey water was climbing up our own side, lapping the fresh paint higher and higher with successive happy tide-marks. One by one our props lurched free and drifted off, and were retrieved with eighteen-foot boathooks by men now reaching out from the edge of the dock.

There was a long hopeful pause while the whole basin swirled and filled; then the last timber floated sluggishly up and away, and became the last prize for the shore-gang; with a maidenly tremor, not too convincing, and a small stagger to celebrate her liberty, *Campanula* was released; and thus, on the next tide, we returned to our war.

3

I had hoped that I had already survived the most punishing convoy of the war. But I was wrong, and was smartly proved so, as soon as we had spring-cleaned the ship.

We now embarked on the most horrible voyage of all, made especially foul by the fair weather which blessed us throughout the trip.

This time our run was south to Gibraltar, to calm seas and hot sunshine, and to the longest gauntlet of murder we were ever likely to encounter.

There is no temptation to fight this one again, particularly as we lost it so brutally; but there were such contrasts, astonishing and appalling, in that convoy that memory remained infected for ever, and can stand an airing, if only for pity's sake.

We were routed far westwards, in a great arc which curved out for hundreds of miles into the Atlantic, so as to take us out of bomber range of the French coast. The weather, as the smoky hills of western Ireland faded astern and we made the latitude of the Bay of Biscay, grew peerless: the sort of 'sunshine cruise' conditions which, even in the mid-thirties, the advertisements had no trouble in selling to the privileged.

We were all in good heart, after the long lay-off. We liked our newly-furbished ship; we had the radar to fiddle with; above all, there was this canopy of sky and carpet of calm sea which, after the snuffling gloom of Liverpool, seemed far out on the profit side of paradise. There was a new, sensual pleasure in that southward journey which seemed to take the whole ship away from the war and into the simple warming joys of being alive and afloat.

We passed whales, and basking sharks, and once a lone turtle, paddling towards its first and only landfall—Florida, four thousand miles away. Flying fish were reported; in the dog watches the hands sun-bathed. All I had to do was to maintain the zigzag pattern by the clock; to answer 'Very good' as the look-outs changed at the half-hour and the helmsman was relieved; to keep up the deck-log (our course and speed); and translate the weather pattern into the required officialese: 'Wind light, variable: Sea smooth: Cloud nil: Corrected barometric pressure in millibars, 1004.'

Sometimes the coxswain, totally unemployed in such a benevolent world, came up to the bridge to gossip with me. He would begin with a formal salute, continue with a confederate grin and, invariably, fire off one of his awful jokes:

'Did you hear about the sultan's ninth wife, sir?'

'No, coxswain, I don't think I did.'

'She just got the hang of it.'

'Coxswain. . . .'

But in fact I welcomed the variation; I thought it was going to be: 'She had it pretty soft.'

Sometimes there would be a signalman washing out his flags and pendants in a bucket of suds at the back of the bridge, and the coxswain could never resist a comment.

'Eh Bunts!' 'Bunts' was short for 'bunting-tosser': the coxswain pronounced it 'Boonts.' 'Eh, Bunts! You're making a proper snakes' honeymoon of that lot!' Then he would turn back to me. 'You don't know whether to laugh or cry, do you? How are we going on, sir?'

'All right. Pretty slow.'

'Slow all right.' He looked across at our drifting convoy and astern at our gently furrowing wake. 'Six knots and a Chinaman, I'd say.'

This was a new one to me. 'What on earth does that mean?'

'Old sailing ship yarn.' He was always glad when I asked a question, because he always knew the answer. 'Like, there was this Chinaman streaming the log to find out how fast the ship was going. He dropped it over the side, and the line ran out too strong for him and jerked him overboard. Never saw his little yellow botty again. The Captain says to the mate: "How fast are we going?" and the mate says; "Six knots and a Chinaman." '

The joke, totally goodhumoured, totally heartless, seemed just right for our own secure voyage.

The sixth dawn came; the luck seemed good, the life wonderful. Dawn was never quite included in my middle watch, even at high summer; but I always stayed on, at the back of the bridge, to watch and wait for it, until at fifteen or twenty minutes past four o'clock the longed-for miracle happened. The change was always swift: at one moment the sea was silvery, the sky black, the stars brilliant, and then, when one next looked round, the colours had all turned pale grey—the grey which was the day's first signal.

Campanula's outline took shape with swift decision, along her whole length; the men on the bridge became faces and figures instead of shadows or voices unseen. The duty steward climbed the bridge ladder, to collect the middle watch's plates and cups. It was the best hour of the twenty-four. We were all still alive, and safe, and 168 miles nearer harbour; the barometer was rock-steady, and the sun on its way—and then, even as I turned to go below, one of the new look-outs sang out 'Sound of aircraft, sir!' and within a second or so I had got it myself, and the sick fear that went with it—the steady hateful drone, somewhere out on the pale fringes of the dawn, which meant that we had alien company.

Some finger, prompt and itchy on the trigger, was already pressing the alarm bell, and *Campanula*, lately so sleepily content, jumped into urgent action. My place of duty, instead of snug between the blankets, was now the anti-aircraft gun-turret aft, where there was newly installed a four-barrelled 0·5-inch pom-pom, nicknamed a Chicago Typewriter. (A Chicago Piano had eight barrels.)

The gun's crew of five was there almost as soon as I was: five young men, steel-helmeted, their faces puffy with sleep, the white tops of their sea-boot stockings standing out in the faint light of dawn. We closed up round the gun, and tilted its multiple snout skywards, and waited: watching, listening to the snarling anonymous intruder, peering about as the gaining light gave us more to peer at, for a full hour; and then there was a sharp call on the bridge voice-pipe—'Aircraft, red four-five!'—and we all swung round, to find, far away on the port beam, the author of our harassment.

It was not a true enemy, but a spy—yet the worst spy we could wish to see; one of the Focke-Wulf long-range reconnaissance planes, circling round and round the convoy, far out of range even of a destroyer's guns.

We had been discovered, and beyond doubt reported; and before long the cutting edge of war sliced our brief paradise to bloody rags. The last warning for action was signalled to us, in a disgusting way, that same afternoon; the sighting of some fresh human excrement on the surface of the water, where no honest ship had travelled for many a long day. U-boats. . . . As dusk fell, violence began to split our whole universe.

We lost fourteen merchant ships in the next five days; fourteen of our small stock of twenty-one—a percentage so appalling that the cold print seemed almost worse than the sights and sounds of action. We lost four tankers. We lost a small cargo-liner called the *Aguila*, which had on board the first draft of Wrens going out to Gibraltar. We lost the rescue-tug which, the previous night, had picked up the last four or five surviving girls. We lost a Norwegian destroyer full of orphaned exiles far from home. We lost one of our own cherished sisters, a corvette-in-arms for more than a year, H.M.S. *Zinnia*.

Zinnia was commanded by a tall, friendly, capable man called Cuthbertson, whom, as an occasional visitor to our wardroom, I liked very much, if only by reason of contrast; and when I saw her go up in one quick stab of flame, far out on the wing of the convoy, and knew it could only be *Zinnia*, I was saddened and sickened far beyond any ignoble thought that at least it was only them and not us. What a waste, what a waste. . . . The extent of that waste was made apparent next morning, when as soon as we could be spared we were sent back to pick up the bits.

There were only fifteen men alive; Cuthbertson himself (rescued by another ship) and fourteen wretched members of his crew of ninety, and corpses a-plenty. I was in charge of the scrambling-nets aft; it was my pride and privilege to yank from the water half-a-dozen shipmates of this admired man, this oily half-dead master mariner—as I found him to be when he came on board at Gibraltar.

He had nothing much to say except thank you: what man could have had anything to say, who had just lost seventy-five of his crew and a corvette which, turning under full helm, was hit below the boiler-room and broke in half while those left alive on the upper deck were still shocked and staring? I could only tell him that I had looked after his stunned survivors, and buried his dead: those rows of sailors like ourselves, their badges proclaiming their faithful service, their wide-open eyes attesting their last surprise.

Cuthbertson may have forgotten all this quite soon, but, movingly, his mother never did. She must have been, even then, quite an old lady; but when my own son was born she sent a message of congratulation, and for years afterwards, punctually on his birthday, a card arrived, for me as much as for him, sending her best wishes, still saying thank you.

Lieutenant-Commander Cuthbertson occurred later—I made him occur later in a novel. But on that day in Gibraltar he was only a shrunken hostage from the sea, one of the witnesses to the last act of this rotten play when, with the tatters of our convoy—our seven remaining ships—we beat our retreat.

Faced with reports of 'U-boats joining', and old and new enemies still waiting astride our route to Gibraltar, we fled the scene. We took what was left of our flock and led them up the River Tagus towards Lisbon, within the safe, neutral, prudent waters of Portugal—as bitter an act of surrender as could ever come our way. Then—only a clutch of escorts in line abreast, not a convoy any more—we made all speed for Gibraltar, past Cape St Vincent and other honoured names, to tell our wretched story.

The last entry I made in the deck-log, on my last middle watch, was; 'Cape Trafalgar bearing due east, twenty miles.' We were thus crossing the very shoals where lay all the iron shot of 1805 and the bones of the French 74 *Redoutable*, from whose cross-trees a sharpshooter had taken aim on an admiral's emblazoned coat; where Nelson, dying, yet hearing with a sailor's faithful ear the surf growling under *Victory's* lee, had given his last recorded order: 'Anchor, Hardy! Do you *anchor!*'

But that had been *Victory*, victory.

We were barely past the Straits of Gibraltar, with Spain on the port hand, Morocco on the starboard, the scorched smell of Africa in between, and a distant view of the Rock to lure us homewards, when we were told to turn round again and start a two-day 'anti-submarine sweep' through the waters of our defeat: perhaps to teach us the virtues of discipline and fortitude, or to recall a long-ago signal: 'England confides that every man will do his duty', or to drive home the disgrace of still being afloat.

We felt we knew enough of all these things already.

It must be admitted that most of us were a little cracked, in all senses, by the time we made harbour. It had all gone on too long; we had been nearly a week at action stations, missing meals, missing sleep, with nothing to show in return save a shameful tally of lost ships climbing past the 60 per cent mark.

Indeed, we had done nothing more martial than to kill, with a depth-charge, some diving seabirds. Yet Gibraltar proved a healing balm, in a way I would never have thought possible.

There was literally nothing to worry about here, except keeping a look-out for Italian midget submarines which were rumoured to be trying to break into the harbour. There was nothing much to do, especially since the official mail had not caught up with me, and could not do so. The sun shone all the time; we wore the Navy's tropical kit which was itself a tonic.

I swam in what truly seemed a rich man's playground, Rosia Bay, not quite shadowed by the Rock, in the warm Mediterranean water which really could caress an exhausted body. We travelled round the town by gharry. There was no blackout. We took our *aperitif* on a balcony overlooking Main Street.

Gradually the war faded from this blessed scene. We could not quite forget *Zinnia*, but we began to forget all the rest. We could even recall, with laughter instead of embarrassment, an answer which our captain had sent to another corvette whose signal he had not understood. It had been: 'Snow again. I don't catch your drift.'

Campanula was berthed in the very shadow of *Ark Royal*, the huge towering aircraft-carrier which was the target of two angry air forces, German and Italian, as long as she was in harbour, as well as of U-boats' spite whenever she put to sea. It must have been strange to serve in such a notorious 'hunted ship', but it seemed that her crew were inclined to relish their notoriety, as an extra source of pride.

They used to listen to Radio Hamburg, and especially to William Joyce (hanged for treason, 1946).

Latterly, Joyce (nicknamed Lord Haw-Haw from his curious, fake upper-class accent) had taken to asking, over and over again, on a menacing snarl: 'Where is the *Ark Royal*?' and in the *Ark Royal*'s mess-decks they took an answering delight in roaring back: 'HERE!'

In fact, William Joyce must have known very well where the *Ark Royal* was; or if he did not, some little man just down the corridor could certainly have told him. For we knew all the time that Gibraltar was totally open to the spying eyes of the enemy across the bay, in neutral Algeciras.

I was Acting Duty Captain at the Admiralty, charged (on a strictly sub-contractual basis) with Britain's entire naval destiny, on the last night of our war.

Even inside the massive building one could hear the tremendous noise from Trafalgar Square. Coming on duty at 8 p.m., I had already seen the crowd roaring, dancing, swaying: a crowd sampling the magic taste of the first evening of peace.

I had carried the enormous happiness of that moment, the choking relief, with me into the Admiralty, where everyone else I met was happy, because, at least from the Atlantic and the Mediterranean, there would be no more news of U-boats ('Up to nine in your area'), no more terrible tidings of disaster ('Following six ships in convoy sunk last night'), no bells tolling across a thousand miles of the worst widow-maker of them all.

I would have given big money (well, medium-sized money, suitable to my station) for a celebration drink on this night, but no such facilities were on tap in our humble area. Instead, I said 'Enjoy yourself' to the fortunate man whom I had relieved, leafed through the last hour's signals, and settled down in the consequential armchair normally occupied by the Duty Captain.

But by midnight the crescendo of noise and cheering was very hard to resist. My telephone had not rung for the past hour. The signal-log was almost bare. Nothing was happening, because we had won the war.

On a guilty impulse I deserted my post, and climbed up the devious stone pathway to the top of Admiralty Arch.

There were lights! There were lighted windows, unmasked headlamps, gaping doorways stripped of their black-out screens. Both Buckingham Palace and the Admiralty Arch itself were floodlit. There were actual lights, for the first time since September 1939.

I stood there for quite a long time, listening to the crowds, laughing at them and with them; leaning against the parapet which was like the bridge of a ship, except that in front and below me was not the sea, calm or cruel, peaceful or murderous, but an ocean of people with its own surging wave-pattern, its *life*. Then, on a half-turn, I became aware that I was not alone on top of the Admiralty Arch.

There was someone standing within five yards of me, also staring down at the crowds, and oblivious of close company for the same reason as I had been—because we were both entranced by the magnet of what was going on below. With that perceptible twinge of nervousness which had been built into my life for so many years, I recognized, first the rank and then the man.

The massive display of gold braid told me that he was an admiral, like his brave and lonely brother on top of Nelson's Column. Then I realized that this was a very superior admiral indeed. I counted one thick band of gold, and *four* thinner ones. He was an Admiral of the Fleet—the highest any sailor could go.

In fact, I suddenly recognized, he was *the* Admiral of the Fleet. The man in my company was the First Sea Lord and Chief of Naval Staff, Admiral Cunningham.

Cunningham had been a legend with us all for years; he was in command at the Battle of Matapan and Commander-in-Chief of the Mediterranean when, between the onslaught on Malta and the brutal ebb and flow of the North African campaign, it was an ocean which had to be cleansed before we could make any headway at all.

He had done that, and then moved on. In fact, he had probably done more for our side than any other living sailor.

We had won. *He* had won. It must be quite a moment for him.

It was. I watched him surveying the raucous happy crowds. Then he looked up at Nelson. Then he leant forward, his knuckles planted squarely on the parapet. The movement brought his face into the floodlights shining from below, and I saw, in one bare, glistening fraction of a second, that he was crying.

I returned to duty forthwith.

The Ship That Died
of Shame

THERE ARE A LOT OF THINGS ABOUT THIS STORY THAT I STILL don't understand. I've had a good deal to do with ships—too much, maybe—and if there's one thing I know about them, it is that they are *not* alive. They are made of wood and metal, and nothing else: they don't have souls, they don't have wills of their own, they don't talk back. In fact, they're not like women at all. Writers of nautical romances may pretend—but I'd better start at the beginning.

The beginning, like almost everything in my life, goes back to the war.

My name is Bill Randall, and, if you used to read the naval communiqués with any sort of attention during the recent contest, you might just remember it. I spent nearly all the war in Coastal Forces, which meant, for me, mucking about in motor-gunboats and having hell's own fun in the process. The Beat-up Boys, they used to call us—and the name tells you just about all you need to know. We had been hired, it seemed, for the specific purpose of nipping across to the French, Dutch, and (later) German coasts, shooting up everything in sight, and nipping back again, cheating the dawn each morning by a few short minutes.

Our targets might be anything. It depended on our own luck. Sometimes it was a coastal convoy making for the Scheldt, sometimes German E-boats, sometimes mine-layers off Calais, sometimes fishing craft, German-chaperoned, trying their luck east of the Dogger Bank. (If you even *fished* for the Germans, as far as I was concerned, you were a legitimate target.) Once it was a lighthouse, once it was a camouflaged gasometer, once (glorious moment) it was a train coming out of a tunnel north of Boulogne. We were sent over the other side to make trouble, any trouble, and we did just that, using (in Their Lordships' convenient phrase) 'the widest possible discretion' in the process.

In between times, we escorted our own East Coast convoys, and picked up clumsy R.A.F. types who had come down into the sea, and touched off drifting mines, and acted as target-towing ships. Motor-gunboats could do anything—and that was especially true of mine, M.G.B. 1087. Which brings us to the ship in this story.

M.G.B. 1087 was a special honey. All gunboats are hit-and-run weapons, of course, and mine could do both to perfection. She was a hundred feet long, with four Packard engines of 5,000 brake-horse-power, able to shove her along at nearly thirty-five knots. She was armed with a few depth-charges, in case we got on the track of a submarine (we never did), six Oerlikons and eight smaller machine-guns, and two six-pounders—a gun that makes a hole approximately a foot wide in any metal, and more in a man. We had plenty of examples of both, in those wonderful years.

M.G.B. 1087. . . . I raised that boat practically from a toy yacht, and there wasn't a better one in any flotilla operating from any base; we must have finished the war with as good a record as you could find anywhere. On the shield of the forward six-pounder—the obvious place for scoring up 'trophies'—we painted the following tally:

Mines	126
Gasometers	2
E-boats	7
Steam Locomotives	1
Aircraft	8
Trawlers	3

Those were definite kills, the fruit of hundreds of nights of watching and waiting, hundreds of hours of cutting spray and pinching cold. There seemed no harm in being proud of them.

We were also well decorated. Hoskins (my First Lieutenant—I'll tell you about him in a minute) once suggested that we enlarge the trophy list to read:

D.S.O.	1, *and bar*
D.S.C.	1
D.S.M.	3

That didn't seem a very good idea, either then or now. . . . But we *did* get those aircraft, and we did get those seven E-boats, and all the rest, and I suppose the medals were, in a way, the same sort of trophies. It seemed to me, though, that it needed a special kind of outlook, unusual in our job, to paint them up in black and white for all the world to see.

The ship carried a crew of twenty-two, mostly gunnery-ratings, and two officers. I was the Captain of M.G.B. 1087; the other officer, for nearly three years, was my First Lieutenant, George Hoskins.

It's extraordinary how close you can be to a man and how many times you can owe him your life (and vice versa), and still know nothing about him. I liked Hoskins for his good qualities, exhibited on many occasions—his guts, cunning, and ruthlessness, all essential 'beat-up' attributes—and I shut my mind to the rest. He ran the ship efficiently—the guns were always clean, the engines smooth as machine-oil, the ship's company well organized and well looked after. But there was always something else, something I didn't know about and didn't want to know.

Perhaps it was in his eyes. Hoskins was a small man, neat, an R.N.V.R. Lieutenant who had been some sort of salesman before the war. We were together during all those three years, and he never let me down on any of the dozens of occasions when that might have happened. He won his D.S.C., the one he wanted to chalk up as an advertisement on the six-pounder gun-shield; and he deserved to win it. But somehow his eyes said that the thing was *all* advertisement: that the point of the war was not really sinking E-boats and downing aircraft and killing Germans, but selling M.G.B. 1087, and Lieut.-Commander Randall, D.S.O., and Lieutenant Hoskins, D.S.C., to the Admiralty and, through them, to the public, as the ace outfit of Coastal Forces.

In a way he had plenty of facts to support him. She *was* a wonderful ship, with a wonderful record. We *did* make the headlines, on a lot of occasions. The basic virtue of that, however, was not in the headlines, but in what we did to earn them: the actual sunk ships, the actual dead Germans, the actual few steps nearer to winning. I don't think Hoskins ever saw it like that. . . .

Whenever we came back into harbour, with the dawn breaking behind us, and the ship perhaps scarred by machine-gun fire, and an entry in the deck-log such as '0125: sank one E-boat' to tell the story of a wild, nerve-testing night, something in his eyes seemed to say: 'This ought to get us into the newspapers again. We ought to get another medal. I ought to get my half-stripe, with more money. We might even make it *two* E-boats. . . .'

Hoskins had a recurrent joke (if you can call it a joke). Whenever I remarked on the way he boosted the ship's reputation, he used to answer: 'In this war, you've got to look after number one.' Number One, as you probably know, is the Navy slang for the First Lieutenant. He was the First Lieutenant.

Perhaps it wasn't a joke, after all.

My doubt of his 'genuineness' was often there, but I had only one concrete example to go on.

It was a very small matter, when you look back on it: the question as to whether or not we had shot down an aircraft, and whether we should claim it as a 'certainty'. We had been caught, one morning at first light, still on the wrong side of the Channel, and still searching for the crew of a Lancaster bomber which had come down into the sea off Dunkirk.

We never picked them up, but we were picked up ourselves—by a patrolling Ju.88 which nipped in from seawards and tried to dive-bomb us. On his way down he was squarely hit by our Oerlikons—we were *very* ready on the trigger that morning; you could see the bits flying and scattering behind him, and then he levelled off overhead, without letting his bombs go. With a thin plume of black smoke streaming out of his tail-assembly, he disappeared inshore and out of our lives.

I never thought for a moment that we could claim that Junkers as shot down, since he was still going strong, and it was obvious that he would at least reach his own coast-line. But Hoskins, writing up the deck-log as we set course for Dover, entered the incident, without batting an eyelid, as 'One enemy aircraft destroyed'.

I said: 'Oi!' and then: 'We can't put that, Number One. He was still flying for home, happy as a lark.'

Hoskins eyed me, smiling. 'A lark with a pretty sore tail. . . . He'll never make it, I'm damn' sure.' We both had to shout, above the sea noises and the roar of the Packards going full out. 'You saw the bits and pieces. He was on his way down.'

I shook my head. 'He was losing height very slowly. You can't call it a confirmed kill.'

'As good as.' Hoskins was still smiling, in a vaguely encouraging way, as if I only needed a bit of jollying-along to see it from his angle. 'I wouldn't give much for his chances.' But then he added: 'What's the harm, anyway?'

I stared at him—the small man, bright as a button even at five o'clock in the morning, looking up at me with those encouraging eyes. I wanted no part of any of this.

'People rely on our reports,' I said shortly. I didn't want to touch on anything more definite, like honesty or truth; though I was still keyed up after the action, and felt the thing very simply and clearly myself. 'There's a man at the Air Ministry adding these things up, and we don't want to muck up his figures.' I pointed down at the deck-log. 'Call it "damaged".'

He shrugged, looking away from me. 'We're missing a good chance.'

I didn't like that, either. 'A good chance of what?'

'I mean,' he said elaborately, 'we *did* hit it and it *was* going down, and we want to keep our *own* record straight, just as much as some chair-borne clot at the Air Ministry.'

Listening to the careful phrases, watching him, I could almost see the headlines in his eyes, the headlines he wanted so much: '*Randall and Hoskins Again: Ju.88 Destroyed in Dawn Action.*' I could almost see his private dream of the Admiral shaking hands with him, and the 'Mentioned in Despatches' citation coming by the first post in the morning. . . . Without a word, I scored out his entry in the deck-log, wrote in my own, and said: 'That straightens *our* record.'

Then I walked to the front of the bridge, glad as never before to feel the ship bucking under my sea-boots and the fresh air coming inboard over the dodger.

But no piece of near-crookery by Hoskins could spoil those years, nor diminish the weight of tough achievement that M.G.B. 1087 piled up. Let me just tell you one thing we did in that ship at that time, to give you the measure of it.

It happened some months after the invasion, when our job was to look after the 'shuttle-service' of Allied shipping that went to-and-fro, to-and-fro between England and Normandy, twenty-four hours of every day of every week: keeping the men alive and the weapons served, away eastwards at the tip of the spear-head now approaching the Rhine, the place where it really mattered.

No convoys were ever so important as those cross-Channel ones—I know the Battle of the Atlantic boys will argue the toss about that, but if the flow of materials to France and Germany had ever been checked, even for half a day, we might have been driven back into the sea, and so lost the war in a prolonged and bloody stalemate. You've got to remember that there were things called V-Ones and V-Twos, robot-weapons aimed at London and tearing the heart out of it every hour on the hour, until we got a grip on the Calais coast-line. . . . That invasion just had to stick.

I should explain also that it took place shortly after my wife had been killed in an air-raid, when I didn't mind what went on so long as I could hit back and draw blood. That feeling came in very useful.

We were on independent night-patrol when it happened, near the opposite coast, and drifting with our engines stopped about six miles north of Mulberry Beach. We lay a little to the side of the 'fairway'—the buoyed channel that marked the way into the landing-beaches. It was a calm night, dark, with an edge of moon still showing above the horizon.

On our hydrophones there had been, for hours on end, nothing save water noises, and the occasional boiling sound made by a nearby shoal of fish. No shipping moved within miles of us, though there was a south-bound convoy—including troopers—due to pass through our sector some time after five in the morning. Waiting and listening, for hour after hour, we did our best to believe that, in spite of the tight coastal blockade, there might still be something for us that night.

Then, a little after one o'clock, with the moon nearly down, we suddenly picked up the sound of engines coming towards us from the south—the French coast. It was a whisper at first, then a steady purring, then the loud beat that meant fast-moving diesels.

The leading seaman on the hydrophones pressed the earphones closer to his head for a moment, frowning. Then he said: 'Uneven beat, sir. Must be two of them. Approaching one-nine-o degrees.'

We trained our glasses and watched the bearing. One-nine-o degrees was up-moon, which gave us an initial advantage: it meant that we lay hid in an outer ring of darkness, looking towards the footlights. . . . Presently something came into view—two somethings, two vague blurs in the darkness, with two slivers of light gradually widening beneath them, the creaming of their bow-waves. They were two ships, chugging towards us down the fairway as if they were driving along the Brighton Road.

They were small. They looked like us—or like E-boats.

I began to think quickly. It was far too early for our own mine-sweepers; they couldn't be other British gun-boats, because this was *our* sector; and the Yanks, however far they strayed from Omaha Beach, could hardly stray as far as this. In fact, it couldn't be *anything* belonging to our side: there was nothing due and there had been no emergency signal to alter the schedule. They *couldn't* be ours—or, if they were (for this was how I felt, after Lucille died), it was going to be just too bad for all concerned.

Hoskins, crouching by my elbow at the front of the bridge, said suddenly: 'I think they're laying mines.'

That of course was the obvious, the only answer, the sort of thing Hoskins always worked out, seconds ahead of me. I did not mind. Mine-laying E-boats in the approach channel, with a convoy on the way. . . . They must have come in fast down the Dutch and French coasts, lying hid for one night on the way (though how they had got past our destroyer patrols wanted a lot of explaining), then slowed down, turned north up the marked channel, and set to work.

I called softly: 'Signalman . . .' and dictated a warning signal for the incoming convoy. They would have to send mine-sweepers on ahead, or perhaps divert it altogether. But that was someone else's worry. Ours was here, and nearly within our range.

The blurred shapes were clearer now, resolving themselves into two small ships of our own size, fifty yards apart. If they were E-boats, they would be armed like ourselves: the odds were thus two to one against us, but we had the moon and the surprise, and above all, we had M.G.B. 1087.

I said: 'We'll go in, Number One. The starboard ship first. Then circle inshore and come back for the other one.'

Hoskins said: 'If we went between them, going very fast and firing to port and starboard at the same time, and then ducked out, they might start hammering at each other.'

That, again, was Hoskins at his best: cunning, resourceful, ready to take a chance. It *was* a chance, because if the E-boats were wide-awake, we might be caught in their cross-fire—but then again they might hold their hand for fear of hitting each other. If only we could confuse them a bit. . . .

The thing suddenly clicked into place, and I said: 'As we go through, we'll drop a depth-charge between them. The spray will hang for a bit. We'll turn quickly, and fire at one of them through it. They'll both answer back—and with any luck there'll be a riot and they'll start beating each other up.'

Hoskins said: 'Genius.'

I pressed the button.

The roar with which our engines burst into life always startled me: it startled me now. 1087 jumped, then began to rip forward, the bows lifting, the spray whipping upwards and outwards. We started to weave towards the gap between the two E-boats, going our full thirty-five knots, the engines rising to a thick, solid howl as the screws took hold, and the whole ship bumping and shuddering as we drove onwards. Hoskins shouted his fire orders through the inter-com.; presently I pressed the firing-bell, and all our guns opened up, half on one side and half on the other as we'd arranged, the red tracer-bullets fanning outwards in the darkness like the last, most decorative moment of a firework display. Other tracers—theirs—now began to come towards us, but sluggishly and wide of the mark: clearly the E-boats had been caught with their trousers way below their ankles, and we were scoring hits on both targets.

Just before we were level with them, our depth-charge went down, and then up! up! in a colossal cloud of spume and dirty water, hanging livid in the moonlight, obscuring the battlefield.

We came hard-a-port, turning behind them in a tight circle and a fifty-degree heel, and began to fire *over* one E-boat, *through* the spray cloud, *towards* the second ship. Presently the latter, confused and hurt, started to blaze away at her best friend.

We slowed and came to a stop, our guns silent. I began to laugh, standing there on the bridge watching one set of Krauts lacing into another. One could only hope that it would be a very level battle, with both sides selling their lives most dearly. . . . We could see that hits were being scored by both E-boats, but the battle was *not* running level: soon the nearest E-boat, which was engaging us as well as its chum in a bemused sort of way, lost heart, and the other closed in, intent on the kill.

The kill could not be denied. There was a rumbling explosion, and the losing E-boat glowed red as though in sudden anger. Her fore-deck flickered as the flames took hold, and she began to settle in the water. The victor ceased her fire, and edged nearer, hungry for prisoners. She was trying to signal us all the time, probably to get us to pick up prisoners with her.

There was something of an uproar as she found what sort of prisoners she was picking up. Shouts of wrath and pain, guttural cries of reproach, reached us across the water, sweeter than any music. While they were still sorting it all out, we started up our engines, closed in to fifty yards, and turned to starboard so that all guns were bearing. Then I pressed the firing-bell again, and we opened up with everything we had.

Two six-pounders, six 20-mm. Oerlikons, eight machine-guns—it's a hell of a lot of metal in one place at one time, and it was far too much for this target. It seemed to hit that E-boat in one solid thunder-clap; there was a small pause, and then she disintegrated, with a quick, short-lived growl like an animal falling into a pit. Her main magazine bore the remnants skywards. . . . There were splashes, as bits of everything fell back into the sea, and then complete silence—the silence of victory.

The score was two E-boats, two complete crews, and our only casualty a seaman who, catching his finger in the depth-charge release gear, lost a nail for King and Country.

I'd never felt so good before—or since.

Six years later I sat in the bar of the Coastal Forces Club, tankard in hand, and wondered why I was unemployed.

It was a familiar train of thought, and entirely suitable to my surroundings. . . . I had always found the Coastal Forces Club depressing, not only because it was shabby and run-down, but because

it was full of chaps like me—good at war, not much good at anything
else, and so returning again and again, in thought and conversation, to
the successful past, the only thing that was real for them.

Of course it *was* depressing, physically, with its cheap-looking bar,
its indifferent servants who were always being replaced, and its
members—mostly ex-R.N.V.R. types like myself—gathering there
every night and getting noisy or morose over their watery beer. But
though I knew all this, I never stayed away from it for more than a few
days. 'Keeping up the old war-time comradeship,' we called it, slapping
each other on the back and using carefully preserved slang. (The bar
was the 'wardroom', the wretched rooms upstairs 'cabins', the
inaccurate telephone messages 'signals'.) 'Whistling in the dark' might
have been a more accurate description, for that was what we were doing:
keeping close together, going through a dead ceremonial like a court in
exile, because the past was our whole life, and it was now too tough
outside.

But why *was* it too tough, I wondered, not for the first but for the
hundredth time? What sort of men were we, that the war had been so
good to us and the peace so rotten? Why was it, for example, that in
1944 I could be trusted with a ship worth ninety thousand pounds and
the lives of twenty-two men, and yet, in 1950, no one would trust me
with a suitcase full of samples? Why had I been able to do such skilful
and accurate things six years ago, while now I could hardly put a fresh
ribbon in a typewriter? Why had it all dried up so soon? Why was I, in
peace-time, such a dead loss?

I was trying not to be sorry for myself, but I *was* puzzled.

I sipped my beer, not looking at the hearty types round the bar who
were showing signs of wanting to sing. Life had been fine at first, when
we were newly demoblized: we all had a bit of money saved up, we all
had our war gratuities, we all had a future as bright as the past we had
been able to conquer so royally. I 'looked around' for a bit, loafing
unashamedly, and then took a job in a firm of travel agents; it was all
right to begin with, except that everyone seemed to know a lot more
about it than I did, and then suddenly I got sick of it, and it didn't seem
worth doing any longer, and I walked out. That was the first of many
such walk-outs.

I couldn't settle down anywhere. The succession of shoddy jobs
multiplied, grew, faded, and disappeared behind me: I was salesman,
clerk, courier, tutor, salesman, yacht-broker, club-secretary, and
salesman again. The level drifted a little lower each time: the

deterioration, though never too marked, was always there, always progressive.

Pretty soon I stopped being choosy about jobs, and started to wheedle and to agree with everybody who might have work to offer, and to call them 'sir' again. But by then it seemed to be too late, or else I had lost the trick, or I just *looked* no good. Whatever it was, the shutters were coming down, and even the foot in the door was being squeezed out into the cold again.

Only in the Coastal Forces bar, 'keeping up the old spirit' with a lot of other dead-beats, was life anything like a living thing at all.

If Lucille had been by my side, it would all have been different; she would have taken me in hand, and organized things and seen that I climbed instead of slipped. But she wasn't by my side; she had been dead these seven years, and I *had* slipped, nearly all the way down.

Now, on this summer evening in London, I was shabby, and out of work, and broke; and I knew it all.

The man next to me, a beefy boozer who tried to sell you insurance unless you shut him up straightaway, said:

'Do you remember that show at Walcheren, when old Jack Phillips bought it?'

He droned on, while I said 'Yes' at intervals. We both knew it all by heart, and it hadn't been nearly as well-handled or as successful as we now made out. Then there was a stir at the door, and someone said: 'Of *course* I'm a member,' and a man walked in. It was George Hoskins.

We saw each other immediately. I rose, and he came across the room towards me. I said 'Hallo, George,' and he said: 'I thought I'd find you here.'

We looked at each other. I knew well what he saw—a tall, thin man in an old grey suit, scuffed rubber-soled suede shoes, and a frayed R.N.V.R. tie. What *I* saw was very different: different from myself, and different from what the picture had been in the past.

Hoskins had blossomed. He looked enterprising, slick, confident —all the things I was not. He was well dressed, in a neat dark suit and a grey tie; he carried himself with assurance, and glanced about him with a wonderfully good-humoured air, as though to demonstrate that there was no shame in being a small man if you were a successful one also. I knew, from the past, that there must be something snide about him—that, whatever he was doing, it was not quite straightforward. But it seemed to pay all right.

I felt him taking me in, swiftly, as we faced each other in the centre of the room. His eyes, I noticed, were still encouraging, but now they were slightly ironic as well, as if we must both realize that much of the ground between us had altered. We hadn't met for five years, not since I was the Captain, and he the First Lieutenant, of M.G.B. 1087. Things, he seemed to be saying, had moved on, hadn't they?

He looked round the bar, taking *that* all in, too. Then he said: 'Chaps still fighting the war?'

It was what I had often thought myself, but it nettled me to hear it from him. I said, shortly: 'Something like that,' and asked him what he would drink.

'A large pink gin, please.'

I ordered it, and beer for myself, rather glumly, while the other people at the bar eyed us in morose speculation. No one drank gin in the Coastal Forces Club any more. Gin was six-and-sixpence.

Hoskins faced me easily, legs crossed, one elbow on the bar—a negligent man at ease with all the world.

'Nice to see you again, Bill.' He had never called me Bill. 'What are you doing these days?'

I said: 'Nothing much.'

He nodded, as if recognizing one of his own thoughts in my answer. But he said: 'That must be nice. Wish I could afford it.'

I looked at him without saying anything; the suit I was wearing, and the shoes, and the tie, had all proclaimed the answer to his remark before it was made, putting it in a special category of insult. But it might be worth sweating this sort of thing out. . . . We talked idly, reminiscing in the best tradition of the Coastal Forces Club.

Presently I said: 'What are *you* doing?'

'Oh, this and that.' He waved his hand vaguely. 'You've got to scratch a living where you can, these days. It's not so easy either, with all these bloody restrictions.'

'I suppose not.' The comment meant nothing to me, but from long experience I could tell that something was coming; and I wasn't prepared to balk him in any way, however much of a spiv he sounded.

Hoskins bent towards me. 'If you're not fixed up permanently,' he said, 'I've got an idea for a sideline that might be interesting. It needs someone like you.'

I grunted noncommittally. It was nice to hear that one was needed, anywhere. I imagine that Hoskins knew that.

'It would take a boat, a first-class boat, and someone to run it. Two people, in fact—you and me.' Round us, conversation had broken out again, and his voice was now masked by others. 'A fast motor-boat, to make trips across the Channel and back.' He smiled engagingly. 'We've made enough of those in our time, God knows.'

'What sort of trips?' I asked, though I knew the answer already. 'Passengers? Freight?'

He nodded. 'You could call it that. Fast freight.'

'But what about the boat? Who'll put up the money?'

He gestured again, his eyes meeting mine with particular directness. 'I've got some friends. There are a lot of *other* people around here who don't like restrictions. . . . Are you interested?'

'Yes.'

'Good show.' He smiled, as if he too knew the answers before they were given. Then he looked round the bar. 'The house should now go into secret session. Isn't there anywhere else we can talk?'

'There's a writing-room upstairs. It's usually empty.'

'O.K. Let's take our glasses up.'

As I felt in my pocket to pay for the drinks, he put a pound note down on the bar and said: 'That's all right, old boy—expenses.'

On the way upstairs I said: 'I suppose you mean smuggling,' and he said: 'Yes.'

I didn't make much objection when it came down to it: I was broke, and past caring much what I did, as long as I could pay the long list of debts I owed and organize myself a bit of elbow-room. Hoskins, expanding his ideas in the down-at-heel writing-room, painted a very rosy picture of our joint future: what fun we would have, how much we could clear each trip, how enormous a demand for our services there would be, from those vague people who 'didn't care for restrictions'.

So far, life in the Welfare State had given me nothing; but all that was now to be changed. Shortages, rules, regulations, import control— these, apparently, could combine to give us a very generous living.

I thought fleetingly of England, struggling with her screwed-up economics for year after year, trying to butt her way through the post-war mess, relying on people to go fair shares and not swindle on the rations. Then I thought of myself, struggling with *my* economics; and the shabby, shoddy life which was all I had won for myself in the process.

There was no doubt which was the more compelling picture.

It would be wrong to say that I hesitated for very long; or even at all. Sometime during the evening I said:

'I wonder if we could possibly get hold of the old ship. She'd be ideal.'

Hoskins nodded, as if once more recognizing his own thoughts.

'Funny you should say that,' he answered. 'I happen to know where she's lying. And she's for sale. . . .'

It was wonderful to see M.G.B. 1087 again; though there was no doubt that she looked like hell.

She was lying in the yacht basin on the Lymington River in Hampshire. When Hoskins and I crossed the plank that served as a gangway and stepped aboard her, it was like stepping into the decayed past. She wore an air of old-womanish neglect: unwanted, uncared-for, unloved. The paint was blistered and flaking off, all the metalwork rusty or green with verdigris; at the water-level, a filthy fringe of weed killed the clean sweep of her lines. She had nothing left to show for the proud years; if it had not been for the deep scored furrow made by a two-pounder shell in her fore-deck, I would not have recognized her, would not have claimed her as my own.

'Plenty to do,' said Hoskins, looking round him with a faint—a very faint—return of professionalism. 'But the builders swear the hull's still sound.'

'We won't need four engines,' I said. 'Too expensive to run.'

Hoskins grinned. 'And we can use the space, too.'

Down in the tiny wardroom, long closed and musty, we sat at the table where we'd both sat on hundreds of occasions in the past—sometimes safe in harbour, sometimes within gun-shot of an enemy coast—and listened to the water lapping against her bows, and planned a future for her. It wasn't going to be as worth-while as the past, but we owed it to her to make a success of it.

I worked for nearly three months down at Lymington—and that was wonderful, too. Hoskins remained in London, organizing our affairs and, I suppose, drumming up custom for the future; it was my job to dish up M.G.B. 1087 so that she could face her curious assignment. Sometimes I caught myself thinking: all this is the First Lieutenant's job, really. . . . But it was clear that the war-time roles were now reversed, and that when Hoskins had said, looking at the ship, 'There's plenty to do', he had meant that there was plenty for *me* to do, and I'd better get on with it because that was what I was going to be paid for—by him.

It would have been irksome, a few years back, but now it was not—the intervening time had been too unsuccessful, too defeating, for me to cling even to the shreds of hierarchy. And, anyway, I soon found that I didn't really mind what label I wore, because I was working again, and close to the sea, and back home in M.G.B. 1087.

The first things to be fixed up were the engines, which, having been grease-packed and sprayed, were still in good shape. We took two of them out; the remaining two, I calculated, would still give us a speed of between twenty-five and thirty knots—enough for most emergencies. But a more important thing was to simplify the controls, since there would only be two of us aboard to work the ship. In the end we led everything up to the bridge: the steering-wheel, the engine-controls, the lighting system—they were all there under the hand of one man, leaving the other half of the crew free to sleep, or to work round the ship, or (when we came into harbour) to see to the mooring-wires or the anchor.

A general clean-up followed this reorganization: the ship was hauled out of the water, and scraped and repainted: the woodwork was sand-papered smooth, and all the metal cleaned and polished. With a spring-cleaning down below, and some extra lockers fitted in place of the two engines, that completed a refit which turned M.G.B. 1087 from a hulk into a ship again. She wasn't a ship of war, of course: she couldn't hit her thirty-five knots, or punch holes in E-boats and aircraft, or scare the hell out of the fish with her depth-charges; but she was shipshape once more, and clean inside and out, and workmanlike, and I knew she would not let us down.

As soon as she was ready, I telephoned Hoskins in London, and when he came down at the week-end we took her for a trial run, down-river and out into the Solent.

It was grand to be at sea again, and we were lucky in our weather, which was clear, sunny, and calm. We crossed to the Isle of Wight, and then turned westwards down-Channel; the ship handled easily, in spite of the loss of power, and she remained as dry as a bone inside. We spent nearly the whole day at sea, alternately speeding and idling, testing her engines, her steering, her electrics, her general seaworthiness. At the end, in spite of the long lay-off, there was nowhere we could fault her.

'She's still good,' I said at last, when we had seen enough and were setting course for Lymington River once more. 'She'll take us anywhere.'

Hoskins, who had been checking the small radio we carried, joined me at the front of the bridge, where I was steering by the remote-control wheel. The spokes of this, I could not help remembering, were hollowed out—'for small jobs', as Hoskins had put it. There were a lot of such hiding-places all over the ship, covertly installed by our own carpenter ('One of the boys,' Hoskins explained): tucked inside the navigation lights, and disguised as spare petrol tanks, and hidden in a false beam down in the wardroom, and masquerading as a cold-storage space; even the pint-sized lavatory forward had a cistern that was something quite different. M.G.B. 1087 had now become a high-class conjuring apparatus, as well as a working ship.

Hoskins looked at me and grinned suddenly. I think he had enjoyed the day, too, and our re-encounter with the past. He gestured round M.G.B. 1087, and then at the wide horizon.

'Randall and Hoskins again, eh?' he said cheerfully.

I supposed we could call it that, in a way. In spite of the details.

From the start, Hoskins handled the business side: I was employed on a salary basis, plus a commission on 'results', which the future would determine. Hoskins did all the accounting, as well as fixing up the various jobs; and I never had any sort of complaint in that line, since, from the very beginning, we made a lot of trips, and a lot of money very fast.

'What do people need most?' Hoskins had once asked when we were working out our plans. 'That's what we want to find out—then we'll give it them.'

Put like that, our operations were practically a moral crusade, since our only aim in life was to see that people were happy. Why, we were almost on the side of the Government. . . . I must say that 'what people wanted most' covered some damned queer things, particularly later on, when we started to extend a bit; but to start with, it was in a way true that we were, as smugglers, quite respectable characters.

Brandy was our principal cargo on the first few trips: that, and French wines, and nylon stockings, and tinned ham, and cigars; all the little things, you see, that make the difference between life and the 'gracious living' that one sees in the ads. I used to think what a great deal of pleasure, and how little pain, we were giving; and, at the same time, what a lot of money we were making, in this innocent fashion. . . . Sometimes we made it in one quick trip—from near Dover, across the thirty-odd miles to France, and back again in one night; sometimes we took it more easily, cruising along the northern French coast, or as far south as St Malo, in the guise of English yachtsmen who could hardly bear to tear themselves away from so hospitable a playground. But as soon as we were loaded, we tore.

Hoskins had plenty of contacts in England and plenty in France: that much I could tell, though I never asked him about the details, preferring to be just the dull sailor who ran the boat. That part did not prove difficult. We never had any trouble with M.G.B. 1087 in those days: she handled perfectly, my coastal navigation was still adequate, and Hoskins, who could tinker effectively with most engines, kept ours running smoothly.

We had our share of excitement in other ways. Let me tell you one thing we did in that ship at that time, to give you the measure of it.

It was about four o'clock one morning, when we'd just got back from a Cherbourg trip, and were feeling our way up the Lymington River to our anchorage. There were no shore-lights, and we showed none ourselves: M.G.B. 1087 inched her way upstream against the gently falling tide, creeping past the stakes that marked the channel, and the mud-flats that smelt richly of the sea, and the other boats at their moorings, and the beginning of the sheds and houses grouped round the anchorage. It was our own front drive, and we knew it well, even in the pitch blackness which shrouded the hour before the dawn.

It reminded me of other nights in this same ship, when we crept our way along the Dutch coast, or up the little estuaries, probing the defences, not looking for trouble, hoping for a quiet run in—and out again. Then, the enemy had been the Germans. But now. . . .

We were just rounding the last bend, and shaping up for the ferry-boat slipway, when a searchlight was switched on, dead ahead, and a voice shouted:

'Motor-boat ahoy! Stop your engines!'

Instinctively I swung the wheel and took the ship across to starboard: I knew we were near the right-hand river-bank, but I didn't want to risk a collision—nor another boat taking too close a look at us. But the searchlight followed our sheer to starboard; at my elbow Hoskins said softly: 'Keep her going—this looks official.' The hail was repeated, this time on a peremptory note; and knowing what was bound to happen I eased back the throttle and threw the engine out of gear.

We grounded gently on the mud, and came to rest, the stern swinging, the bows caught fast in the sucking clay.

Hoskins, not at a loss for a moment, faced the blinding searchlight, and shouted: 'You stupid clots! Where the hell do you think you're going?'

A stolid voice, unimpressed, answered: 'Take our line. We're coming aboard.'

There were two men, one small, one big. They brought their fast open launch alongside, and clambered aboard, with an air of competence and authority which I did not relish. But we still had a part to act.

'What's this all about?' I asked peevishly, as soon as they were on deck. 'I thought we'd collide—and now we're aground.'

'You'll float off all right, at the next tide,' said the small man.

'That's not the point. . . . What was the searchlight for, anyway?'

'Customs,' said the small man briefly.

Hoskins said, surprised: 'In Lymington?'

'We're not from Lymington,' said the big man. 'Let's see your log.'

A prickling silence fell, while the two of them peered at the deck-log on the chart-table. Luckily it was written up every hour—a habit from the respectable past which now paid a dividend; and there was nothing wrong with our clearance papers. But I wondered, as we waited, if Hoskins felt as tight about the throat as I did. This could be total disaster.

'Cherbourg,' said the small man presently. 'Why so late getting in?'

'We were held up,' said Hoskins. 'We could have anchored down river, but I didn't want to hang about.'

'And why no navigation lights?'

'They're fused,' answered Hoskins promptly. 'I'm sorry—I know *that* was wrong.' And then: 'Look, let's get this sorted out in comfort. Come along down to the cabin, out of the cold.'

I must say that, during the next hour, Hoskins was superb. We sat round the table, and talked and smoked; presently Hoskins produced a bottle of brandy, winking, and said: 'This hasn't paid any duty—yet,' and poured out some generous drinks. We found out where they had both been during the war, and reminisced about that, and about smuggling generally, and some of the war-time Navy scandals in connection with duty-free cigarettes. . . .

The two men were suspicious—you could see that a mile off: and they were also good at their jobs and, of course, incorruptible. But to listen to Hoskins, we might have been safe in a pub ashore, with a couple of chance acquaintances who had turned out to be good company.

In spite of the ease which began to prevail, however, I found myself starting to sweat. The Customs men were certain to 'take a look round', if only as a matter of form; and on this trip we couldn't stand even the most cursory look. Perhaps we had become careless, but this time the ship had been loaded on the supposition that we *wouldn't* run into trouble. As well as a lot of Dutch cigars and some lengths of cloth in the lockers aft, we had thirty-six dozen bottles of wine—claret and burgundy—hidden under the floor-boards, and in the fake buoyancy chambers and under the seats at the back of the bridge. We were crammed with the stuff: to all intents and purposes, M.G.B. 1087 had red wine running out of her ears.

I began to sweat some more.

The hour passed; the convivial party must soon draw to a close. Presently, I knew, the small man would point to the brandy bottle and the cigars, and ask: 'Have you got many more of these?' and the big man would rise, and stretch, and say: 'I'll just take a look round. . . .' And we would listen to him walking about, and lifting things, and then after a pause he would call out: 'Joe—just come here. . . .' The party was convivial, but not convivial enough: duty lurked round the corner, and the big man and the small man were not the sort of people to forget it. No British Customs men ever were.

Hoskins said: 'Excuse me, chaps—nature calls'; and I heard him walk forward to the lavatory. There was silence round the cabin table while he was away—in spite of the brandy, my tongue was dry as bleached sand—and then he came back, and stood in the doorway, not looking at me, and said:

'It's up forward, if anyone else wants it.'

The small man nodded, and said: 'That's for me,' and disappeared. When *he* came back, the big man rose, and stretched, and said:

'I'll just take a look round before we go.'

Hoskins said: 'Sure—help yourself,' and then he suddenly looked down at his feet, and called out: 'For Heaven's sake—we're half full of water!'

It was true, like a nightmare that suddenly takes an incomprehensible turn; water was seeping across the cabin floor-boards and starting to gurgle round our feet; even as I looked, the boat gave a lurch, and more water sprayed in, in a solid cascade, from forward. M.G.B. 1087 was awash, fore and aft.

The ensuing chaos, ably promoted by Hoskins, was our salvation.

'We must have holed ourselves when we went aground!' he shouted, and immediately, for no very clear reason, he darted up on deck, as though he could find the answer there. Then, inexplicably, all the lights went out: I could hear Hoskins blundering round above our heads, and then jumping down again, through the forward hatch. He shouted: 'It's coming in fast—you'd better get on deck!' and the Customs men, groping in the dark, stumbled up the ladder to the bridge. The ship was settling down, though it was clear that she would not settle very far: ahead of us, the moon gleamed on the uncovered part of the mud-bank that held our bows, and there could not have been more than three feet of water round our hull.

Hoskins shouted again: 'The pumps—get the pumps going!' and helped by the Customs men I started the small auxiliary pump in the after-part of the ship. There was still a lot of noise, and movement, and fluent cursing from Hoskins as he searched for the leak. Then I heard his voice once more, above the putt-putt of the motor pump, calling out: 'She doesn't seem to be holed—I wonder if it's that damned valve in the lavatory,' and then, with a loud shout like a man lighting on a burglar in the basement: 'That's it—it's been left open!'

There was another long pause, and then Hoskins joined us on deck, his sea-boots clumping like thunder. 'Just got to it in time!' he gasped, as though he had run five miles to tell us the news. And turning to the small Customs man, reproachfully: 'You have to close the inlet valve after you've used the lavatory. Otherwise it floods in—it's below the water-line.'

'Oh,' said the Customs man, crestfallen. And then: 'I'm very sorry—I didn't know.'

'I should have told you,' said Hoskins magnanimously. He looked round at the rest of us. 'There's not much harm done, anyway. She's flooded about eighteen inches all round, but I've shut the inlet valve and we can pump her out quite easily by the morning.'

'I'm very sorry,' said the Customs man again. 'I should have thought of it.'

'We'll send you a bill for a new carpet,' said Hoskins jovially. He peered down the ladder into the wardroom, where the water gently lapped and swirled. 'Looks like the party's over,' he went on. 'We'll have to doss down in the wheel-house tonight.'

'Are you sure you're O.K.?' asked the big Customs man, solicitously. He had not spoken for some time, and I had been afraid that he must be brooding, not without suspicion, on the turn of events; but apparently his silence was due to embarrassment only. 'We can give you a shake-down ashore, easy enough.'

'We'd better stay aboard,' said Hoskins. 'Thanks all the same, but I'd like to watch that pump. We want to get her dried out before the tide comes up again.'

We waited, in reflective silence. Perhaps it was only my conscience which made me think: they *can't* have been put off from what they were going to do—they must still want to search the ship. But it was not so. Noise, movement, crisis, and their own sense of social guilt had altered the picture altogether. When the small Customs man shifted his feet, and said: 'Well, in that case . . .' I knew that we had won the round, after all.

The two of them climbed into their launch very shortly afterwards, still apologizing, still offering hospitality, still wishing us the best of luck, and cast off. Then their boat chugged away up-river, while M.G.B. 1087 settled comfortably on the mud, and the tide slackened, and away to the east the dawn came up to cheer us, as we stood safe on our own deck.

I ran my hand over my face—grey, bristly, at least ninety years old. 'That was a stroke of luck.'

I could just make out Hoskins, in the cold half-light, bending over the motor pump aft. He straightened up.

'You've got to keep your head, that's all.'

I was still puzzled. 'But surely that valve in the lavatory is automatic. You don't have to close it yourself.'

'It *was* automatic.' I could see him grinning as he walked towards me. 'And it is now. . . . There was just a short time this evening when it kind of got stuck. Anyone who used the lavatory after me was bound to start it flooding.' And he said again, as if to a child: 'You've just got to keep your head.'

Hoskins handled the business side. Judging from the size of the cheques that went into my bank account, he was doing it very well: in one period of four months I banked nearly three thousand pounds, and the average throughout that year was over four hundred pounds a month. I could not help being aware that we were branching out, extending markedly the basis of the brandy-and-nylon run with which we had started operations. I could not help being aware, also, that we were handling some very questionable cargo in the process.

That much was obvious, simply from the look of the people who came down to see us whenever we berthed, whether it was in England or in France. Glorified barrow-boys, I would have called them, if it had not been clear that they would never do anything as straightforward as push a barrow; smart, slick young men in black overcoats and curly-brimmed hats, who manhandled their cigars and paid us out in great greasy bunches of fivers. It was not pleasant to see them aboard M.G.B. 1087. . . . I can't claim that I gave a great deal of attention to the details of these transactions, because, basically speaking, I just didn't want to know; but I *did* know that during that time we carried, among other items, some crates labelled 'Scrap Metal' which actually held Thompson sub-machine-guns: and an innocent-looking trunk crammed with faked ration-cards printed in Bordeaux; and case upon case of bottles which, though hailing from a second-rate wine merchant in Paris, yet bore the ornate practically genuine label: 'JOHN HAIG'S VERY OLD SCOTCH WHISKY'. . . .

When I protested, not very strongly because I was getting too deep in and too aware of that mounting bank balance, Hoskins simply said:

'We're in the cash-and-carry business—and there's plenty of both. You just leave it to me.'

I left it to him. There had been a time when I seemed to have a choice in the matter; but that time, along with a lot of other things, was vanishing.

It was during this period that I became aware of something else: that M.G.B. 1087 was not behaving as well as she ought to.

It showed itself in little things: things that ought to have gone right and actually went wrong. Once we suffered from oiled-up plugs, which kept the engines coughing and spluttering all the way back from Calais. Once we had a steering breakdown which very nearly put us ashore between St Malo and Dinard. On another occasion we spent six precious hours of darkness, when we had hoped to clear harbour unobtrusively, trying without success to start the engines; thus losing the tide, the cover of night, and (very nearly) our clean record. Once, water in the switchboard put every moving thing out of action, and cost us five hundred pounds for an unfulfilled contract.

There was absolutely no reason why M.G.B. 1087 should start behaving like this: she was as good as the day we bought her, both Hoskins and I lavished hours on her maintenance, and each breakdown won her a thorough overhaul. But it was certainly true that she was giving us a lot of trouble; and even when there was no ascertainable mechanical fault, she seemed to act in a curiously sluggish way, as if she were beginning to lose heart. . . . I knew it was silly to endow a ship with a heart, of course. Perhaps my nerves were getting a bit out of hand, with the continual risks we were running; but that was how she seemed sometimes—human, unreliable, inexplicably disinclined to try.

One of the worst times was when the engines failed, in bad weather, when we were off the entrance to the Lymington River. Something in Hoskins's manner when we left the other side had told me that this was a special trip—which must mean either a very ticklish or a very expensive cargo; but as usual I had paid little attention to what we were carrying, and I only discovered what it was at the very end. Before I found out, we had almost run aground. M.G.B. 1087 could not have chosen a worse moment to pack up, and if it had not been for a change of tide, which carried us away from the point again and gave us some sea-room to play with, we would have gone ashore, and probably broken up. As it was, we drifted for nearly three hours before we got going again.

As soon as we got in, Hoskins said: 'I'm taking the steering-wheel ashore for repairs. It may have to go up to London.'

I stared at him. 'The steering-wheel? There's nothing wrong with that. It's those blasted engines that keep playing us up.'

'The steering-wheel,' he repeated, with a sort of false impatience, as if he couldn't be bothered to argue.

Then I remembered the hollowed-out spokes, the hiding-place that we had never used. Light broke in.

'Why didn't you tell me?' I asked. 'What's inside?'

Hoskins said: 'Very small mink coats.'

I grinned. 'Don't be a sap. What have we brought over this time?'

Hoskins said: 'Dope.'

I thought he was still fooling. I said: 'It's you that's the dope . . .' and then the bell rang again. 'Good God! Do you mean drugs?'

Hoskins nodded. I could see that he was already gauging my mood, knowing that I was bound to kick up a fuss, not knowing how seriously I would take it. Just before I started to speak, he said: 'It's *very* remunerative. I can assure you of that.'

We did have a blazing row; but I remember it chiefly because it was the last time I objected to anything we did. I was damned angry—because I now realized without any doubt that Hoskins did not care how far he carried this game. At one point, when I said I wanted to get out there and then, he came back very toughly indeed:

'You can't get out—you're in this, boots and all, and don't you forget it!'

'But drugs,' I repeated, still appalled. 'It's so—rotten.'

He swore vividly, and then: 'Don't be so ruddy moral,' he said. 'It gets you nowhere. . . . By God, I remember when I wanted to claim that Ju.88, and you bawled me out like a blasted clergyman. I thought you'd got wise to things, these last few months.'

I said: 'Perhaps I have.'

'Well, you'd better stay that way.' He came close to me, a small man no longer unsure of himself and violently determined to keep me in his grip. 'You haven't done so badly, this last year, have you? You'd have a hard time talking yourself out of this, if it ever came to a show-down.' His eyes were holding mine with extraordinary menace. 'Don't get any funny ideas, will you? We're both in this, up to the eyebrows, and we both stay in. . . . Now get that steering-wheel unshipped.'

It was, as I said, the last time I made any sort of protest.

After that, things went from bad to worse. It was as if Hoskins, given virtually a free hand, was determined to go to the very limit in order to demonstrate that he was master of a dangerous trade—and of me. I can hardly tell you the sort of jobs we did, during those horrible months.

Narcotics became nothing special in our cargo lists, and adulterated liquor a pleasing variation on an evil theme. Once there was a tough-looking woman with two terrified girls, who cried the whole way across and were taken ashore in a drugged stupor. When I asked Hoskins who they were, he said: 'Meat. . . .' Once there was a coffin, a lead coffin, which we lashed to the back of the bridge—and dumped into deep water off St Catherine's Point. Once, we gave passage to some wretched stateless Jews, without papers of any sort, who went ashore at Southampton and walked straight into the arms of the police at the end of the jetty. Hoskins, when he saw this, only remarked: 'What a waste of money—their money.' I wondered if he had organized *that* as well.

Such were the outlines of this infamous period, such the sort of exploit we had worked our way up to.

Perhaps it was just a coincidence that M.G.B. 1087 seemed to be deteriorating at the same pace during all this time; but it was certainly true that she was not the ship we had known in the old days. I found that I couldn't trust her any longer; she was like a sulky, ill-bred child whom one remembered, only a few years back, as having been a positive angel, exhibited proudly even at grown-up events. . . . Now she broke down on dozens of occasions, sometimes when it did not matter, sometimes when it mattered a great deal; she was sluggish, she wallowed heavily in any sort of a sea, she broached-to and shipped water no matter how carefully she was handled. Life aboard her had become a chancy and uncomfortable affair; and occasionaly, as on one of the last trips we made in her, it was highly dangerous as well.

I remember that trip very well; except for our final one, it marked the worst thing we did in M.G.B. 1087.

The ship had been under repair for a fortnight, down at Portsmouth, when Hoskins telephoned me from London.

'How's our little friend?' he asked, as soon as I reached the hotel call-box.

'She's O.K. now,' I said.

'She'd better be. . . . We have a trip to make, two days from now. It's got to go like clockwork.'

'All right,' I said.

'Now, listen. . . . About ten miles west of Hythe'—and he gave more particular directions—'there's a creek running right up into the marshes. It has plenty of water at high tide. There's a side lane, off the main Folkestone road, that goes right down to the water's edge.'

I said I could find it from the chart.

'I want our friend in there, at eleven o'clock at night the day after tomorrow. Can you bring her round by yourself?'

'Yes.'

'That's fine, then.' And he repeated: 'But it's got to go like clockwork.'

'What is it this time?' I asked after a pause. I didn't really care.

'Something special.' Hoskins sounded nervous and jubilant at the same time. 'The biggest thing we've ever done.' Then I heard him laugh, unpleasantly. 'You could almost retire after this one. Does that tempt you?'

I said: 'I'll be there,' and rang off. There were no jokes between us now—and that hadn't been a joke, anyway.

Waiting with M.G.B. 1087 among the briny, low-lying marshes, with the moon glistening on the wet fields and the seabirds crying like anguished ghosts all round me, I found myself hoping that this time something would go wrong, and that Hoskins would not show up—or that the police would do so in his place. But punctually at eleven o'clock I saw the dimmed headlights of a car turning off the main road towards me, and the purr of a heavy engine growing louder as it approached. I waited. Presently a dark shape came into view, bumping unevenly down the rough farm lane. It was a small truck; it stopped and turned, and backed towards the ship's side, as if the whole thing had been rehearsed.

A man jumped down from the tailboard, and another—Hoskins— ran round from the driving cabin. Without a word the two of them started to unload something from the back of the truck—small oblong boxes, eight of them. Still silent, breathing deeply with the effort, they manhandled the consignment aboard, and then down into the cabin. I did my share of the work, levering the heavy shapes over the edge of the coaming, and down the steep ladder.

In the faint glow from the shaded cabin-light, I saw that the boxes, wooden but securely bound with steel, were all identically marked with two intertwined letters—the Royal cipher that the Post Office used.

Not till the last one was aboard did anyone speak. Then the unidentified man said gruffly: 'Eight of them. O.K.?' and Hoskins answered: 'Eight. Yes.' That was all. The man walked back to the truck; the engine started; and it bumped away again towards the main road.

Hoskins, beside me on the bridge, said: 'Let's get going. I want to be in mid-Channel by daylight.'

That was a hell of a trip, the worst we had had so far. We were headed for a beach some miles to the south of Le Touquet, a safe 'outlet' which we had used many times before. We should have completed the crossing at easy speed, in time to close the French coast at dusk and keep our rendezvous at midnight. As it was, we were a full twenty-four hours late on the assignment; and only with great good luck were we able to make delivery on the other side.

I learned afterwards that the French 'contacts' were convinced we had made a break for a Spanish port, and that a reception committee had been warned to stand by at San Sebastian. Such were our friends and such our reception. But our failure to turn up the first night was certainly none of our own choosing.

Once again, M.G.B. 1087 just would not play. Within ten minutes of starting out, we were brought to a dead stop by weed wrapped round the screws. It took me two hours of alternate diving, hacking away for a few seconds with a knife, and then coming up for air, before I could clear it.

It had to be me that did the work, because Hoskins said he could not stay under water at all; but perhaps it was better to have something definite to do, even something as cold, wet, and miserable as this, rather than to wait inactive for the ship to get moving again. Hoskins was in a remarkable state of nerves during all this period. We were still land-bound near the mouth of the creek, and every time a car's lights travelled along the coast road, he watched them as if they were a gun pointed at his stomach.

I wondered what on earth we could be carrying, for him to have so obvious a dose of jitters. . . . But when I asked him, all he would say was: 'Don't you worry about what it is. I can tell you this, though; if we're caught with it, we'll each have about ten years to worry in—if not rather more.'

I remembered those Post Office ciphers, and the weight of the steel-bound boxes. For the first time, I really felt like a criminal on the run.

Presently we got the ship going again, and headed out into the Channel on our course for Le Touquet. Though we had lost two hours, it shouldn't have been difficult to make them up: M.G.B. 1087 had plenty of speed in hand for an occasion like this. But now, it was clear, she had other ideas. . . . Everything happened to us on that trip: an oil leak, a short circuit, dirty petrol, horrible weather, and a loose rudder-pin. The compass went completely haywire: the first shore-light we saw was Dieppe—at least seventy miles off our course. We were stopped, at one point, for nearly nine hours, while I tried to trace an electrical fault. Hoskins was seasick (that, I didn't mind). The Primus stove wouldn't work at all. The least pressure on the steering-wheel threatened to tear the rudder loose altogether.

M.G.B. 1087, in fact, behaved all the time as though she could hardly bear to be touched.

Perhaps it sounds odd to say that I found out the reason for all this when we reached the other side. But that was how it seemed.

We made our delivery just as Hoskins must have planned, even though we were twenty-four hours late. I took M.G.B. 1087 limping into the little bay south of Le Touquet, and ran her aground on a gently shelving beach from which we could retreat quickly if necessary. Four dark figures rose to meet us, four men who first flashed torches in our faces, as though they could hardly believe we had turned up, and then set to work unloading the boxes in total silence. When this was completed, still without a word spoken, we backed off again, and then turned quickly southwards for St Valery.

We reached harbour at first light, nearly out of fuel and dead tired. Neither of us had shut our eyes for two and a half days.

I slept late, in the little cabin under the shadow of the tall quay wall. I was roused by Hoskins clambering down the ladder, with his arms loaded. He seemed in good spirits; he carried loaves, cheese, fruit, and a copy of the *Continental Daily Mail*.

There was something in the careful way he put the paper down on the cabin table that caught my attention immediately. It was as if he were saying: 'Now you're going to find out what this is all about. . . .' The paper lay between us like the dividing line of a frontier: I knew that if I picked it up and read it, I would be in Hoskins's country for ever.

'Hallo,' I said, blinking. 'What's the news?'

He grinned amiably. He said: 'You're famous. But they don't know your name yet.'

At that, I flipped the newspaper open without lifting it, and bent towards it.

There was little room for anything on the front page, save the story of the daring daylight hold-up of a Post Office van in London three days before. It made tough reading. The van had been forced into a side street by a car full of masked gunmen while on its way from the Bank of England, and the contents, a shipment of bar-gold, transferred immediately to a second waiting car. The thieves had got clean away, though not without a brief and bloody struggle. Two men had been killed, shot down in cold blood—a bank messenger, and a Post Office driver who bravely tried to tackle his assailants.

The escaping car, in an eighty-mile-an-hour chase, had knocked down a child outside Edgware Road Station; a girl of five, who was critically injured and was not expected to live. The trail had been lost somewhere in South London. It was thought that the gold might already have reached the Continent.

The thieves, *concluded the newspaper*, have thus brought off the biggest haul of its kind for many years. Bank officials now disclose that the consignment of gold was on its way to Heathrow Airport, *en route* for America. Its value is estimated at £400,000. It was contained in eight wooden boxes, marked as usual with the Royal cipher.

We lay low for a long time after that. With the spectacular hue-and-cry which the gold robbery set in train, it was a bad moment to attract any sort of attention; and we could certainly afford to take a rest.... We were paid, I learned from Hoskins, four thousand pounds for that trip to France—only one per cent of the total haul, but a lot of money, anyway. With all the rest of what we had banked, it was enough for me to suggest to Hoskins, once more, that we get out and stay out.

'It can't last for ever,' I said. 'We've had hell's own luck all the time, and we've done very well out of it. I want to call it a day.'

'You can't,' he said, not for the first time. We were sitting in the Berkeley Buttery in Piccadilly, spending, elegantly, some of our winnings. 'And, anyway, what's the point? We're on to a wonderful racket. Why not make a career out of it?'

'Because we're bound to be caught in the end.'

'Why? If we do just one good job a month in future—and with the contacts I've got now, that shouldn't be hard—we can still make all the money we need. One job a month, carefully planned, isn't likely to land us in trouble.'

'They'll get wise to us in the end,' I insisted. 'In fact, I don't know why they haven't done so already. It *must* attract attention, the amount of travelling we do in the ship.'

'Don't you believe it.' Hoskins tossed back his drink and beckoned a waiter for another. 'They're not as smart as that, not by a hundred miles. As long as we keep on looking like amateur yachtsmen who can't resist the call of the sea, we're quids in.'

The call of the sea. . . . The way Hoskins said it excited my special loathing. The sea did have a call for me; it had always done so; and to hear the phrase drip thus smugly from his tongue seemed to cheapen intolerably one whole side of my life.

'Well, I'm not staying in for ever,' I said shortly. 'You can do what you like. I'm getting out pretty soon.'

'That,' said Hoskins after a pause, 'would be very unwise.'

We were staring at each other across the bar table, in such naked mutual dislike that it seemed absurd that we could be committed to any joint enterprise. I found myself wondering if other criminals found that they were tied to each other in the same disgusting way. . . . I knew, in the back of my mind, that what he said was true: that he held the whip-hand, and that, having made me his accomplice, he would never let me go. If I did walk out, now or at any time in the future, he would find some way of seeing that the police got on to my track. How he would do it, without involving himself at the same time, I didn't know. But I knew he *would* do it. I was in that sort of position, and he was that sort of man.

I said, feebly: 'We'll see.'

I knew then that relief must come from somewhere else: not from my own efforts, and not from Hoskins's good offices. There was no such thing as the latter. In some way, I must be rescued—by fate or by accident. Or by something.

The revolting series of crimes which came to be known as the 'Raines Murders' filled the front pages of all the English newspapers, and of many others, for several weeks. From the newspaper point of view, the story had everything: blood, sex, mystery, a quaking public, and a resounding official scandal—in that Raines had been committed to an asylum some years before, and had then been pronounced sane, and set at liberty, by a panel of Home Office doctors.

But sane or not—and it was always fun to confound the experts—the facts were that Raines had recently, within the space of ten days, criminally assaulted and then strangled four children, none of them over eight years of age, and had then disappeared completely.

He was, of course, reported from scores of places, being identified from the 'Wanted for Murder' photograph in the newspapers, which showed a pudgy, bald, egg-shaped man looking for all the world like a stage bishop. He was 'an obvious gentleman', the papers always said, with carefully manicured hands; a man, as one bereaved mother described him, who talked like kindness itself.

Kind he may have been—he was certainly free enough with bags of sweets and offers of a nice ride in his car; but 'gentleman' was a trifle off the beam. Four children was Raines's current score: four children all killed in the same unprintable way, followed by a month of nation-wide man-hunting, a torrent of clues, evidence, near-arrest, and public outcry, and then—silence.

Though it was dusk, I recognized Raines as soon as he came aboard.

Hoskins brought him down, of course, ushering him on board as if he were the rich owner's favourite son. Standing on the bridge, watching the back of Raines's head as he minced down the ladder, I found myself thinking: no, this is too much—and then I followed them below, in order to be introduced. . . . I remember that handshake, across the table of the half-lit cabin, as something specially degrading; his hand—plump, smooth, slightly moist—closed round mine with an embracing warmth, as though he were sure that this small contact would make us friends. I thought of what had lain within that hand, only a few weeks before, and my throat and tongue were dry as I withdrew my own hand from his grasp. The police doctor's phrase, I remembered, had been 'manual strangulation'. Now it wasn't a phrase any more.

Raines did not speak—indeed, I never found out what sort of a voice he had. After half-rising for our greeting, he sat hunched in one corner of the wardroom, with the look of a doomed man about him—a man living in an ultimate kind of hell which, after showing him briefly the bright lights of conquest, had left him alone in a pit of fear. You're on the run, I thought, with *that* on your conscience and the police of many countries searching for you; and we are helping you because our help has been bought, and we may be the last and best friends you make on this earth.

I took one more look at the smooth bald head and the drooping, egg-shaped face below it, and then I broke for the open air.

When Hoskins joined me on the bridge:

'How could you?' I asked him, in a frenzy of disgust. 'You must be crazy!'

'It's a job.' His voice was off-hand, but I knew that he did not really feel like that about it; he realized that this was very near the last margin of evil, even for him, and the only way to endure it was to turn aside from its implications. 'He's a piece of cargo, just like anything else.'

'He's not like anything else! He's wanted for rape and murder, and he did them both—four times, with kids of seven and eight—only a few weeks back,' I swallowed. 'This is the most horrible thing we've ever done.'

'Look,' said Hoskins. He came closer to me, dropping his voice. 'We both know he hasn't a hope in hell of getting away. The police in France will pick him up, the same day as he lands. And in the meantime——' He made a curious fluttering movement of his right hand, as though he were handling bank-notes. 'In the meantime, we cash in.'

'No matter what he pays——' I began.

'Raines was a rich man,' said Hoskins, interrupting. We were both whispering now, mindful of the obscene figure sitting within a few feet of us at the bottom of the ladder. 'Look here, that man had twenty-five thousand pounds tucked away. Twenty-five thousand pounds. Now it's going to be ours—all but five thousand.'

He was watching me closely, his eyes gleaming in the darkness;

probably he was trying to persuade himself as well. . . . I knew suddenly that nothing he was saying was making any difference to me, *because it didn't have to*. I was still sick with disgust, but in the back of my mind I knew that we would make the trip as planned. It wasn't the money, it was the whole horrible machine that I was caught up in; we were in the cargo business, and Raines was cargo, and we would carry him, as we had carried liquor and drugs and dead bodies and stolen gold and illegal immigrants in the past. I knew, once more in deep disgust, that I was simply going through the motions of dissent; and that I would stay in this business, with Hoskins by my side, until the sea or the law caught us and dealt with us.

When I had said: 'This is the most horrible thing we've ever done,' I had already known that we would do it.

Something made me walk a few steps forward and peer down the ladder into the cabin again. Raines was still sitting where we had left him, his body hunched, his hands hanging slack between his thighs. He noticed my movement and his eyes rose to meet mine. There was no expression in them; I might have been exchanging glances with a slug. Yes, I am Raines, he seemed to be saying: you may not like me—nobody does—but you are taking twenty thousand pounds of my money to get me out of this. When do we start?

I drew back again and moved across to the controls. Poor old M.G.B. 1087. . . . Just before I started the engines, I said:

'I don't think she'll stand for this.'

It began to blow as soon as we left the shelter of Lymington River; a tough, blustering south-easterly wind that was clearly going to give us a lot of trouble.

We had a long way to go—across the Solent, westward of the Isle of Wight, over to the French coast near the Cherbourg peninsula, and then south towards St Malo. That was where Raines said he wanted to be put ashore, Hoskins told me—in a country district that would give him a better chance of slipping past the police than anywhere north of Paris. So, St Malo it was to be. But before that, we had to cross about a hundred miles of the most open part of the Channel, in the teeth of a rising wind and a short steep sea that was already seamed and flecked with white foam.

There was nowhere round the whole coast of Britain where the weather could so swiftly deteriorate.

We sailed at about ten o'clock that night, and by dawn we had crossed the Solent and were rounding the Needles, the westerly tip of the Isle of Wight. But now we started to meet the full force of the wind and the main anger of the sea. M.G.B. 1087 began to labour, as the waves tossed her about blindly, throwing her many degrees off her course; sometimes she buried her bows deep in the trough of the sea, sometimes she rose high on the crest of a wave, and her screws, shuddering and racing wildly in the free air, shook the whole ship. Ahead of us, a lowering sky and a torn sea was now our only horizon.

We wrestled with these enemies for over three hours before I began to have doubts about the outcome. Raines remained below, 'sick as a dog', as Hoskings told me spitefully. Hoskins himself was beside me on the bridge, tending the engine-controls and occasionally taking a spell at the wheel.

We were both very tired already and drenched to the skin; though even now we had hardly left the English coast, and there were hours of this battle, and of worsening weather, ahead.

'I don't think we can do it!' I had to shout to make myself heard, bending towards Hoskins under the lee of the bridge-rail. 'We're not making more than two or three knots headway, and the sea's getting worse. If anything goes wrong with the engines, we're sunk.'

Hoskins looked round him at the flurry of foam and dark water that contained and threatened us. 'Sunk is a good word!' he shouted back, and grinned. I almost liked him at that moment. He sounded something like the old Hoskins, at his best when we were in a rough corner, with things going wrong.

But we *were* in a rough corner. M.G.B. 1087 was now taking huge punishment with every wave, and labouring exhaustedly under it. Everything above decks ran with water, and we had shipped a lot of it below, in the cabin and the engine-space.

The wind had begun to howl at us; under the livid sky the waves seemed to race and roar against the ship, throwing themselves against her with the full shock of malice. Even if we turned round now, we would have a wild fight getting back to shelter; and if we didn't turn, there would come a moment when we would bury our bows beneath tons of water for the thousandth time, and not come up again.

Tough as she was, she was not built for this sort of thing, and we knew it, and so did she.

M.G.B. 1087 settled the question for us. Towards midday, the engines began imperceptibly to fail.

It was sea-water, I suppose; or the harm done whenever the screws raced free; or the oil-level, which was erratic; or the terrific weight of the sea surging perpetually against us. Or perhaps she was just ashamed of us all. . . . Whatever it was, she started to miss successive beats, and the revolutions dropped steadily.

Hoskins and I looked at each other. In that horrible sea, the inexorable falling of the engine-speed drained the heart of its courage.

'We'll have to turn back!' I shouted. The wind was plucking the words from my mouth as I spoke them, and again I bent towards him behind the shelter of the bridge. 'Maybe she'll pick up again if she's running with the wind.'

Hoskins stared at me, his face taut. I could tell that he was starting to be afraid, as I was. We were then twenty miles south of the Needles, twenty miles from any sort of shelter; and to reach it we would have to bring M.G.B. 1087 round, beam on to this villainous sea, with the engines failing, and then struggle for home, with all the fury of the storm on our trail. Even if she came round without mishap, we would be taking a frightful chance, running before such a gale with the cockpit being swamped by every second wave.

But the turn had to be made. If we didn't make it and make it soon, it would be too late, and we would simply keep on until we headed for the bottom.

Whether or not M.G.B. 1087 could in the future complete the journey, she had now been beaten back in surrender, and we had to face the fact that we were in her hands.

I had a wicked time, working to bring her round; it took nearly an hour of successive attempts, with never enough power to complete the full turn. Time and again she came half-way round, until she was lying in the trough of the waves; time and again she stuck there, with the screws thrashing ineffectually, and the sea dealing her blow after blow as she lay broadside on. She would reach that certain point, with the rudder hard over and the engines feebly pulsing, but she always lacked the power to complete the half-circle and turn her stern to the wind. Time and again we would abandon the effort, and bring her bows up to the wind again, preparatory to another try, another wild stab at it.

All the while, the ship suffered fearfully: pounding, shuddering, shipping solid black cataracts of water, unloosing below decks a frightful clatter as spare gear and crockery and oil-drums broke adrift and thrashed about.

Finally she made it. There must have been a lull, or else the engines summoned a few extra revs. She did come round, after a terrible moment of indecision, and turned her back to the storming sea. Then the worst part of the voyage began.

I had a feeling that she would never live. There was something in the touch of her, in the way the wheel spun loosely in my hands, in the sound of the dying engines, that told me that M.G.B. 1087 was not going to make harbour. Our progress grew slower and slower; far away ahead of us I could see the vague outlines of the land, but it was like a promise that would never be fulfilled—it came no nearer, grew no clearer to the eye.

More and more often the solid seas crashed down upon our stern, driving it deep under water, and then roaring along the upper deck with the sound of unloosed thunder. Hoskins and I clung helplessly to the bridge-rail; I found that my hands, clawing at the wheel, were without feeling, and my whole body cold to the bone. The engine-beat dropped further, as the whole ship was invaded and swamped. Already she seemed to have grown smaller under the triumphant attack of the sea, and shrunken in defeat.

She was lying down under it all; as if now, at last, she had had enough of us and the things we had done to her. She was not trying any more.

There was a sudden confused noise from below, above the groaning and the clatter, and the door at the head of the cabin-ladder burst open. Raines appeared. He was a fearful sight—grey-green with seasickness, glistening with terror. He had upon his face an extraordinary luminous pallor, as if he were already dead. He reminded me of the children he had killed. . . . He tottered towards us, looking round about him fearfully, and gestured at the roaring sea as though he could not believe what he saw.

The engines spluttered and died.

Now we lay there helpless, taking every blow that fell, settling lower beneath the scudding spray. M.G.B. 1087 had become a waterlogged wreck, drifting down-wind uselessly as the gale screamed round her rigging and the sea slugged and slugged at her hull. Hoskins touched Raines on the shoulder, and pointed to the land, still a long way away, vaguely glimpsed through clouds of flying spray.

It was doubtful whether he meant anything special by this pointing, but Raines took it as a definite directive. He nodded, and seemed to be gathering himself together. Then, as yet another sea swept unchecked along the deck, and drenched us all, he jumped.

It was perhaps the best thing to do, though not for him. He had not the build for swimming, nor the strength, and we could only watch him drown. I had never before seen a bald head sinking lower and lower in the water, surrounded by thrashing arms. There was a moment when he seemed to be bubbling fantastically at surface-level, like a suspect, simmering egg. . . . I found that I still hated him, even as he disappeared.

I hated Hoskins, too—the man who had brought us all here, who had done all this to me and to the ship. M.G.B. 1087 was heading for the sea-bed now—full of water, all her buoyancy lost, the great weight of the keel and the engines starting to drag her down. Thus we were all dead or dying: Raines, Hoskins, the ship, and I; dying in hatred and shame and anger, amid the raging sea.

Hoskins clutched my shoulder. When I turned, his face was close to mine, and enormous—the face I had grown to loathe, constricted now with cold and fear. Honour had caught up with him—with both of us. The ship trembled under our feet, and slid lower.

Hoskins cried out: 'I can't swim.'

I wanted to laugh, but much more I wanted to save my breath. I said: 'That's all right with me,' and as the ship foundered I struck out for the shore. I never saw him again.

Well, that's the story, and probably you see what I meant when I said, at the beginning: there are things about it that I don't understand. I've got plenty of time to work it out—ten years, as Hoskins once forecast. (They traced the payment for the gold robbery to my bank account. Perhaps I was lucky—three of the principal characters were hanged.)

What made M.G.B. 1087 lie down and die? For that was what did happen, after all—not suddenly but progressively; in spite of all the care we spent on her, she did grow less and less dependable, and in the end she just gave up, without fighting. It was as if the last trip, the worst thing we ever asked her to do, decided the matter for her.

But that's surely a fanciful idea. There was no *real* reason for her giving up, even on that final voyage; the weather was terrible, but we'd had terrible weather on lots of occasions, particularly during the war, and she had always survived it—and even seemed to thrive on it.

Of course, during the war we had to fight the weather for different reasons. There was usually a stake that the M.G.B. 1087 could be proud of then—in fact, many such stakes, for years on end.

Perhaps it was I, and not the ship, that was at fault. Perhaps I handled her badly, or forgot things, or just lost the knack; perhaps I was ashamed of the frightful things we did, and the shame became translated into action—or lack of action.

It may have been my fault we were wrecked. But I don't think so. I was always trying my very best, I'm afraid.

Sources

THE LONGEST LOVE, THE LONGEST HATE: Copyright © Nicholas
Monsarrat 1974

Published in *The Observer Magazine* under the title *The Longest Love
Affair*.

THREE CORVETTES: © Nicholas Monsarrat 1945

H.M. Corvette

Serialized in: *Daily Telegraph* (1942), *Harper's Magazine* (1943), *Toronto
Star* (1944).

As book: Cassell, London (1942), Lippincott, New York (1943).

Broadcast: by B.B.C. (1943).

East Coast Corvette

Serialized: in *Daily Telegraph* (1943), *Daily Despatch* (1943), *Sunday
Express* (1944), *Argosy* (1944), *Maclean's Magazine* (1944).

As book: Cassell, London (1943), Lippincott, New York (1944).

Corvette Command

Serialized: *Trident* (1944).

As book: Cassell, London (1944).

AS THREE CORVETTES

Cassell, London (1945), Presses de la Cité, France (1955), Panther (1957),
Danish Pocket Books (1960), Ballantine, U.S. (1962), Mayflower Books
(1972).

I WAS THERE: © Nicholas Monsarrat 1957

Atlantic Monthly (1957), *Aftenposi*, Norway (1957), *Everybody's Weekly*
(1958), Danish Radio (1960), American Book Co. (1962), *Reveille* (1967).
Published in THE SHIP THAT DIED OF SHAME, Cassell, London (1959).

A SHIP TO REMEMBER: © Nicholas Monsarrat 1970

Published in *The Daily Telegraph Magazine* (1970) under the title *Epitaph
for Forgotten Thousands*. Reprinted in *Weekly News, Boston Herald-
Traveler, New Cunard, Midwest Magazine* (all 1970), *Junior Statesman*
(1971).

H.M.S. *MARLBOROUGH* WILL ENTER HARBOUR: © Nicholas Monsarrat 1947

Published in DEPENDS WHAT YOU MEAN BY LOVE, Cassell, London (1947), Alfred Knopf, New York (1948), Dassie Books, South Africa (1950), Signet, U.S. (1954), Bonnier, France (1954), Panther (1956), Ballantine, U.S. (1963), Mayflower (1972).

As story: *Argosy* (1951), *Liverpool Echo* (1952), *Western Mail* (1952).

As separate book: Cassell, London (1952), Elsevier, Holland (1953), Stabenfelt, Norway (1954), Schonbergske, Denmark (1954), Otava, Finland (1958), Jackson, Spain (1964).

Broadcast: by B.B.C. (1954, 1957 and 1969), Australia (1954), CBS–TV (1954), South Africa (1955).

IT WAS CRUEL: © Nicholas Monsarrat 1970

Extracted by *Sunday Times* (1970) from LIFE IS A FOUR-LETTER WORD Vol. II, Cassell, London (1970), Pan Books, London (1972), and BREAKING IN, BREAKING OUT, Morrow, New York (1971).

THE SHIP THAT DIED OF SHAME: © Nicholas Monsarrat 1952

As story: *Lilliput* (1952), *Saturday Evening Post* (1952), *Sunday Chronicle* (1953), and in Australia, South Africa, New Zealand, Germany and Sweden.

As book: Cassell, London (1959), Presses de la Cité, France (1964), Skrifola, Denmark (1954), Schonbergske, Norway (1954), Elsevier, Holland (1955), William Sloane Associates, New York (1959), Pocket Books, U.S. (1961), Pan Books, London (1961), Juventud, Spain (1964).

Broadcast: by the B.B.C. (1954), Australia (1954), and South Africa (1956).

Filmed: by Ealing Studios (1955).